BEYOND
ORIENTALISM

BEYOND
ORIENTALISM

Essays on Cross-Cultural Encounter

Fred Dallmayr

State University of New York Press

© Cover illustration:
 "Buddha in Meditation" Balawaste, New Delhi
 Central Asian Painting, Editions d'Art Albert Skira S.A. Geneva
A greatly condensed form of chapter 2 appeared in *Yale Journal of Law & the Humanities,* Volume 5, Number 2 (Summer 1993).
An earlier version of chapter 6 appeared in *Philosophy East & West,* Volume 44 (1994).
An earlier version of chapter 7 appeared in *Alternatives,* Volume 17, Number 4 (Fall 1992). Copyright ©1992 by Alternatives, Inc. Used by permission of Lynne Rienner Publishers, Inc.

Published by
State University of New York Press, Albany

© 1996 State University of New York

For information, address the State University of New York Press,
State University Plaza, Albany, NY 12246

Production by Dana Foote
Marketing by Dana E. Yanulavich

Library of Congress Cataloging-in-Publication Data

Dallmayr, Fred R. (Fred Reinhard), 1928–
    Beyond orientalism : essays on cross-cultural encounter / Fred Dallmayr.
        p.   cm.
    Includes bibliographical references and index.
    ISBN 0-7914-3069-3 (hc : alk. paper). — ISBN 0-7914-3070-7 (pbk. : alk. paper)
        1. Multiculturalism.   2. Intercultural communication.   3. Philosophy,
Comparative.   4. East and West.   5. Civilization.   Modern—20th century.
6. Philosophy, Modern—Forecasting.   I. Title.
    BD175.5.M84D35   1996
    303.48'2'01 — dc20   96-12033
                                                                        CIP

1 2 3 4 5 6 7 8 9 10

For Edward W. Said
and for Hans-Georg Gadamer
in respectful admiration

*The man who finds his homeland sweet is still a tender beginner;
the man for whom each country is as his native soil is already
strong; but only the man for whom the whole world is as a foreign
land is perfect.*

— Hugo of St. Victor

Us and them. Who is us, now, and who them?

— Godimer, *July's People*

CONTENTS

PREFACE

On the surface at least, this book signals a shift in the focus of my intellectual concerns. Readers familiar with some of my previous writings or scholarly attempts may well wonder what prompted someone rooted in Western, especially Continental, thought to turn his attention to "cross-cultural encounters," particularly encounters with non-Western perspectives and life-forms. If I were asked to account for this shift, I would point to two main factors or developments: one more overtly political, the other more recessed and intellectual. Politically, one of the most dramatic developments of the past half-century has been the steady advance of globalization, that is, the emergence—buttressed by markets and information breakthroughs—of something like a cosmopolis or "global village." In a new and stunning Copernican revolution, the Eurocentric world view of the past—with its corollaries of colonialism and "Orientalism"—has been replaced or at least challenged by the rise of a global arena in which non-Western cultures and societies are increasingly active participants in shaping the future of the world.

As it happens, this political transformation has been seconded or abetted for some time by a more quiet, subterranean process: the internal self-questioning or self-decentering of European or Western thought. This decentering is particularly evident in recent Continental philosophy, especially in those intellectual perspectives commonly grouped under such headings as poststructuralism, postmodernism, and deconstruction. Despite diverse accents, what is common to these orientations is the preoccupation with "difference" or "otherness," more specifically with the intrusion or irruption of the alien and undomesticated into familiar types of thought and practice. Reared in central strands of Continental philosophy, my own work has reverberated for several years now with these kinds of intrusions or irruptions—with what Michael Theunissen, in a felicitous phrase, has termed *"Veranderung"* (alteration). More recently, however, I have been made uneasy by a certain flattening out of difference, that is, by the tendency to turn otherness into an oracle or else into a facile and empty rhetorical formula devoid of concrete implications. To counter this tendency, I have increasingly shifted attention to concrete modes of difference both at home and abroad: to life-forms and cultural patterns able to contest dominant metaphysical premises and habitual practices. Quite naturally (or so it seems), I was thus led in the direction of cross-cultural encounters at the limits or boundaries of traditional Western world views. Seen against this background, the change of focal concerns certainly was not whimsical or haphazard, but prepared and sedimented by motives of *longue durée*.

Among non-Western cultures, primary attention is given in this volume to South Asia, chiefly to the traditions linked with, or emanating from, the Indian subcontinent. The motives for this emphasis are partly personal or fortuitous, and partly philosophical in character. More than a decade ago, in 1984, I visited India for the first time—a visit which had a deep impact on my thought and life. Subsequently, I returned to the country repeatedly for conferences or lecture tours. In 1991, I spent a more extended period in India under the auspices of a Fulbright research grant, an arrangement which allowed me to solidify my connections with colleagues and friends and to undertake visits to a great number of educational and cultural centers across the subcontinent. Many of the chapters in this book owe their inspiration to these experiences. Philosophically or intellectually, India deserves attention as one of the oldest living civilizations on earth: a civilization where older and oldest strands of culture are overlayered by newer and more recent strands, but without being smothered or eradicated in the process. Thus, the Indian subcontinent offers an enormous site for cultural exploration: in fact, for a nearly unparalleled "archaeology of knowledge" attentive to multiple forms of historical or temporal otherness. Moreover, throughout the centuries, the subcontinent has generated a panoply of diverse cultural traditions, including Hinduism, Jainism, Buddhism (and others)—in addition to being host to Islamic penetration and later a victim of European colonialism. In many ways, South Asia thus represents a crossroads of life-forms: between East and West, between polytheism and monotheism, and also between tradition and modernity.

This book is a collection of essays rather than a systematic treatise—for reasons having to do with the topic of inquiry. Proceeding in linear fashion from start to finish, a systematic treatise presupposes a standpoint outside or above the welter of competing cultures and life-forms, a standpoint permitting an objective and "totalizing" overview. This assumption goes against the very grain of cross-cultural encounter, which has to start "from the ground up" and in a dialogical fashion, offering only the uncertain prospect of a learning experience. Coming from a European or Western background, I certainly cannot pretend to a superior or encompassing perspective; all I can claim is to have been sometimes the instigator and always the beneficiary of cultural learning—in a manner which hopefully will also be beneficial to readers. In the contemporary political climate, I definitely do not wish to give aid and comfort to a homogenizing globalism or universalism, which often is only a smokescreen for neocolonial forms of domination.

Although a collection of essays, this book is not simply a string of haphazardly linked vignettes. In a cautious and subdued manner, the sequence of chapters is held together by a line of argument which moves forward (without being coercively systematic). The opening chapter discusses the broad range of possible "modes" of cross-cultural encounter in a historical perspective. Following a path of normative-ethical ascent, the discussion ranges from strategies of conquest, conversion, and assimilation to more benign forms of interaction, culminating in a model of dialogical reciprocity and exchange. Drawing its inspiration chiefly from Gadamer and Derrida, the book then develops as preferred option the notion of a 'deconstructive dialogue' or a 'hermeneutics of difference' where dialogical exchange respects otherness beyond assimilation. Concentrating on the relation between India and the West, subsequent chapters examine the work of several prominent bridge builders across cultures, primarily the Indian philosophers Radhakrishnan and J. L. Mehta and the German-American philosopher and Indologist Wilhelm Halbfass. Proceeding to a broader comparative level, a centerpiece of the book juxtaposes Western thought and Indian thought along the lines of a distinction between decontextualized and context-bound modes of cultural discourse. The remaining chapters shift the accent to more concrete social-political problems, including the issues of social development (or "modernization"), multiculturalism, and the prospects of a globalized democracy. The theme of democracy, in particular, is elucidated through recourse to the Buddhist notion of 'emptiness,' or *sunyata,* a notion which entails that political power and identity can never be fully grounded or fixated and thus remain open to democratic contestation and dialogical negotiation.

Taken as a whole, the book does not seek to offer a global blueprint, but rather to venture some steps beyond Eurocentric arrogance and hence "beyond Orientalism"; as a corollary, it also seeks to move beyond Samuel Huntington's vision of a looming "clash of civilizations." In the attempt to transgress "Orientalism," I am strongly and lastingly indebted to Edward Said whose book of the same title opened the eyes of readers to the complicity of much traditional scholarship with European colonial expansion. As Said more recently has taught us, the end of colonial empires has not by itself ushered in the demise of subtler forms of Western economic and military hegemony. In subscribing to the model of cross-cultural encounter and learning, as an alternative to Eurocentrism, I am deeply in the debt of Hans-Georg Gadamer whose philosophical hermeneutics has always accentuated the dialogical exchange between reader and text and between the present and the past. Taking some cues from Jacques Derrida, Gadamer's recent writings have shunned the telos of consensual convergence in favor of a nonassimilative stance of "letting-be." Appropriately, I think, the book is hence dedicated with respect, gratitude, and admiration both to Said and Gadamer.

Apart from these two mentors, my indebtedness and gratitude extend to a broad circle of people, not all of whom I can mention or acknowledge here. Among Indian friends and colleagues I want to single out especially the following for having greatly contributed to my cultural learning, and also to the pleasantness of my visits to India: Thomas Pantham, Prafulla Kar, and Ganesh Devi in Baroda; Ashis Nandy, Rajni Kothari, and Rajeev Bhargava in Delhi; Sundara Rajan in Pune; Partha Chatterjee in Calcutta; and Padmanabhan in Madras. With Thomas Pantham, in particular, a steady friendship has been cultivated over the years between our families. Among younger Indians I want to mention with special fondness Hitesh Soni whose friendship has been for me a source of much happiness. Closer to home I acknowledge Wilhelm Halbfass from whom I have learned a good deal and whose work has at least in part encouraged me to venture beyond Orientalism. Among American colleagues, these have been particularly generous in providing advice and support: Jean Elshtain, Hwa Yol Jung, Stephen White, and Calvin Schrag. In still closer proximity, at my home university of Notre Dame, a circle of friends has enriched my life and broadened my horizons; this circle includes, among others, Stephen Watson, David Burrell, Gerald Bruns, Joseph Buttigieg, and Eva and Chris Ziarek.

My deepest gratitude, of course, goes to my family, particularly my wife, Ilse, who graciously accepted my often prolonged absences from home so that I could engage in my cross-cultural explorations. I can only hope that, by struggling in my limited way against cross-cultural conflicts or the "clash of civilizations," I have made a small contribution to a brighter and more peaceful future for our children—to what Indian sages have called *"lokasamgraha,"* world maintenance.

Note: Since this book is addressed to a general audience rather than a small circle of Indological experts, diacritical marks have been omitted throughout the text.

INTRODUCTION

In a recent interview with the Indian political theorist Thomas Pantham, Hans-Georg Gadamer made these comments:

> The human solidarity that I envisage is not a global uniformity but
> unity in diversity. We must learn to appreciate and tolerate plu-
> ralities, multiplicities, cultural differences. The hegemony or un-
> challengeable power of any one single nation—as we now have
> with just *one* superpower—is dangerous for humanity. It would
> go against human freedom. . . . Unity in diversity, and *not* uni-
> formity or hegemony—that is the heritage of Europe. Such unity-
> in-diversity has to be extended to the whole world—to include
> Japan, China, India, and also Muslim cultures. Every culture, every
> people has something distinctive to offer for the solidarity and
> welfare of humanity.[1]

In these comments, Gadamer reiterated and underscored the vision of
cultural diversity he had articulated a few years earlier in *The Legacy
of Europe (Das Erbe Europas)*, projecting that vision now onto a global
scale, the scale of the emerging global community or *cosmopolis*. The
latter projection, one should add, was not simply an off-hand remark
or an afterthought tagged on to a primary focus on Europe or the West.
For many years, Gadamer had encouraged students of European philosophy to expand and enrich their horizons through contact with non-
Western modes of thought. In his *Heidegger's Paths (Heidegger's Wege)*,
he strongly insisted that some of these paths were pointing the way toward an encounter and possible dialogue between Europe and Asia
or between West and East.[2]

In encouraging this broadening of horizons, Gadamer was following the lead of his teacher, Martin Heidegger, whose thinking throughout his life was progressively attuned or attentive to non-Western life-
forms. During the interbellum period, Heidegger's lectures in Freiburg
were attended by numerous students from Asia, especially Japanese
students associated with the so-called Kyoto School which then was
engaged in the effort of probing the relation between (Zen) Buddhism
and Western philosophy. According to some accounts, Heidegger's
acquaintance with Taoist texts also dates back to the same period. In
the years immediately following the war, Heidegger was engaged with

a Chinese scholar in the laborious effort of providing a German translation of the *Tao Te Ching* (an effort that did not reach final fruition).[3]

In subsequent decades, Heidegger became increasingly preoccupied with the growing "Europeanization" or Westernization of the
world, especially with the standardization of the globe under the rule
of Western technology *(Gestell)*. In a letter addressed to Ernst Jünger
in 1955, he urged the cultivation of a new kind of "planetary thinking" as an antidote or counterpoise to the spreading technological
world civilization (seen as a corollary of Western "nihilism"). In 1969,
on the occasion of Heidegger's eightieth birthday, it was the Japanese
philosopher Koichi Tsujimura (a product of the Kyoto School) who
presented the keynote address to a gathering in Messkirch. Roughly
at the same time, a symposium on "Heidegger and Eastern Thought"
was held at the University of Hawaii as a meeting ground for philosophers from West and East. In a letter sent to the organizers of the conference, Heidegger himself stated at that juncture: "Again and again
it has seemed urgent to me that a dialogue take place with the thinkers
of what is to us the Eastern world."[4]

In the meantime, Heidegger's comments have gained added weight
by the accelerated pace of globalization proceeding under the ban-
ner of Western science, technology, and industry; as an antidote to
facile "one-world" formulas, dialogue and cross-cultural encounter
have acquired both intellectual and political urgency. To be sure, meeting this urgent demand requires more than a repetition of Heidegger's
plea or a simple recapitulation of Heideggerian and Gadamerian teachings. Despite the importance of scholarly exegesis, what is needed
today is a willingness to venture forward into the uncharted domain
intimated in their writings, and thus in a sense a readiness to "cut
loose" from their moorings.

Such a cutting loose is by no means contrary to the spirit of their
work. In one of his late fragments, Nietzsche remarked: "Once you
have discovered me, it seems to have been no great trick to find me;
but now the difficulty is how to lose me." Elaborating on Nietzsche's
statement, Heidegger made it plain that "losing" here was not a form
of abandonment but rather a mode of remaining faithful or loyal to a
work by pursuing its untapped potential or future possibilities. In his
words: "And this, to lose, is harder than to find; because 'to lose' in
such a case does not just mean to drop something, leave it behind,
abandon it. 'To lose' here means to make ourselves truly free for that
which Nietzsche's thinking has thought."[5] In a similar vein, remaining
faithful to Heideggerian and Gadamerian teachings involves a free continuation of their journey and thus a transgression of their European-
style discourse in the direction of broader, cross-cultural engagements.

Such a continuation and transgression is today no longer an isolated venture but a shared enterprise of numerous thinkers both in the West and in the East. Among Western thinkers indebted to Heidegger's work, important steps along these lines have also been undertaken by Jacques Derrida, especially in his recent book *The Other Heading: Reflections on Today's Europe*. As Derrida observes in that text, Europe has always tended to consider itself as the cultural "capital" (from *caput,* head) of the world, that is, as a "heading" or promontory not only in a geographical sense but in the sense of providing a lead for "world civilization or human culture in general." However, this self-understanding is today under siege or in crisis due to the combined effect of a number of factors: chiefly the influence of internal scrutiny and self-doubt calling into question Europe's traditional identity, and the impact of a radically changed global context. In Derrida's account, the point today is neither simply to dismiss Europe's cultural aspirations—thus making room for self-seclusion and Balkanization— nor to cling to Europe's legacy in a domineering or imperialistic way. As he writes, Europe today is faced with a profound aporia or double injunction: on the one hand, European cultural identity cannot or should not be disassembled into "a myriad of provinces," a multiplicity of "petty nationalisms, each one jealous and untranslatable"; on the other hand, Europe cannot or should not erect itself into "the capital of a centralizing authority" that, by means of "trans-European cultural mechanisms," would attempt to "control and standardize" both its constitutive elements and the rest of the world.[6]

Derrida's observations can without great difficulty be extended to Western civilization in its relation to the non-West or the array of non-Western cultures co-inhabiting our contemporary "global village." But how can Europe or the West approach these cultures? More specifically, how can it advance itself toward the "other heading," which, as Derrida intimates, would be something other than a straightforward heading or *telos* and perhaps an altogether other shore? Historical experience on this score is not encouraging. Traditionally, Europe or the West has tended to approach other cultures from a superior intellectual and political vantage, that is, from the perspective of a master-spectator able to construct a model of the other best suited to purposes of domination and domestication. In his justly famous study, Edward Said has summarized Europe's historical relation to Islamic culture under the heading of "Orientalism," meaning by this title a way of "coming to terms with the Orient" based on the latter's "special place in European Western experience." More specifically, Orientalism denoted for Said a "corporate institution" erected in the West for dealing with the Orient "by making statements about it, by teaching it,

settling it, ruling over it": in short, a "Western style for dominating, restructuring, and having authority over the Orient."[7]

As portrayed in Said's study, the rise of Orientalist learning, institutions, and literature coincided roughly with the expansion of Western colonialism and imperialism: that is, the period between 1815 and
1914 when European colonial dominion extended to 85 percent of
the earth's surface. Pondering the close linkage between academic
learning and colonial power, Said in his study was led to associate
Orientalism with a quasi-Nietzschean "will-to-knowledge" or "will-
to-power"; seen from this angle, Orientalist discourse reflects not a serious engagement but rather a social "imaginary" or mode of "representation" imposed for purely strategic ends. "My contention," he
stated, "is that Orientalism is fundamentally a political doctrine willed
over the Orient because the Orient was weaker than the West, which
elided the Orient's difference with its weakness. . . . As a cultural apparatus Orientalism is all aggression, activity, judgment, will-to-truth,
and knowledge."[8]

Written at a time of accelerating globalization, Said's text issued a
dramatic appeal for intellectual reorientation (perhaps also for a political restructuring of East-West relations). Despite its importance and
attractive élan, however, *Orientalism* was not free of quandaries or
theoretical dilemmas. For one thing, endorsement of certain Nietzschean (or quasi-Nietzschean) assumptions tended to blunt the book's
critical edge or its pathos of indictment: if interpretation of alien cultures always and necessarily proceeds from a strategic will to power,
European or Western students of the East could not possibly help but
"Orientalize" their subject matter in an exercise of intellectual imperialism. On the other hand, Said himself did not entirely subscribe to
the equation of power and knowledge, preferring instead to oscillate
between exegetic constructivism and a bland sort of realism. On repeated occasions, the study juxtaposed and contrasted the Orient as
constructed by Orientalist discourse with something else elusively
called the "real Orient," the "true Orient," or the "Orient itself."

"It would be wrong to conclude," Said noted at the beginning of
his book, "that the Orient was *essentially* an idea, or a creation with
no corresponding reality"; for clearly there were (and are) cultures and
peoples in the East whose lives and histories have "a brute reality obviously greater than anything that could be said about them in the
West." At another point, the different elements of Orientalist discourse
were described as "representative figures, or tropes" which were said
to relate to the "actual Orient" in the same way as "stylized costumes"
relate to the characters in a play. In fairness, *Orientalism* was not entirely devoid of glimpses pointing beyond the polarity of construction

and realism. Perhaps the most important task of all, Said states in passing, would be to undertake studies in "contemporary alternatives to Orientalism," that is, to inquire how one can study other cultures from a "nonrepressive and nonmanipulative perspective," something which would demand a rethinking of "the whole complex problem of knowledge and power."[9] As it happens, Said in the meantime has undertaken important steps oriented precisely toward such a rethinking, steps which point (however haltingly) in the direction of hermeneutical interrogation and thus beyond the confines of Orientalism as a delimited historical and analytical paradigm.[10]

To be sure, critical comments on Orientalism cannot in any way screen from view one of Said's central concerns: the prevalence of hegemonic and exploitative power relations in the world. As in the past, cross-cultural encounters today are deeply overshadowed by political and economic asymmetries shaping the respective status of West and non-West, of Northern and Southern hemispheres, and of "developed" and "developing" societies. Commitment to dialogue and hermeneutical interrogation cannot cancel awareness of these asymmetries. The present study opens with a chapter devoted to "Modes of Cross-Cultural Encounter," a chapter whose point of departure is one of the most dramatic and devastating forms of cultural contact: conquest and physical subjugation. The chief example chosen to illustrate this mode is the Spanish take-over and annihilation of the Aztec and Mayan cultures, as discussed mainly in Tzvetan Todorov's magisterial *The Conquest of America*. In Todorov's presentation, the Spanish conquista involved a clash between two radically opposed paradigms of cultures: one (the Indian) wedded to a cosmic-holistic world view, the other bent on transgressing existing cultures in the direction of decontextualized universal rules and rationalized structures of government. Seen in this light, the clash carries a broader "exemplary" significance: by foreshadowing the long sequence of encounters between West and non-West culminating in the contemporary process of globalization—a process which, for Todorov, reveals the grandeur and tragedy of Western culture (as a variant of the "dialectic of Enlightenment").

In the opening chapter, the story of conquest is pursued beyond 1492 to later instances of military expansion and annexation, especially the Spanish take-over of the Philippines seen as forerunner of the rise of Western (European and North American) colonialism. From conquest, the discussion moves on to less direct or overt forms of cultural domination, chiefly to practices of religious or ideological conversion and to policies of assimilation and acculturation, as exemplified both in Western and in non-Western societies. Leaving behind domineering expansion altogether, the chapter next turns to reduced or attenuated modes of cultural contact or co-existence, focusing for this purpose on instances of cultural borrowing and on the model of neutral abstinence and nonengagement as promoted by (strands in) Western liberalism. By way of conclusion, the chapter concentrates on two types of intense cross-cultural or self-other engagement: the cases of radical conflict and of dialogical reciprocity. While the former type is particularly relevant in situations of insurgency against imperial (or class) domination, the second type provides the chief avenue for attempts at fostering nonviolent or nonmanipulative ways of cultural interaction. In *The Conquest of America,* Todorov himself grants normative preference or priority to a "dialogue between cultures," a preference predicated on the view that our emerging global village entails unparalleled opportunities for cultural cross-fertilization while at the same time placing a stigma on overt forms of colonial domination.

As one should note, however, dialogue in this context does not mean the enactment of a ready-made consensus (the subsumption of particulars under a universalist umbrella) nor the conduct of random chatter. As invoked by Todorov, dialogical exchange means an effort at bridge building across a vast abyss, an effort which does not erase the abyss nor domesticate the "other shore." In terms of self-other relations, dialogue means exposure to an otherness which lies far beyond the self (without being totally incommensurable); it signals an alternative both to imperialist absorption or domination and to pliant self-annihilation (a surrender to an "essentialized" other). Wedged between surrender and triumph, dialogical exchange has an "agonal" or tensional quality which cannot be fully stabilized; as a corollary of self-exposure, it requires a willingness to "risk oneself," that is, to plunge headlong into a transformative learning process in which the status of self and other are continuously renegotiated.

Among contemporary Western philosophers no one is more closely associated with dialogue and dialogical learning than Hans-Georg Gadamer; but his approach is sometimes too narrowly identified with consensualism or a pre-established "fusion of horizons." Despite traces of fusionism in his earlier work, this assessment does not begin to do justice to the complexity of Gadamerian hermeneutics, especially as articulated in his later writings. To provide some "methodological" guideposts, chapter 2 explores Gadamer's views on self-other as well as cross-cultural relations, views which—especially when conjoined with parallel arguments of Jacques Derrida—yield something like a "hermeneutics of difference." The opening section of the chapter focuses on a small, so far untranslated book *Wer bin Ich und Wer bist*

Du? in which Gadamer offers an interpretation of one of Paul Celan's cycles of poems. In approaching Celan's poetic world, Gadamer does not even attempt to achieve a fusion of horizons which would reduce that world to the level of common-sense understanding. Proceeding haltingly along the path of exegesis, Gadamer's reading carefully respects the distance or otherness of Celan's poems and of their coded "message in the bottle" *(Flaschenpost)*. Respecting poetic distance also implies a willingness to refrain from willful penetration, that is, a readiness to leave blank spaces intact and thus to honor the interlacing of said and unsaid and of word and silence—which is not synonymous with a simple abandonment of interpretation.

In accepting the link of word and silence, Gadamer's approach approximates to a degree Derrida's critique of "logocentrism" and of the cult of rational or epistemic transparency, thus paving the way to a limited complicity (at least) of hermeneutics and deconstruction. From the topic of poetic and interpersonal understanding, the chapter moves on to more overtly cross-cultural issues as they are broached both in Gadamer's *Das Erbe Europas (The Legacy of Europe)* and in Derrida's *The Other Heading.* Far from endorsing the dystopia of a unified or monolithic European culture, the two texts accentuate precisely the diversity and multiplicity of European cultures—in fact the difference of Europe from itself—while suggesting that diversity can be bridged only through a (deconstructive) hermeneutics respectful of difference. Without neglecting the impact of European colonialism and of the ongoing "Europeanization" of the world, both Gadamer and Derrida thus seek to salvage a nondomineering cultural potential under the debris of Eurocentrism and traditional Orientalism.

Cross-cultural inquiry and exegesis today is no longer the monopoly of Europe or the West; in our century, non-Western voices have increasingly come to infiltrate the "conversation of humankind," thus correcting (at least in part) the monological privilege chastised by Said. Chapters 3 and 4 deal with two leading Indian philosophers and intellectuals who, in different ways, have been bridge builders between Western and non-Western cultures. A contemporary and friend of Gandhi and Nehru, Sarvepalli Radhakrishnan held important teaching posts in India and the West (chiefly Oxford), in addition to serving as ambassador of his country to the Soviet Union and, for a period, as president of the Republic of India. A spokesman of neo-Hinduism, Radhakrishnan drew inspiration chiefly from German idealism and *fin-de-siècle* life philosophy in an effort to gain fresh insight into classical Indian teachings and scriptures. Chapter 3 seeks to highlight both the stimulating promise and the intellectual drawbacks implicit in this synthesizing or harmonizing approach.

While, in Radhakrishnan's case, bridge building sometimes courted the danger of syncretism, his younger compatriot J. L. Mehta was more keenly sensitive to cultural difference (without subscribing to incommensurability). Relying chiefly on Heideggerian and Gadamerian hermeneutics, Mehta sought to liberate Indian texts from the tutelage both of Western metaphysics and of Orientalist "Indology," thereby paving the way to a postmetaphysical (and postmodern) understanding of Indian experience. In proceeding along this route, Mehta actively participated in an agonal dialogue between cultures which avoids both uncritical acceptance and uncritical rejection of Western learning.[11] Chapter 4 is devoted to a review of Mehta's complex navigation between recent Western philosophy, on the one hand, and the legacy of classical texts (especially Vedas and Vedanta) as well as popular Hinduism, on the other.

Cross-cultural conversation and sensitivity in the meantime have penetrated into the very heartland of academic Indology. Chapter 5 deals with one of the leading contemporary participants in the conversation: the German-American philosopher and Indologist Wilhelm Halbfass. More deliberately and resolutely than many of his peers, Halbfass in his studies has made an effort to "exit from Orientalism" and thus to transgress the "essentialized" images of Western and Indian culture. Relying in part on Heideggerian ontology and Gadamerian hermeneutics, these studies offer challenging and refreshingly innovative readings of traditional Indian thought, with a focus on the teachings of the classical and postclassical schools of Indian philosophy. The chapter concentrates on three main issues in Halbfass' recent work: his approach to cross-cultural understanding, particularly his relation to Heideggerian and Gadamerian teachings; his application of hermeneutical insights to the study of classical Indian texts, with special attention to the empiricist tradition in India; and finally his thoughts on the compatibility (or incompatibility) of classical Hinduism with modern Western conceptions of democracy and political equality. In each instance, his views are profiled against the backdrop of more conventional "Orientalist" doctrines.

Turning from individual thinkers to the broader plane of comparative philosophy, chapter 6 takes up the general question of the differential relation between "Western Thought and Indian Thought." Shunning the temptation of "essentialist" simplifications, the chapter takes exception to popular construals of the difference in terms of the oppositions of reason versus intuition, materialism versus spiritualism, argumentation versus scriptural authority. Following a suggestive proposal advanced by the Indian poet and linguist A. K. Ramanujan, discussion in the chapter focuses on a distinction between different types of world views and modes of communication: namely, the distinction between "context-bound" or holistic and "context-free" or linear-horizontal forms of thinking and discourse. In Ramanujan's formulation, Indian culture, art, and literature are basically contextual or embedded in concrete life worlds, whereas Western thought and discourse lean toward decontextualization and thus a spectatorial "view from nowhere." While on the whole endorsing Ramanujan's suggestion, the chapter also voices some critical reservations (especially concerning points where Ramanujan seems to succumb unwittingly to Western metaphysics).

Adopting a temporal-historical perspective, chapter 7 examines a topic that has been in the limelight of social-scientific literature during the past several decades: the status of Western and non-Western societies as seen from the angle of their respective "development," modernization, or historical teleology. With specific attention to the Indian subcontinent, the chapter reviews Indian socioeconomic and cultural development from the vantage of three alternative frameworks: those of empirical "modernization theory," of an Enlightenment model of modernity, and of "postmodernization." While modernization theory (prevalent during the postwar decades) embraced a blatant form of social-scientific Orientalism by erecting Western society into a universal standard, the Enlightenment model postulates universal or global rules of human emancipation—without, however, mediating these rules through agonal dialogue with diverse cultural traditions (especially of a non-Western vintage). Such mediation is precisely at the heart of "postmodernization," a term which must not be seen as involving a simple rejection of Western modernity. To illustrate the sense of this latter approach, the chapter offers examples from contemporary Indian writings as well as from traditional Indian literature.

Sociopolitical concerns are also at the heart of the remaining chapters assembled here. Chapter 8 analyzes the meaning and status of democracy in the light both of Western and of non-Western theoretical contributions. Relying on the customary distinction between "politics" and "the political"—where the former denotes manifest activities and the latter the stage or arena enabling such activities—the chapter first reviews salient transformations in the Western conception of sovereignty, transformations which ultimately yield a view of popular sovereignty as an "empty place" or a space of "absent presence." This view is then compared with Buddhist teachings regarding "emptiness" or *sunyata,* teachings whose historical evolution is traced from the classical age of Buddhism (Nagarjuna, Dogen) to recent reformulations by Keiji Nishitani and Masao Abe (members of the Kyoto School of Zen Buddhism).

The confluence of Western and Eastern theoretical initiatives opens the path to a conceptualization of democracy and democratic sovereignty as a regime form hovering precariously between affirmation and negativity, that is, as a mode of political will formation that can never be stabilized into a solid identity (without on this account becoming a mere playground of strategic interests). The issue of identity and diversity is further pursued in the concluding chapter 9, which is devoted to "Democracy and Multiculturalism." Returning to Todorov's suggestion of distinct cultural paradigms, the chapter first highlights recent developments in Western democratic theory and political ethics, with special attention being given to the role assigned to a "politics of (cultural) difference." These theoretical reflections then set the stage for a more detailed examination of multiculturalism in a number of political contexts, primarily in Canada and in some non-Western, developing societies. Experiences in these contexts are finally presented as incentives both for political-institutional experimentation and for theoretical innovation pointing beyond the conundrums of universalism and particularism or of globalism and local parochialism.

What all the successive chapters point to, and plead for, is a move beyond Orientalism, but one which does not end up in a bland assimilationism or a melting-pot cosmopolitanism. As it seems to me, global development can avoid turning into a global nightmare only if it is accompanied by a cultivation of deeper human potentials and aspirations, aspirations foreshadowed in different ways in the plurality of cultural traditions. Such potentials also hold the key to a genuine cross-cultural hermeneutics whose direction has been charted by Gadamer, J. L. Mehta, and others. To listen again to Gadamer, in the cited interview with Thomas Pantham: "I firmly believe that the global *status quo* [its built-in hegemony] must be changed and that a new world order of human solidarity must be brought about"; to this end, philosophical hermeneutics can contribute by fostering a "politics of dialogue and *phronesis* (practical wisdom)." These sentiments are echoed and further developed by Mehta in an essay on "The Will to Interpret and India's Dreaming Spirit":

> We live in a world in which the hitherto relatively closed horizons of the different traditions of mankind are opening out to each other and our divided histories are being joined together, or are being rejoined, in strange, unheard-of ways. . . . But so far we have no hermeneutic of a global "we," appropriate to a world factually in process of unification under the common destiny of the *Gestell* [technological enframing], and aspiring to learn to speak a common language and share in a heritage which is no

longer sharply partitioned. . . . [What is needed is] a renunciation of the voluntaristic metaphysics of the will to interpret the
other, a willingness to let the other be, only inviting him to engage in the exciting and creative task of reappropriation that lies
ahead, for him and in respect of his own tradition, endlessly open
to the future and its promise. The non-Western intellectual is
brought to see that by joining in this enterprise he may let his tradition deliver him into a truth, new and fresh, and freed from the
contingencies of its historical context, by delivering to him its
treasures of the unsaid and unthought, the treasure of the *zukün-
ftige* that lies hidden, conserved, held in reserve, in all living past.[12]

MODES OF CROSS-CULTURAL ENCOUNTER

Reflections on 1492

Just a short while ago, the Western world celebrated the quincentennial of the discovery of America. In many places, public ceremonies were conducted to commemorate a remarkable feat in Western history: the fact that (as the saying goes) in 1492 "Columbus sailed the ocean blue." Irrespective of the manifest intent of public celebrations, the latter event is properly momentous because it signals a turning point in the history of the West: a turning from an age of relative containment or self-confinement to an era of expansion, outreach, and unlimited exploration. The "Old World" at this point gave birth and extended itself into the "New World," which is only a stand-in for a series of new worlds and an infinite horizon of new frontiers. As a contemporary of Copernicus, Columbus exemplifies the Renaissance spirit of his time: the spirit of inquiry, of human self-reliance and critical defiance of customs. But his exploits also foreshadow a longer-range trajectory: by emphasizing inquiry and human autonomy, the "age of discovery" paves the way to the Reformation and the age of the Enlightenment and, still later, to the industrial and technological revolutions of modernity. As members of modern Western civilization, we all are heirs and beneficiaries of this historical trajectory and ultimately of Columbus's voyage. How can we fail to appreciate and be impressed by his journey—its daring, its sense of inquisitiveness, its technical know-how, and its sheer bravado?

Yet, as we realize, this is only part of the story. Columbus's voyage is not only historically momentous but also thought provoking—in the sense of being troubling or giving us pause to think. The story of human progress and rational emancipation is offset or counter-balanced by a radically different narrative: a narrative of domination, exploitation, and extermination, and the two stories (we vaguely sense) are not accidentally correlated. In the midst of commemorating Columbus's voyage, we are haunted by a dark sense of guilt and complicity: complicity in one of the most horrendous episodes of genocide in human history. We know today—historical evidence is overwhelming—that the expansion of Europe into the New World or rather the "conquest" of the Americas by European powers resulted in the course of less than a century in the deaths by killing, starvation, and disease of some 70 million native inhabitants.[1] In the face of these staggering figures, our celebration of 1492 is prone to be muted; likewise, our self-congratulatory exuberance as members of advanced Western civilization is liable to be debunked or at least seriously deflated. What gives us pause is not only remorse over past atrocities, but the thought of another complicity: the complicity (perhaps dialectical in character) of Western progress and domination, of rational liberation and subjugation. We are bound to wonder if there is a linkage between Western outreach or exploration and colonial and imperialist ventures. More troubling still, are scientific and technological advances intimately tied to a project of mastery over nature, including mastery over "natural" or backward people (in the sense of native, indigenous populations)? Put more generally, is progress in rational autonomy inevitably purchased at the price of a truncation of "inner nature" (as Freud surmised in *Civilization and Its Discontents*)? Seen from this angle, the year 1492 gathers in itself all the ambivalence of Western culture. Grandeur and tragedy of that culture are epitomized in Columbus's voyage.

These comments are not merely retrospective historical ruminations; as always, the past is active or sedimented in the present. Indications are that we are again in the midst of an age of Western outreach and exploration—this time of genuinely global dimensions. While during the Renaissance Europe was extending herself to the New World, our age witnesses Western extension to the world at large, through a process commonly labeled "modernization" or Westernization. Despite obvious differences of scale, the historical parallels can hardly be overlooked. Just as in the time of Columbus, Western outreach today is animated by a sense of mission, although this mission is expressed no longer in religious terms but in the secular idiom of progress and development. Again, as in 1492, exploratory outreach is accompanied or backed up by military and economic power or a structure of hegemony, with the Renaissance supremacy of Spain having been replaced by the world-wide hegemony of North America and its Atlantic partners.

In light of these historical parallels, Columbus's voyage surely must give us pause today. What—we need to ask—are the goals and likely consequences of Western expansion in our time? Is Western outreach necessarily and inextricably linked with a policy of conquest and domination, entailing the subjugation and even extermination of alien lifeforms and cultures? Are there alternatives to the Spanish and European legacies of colonialism? These questions are at the heart of this chapter. The endeavor here is to offer an overview of different possibilities or modes of cross-cultural encounter, ranging from outright domination over a number of intermediary stages to benign or empowering forms of self-other relations. Although relying (wherever feasible) on historical examples, the accent is not so much on historical scholarship as on theoretical-philosophical understanding. One further aspect should be noted: while proceeding in a classificatory vein, the presentation exceeds pure description by clinging to a normative standard, specifically the standard of mutual recognition. In Heideggerian language, the standard demands "emancipatory care" and a policy of "letting be," a "letting" that allows the other to gain freedom and identity while making room for cultural difference and diversity.[2]

Conquest

Incorporation of alien territories and populations through conquest is a long-standing practice in human history. Historical accounts of ancient and medieval politics are replete with stories of invasion, forceful occupation, and subjugation, from the Persian wars to the sacking of Rome and the later Norman Conquest. These stories are reflected in traditional political and legal theory which habitually distinguishes between government by conquest and regimes based on consent or inveterate custom. Still, not all forms of incorporation are alike. In earlier times—apart from the Islamic expansion during the Middle Ages— conquest was chiefly the outgrowth of brute aggression guided by passion or the sheer lust for power and spoliation; by comparison, modern forms of take-over tend to be more deliberate, planned, and systematic. When bent on territorial expansion, modern civilization in the West engages in what one may call a "studied" or calculated type of conquest, a type animated by general or universal ideas and geared toward the dissemination of rational principles (including rationalizations of religious beliefs). To this extent, the Spanish conquistadors— despite amazing displays of wanton brutality—were pioneers of colonial administration and early forerunners of later "development" strategies.

In his study *Culture and Conquest: America's Spanish Heritage,* G. M. Foster uses the label *conquest culture* to characterize the cultural mold imposed by the conquering power. As Foster points out, a conquest culture can be thought of as "artificial, standardized, simplified, or ideal" in that it is "at least partially consciously created and designed to cope with recognized problems." This standardized character was plainly evident in Hispanic America, given that Spanish policy was marked by "a consistent and logical philosophy of purposeful guided change that extended over a period of three centuries." The conquest culture in the Americas, according to Foster, must be clearly distinguished from the Spanish culture prevailing in the European homeland, a homeland which traditionally exhibited a high degree of diversity and of regional and local autonomy. To counteract this diversity, the conquistadors imposed on the Americas a streamlined version of Spanish politics and religion:

> A conquest culture is the result of processes that screen the more dynamic, expanding culture, winnowing out and discarding a high percentage of all traits, complexes, and configurations found in it. . . . [Thus] by administrative decision many elements of culture were withheld and new elements were devised to take their place. Formal processes, for example, produced standardized municipal organizations, as contrasted to the variety of local Iberian forms, and the grid-plan town in place of the loosely planned or completely unplanned Spanish community of the sixteenth century. Formal processes likewise congregated Indians in villages, governed commerce and trade, and introduced an ideal or theologically purified Catholic dogma and ritual to America.[3]

The systematic and standardizing outlook of the Spanish invaders was a major factor in the swift execution of the conquest and in the efficient expansion of administrative control over American territories; the same outlook also shaped decisively the encounter of the conquest culture with the native Indian populations. By all standards, the pace of the take-over itself was staggering. Barely thirty years after Columbus's voyage, Hernando Cortés had overrun and subdued the Aztec empire of Mexico, by capturing its traditional leaders (including Montezuma); a mere two decades later, Francisco Pizarro had conquered in a similar fashion the Inca kingdom centered in Peru. Placed under the aegis of the Spanish crown, these exploits became the cornerstones of the administrative viceroyalties of Mexico City and Lima, which, in turn, were only the launching pads for Spanish expansion throughout Central and South America. These exploits were greatly facilitated by the "studied" or calculating character of the conquest, that is, by the sense of rational-spiritual mission propelling the Spanish invaders— a mission which could in no way be obstructed or derailed by the distinctiveness of native Indian cultures and customs.

In his study *The Conquest of America,* Tzvetan Todorov offers a thumbnail sketch of the colonial mentality in its encounter with native cultures, a sketch focused mainly on general Cortés. As Todorov shows, Spanish colonizers were not unfamiliar with or callously disinterested in indigenous life-forms; on the contrary, they (at least the more far-sighted among them) made it a point to study and comprehend Indian culture, though with the aim of subjugating it more efficiently, not of appreciating its intrinsic worth. Emulating Bacon's dictum, the Spaniards keenly perceived the linkage of knowledge and power. In his entire behavior, Todorov notes, Cortés affords us "a splendid example" of this outlook:

> Schematically this behavior is organized into two phases. The first is that of interest in the other, at the cost of a certain empathy or temporary identification. Cortés slips into the other's skin. . . . Thereby he ensures himself an understanding of the other's language and a knowledge of the other's political organization. . . . But in so doing he has never abandoned his feeling of superiority; it is even his very capacity to understand the other that confirms him in that feeling. Then comes the second phase, during which he is not content to reassert his own identity (which he has never really abandoned), but proceeds to assimilate the Indians to his own world.

Todorov at this point offers some general observations on the (tendential) relation of European or Western culture to the rest of the world: "The Europeans exhibit remarkable qualities of flexibility and improvisation which permit them all the better to impose their own way of life."[4]

The colonizers' attitude—though on a more inchoate or unsophisticated level—was evident already in the case of Columbus and his dealings with the natives. In Todorov's portrayal, Columbus was entirely unable or unwilling to acknowledge the distinctive difference of the Indians. True to his mission and his Western-universalizing bent, he admitted only two options: either the Indians were as human beings equal to or identical with the Spaniards—in which case they were known (or knowable) and did not require a special effort of comprehension; or else they were radically different, in which case they were reduced to savages and on the same level as animate or inanimate objects of nature. This dualism was reflected in his failure to recognize linguistic diversity. When confronted with a native tongue, Todorov notes, Columbus had available only two reactions: either "to acknowledge it as a language but to refuse to believe it is different"; or "to acknowledge its difference but to refuse to admit it is a language."

The second reaction was elicited by his first encounter with Indians in October of 1492, when he wrote in a note addressed to the Spanish crown: "If it please Our Lord, at the moment of my departure I shall take from this place six of them to Your Highnesses, so that they may learn to speak." The refusal of linguistic diversity was indicative of a deeper schism in the Spanish-Indian encounter and more generally of a basic fissure in self-other relations. According to Todorov, the Spanish-Indian confrontation was a failed encounter from the start, because it was predicated on two alternative strategies: either complete assimilation or complete rejection and subjugation. These two alternatives, he muses, are not confined to the Spanish conquest but are prototypical of the behavior of "every colonist in his relations to the colonized" down "to our own day." Returning to Columbus, his study sharply delineates the main options:

> Either he conceives the Indians . . . as human beings altogether, having the same rights as himself; but then he sees them not only as equals but also as identical, and this behavior leads to assimilationism, the projection of his own values on the others. Or else he starts from the difference, but the latter is immediately translated into terms of superiority and inferiority. . . . What is denied is the existence of a human substance truly other, something capable of being not merely an imperfect state of oneself.

Drawing out broader philosophical implications, Todorov finds that the two modes of "experience of alterity" are both equally grounded in "egocentrism," that is, in the "identification of our own values with values in general, of our I with the universe—in the conviction that the world is one."[5]

By comparison with Columbus, Cortés was a more farsighted colonizer and a more efficient administrator, although his home country in the end disowned his accomplishments. As previously indicated, Cortés studiously connected knowledge and power, buttressing the latter by the former. Although falling far short of an ethnographer's talents, his policies and letters reflect a subtle grasp of the Indians' customs and beliefs, to the point of enabling him to exploit their religion to his advantage. Yet, as noted before, knowledge here does not entail mutual engagement, but is placed entirely in the service of the pursuit of economic wealth, of subjugation, and ultimately of physical destruction. In his study Todorov ponders the "dreadful concatenation" that prevails in this case between understanding and destruction. Should not understanding, he asks, "go hand in hand with sympathy?" And should not even the desire for plunder imply a desire "to preserve the other as a potential source of wealth and profit?" The attempt to unravel the concatenation is complicated by repeated expressions of admiration for the Indians on the part of Cortés and his followers; far from simply dismissing them as contemptible, the Spaniards often praise the Aztecs for their cultural accomplishments. As Todorov is quick to observe, however, such expressions of praise are striking for one feature: "with very few exceptions, they all concern *objects:* the architecture of houses, merchandise, fabrics, jewelry." Thus, Cortés and his followers behave like "today's tourists" who admire the quality of exotic craftsmanship but remain untouched by the notion "of sharing the life of the craftsmen who produce such objects." While going "into ecstasies" about Aztec products, Cortés refuses to acknowledge their makers "as human individualities to be set on the same level as himself." This leads Todorov to another philosophical observation of broader import:

> To formulate matters differently: in the best of cases, the Spanish authors speak well *of* the Indians, but with very few exceptions they do not speak *to* the Indians. Now, it is only by speaking to the other (not giving orders but engaging in a dialogue) that *I* can acknowledge *him/her* as subject, comparable to what I am myself. . . . Unless understanding is accompanied by a full acknowledgment of the other as subject, it risks being used for purposes of exploitation, of "taking"; knowledge will be subordinated to power.

This linkage of knowledge and power still leaves obscure one outstanding feature of the Spanish conquest: its resort to wonton brutality and physical destruction. Faced with staggering accounts of massacres, Todorov's study can find clues only in geographical distance, in the uprooting of the conquistadors from customary constraints: "What the Spaniards discover is the contrast between the metropolitan country and the colony, for radically different moral laws regulate conduct in each: massacre requires an appropriate context."[6]

The story of the Spanish conquest (recounted here largely through Todorov's lenses) is instructive beyond its immediate historical setting for the future of European or Western colonialism. To be sure, none of the subsequent colonial ventures can match the original Spanish exploit in the boldness and novelty of discovery, in the starkness of cultural contrasts, and (perhaps) in the extent of physical brutality. Subsequent colonizers absorbed indeed the lessons of the Spanish precedent; but on the whole they sought to emulate Cortés more in his calculating foresight than in his fits of anger. In the felicitous phrase coined in *The Conquest of America:* A "new trinity" replaces or supplements "the old-style soldier-*conquistador:* it consists of the scholar, the priest, and the merchant"; among the three, the first collects information about the country, the second promotes its "spiritual annexation," and the third "makes certain of the profits."[7]

Actually, during ensuing centuries, this trinity was further modified by additional shifts of accent; progressively, the linkage of knowledge and power was rendered more subtle and circuitous, without ever losing its cutting edge. As it happened, despite its standardizing and rationalizing bent, Spanish colonialism was never quite congruent with the demands of modern rationality; as a Catholic power, Spain was never fully in tune with the central guideposts of modernity: individual freedom (of conscience and belief), capitalist free enterprise, and political liberalism. Apart from historical contingency, this incongruence was one of the main reasons for the decline of Spanish hegemony (after 1588) and for the progressive shift of hegemonic leadership to northern European powers and ultimately to North America. Like Spain before them, these new hegemonic powers were guided in their colonizing efforts by standardizing-universal principles or ideas, but these principles were couched not in the language of church dogma but in a more secular-progressive idiom (sometimes the idiom of linear progressivism); as a corollary, Christian faith steadily gave way to, or was fused with, overarching ideologies or "world views." To this extent, the trinity of scholar-priest-merchant was gradually transformed into the triad of missionaries, entrepreneurs, and intellectuals.

To round out this discussion of conquest, we turn briefly to another Spanish colonial exploit, one that happened barely half a century after the conquest of Mexico: the Spanish take-over of the Philippines. Tellingly, the old-style reliance on the soldier-conquistador was already greatly muted in this case in favor of (Todorov's) new trinity. Apart from this shift, the Philippine take-over is noteworthy both for giving evidence of Spanish "universalism" and for demonstrating in the long run the transfer of hegemonic rule from Spain to North America. The Philippine story has been recounted in some detail by John L. Phelan (in his *The Hispanization of the Philippines*). As Phelan points out, the conquering troops this time were under strict instructions from the Spanish crown (and also from the Vatican) to replace the sword with the gospel, or at least to foreground the gospel over the sword; somewhat euphemistically, the colonial policy was now termed "pacification" or "peaceful occupation."

Regarding the objectives of the take-over, Phelan lists three main purposes, in an ascending order of universality: the first was the economic goal of gaining a share in the spice trade; the second was the mission to Christianize the inhabitants of the archipelago; and the third (astonishingly) was the aim "to establish direct contacts with China and Japan" in the hope of converting them to Catholicism. The latter aim was predicated on what Phelan calls an "almost unlimited faith" among Spaniards in their nation's power and prestige:

> The Spanish race appeared to them as God's new chosen people,
> destined to execute the plans of providence. Spain's mission was
> to forge the spiritual unity of all mankind by crushing the Protes-
> tants in the Old World, defending Christendom against the on-
> slaughts of the Turks, and spreading the gospel among the infi-
> dels of America and Asia. . . . With the conversion of the peoples
> of Asia all the races of mankind would be brought into the fold
> of Christianity, an event which some interpreted as foreshadow-
> ing the approaching end of the world.

As we know, the Spanish dream of world dominion did not material-
ize, despite remarkable strides in that direction and a stubborn display
of persistence. According to Phelan, the Spanish take-over of the Philippines began in 1565 and reached its completion only in 1898. The
entire process can be grouped into three major phases. The first was
marked by the successful occupation of the northern and central por-
tions of the archipelago; the second brought sustained offensives against
two pockets of resistance in Mindanao and northwestern Luzon. Curiously, in the third phase the entire process reached both its final culmination and its demise in the latter part of the nineteenth century. By
1898 the backbone of resistance had been broken, but this happened
"on the eve of the overthrow of the Spanish colonial regime by the
combined efforts of a Filipino nationalist revolt and the more decisive
intervention of the United States."[8]

Conversion

In its typical form, conquest entails the physical subjugation of alien
populations and sometimes also their forced cultural assimilation;
where the latter feature predominates, conquest gives way to conversion. Although often closely linked, conquest and conversion are not
always or necessarily connected. History teaches that there have been
conquests without any overt efforts of assimilation, although modern-
style take-overs usually involve also the dissemination of general ideas
(religious or ideological); conversely, there have been conversions in
the absence of conquest or forced subjugation (and sometimes even
as counter-moves to political and cultural domination). Although distinguishable, the two modes of outreach share one prominent feature:
the denial of meaningful human difference. In the case of conquest,
difference is actually affirmed but in a radical-hierarchical way which
sacrifices mutuality in favor of the rigid schism of mind and matter,
culture and nature, civilized people and savages. In the case of conversion, difference is denied through the insistence on a common or

identical human nature—an identity which predestines native populations to be willing targets of proselytizing missions.

As one should note, conversion is not an inextricable ingredient of
religious faith. Several of the leading world religions have been strongly
averse to missionary practices. This is true among Western religions
of Judaism and among Eastern religions (or quasireligions) of Hinduism,
Taoism, and Confucianism. In the latter category, only Buddhism has
engaged in large-scale missionary outreach, but in a manner typically
shunning conquest in favor of teaching and practical example. This
leaves as missionary world religions of a militant type only Islam and
Christianity. Among the two, Christianity has been historically more
successful, mainly because of its closer kinship with the modern spirit
of individualism and progress (enshrined in the "Protestant Ethic").
While the heyday of Islamic expansion occurred during the Middle
Ages and before 1492, Christian expansion started with the voyage of
Columbus and later merged with the secular aspirations of Western
modernity.[9]

The story of the initial growth and dissemination of Islam in the
Near East and along the Mediterranean has often been told in considerable detail, sometimes with close attention to its encounters with
pre-Islamic, animistic forms of belief.[10] The same cannot be said of the
early growth and dissemination of Christianity throughout Europe. We
have accounts of the missionary "acts" of the apostles and we also
have accounts of Christian martyrdom at the hands of nonbelievers
(Jews and gentiles); but we lack detailed narratives shedding light on
the triumphant expansion of Christianity after the conversion of Emperor Constantine. What is obvious is that the expansion occurred at
an amazing speed and that in the end hardly a trace was left of earlier modes of worship or "pagan" beliefs (despite instances of local accommodation). Given the scope of the process and the long duration
of pre-Christian beliefs, one cannot assume that the transformation
happened without conflict or resistance and without recourse to deliberate strategies of subjugation—strategies which (perhaps) foreshadowed later policies of "pacification."

On the whole, the attitude of the early church alternated between
outright rejection of pagan beliefs and selective "utilization" (chresis)
of pagan traditions and teachings, that is, their modified incorporation
into Christian doctrine. Although practiced by some eminent theologians, utilization always remained suspect in the eyes of the church
hierarchy; in case of doubt, or where necessary for the defense of orthodox faith, incorporation always had to cede to condemnation. The
writings of many of the church fathers still reflect the intensity of the
struggle—at least on the intellectual (though rarely the political) level.

Tertullian and Origen have left us lengthy treatises directed against *(contra)* the pagans or gentiles—treatises which are exercises in apologetics and hardly based on mutuality or dialogue (the term *pagan* is itself part of Christian nomenclature). In his *City of God,* St. Augustine goes to great length to defend Christianity against the charge of having contributed to the downfall of Rome. His strategy is simple: he blandly pits Christian virtue against Roman vice, divine salvation against mundane-pagan corruption. While successful in combating a Caligula, this argument notably runs into difficulties when dealing with an upright Roman like Varro who, in his writings and life, upholds traditional Roman virtues and religious beliefs (without being proto-Christian). At this point, St. Augustine—in a curiously modernist move—appeals to the more enlightened rationality of Christian faith in comparison with pagan ignorance and superstition. In the words of the Spanish missionary Bernardino de Sahagún:

> Saint Augustine did not believe it would be a vain or superfluous affair to treat of the fabulous theology of the gentiles, in the sixth book of the *City of God;* because, as he himself says, the fables and vain fictions of which the gentiles made use on the subject of their false gods, once being known, it would become easier to make them understand that these were no gods at all and that, from their essence, nothing useful should proceed for beings endowed with reason.[11]

Sahagún was a Franciscan missionary who arrived in Mexico a decade after its conquest by Cortés. By this time, conversion of the indigenous populations was well under way and had already reached its more subdued or "pacifying" stage. Actually, conversion was an intrinsic feature of the Spanish invasion from the beginning and—next to the desire for plunder—served as its chief justifying rationale. This rationale was already embraced by Columbus himself, albeit in a somewhat intuitive and unsystematic fashion. On his first return to Spain he decided to take some native Indians with him so that, through their exposure to Spanish ways of life, they "might adopt our customs and our faith." In a journal entry of December 1492, he recommends these Indians to the attention of the Spanish crown, saying: "Your Highnesses may have great joy of them, for soon you will have made them into Christians and will have instructed them in the good manners of your kingdoms"—these good manners including the profession of (Catholic) Christian faith and the habit to "wear clothes." As indicated before, missionary efforts—once deliberately undertaken—were generally predicated on the assumption of a shared human nature and hence on the belief that native populations were basically predisposed to Christian faith and thus ready and eager to accept the opportunity of salvation offered to them. As it happened, this expectation was occasionally rudely disappointed. Todorov recounts an episode which sheds light on the difficulties of the conversion process and also on some hazards of Christian charitableness:

> In the course of the second expedition, the priests accompanying Columbus begin converting the Indians; but it is far from the truth that all of them submit and consent to venerate the holy images. "After having left the chapel, these men flung the images to the ground, covered them with a heap of earth, and pissed upon it"; seeing which, Bartholomé, Columbus's brother, decides to punish them in quite Christian fashion. "As lieutenant of the Viceroy and governor of the islands, he brought these wretched men to justice and, their crimes being duly attested to, he caused them to be burned alive in public."[12]

As it seems, incidents of this kind were not rare but recurrent, which may account in part for the extreme savagery characterizing the colonization or Hispanization of America well into the period of pacification. This savagery was uppermost in the mind of one of the most perceptive and affable Christian missionaries of that era: the Dominican Bartolomé de Las Casas. For Las Casas—as later for Sahagún—the atrocities committed by the Spanish were an indictment of the military method of colonization and a compelling motive for replacing that method with missionary endeavors more in tune with the teachings of the gospel. In his *Brevissima Relación (The Tears of the Indians)*, Las Casas offers a gripping account of Spanish cruelties: hangings, mutilations, burnings—which was meant as an appeal to the Spanish crown for a change of policy (and which later provided welcome ammunition to the Protestant enemies of Spain in northern Europe). In a truly historic encounter, Las Casas entered into an intense and remarkable debate with the historian Ginés de Sepúlveda at Valladolid (in 1550). Relying in part on Aristotelian teachings, Sepúlveda justified the subjugation of the Indians on the basis of their natural inferiority, thereby submitting conversion to the logic of conquest. Politics as well as religious salvation in his view were governed by the same principle: the dominion "of perfection over imperfection, of force over weakness, of eminent virtue over vice"; seen in this light, the Indians were related to the Spaniards in the same way as "children are to adults" or "women to men" or savages and "wild beasts" to civilized people.

On all these counts, Las Casas opted for a radically opposite out-look, namely, for a strictly egalitarian conception according to which all humans are equally endowed with a soul and hence equally called to salvation through Christian faith. As he expostulated in his re-joinder to Sepúlveda (published under the title *Apologia* or *In Defense of the Indians*): "Aristotle, farewell! From Christ, the eternal truth, we have the commandment 'You must love your neighbor as yourself.'. . . Christ seeks souls, not property." Animated by this spirit, Las Casas advocated a complete shift of strategy: specifically the abandonment of military conquest, of forced land acquisition *(encomienda)*, and of Indian slavery. Still, despite these humanitarian pleas, Todorov is probably on safe ground when he charges Las Casas with spiritual colonialism, that is, with continued support for His-panization or the "annexation of the Indians," provided the latter was "effected by priests rather than by soldiers." Todorov also casts doubt on neighborly love if accompanied by missionary conversion: "Can we really love someone if we know little or nothing of his identity; if we see, in place of that identity, a projection of ourselves or of our ideals? . . . Does not one culture risk trying to transform the other in its own name, and therefore risk subjugating it as well? How much is such love worth?"[13]

Las Casas was not successful in transforming colonial practices, al-though he did manage to instill in colonial administrators the need for greater subtlety, circumspection, and (perhaps) subterfuge. Following the Reformation and as a corollary of the rise of capitalist markets, colonial hegemony tended to shift from Spain (and Portugal) to north-ern European powers, especially to England and the Netherlands. As in the case of Spain, colonial expansion by these powers was accom-panied or closely followed by missionary endeavors intent on spread-ing religious beliefs as well as cultural and ideological preferences. Seen as the "white man's burden," the civilizing mission of the West came to affect increasingly the entire fabric of life (from worship to politics and economics) of non-Western populations in a manner fore-shadowing later strategies of development and modernization. In the field of religious conversion, Christian missionaries working in tan-dem with colonizers concentrated their efforts on Africa, India, and the Far East, often pursuing a path which navigated ambiguously be-tween Cortés and Las Casas.

To resume a point made earlier, conversion does not always serve the purposes of colonizers or colonial rule, but may occasionally have oppositional and even subversive connotations. This has to do with a central feature of religious faith: the ability of such faith to transcend prevailing social and political conditions and hence to become a resource for liberation rather than domination. Thus, in the case of India, Mahatma Gandhi was able to invoke the Hindu notions of *'swaraj,'* *'satyagraha,'* and *'ramaraja'* as guideposts in his struggle against British colonial oppression. On the other hand, especially after the accomplishment of independence, various groups in Indian society disenfranchised by the prevailing caste system became willing targets of conversion to Islam and Buddhism (occasionally to Christianity), sometimes on a large scale. As Lloyd and Susanne Rudolph have reported, in 1956 at least 3 million and perhaps as many as 20 million untouchables were converted to Buddhism in the state of Maharashtra alone. Again, during more recent decades, entire villages of untouchables have reportedly been converted to Islam, especially in the state of Tamil Nadu. Although in all these cases the role of political and financial manipulation cannot be entirely ignored, the deeper reason for these events was surely the desire of disadvantaged people for greater freedom and respect (however elusive this goal may be under the circumstances).[14]

Assimilation and Acculturation

As we have noted, conversion is not always a corollary of conquest, nor is it necessarily restricted to the dissemination of religious beliefs. Apart from colonial expansion in foreign lands, cultural hegemony may also be exercised in a "domestic" (that is, politically more or less settled) context and, in this case, may involve the spreading of diffuse cultural patterns or ways of life (of religious and/or secular vintage); the targets of such hegemonic outreach are typically marginalized ethnic, national, or linguistic groups (sometimes composed of immigrant populations). In contradistinction from external colonialism, domestic colonization of this kind tends to be discussed by social scientists and anthropologists under the headings of "assimilation" or acculturation. Some broad definitions may be in order here. According to Robert Park and Ernest Burgess, assimilation may be seen as "a process of interpenetration and fusion in which persons and groups acquire the memories, sentiments, and attitudes of other persons and groups and, by sharing their experience and history, are incorporated by them in a common cultural life." While assimilation is usually applied to policies in some Western or Westernizing nations, the term *acculturation* tends to have a broader and more indefinite application, extending from domestic contacts to global interactions between the hegemonic Western culture and developing non-Western societies.

In our century, assimilation and, to some extent, acculturation have been greatly abetted and intensified by nationalism and the idea of the nation-state. In the well-known words of Rupert Emerson:

> In the contemporary world, the nation is for greater portions of
> mankind the community with which men most intensely and most
> unconditionally identify themselves. . . . The nation is today the
> largest community which, when the chips are down, effectively
> commands men's loyalty, overriding the claims both of the lesser
> communities within it and those which cut across it. . . . In this
> sense the nation can be called a "terminal community."

The hegemonic influence of nationalism and the nation-state, one
should note, is not confined to advanced Western countries but extends to non-Western, postcolonial societies. While initially opposing
the "state" as an alien, colonial apparatus, independence movements
quickly adopted a nationalist rhetoric geared toward the acquisition
of state power. "In seeking the mandate," Crawford Young writes, "the
anticolonial leadership began the process of transforming the often-
arbitrary colonial state into a nation."[15]

In the Western orbit, the most frequently discussed and conspicuous examples of cultural assimilation are the United States and Israel. In both cases, large numbers of immigrants from many parts of
the world were progressively integrated or incorporated into the dominant social and political fabric. For over a century now, the United
States has been celebrated as a successful instance of "melting-pot"
policies in practice. Wave after wave of immigrants were steadily
socialized or assimilated into the prevailing "American way of life"
with its accent on individual initiative and the profit motive. Even
where major cracks or fissures appeared in the melting-pot model,
remedy was typically sought not through a revision of that model
but through closer incorporation or "integration" of marginalized
groups—as was evident in the early phases of the civil rights movement. During subsequent years, the cracks continued to widen steadily,
giving rise to intense ethnic rivalries, "black power" movements, and
inner-city riots in many parts of the country. In their study *Beyond
the Melting Pot,* which was written during these developments,
Nathan Glazer and Daniel Moynihan assessed the situation in these
terms: "The notion that the intense and unprecedented mixture of
ethnic and religious groups in American life was soon to blend into
a homogeneous end product has outlived its usefulness, and also its
credibility."

Their comments were seconded by numerous other observers, including Milton Gordon, who pointed to the persistence of "structurally
separate subsocieties" in American culture, and Michael Novak, with
his emphasis on "unmeltable" ethnic groups. In the wake of these
challenges and experiences, melting-pot rhetoric was increasingly
supplemented if not replaced by alternative theoretical formulas, such

as the notions of 'cultural pluralism' or of a confederated 'rainbow coalition' of cultures sustaining a broader social synthesis. In the case of Israel, the assimilation model was simplified from the beginning by the fact that immigrants—although they came from different countries—all shared the same (or similar) religious background. Where such cultural commonality is lacking, melting-pot consensus quickly tends to give way to conflict, as is evident in Israeli-Palestinian relations during recent decades.[16]

Returning to the story of Hispanic America, assimilation became a dominant policy in the newly independent countries which emerged in the early part of the last century. By that time, Latin American societies were already strongly shaped by the cultural patterns of the Spanish (and Portuguese) homeland, patterns carried forward chiefly by "creoles" (European stock born overseas). This hegemonic patterning was intensified during the postindependence period. In the words of Crawford Young:

> During the unstable and tumultuous years of the nineteenth century, the creole elite indelibly stamped its cultural imprint on the new states. The key culture-forming groups—lawyer, *caudillo,* intellectual, or priest—were firmly Hispanic. The nodal points of urban culture—the towns and cities—were a generalized model of the Iberian community, remarkably uniform in spatial configuration and cultural pattern from the Rio Grande to the Straits of Magellan.

During the course of the last century, the hegemonic culture shaped by colonizers and creoles was progressively disseminated through the rest of society, especially to the mestizo, mulatto, and native Indian populations, in a manner approximating the melting-pot syndrome. Usually termed "mestization," this process of assimilation extended even to areas, such as Peru and Bolivia, where Indians formed a large majority at the time of independence. Only in recent times have cracks in the cultural fabric been noted by social scientists and anthropologists; as in the case of North America, analytical models based on assimilation and mestization are challenged today by accounts stressing cultural diversity and ethnic rivalry. The situation in the Philippines was more complicated. Despite the extensive impact of Hispanization and Christian conversion, the relatively small number of Spanish settlers allowed the emergence of a native (or mestizo) Filipino elite which became the backbone of the nationalist movement during the late nineteenth century. This diverse cultural background was compounded subsequently by the American colonial influence with its stress on modern industry and democracy. In its general fabric, Filipino society thus can be said to straddle the models of "integration and cultural pluralism."[17]

These comments on cultural fusion require further amplification. As one should note, assimilation is not only or exclusively a policy imposed from above, that is, a process whereby a hegemonic culture is disseminated by an elite to subordinate segments of the population. Sometimes (perhaps quite frequently), the hegemonic culture holds a powerful attraction for subordinate groups eager to gain social acceptance or recognition and thus to terminate discrimination. Where such acceptance is pursued deliberately and with some promise of success, we are in the presence of acculturation through upward mobility. This phenomenon is well-known in Western societies where members of underprivileged or marginalized groups may be engaged in a struggle for higher social status (sometimes termed *"embourgeoisement"*). In the context of Indian society, the process of upward mobility on the part of lower castes or subcastes has been analyzed perceptively and in detail by M. N. Srinivas under the label "Sanskritization." As Srinivas points out, by means of caste associations lower status groups have often been able to break through established caste barriers by adopting elite cultural patterns, for example, by performing ritual practices associated with the higher (or "twice-born") castes.

Following Srinivas and the Rudolphs, Crawford Young discusses the case of the Nadars in Tamil Nadu in southern India. According to the traditional caste structure, the Nadars were placed below the Sudra category (though not quite at the bottom of the pyramid) and thus were subjected to various ritual disabilities (such as exclusion from certain temples and physical distance from Brahmans). During the colonial period, the Nadars managed to escape the yoke of stark poverty by becoming commercially active; this change in economic well-being was soon followed by the adoption of upper-class cultural patterns (a move at first fiercely resisted by elite groups): women began to wear higher caste clothes, marriage ceremonies copied aspects of Brahmanic ritual, and some members insisted on wearing the sacred thread. Summarizing the metamorphosis, Young observes: "Today, the Nadars are recognized as an 'advanced' community—a status reversal accomplished over the past century through horizontal mobilization of group solidarity, challenge to servile traditional ascription through ritual transformation, effective utilization of modern opportunity through education and commerce, and skillful communal exploitation of the political arena." Young also points to other cases of upward group mobility in non-Western societies outside India. A telling example is the Fur tribe of western Sudan which, over an extended period of time, came into growing contact with Arab groups who were seen as the carriers of the "superior" Arabic or Islamic culture. From these groups, the Fur acquired the religion of Islam, trading practices, a school system, and especially access to the Arabic language. In Young's account, Arabic is associated with "superior force, a religion of great prestige" as well as "social and economic modernization opportunities through school or urban migration." He adds that command of Arabic is "a fair measure of the internal distribution of social mobility opportunity among the Fur."[18]

Partial Assimilation: Cultural Borrowing

Cultural encounter does not always entail merger or fusion, but may lead to partial adaptation or assimilation, through a process of cultural borrowing (and lending). For such adaptation to happen, the respective cultures must face each other on a more nearly equal or roughly comparable basis, in contradistinction to the starkly hegemonic or hierarchical relation characterizing the previously discussed cases. Partial adaptation, in any case, involves a greater subtlety in self-other relations. In opposition to the self-imposition (through dissemination) or self-surrender (through upward mobility) marking hegemonic situations, selective borrowing requires a willingness to recognize the distinctiveness of the other culture, coupled with a desire to maintain at least some indigenous preferences. The outcome of such partial accommodation can be greatly varied. In some instances—which are less interesting because of their affinity to the melting-pot syndrome—the result may be the complete absorption of foreign ingredients in the prevailing cultural matrix, in a process which may be termed partial "incorporation." In other cases, encounter may facilitate a pattern of mutual adjustment or reciprocal give-and-take which, in turn, can engender either an ambivalent form of syncretism or a precarious type of cultural juxtaposition or coexistence. In some instances, finally, exposure to alien cultural strands may initiate a movement of genuine self-transformation, that is, a reassessment of prevailing patterns in the light of newly experienced insights or modes of life. Here as elsewhere, of course, theoretical distinctions need to be applied cautiously: concrete historical examples tend to resist neat labeling and to range frequently across a whole spectrum of possibilities.

Partial assimilation and selective borrowing are familiar to Western culture. Throughout the course of Western history we find many episodes of partial adjustment and incorporation, sometimes to the point of calling into question the very notion of indigenous traditions. Through recent historical scholarship we are acquainted with the extent to which early Greece borrowed from North African and Mycenean cultures. Within the confines of the Greek peninsula, we are also familiar with the intense process of cultural exchange among the various city states, although a sharp cultural barrier was erected by all of them against the "barbarians" in the East. During the period of the Roman Republic, Greek intellectual influence was steadily on the rise: several of the famous philosophical schools, including the Epicureans and the Stoics, were originally founded in Greece before being transplanted to Roman soil. With the expansion of imperial power, Rome came increasingly into contact with alien—especially Near Eastern—cultures and belief systems; despite an official policy of conquest and colonization, the repercussions of these peripheral cultures on the Roman metropolis can hardly be ignored or underestimated. To this extent, the Hellenistic and the imperial periods were times of rampant syncretism.

Accommodation and the practice of cultural borrowing continued into the Middle Ages. The practice of "utilization" *(chresis)*, that is, the partial absorption of pagan teachings by Christianity, has been mentioned before. At a later point, the rise of Islamic culture around the Mediterranean led to the wide dissemination of Muslim philosophical and scientific scholarship, which provided an enormous boost to Western learning and Christian scholasticism during the eleventh and twelfth centuries. Still a few centuries later, the fall of Constantinople triggered a large-scale exodus of Greek scholars from the territories of "eastern Rome," a migration that provided a strong impulse to the European Renaissance. Without question, one of the most significant episodes of cultural borrowing during the later Middle Ages was the "reception" of classical Roman law, especially of the legacy of the *ius civile,* a legacy that subsequently became the cornerstone of jurisprudence in Continental European countries (and their colonies). In this case, borrowing took the form of a complex process of adaptation and partial incorporation, with classical Roman principles being uneasily balanced against historically grown legal customs and local statutory provisions. In the account of one competent observer, whose comments refer specifically to the German situation, the reception of Roman law was "affected with much less strife and opposition than might have been expected from the radical nature of the experiment"; progressively German jurists trained in indigenous common law also became learned "judges in civil law."[19]

Cultural borrowing during the Middle Ages was not restricted to the Continent and Near East, but sometimes extended far afield. In view of the broad acclaim accorded to 1492 and the voyages of Columbus, it may be appropriate to call attention to another explorer and voyager whose travels took him precisely in the opposite direction: the

Italian Marco Polo. About two centuries before Columbus's expedition, Marco Polo set out to visit far-off China which at that time was under the dominion of the Mongol ruler Kublai Khan. Contrary to some Western prejudices, the Mongol dynasty was seriously interested in advanced forms of culture. At the conclusion of an earlier visit by Marco's father, Kublai Khan had sent the traveler back to his homeland furnished with letters to the pope requesting the dispatch of a group of educated scholars to instruct his people in Christian doctrine and the liberal arts. In 1271, Marco and his companions embarked on their long soujourn in the Far East which came to an end only twenty-five years later.

Departing from Venice, the travelers went first to Hormuz at the Persian Gulf with the intent of reaching China by sea; abandoning this plan, however, they turned northward through Persia, following basically the fabled "silk road." Traversing Khurusan they ascended the upper Oxus to reach the plateau of Pamir from where they proceeded to cross the Gobi desert (which Polo called the "desert of Lop") until they finally reached the court of Kublai Khan at Shangtu. On arrival Marco immediately embarked on studying local languages and soon entered the public service where he quickly rose to high administrative positions. Repeatedly he was sent by the Khan to distant provinces or outposts from where he returned with intriguing firsthand reports. On their way back, Marco and his companions voyaged from China to Persia by sea and from there by land to Venice, carrying with them again friendly messages from the Khan to the pope and several kings in Europe. The travelers had not actually recorded their experiences during their visit abroad; it was only several years after his return that Marco dictated his story to a fellow Italian (while he was a prisoner in Genoa). The written account of Marco's travels sparked considerable European interest in the Far East, while also lending impulse to advances in "scientific" cartography. During the Renaissance and Reformation this interest subsided somewhat, being overshadowed by revived concern with classical and biblical antiquity and by fascination with the New World (America). A renewed upsurge of attentiveness to China occurred during the Enlightenment or "age of reason" when enlightened forms of absolutism emulated the bureaucratic practices of the Asian kingdom, while at the same time cultivating a taste for Chinese modes of dress, coiffure (wigs), and courtly behavior.[20]

Explorations and distant voyages are sometimes considered a European or a Western monopoly, but this is far from true. A case in point is the extension of Buddhism to China, Japan, and other parts of the Far East, an extension that constitutes one of the most remarkable instances of cultural borrowing in human history. Borrowing and lending here were closely tied to exploratory voyages. In a well-known study, Erik Zürcher speaks of "the Buddhist conquest of China," but this is surely a misnomer. Buddhism was brought from India to China by traveling monks who faced great hardship, and sometimes even persecution, on their long journeys; they definitely were not accompanied by well-armed troops of *conquistadors* under the command of a Cortés or a Pizarro. The first Buddhist monks arrived in China in the first century (C.E.), bringing with them many sacred texts as well as the Buddhist practices of meditation *(dhyana)* and concentration *(samadhi)*. On their arrival they encountered an alien culture, which in some ways was quite congenial to their own, but in other ways was radically different. One of the principal tasks faced by these itinerant monks was the translation of sacred texts from Sanskrit or Pali into the Chinese idiom, a task which required enormous skills of interpretation, as well as a good dose of cultural flexibility and mutual adjustment. As a result of these exegetic labors, Buddhism was infused or supplemented with prevailing Taoist ideas—especially the wisdom teachings of Lao-tzu and Chuang-tzu—while Taoism in turn was amplified and transformed through the integration of Buddhist ontology and metaphysics. In the words of Heinrich Dumoulin, whose study of Buddhism in India and China carefully traces the complex interaction between elements of Indian and Chinese culture:

> The transplanting of Buddhism from its native soil in India into the culture and life of China may be counted among the most significant events in the history of religions. It meant the introduction of a higher religion—complete with scriptural canon, doctrines, morality, and cult—into a land with an ancient culture of its own. . . . The use of Taoist terms for Buddhist beliefs and practices not only helped in the difficult task of translation but also brought Buddhist scriptures closer to the Chinese people. . . . The "Taoist guise" that Buddhism donned did not remain external but worked deep-reaching changes on Buddhist thought. This encounter with the spiritual heritage of ancient China became a fountainhead that was to nourish the various schools of Chinese Buddhism, all of which were intimately related to one another despite doctrinal differences.[21]

As indicated, cultural outreach here was initiated and carried forward not by generals and merchants desirous of power and wealth, but by learned monks willing to cross or transgress traditional cultural boundaries. One of the earliest itinerant scholars to arrive in China was An Shih-Kao, often described as the "first important known Buddhist translator in China"; among his primary endeavors was the translation of some classical sutras as well as the teaching of Buddhist meditational techniques, which were curiously blended with Taoist practices. Probably the most well known and celebrated Indian Buddhists traveling to China were Kumarajiva and Bodhidharma—the former being a historically well-attested scholar of the late fourth century, the second a somewhat more legendary figure of the early sixth century. A native of northern India, Kumarajiva as a young man entered a Buddhist monastery where he studied both Hinayana and Mahayana literature, developing progressively a decided preference for Mahayana teachings. Having gained great scholarly prestige in his homeland, he traveled in his later years to China where he established a translation institute in Ch'ang-an (the later Xian). Among the most impressive accomplishments of Kumarajiva is the translation into Chinese, in one hundred volumes, of a commentary on the *Mahaprajñaparamita Sutra* (Sutra of Perfect Wisdom) traditionally ascribed to Nagarjuna. It was largely due to Kumarajiva's efforts that Mahayana Buddhism, in its Madhyamika version, gained conclusive ascendancy in China over alternative Buddhist schools.

According to more elusive historical records, Bodhidharma was born into a Brahman family in southern India, but in his youth joined a Buddhist order and then set out on a long and difficult journey to southern Asia. On arriving he is said to have encountered and engaged in verbal sparring with Emperor Wu, founder of the Liang dynasty. Legend recounts that Bodhidharma next crossed the Yangtze River on a reed and for nine years remained seated in meditation before the wall of a monastery until his legs withered away. Less renowned as a translator, Bodhidharma is remembered chiefly for his unconventional teaching and meditational techniques, some of which aroused much opposition at the time. Foremost among these methods was his resort to sharp, paradoxical verbal exchanges *(koans)* geared toward triggering enlightenment. Due to these methods and other accomplishments, Bodhidharma is revered as the founder of Ch'an or Zen Buddhism; actually, Zen practitioners regard him as the first Chinese patriarch (and the twenty-eighth Indian patriarch after the Buddha Sakyamuni). In this capacity he established a long line of descent and an intellectual tradition which eventually leaped beyond the boundaries of China. In the words of a poem ascribed to Bodhidharma himself:

> I came to this land originally to transmit the Dharma
> And to bring deliverance from error.
> A flower opens five petals.
> The fruit ripens of itself.[22]

From China Buddhism spread quickly to Japan, Korea, and adjacent lands in the Far East; again, cultural borrowing and lending were mainly the work of traveling monks and scholars disseminating Buddha's teachings by land and by sea. By the time of Bodhidharma, Buddhism was already beginning to infiltrate Japan; publicly accepted during the following century, it soon flourished in different branches or schools of thought. Still, despite broad acceptance, knowledge and availability of sacred texts tended to be limited; to remedy this defect, Japanese monks set out in the other direction to gain deeper training and insight. Easily the most impressive of these travelers was the monk Ennin, also known in Japan as Jikaku Daishi. Some three hundred years after Bodhidharma and four centuries before Marco Polo, Ennin crossed the sea to China where he spent about a decade, keeping a detailed record or diary of his extensive travels through the vast country (then under the T'ang dynasty); significantly, the diary was titled "Record of a Pilgrimage to China in Search of the Law" (or *dharma).* While Marco Polo was mainly a trader looking for commercial contacts, Ennin was a learned scholar enjoying considerable prestige in his homeland. Comparing the two travelers, Edwin Reischauer—who has translated Ennin's diary into English and also provided an extensive commentary—writes:

> Marco Polo, coming from a radically different culture, was ill-prepared to understand or appreciate what he saw of higher civilization in China. He was virtually unaware of the great literary traditions of the country and, living in a China which was still in large part Buddhist, comprehended little of this religion other than that it was "idolatrous." Ennin, coming from China's cultural offshoot—Japan—was at least a stepson of Chinese civilization, educated in the complicated writing system of the Chinese and himself a learned Buddhist scholar. Marco Polo came to China as an associate of the hated Mongol conquerors; Ennin, as a fellow believer, entered easily into the heart of Chinese life.

In his commentary, Reischauer accompanies Ennin on his manifold adventures, from his early association with the Japanese embassy in China to his religious pilgrimage through the country to his later tribulations during one of the high points of Buddhist persecution in China. Along the way, the reader learns innumerable details about the culture, economy, and political structure of T'ang China. In introducing his own scholarly work, Reischauer offers a general observation that still deserves pondering today. "In the present age," he notes, "in which we are experiencing the painful process of amalgamation into one world, a great historical document of this sort, although medieval in time and Far Eastern in place, is part of our common human heritage, with significance beyond these limits of time and space."[23]

Liberalism and Minimal Engagement

In the cases just mentioned, cultural borrowing involved a prolonged, sometimes arduous process of engagement in alien life-forms, a process yielding at least a partial transformation of native habits due to a sustained learning experience. However, cultural contacts do not always or necessarily entail such engagement. Sometimes cultures are content to live or co-exist side by side in a mode of relative indifference; this is true mainly of contacts occurring under the aegis of modern liberalism, particularly its "procedural" variant. Faithful to its motto of laissez-faire (let it be, do not meddle), modern liberalism has promoted a tolerant juxtaposition of cultures and life-forms predicated on relative mutual disinterest and aloofness. While acknowledging the need for an overall framework (to prevent chaos), liberal spokesmen typically support only a limited procedural rule system or a government that "governs least," while relegating concrete life-forms to the status of privatized folklore. Self-other relations, in this case, are curiously split or dichotomized: while sameness or identity is presumed to persist on the level of general principle (stylized as "reason" or "human nature"), historical cultures and beliefs are abandoned to rampant heterogeneity (tending toward segregation or ghettoization).

Most advanced Western societies are imbued in some fashion with this liberal "ethos." Curiously, the United States is often analyzed in terms of two radically opposed models: those of the "melting pot" and those of liberal proceduralism; while the former model postulates the progressive assimilation of all strands into *one* uniform culture, the latter extols the neutrality or indifference of procedures toward any and all cultures. Although serving as an antidote to melting-pot assumptions, the second model is not necessarily more accurate as an analytical tool or more enticing as a blueprint for cultural encounter. Despite its appealing "open-mindedness," liberal tolerance tends to be purchased at a price: the price of a schism between form and substance, between public and private domains of life. To this extent, the noted move "beyond the melting pot" can (and needs to) be supplemented in our time by a striving beyond proceduralism.

The model of procedural liberalism is sufficiently well known to permit brief summary in the present context. Among American spokesmen of the model, John Rawls, Ronald Dworkin, and Bruce Ackerman are the writers most frequently and appropriately singled out for attention. In his *A Theory of Justice* and other writings, Rawls seeks to develop a conception of procedural fairness (not substantive "goodness") which would transcend, or be impartial with respect to, individual or group-based cultural traditions and religious beliefs. Focusing on prevailing conditions in modern Western society, Rawls notes certain basic cultural features (which he labels "subjective circumstances"), chiefly the fact that "persons and associations have contrary conceptions of the good as well as of how to realize them" and that these differences "set them at odds, and lead them to make conflicting claims on their institutions." In order to mitigate (without in any way trying to eliminate) prevailing contrasts among ways of life, Rawls's study postulates as the chief task of political theory the formulation of abstractly universal principles which could be endorsed by all members of society in a spirit of impartiality; as is well known, the central principles announced in the study are those of "equal liberty" (guaranteeing the free pursuit of life projects) and of "difference" (providing protection against structural disadvantages).

The axiom of equal liberty has been further elaborated by Dworkin under the heading of "equality principle" or "liberal conception of equality." According to Dworkin, modern government in the pursuit of equal justice must be rigorously "neutral on what might be called the question of the good life"; likewise, public policies must be "independent of any conception of the good life or of what gives value to life," whether the conception is held by single individuals or by members of a cultural, ethnic, or religious community. Taking some cues from Dworkin, Ackerman has erected neutrality into the central cornerstone of liberal constitutional theory and legal adjudication. In Ackerman's view, the principle of neutrality would be violated if a ruling or adjudication would privilege one cultural tradition or way of life over another and—more strictly still—if it even acknowledged as legally relevant prevailing differences or contrasts among traditions or cultural beliefs. In this construal, liberal proceduralism—seen as the embodiment of "formal" reason—triumphs completely over historically grown life-forms (which are reduced to contingent accidents or "subjective" preferences); far from being the outgrowth of concrete cultural interaction, liberal justice appears predicated on a cultural *tabula rasa*.[24]

The shortcomings of liberal proceduralism have been frequently discussed—which again permits brevity at this point. On a logical-theoretical plane, the dilemma of proceduralism can be stated succinctly as follows: either justice is truly neutral and universal, in which case it is abstract, devoid of content, and collapses into tautology; or else it is endowed with some content, in which case it is embued with cultural distinctness (where culture denotes a way of life and not merely a "subjective circumstance"). This dilemma has been frankly acknowledged by Rawls, whose candor in this respect might set an example to liberal proceduralists. As Rawls has noted in some recent writings, his theory of justice is not designed for all times and places, but is tailored to the cultural climate of modern, liberal-constitutional societies, a climate that implies distinct assumptions about human behavior, intersubjective (contractual) relations, and secular life styles. However, the problems of proceduralism are not only logical in character; more important are its effects on cultural interaction. Under liberal-procedural auspices, differences of life-forms are either completely bracketed or else they are (more candidly) subordinated to the prevailing or hegemonic liberal culture; in either case, concrete cross-cultural engagement tends to be stifled or circumvented.

This stifling impact is at the heart of a complaint that has been eloquently stated by William Connolly in his *Identity/Difference*. While opposing advocates of assimilation or "collective identity," Connolly also finds fault with "liberal neutralism" or proceduralism. As he points out, liberal neutralism recognizes the "volatility" of competing life styles or identity claims, but would like to "exclude such conflicts from public arenas." In doing so, neutralists bracket those considerations that "move people to present, defend, and reconfigure their identities" in the first place, thus ostricizing "the most intimate areas of life and identity." Opting for a stronger mode of social exchange, Connolly holds that "issues of identity and the good" cannot and should not be banished from public discourse. Shifting the accents to ethical and legal concerns, Michael Perry has launched a blistering critique of liberal proceduralism. Reviewing the arguments of its leading spokesmen (mentioned above), Perry finds that the liberal-procedural project is "spent" and that it is "past time to take a different path," a path which, in his account, is that of a "deliberative, transformative politics." Drawing attention to global-political implications, he writes in a stirring passage:

> The position that a deliberative, transformative politics is beyond the capacity of us Americans is all the more frightening when we realize that although the moral culture of the United States is pluralistic, it is certainly no more pluralistic, almost certainly less so, than the moral culture of the human species. . . . In thinking about problems concerning the relation of morality and religion to politics and law as they arise in a particular pluralistic country like the United States, perhaps we can achieve insights that will help us meet the challenge of conducting productive moral discourse not merely in our own country, but in our pluralistic world as well.[25]

Perry's comments on the global context are insightful because the effects of liberal proceduralism are particularly manifest today in the global arena. It is in the name of liberal neutrality, and of the neutral objectivity of Western science and knowledge, that traditional cultures in developing societies tend to be progressively "defoliated" or shunted aside into folklore. Typically, liberal proceduralism surfaces in these societies in the guise of "secularism" or the secular state, a state whose structure and guiding principles are frequently part of the colonial legacy. Modernizing elites in developing countries often invoke secularism or secular proceduralism as an antidote to native "prejudices" and to the profuse welter of ethnic, religious, and communal traditions. In the argumentative strategy of such elites, secular neutrality is the necessary prerequisite for interethnic and intercommunal toleration and thus for the maintenance of social peace. As in the case of Western neutralism, however, this argument has been strongly challenged by intellectuals in third world countries bent on resisting cultural spoliation. In a remarkable essay titled "The Politics of Secularism and the Recovery of Religious Tolerance," Ashis Nandy has sought to vindicate cross-cultural tolerance through explicit reliance on, rather than ostracism of, traditional modes of belief. Steering a course deftly between liberal neutralism and fundamentalism, the essay critiques the secular state precisely for installing a hegemonic cultural regime and for serving often as a pliant tool of religious politics. In Nandy's words:

> The time has come for us to recognize that, instead of trying to build religious tolerance on the good faith or conscience of a small group of de-ethnicized, middle-class politicians, bureaucrats and intellectuals, a far more serious venture would be to explore the philosophy, the symbolism and the theology of tolerance in the faiths of the citizens and hope that the state systems in South Asia may learn something about religious tolerance from everyday Hinduism, Islam, Buddhism, and Sikhism (rather than wish that the ordinary Hindus, Muslims, Buddhists and Sikhs will learn tolerance from the various fashionable secular theories of statecraft).[26]

Conflict and Class Struggle

Liberal neutralism prefers to leave cultural or religious differences untouched while encircling them with a band of abstractly formal procedures. In the words of Rawls, justice as fairness assumes "that deep and pervasive differences of religious, philosophical, and ethical doctrine remain" as "a permanent condition of human life." Thus, proceduralists take for granted existing contrasts between ways of life, while seeking to mitigate them through a thin consensual layer composed of shared general rules. Once this layer is removed, contrasting life-forms or beliefs face each other in unmediated fashion, which may result either in indifference or (more commonly) in mutual repulsion and conflict. The latter result is prone to obtain under conditions of scarcity and where cultural groups are struggling for predominance or hegemony within a circumscribed territory. In extreme circumstances, struggle entails the transformation of cultural difference into radical otherness, with the contending parties defining themselves through mutual exclusion.

As a mode of social and cultural interaction, conflict (even of the radical sort) occupies a prominent place in the annals of human history and in the literature of social-political thought. In the account of Thomas Hobbes, conflict and mutual enmity are the chief trademarks of human relations in the "state of nature"; given the absence of a deeper sympathy, the "Leviathan" established through rational agreement has to resort mainly to power and to fear (as alternatives to an always fragile cultural consensus). On a more concrete-historical level, social conflict has been accorded centerstage in the political theory of Machiavelli. An ardent admirer of the Roman Republic, Machiavelli perceived the conflictual interplay between patricians and plebeians (or between nobility and common people) as the basic source of the strength and vitality of Roman political life. Surveying the period between the expulsion of the Tarquins to the beginning of the empire, his *Discourses* on Roman history (following Livy) portray inter-group rivalry and conflict as the mainstay of republican virtue and freedom. "I maintain," we read, "that those who blame the quarrels of the Senate and the people of Rome condemn that which was the very origin of liberty." Drawing broader lessons from this example, the *Discourses* chide the critics of these quarrels for ignoring the fact "that in every republic there are two parties, that of the nobles and that of the people" and that "all the laws that are favorable to liberty result from the opposition of these parties to each other, as may easily be seen from the events that occurred in Rome."[27]

Actually, in Machiavelli's account, conflict was not construed in terms of a harsh antithesis since both of the opposing parties were seen as contributing to a common goal: the maintenance of republican freedom. As he writes, the differences between social groups during this period "caused but very few exiles and cost still less blood" and thus cannot be viewed as having been "injurious and fatal" to public life. The radicalization of group conflict into harsh opposition is the emblem of later economic and sociological theories, and mainly of the theory of 'class struggle' as articulated by Marx. In the *Communist Manifesto,* Marx (and Engels) reduced relations between social groups to the antithesis between two main classes, one dominant and the other exploited: the bourgeoisie and the proletariat. While previous centuries had been characterized by multiple and crisscrossing class relations—resulting in a mitigation of class division—the industrial revolution had finally sharpened social interaction into one decisive opposition between exploiters and exploited, an opposition which could only be resolved through revolutionary reversal.

In the words of the *Communist Manifesto,* the nineteenth century has yielded one distinctive effect: it has "simplified the class antagonism." As a result, society as a whole is increasingly "splitting up into two great hostile camps, into two great classes directly facing each other" in a relation of mutual exclusion (what game theorists would call a "zero-sum game"). As the document recognized, the bourgeoisie as carrier of industrialization had unleashed immense productive forces, through a process that was "constantly revolutionizing the instruments of production" and steadily giving a "cosmopolitan character to production and consumption in every country." Yet, the unleashed forces now were straining against the established mode of bourgeois property relations: namely, by indicting the exploitation and expropriation of the real source of productivity, the working class. By engendering industrial wage labor, the bourgeoisie had unwittingly produced its "grave-diggers," forging the weapon that would "bring death to itself." In the end, the long-festering but "veiled civil war" raging in society was bound to reach the point where it "breaks out into open revolution" and where "the violent overthrow of the bourgeoisie lays the foundation for the sway of the proletariat" whose victory is "inevitable."[28]

The model of radical conflict—or of self-definition through mutual exclusion—is not confined to traditional Marxism (whose influence and persuasiveness have notably receded in recent decades). Sometimes, the model also surfaces in intellectual perspectives whose premises and theoretical lineage seem at first glance far removed from the Marxist notion of 'class struggle'—for example, in existentialism and (versions of) poststructuralism. Thus, in the work of the early Sartre, social or interpersonal relations are almost exclusively conceptualized in terms of radical antagonism and conflict. As presented in *Being and Nothingness,* such antagonism is basically the result of mutual "objectification," that is, a process where self and other are alternately or reciprocally reduced to "objects" of consciousness and thus to targets of possible manipulation or domination. In the well-known chapter on "The Look," the appearance of the other and his unexpected gaze annihilate the self's autonomy, by integrating the self as a mere ingredient into the other's world. However, this loss of freedom or autonomy is only temporary because, by casting the look back at the other, the self can reverse the situation by negating or nullifying the other's dominance and constraining world view; in this manner, the other "becomes then that which I make myself *not* be."

The outcome of this process of mutual denial and subjugation is a basic instability of interpersonal relations where the self is "referred from transfiguration to degradation and from degradation to transfiguration" without being able to get a "total view of the ensemble of these two modes of being"; more simply put: "Conflict is the original meaning of being-for-others." Curiously, despite a strong rejection of existentialist "humanism," poststructuralist writers occasionally approximate the Sartrean analysis. In rigorously opposing melting-pot assimilation or "totalitarian" synthesis, the accent on "difference" and multiplicity sometimes shades over into a celebration of self-other separation and unmitigated antagonism. Thus, in his *Postmodern Condition,* Lyotard forcefully chastised the assimilationist striving for a "unified totality" or "unicity," a striving to which even Marxism has tended to succumb (in Communist regimes). Countering all unifying-holistic strategies, Lyotard perceived as trademark of postmodern or poststructuralist policy the "atomization of the social" into diverse networks of language games. Stressing dissent over consensus, his study postulated as a desirable approach a "theory of games which accepts agonistics as a founding principle."[29]

In the global arena, the accent on conflict surfaces in prevailing accounts of international politics among nation-states (accounts typically foregrounding the imperatives of "realpolitik"). Outside the nation-state arena—and on more legitimate grounds—conflict has been a prominent feature in the relations between Western and non-Western societies, especially between colonial powers and colonized populations. In extreme situations, these relations assume the character of that great "simplified antagonism" described in the *Communist Manifesto,* an antagonism predicated on radical otherness and mutual exclusion. It is not surprising that the model of encounter (or rather nonencounter) prevalent in cases of conquest reemerges in these situations—but now seen from the vantage point of the colonized rather than the colonizing power. Some of the dilemmas and agonies of the anticolonial struggle have been pinpointed by Frantz Fanon in his *The Wretched of the Earth,* sometimes in harsh and uncompromising language. "Decolonization which sets out to change the order of the world," Fanon states in his book, "is obviously a program of complete disorder." This disorder derives from the fact that decolonization is the meeting of two forces, opposed to each other by their very nature, which in fact owe their originality to that sort of substantification which results from and is nourished by the situation in the colonies. Their first encounter was marked by violence and their existence together—that is to say, the exploitation of the native by the settler—was carried on by a dint of a great array of bayonets and cannons. . . . In decolonization, there is therefore the need of a complete calling into question of the colonial situation.

To characterize the sense of this "calling into question," Fanon invokes the biblical phrase *The last shall be first and the first last,* giving it a starkly conflictual meaning: "For if the last shall be first, this will only come to pass after a murderous and decisive struggle between the two protagonists." Commenting on these lines, Cornel West finds that Fanon's words, though "excessively Manichean," clearly express "century-long heartfelt human responses to being degraded and despised, hated and hunted, oppressed and exploited, marginalized and dehumanized" at the hands of xenophobic colonial powers.[30]

Dialogical Engagement

To round out this survey—in no way meant to be exhaustive—of modes of cultural encounter, attention should finally be given to a type which appears most genuine and normatively most commendable: dialogical engagement and interaction. This chapter now returns to Tzvetan Todorov from whom these pages began. In his epilogue to *The Conquest of America* Todorov discloses his own normative stance or commitment, a commitment to "communication" or "dialogue," specifically "dialogue of (or between) cultures." As he writes, somewhat hopefully, it is the dialogue of cultures that "characterizes our age" and which is "incarnated by ethnology, at once the child of colonialism and the proof of its death throes." In opting for this stance, Todorov joins a host of other writers in our time who likewise endorse communication and dialogue—most notably Habermas, Gadamer, and Bakhtin—but his outlook is distinctive (for one also has to distinguish between modes of communication and dialogue).

In the case of Habermas, dialogue tends to be stylized as "discourse" and communication as "rational" communication bent on the assessment of "validity claims." In its basic structure, discourse implies or presupposes the observance of universal rules, procedures, and categories (which are notably of a modern Western vintage). To this extent, sameness of form prevails over concrete diversity, at least on the level of the presumed "rationality" of discourse. As one should point out in fairness, sameness in Habermas's theory does not imply cultural assimilation. As in the case of liberal proceduralism, rational discourse only involves a formalized consensus or an agreement in principle, while leaving intact concrete differences; but as in the proceduralist formula again, consensus is purchased at the price of a bracketing of such differences to the extent that they exceed discursive rules. A qualified type of an idealized consensus was espoused by Gadamer in his *Truth and Method* under the rubric of an ultimate "fusion of horizons." However, as one should realize, this fusion was only presented as a regulative idea, as the distant goal of a protracted hermeneutical engagement between reader and text—and analogously, of an interpretive-dialogical engagement between cultural life-forms. Moreover, in Gadamer's later writings, there is a steady distantiation from fusionism in favor of a stronger recognition of otherness in the context of reciprocal encounter.[31]

Among the mentioned writers, Todorov associates himself most closely with Bakhtin's position, especially with the latter's notion of 'dialogical exchange.' Basically, Todorov shares the postmodern or poststructuralist accent on difference; instead of opting for radical separation, however, he blends otherness with a nonassimilative dialogical engagement (which grants the other room to "be"). Todorov speaks of a dialogue "in which no one has the last word" and where "neither voice is reduced to the status of a simple object"—or (one might add) elevated to the status of a superior subject. His own historical account of the Spanish conquest, he notes, has carefully tried to avoid "two extremes": one is the historicist temptation to "reproduce the voices of these figures 'as they really are'" and to "do away with my own presence 'for the other's sake'"; the other seeks "to subjugate the other to myself, to make him into a marionette of which I pull the strings." This precarious middle path—which is that of dialogue—ultimately derives from the human condition or human being-in-the-world which again faces two extreme options: "one where the I invades the world, and one where the world ultimately absorbs the I in the form of a corpse or of ashes."

Using Bakhtin's terminology, the epilogue to *The Conquest of America* speaks of a new "exotopy" which involves an "affirmation of the other's exteriority" (or nonidentity) which goes hand in hand with "recognition of the other as subject" (or as fellow human being). At another point, this exotopic relation is portrayed as a "non-unifying love," that is, as a loving engagement which preserves reciprocal freedom. It is this kind of relation that Las Casas discovered in his old age when he managed to "love and esteem the Indians as a function not of his own ideal, but of theirs." In this respect, Las Casas (and some of his peers) anticipated the attitude of the later ethnologist and, more broadly, of the "modern exile," that is, of "a being who has lost his country without thereby acquiring another, who lives in a double exteriority" or double jeopardy. Yet, for Todorov, exile and exteriority are not synonymous with nomadism or a "generalized relativism" where "anything goes"; for such rootless straying only leads to boredom or indifference rather than engagement. In the words of the epilogue:

> Exile is fruitful if one belongs to both cultures at once, without identifying oneself with either; but if a whole society consists of exiles, the dialogue of cultures ceases: it is replaced by eclecticism and comparativism, by the capacity to love everything a little, of flaccidly sympathizing with each option without ever embracing any. Heterology, which makes the difference of voices heard, is necessary; polylogy is insipid.[32]

Todorov and Bakhtin are not alone in espousing an exotopic engagement in self-other relations (and, by implication, in cross-cultural encounters); a similar outlook can sometimes be found in contemporary social and political thought. In his *Identity/Difference*, Connolly endorses a "discursive ethic of cultivation" or an "ethic of agonistic care" which steers a precarious course between (or beyond) assimilation and atomism, between self-aggrandizing identity and mutual repulsion. In Connolly's account, such an ethic involves both distance and engagement, both recognition of inalienable otherness and genuine "care" for difference. Such caring respect, in his view, is nourished by unsettling dislocations, by the experience of "a life not exhausted by the identity that endows it with definition, predictability, and standing in its society" and that remains open to "loose strands and unpursued possibilities in oneself." Properly nurtured or cultivated, such experiential openness can generate and sustain an attitude of agonal interdependence, more generally, an ethic "in which adversaries are respected and maintained in a mode of agonistic mutuality, an ethic in which alter-identities foster agonistic respect for the differences that constitute them, an ethic of care for life." Turning to the voyage of Columbus in 1492, Connolly finds that the discovery of America actually coincided with another, more important discovery, though one unacknowledged in its implications: the discovery of the other or of the "world of otherness." Thus, the overt expansion of Spain into the New World concealed or sheltered a deeper puzzle or enigma: the enigma of ethical relations between self and other and between disparate cultures. "The most compelling discovery Columbus made," Connolly asserts,

> was that of an enigma, an enigma that resists straightforward for-
> mulation while persistently demanding recognition: the enigma
> of otherness and knowledge of it, of otherness and the consti-
> tution of personal identity, of otherness and estrangement from
> it, . . . of otherness and the paradoxes of ethical integrity. . . .
> Columbus discovered America out of the blue in 1492. But this
> blue now acquires depth beneath its pure, glistening, innocent
> surface.[33]

In Columbus's case, the enigma was never properly broached because it was "subjected to erasure" even while it was being experienced. Yet, the example of 1492 should perhaps not be overly generalized. Throughout human history—both in the West and in the
East—there have been attempts to grapple with this enigma, that is,
episodes of cultural encounter through agonal dialogue or agonistic
care (in at least partial awareness of the implications of such care). In
the Western context, one of the most fascinating examples of agonal
dialogue was the Christian-Jewish-Islamic encounter during the early
High Middle Ages, although the encounter was largely restricted to the
academic plane (which does not detract from the significance of this
cross-fertilization). As we know, classical learning was reaching "barbarian" Europe during this period via Islamic and Jewish translations
and interpretations; thus, Greek sources—especially Aristotelian texts—
were invigorating Western thinking in Christian monasteries and universities after being rendered into Latin from Arabic and Hebrew. The
great thinkers of the time—including Avicenna (Ibn Sina), Al-Farabi,
Ben Maimon (Maimonides), and Albertus—all knew of each other and
often referred (directly or indirectly) to each other's writings.[34]

The medieval episode is important to remember especially in light
of the dismal intercultural situation in the contemporary Near East.
During the Renaissance and the Reformation, cross-cultural dialogue
subsided giving way to interstate and interconfessional conflict and
rivalry—a conflict culminating in internecine religious wars devastating most of Europe (and dwarfing in extent recent ethnic-commu-
nal clashes). In the midst of the Catholic-Huguenot confrontation in
France, Jean Bodin advocated the creation of a public-political space
which would overreach the contending parties (without eliminating
religious differences). Later in his life Bodin composed a treatise or
colloquy titled *Heptaplomeres* which portrayed a spectrum of different faiths—Catholic, Calvinist, Lutheran, Muslim, Jewish, deist and

even Epicurean—as engaged in a week-long agonal dialogue or contestation. Undervalued in his age, the treatise set a standard for tolerant interreligious engagement which was rarely matched in later literature (and even less followed in practice), though exceptions can be found. Some two centuries after Bodin's work, at the height of the European Enlightenment tending toward secularism, Gotthold Ephraim Lessing wrote a dramatic play called "Nathan the Wise," which paid tribute to faith while accepting religious diversity. Like the earlier treatise, the play showed representatives of different creeds—here Islam, Christianity, and Judaism—confronting each other in agonal dispute, the implication ultimately being that salvation transcends doctrinal beliefs.[35]

While relatively intermittent in the Western setting, examples of cross-cultural dialogue are more numerous—and also more closely tied to practice—in the non-Western world. In the context of Indian culture, the most noteworthy instance of interreligious engagement occurred during the reign of the Moghul emperor Akbar the Great who, in the sixteenth century, established political hegemony over most of India. Although himself a Sunni Muslim, Akbar practiced respect for Hindu religion and culture, as well as for other religions, and successively married Rajput princesses. In 1575, at the height of the Catholic-Huguenot conflict in France, Akbar established a "house of worship" *(ibadat-khana)* at Fatehpur-Sikri where Muslims of different sects, Jesuit fathers from Goa, Zoroastrians, Hindu pandits, and others gathered together to discuss religion with Akbar and among themselves. The outcome of these debates was a modified version of monotheism composed of strands from Sufism, Zoroastrianism, and Hinduism which Akbar himself professed—but without compelling adherence to his beliefs throughout his empire.

Historically, intercultural engagement has been even more widespread in the Far East. In delivering his Reischauer lectures in 1986, Theodore de Bary presented the development of East Asian civilization as a "dialogue in five stages." As contrasted to more formalized discourses, dialogue in de Bary's use refers to a "sharing or exchange of ideas in the broadest sense," including the "effect of ideas and institutions upon each other." According to the lectures, the first stage of Far Eastern culture was dominated by the "disputers of the Tao," that is, by the contest between Taoists, Mohists, Confucians, and legalists. During the second stage, the focus shifted to the encounter between Buddhists, Confucians, and the "native traditions of other East Asian countries." While the third stage saw the rise of neo-Confucianism and its confrontation with Buddhism, the fourth stage was marked by the inroads of Western modernity on neo-Confucian tradition (with the last stage witnessing the emergence of Communist China). In their richly detailed accounts, de Bary's lectures provide insight into a complex story of cross-cultural agonies, confrontations, and entwinements. Taking an example from the second stage, they cite a Japanese scholar summarizing the cultural climate of that period as bringing agonally together "the influences of the Taoist *yin-yang* reciprocal circulation principle, the Confucian principle of the Mean, and the Buddhist democratic equality."[36]

In the concluding part of his lectures, de Bary reflects on the future prospects of cross-cultural relations in the global arena. As he points out, those prospects are dim unless cultures are willing to become more genuinely engaged with one another: that is, to undergo a mutual learning process while simultaneously preserving the distinctiveness or difference of their traditions. "No new order can endure," he writes, "that does not draw on the legacies of the past, but no tradition, whether Confucian, Buddhist, or Christian, can survive untransformed in the crucible of global struggle." As he adds pointedly, this struggle or contest cannot or should not involve a striving for planetary control or even extraterrestrial conquest; in our rapidly shrinking global village, what is needed most urgently is the cultivation of a sense of mutual responsibility and of a shared readiness to care for the well-being of this world and its people:

> We have long since passed the last frontier of outward, westward expansion (the bounds of the original New World), but we have not realized that our new frontier must be conceived in terms other than further penetration into others' space. Rather we must learn to live with both ourselves and others as East Asians have been doing for centuries—by a deeper, more intensive cultivation of our limited space. . . . What we need is not new worlds to conquer, star wars and all that, but a new parochialism of the earth or planet.[37]

In his epilogue, Todorov himself ventures some steps beyond historical narrative toward an assessment of prospects and possibilities. Our world today, at the close of the twentieth century, is no longer quite the same as that of 1492, although some frightening parallels still persist in the relentless urge for conquest and domination. Still, global configurations have changed. "I believe," Todorov writes, "that this period of European history"—that is, the period of one-sided colonization—"is coming to an end today." At least, representatives of Western civilization "no longer believe so naively in its superiority" and hence "the movement of assimilation" is beginning to subside.

A similar change is happening on the ideological plane where our time seeks to combine "the better parts of both terms of the alternative," in the sense that "we want *equality* without its compelling us to accept identity," but we also want *"difference* without its degenerating into superiority/inferiority." Taking into account these various changes, the Spanish conquest of America is not or should not be seen as exemplary or as providing a binding model for cultural relations in the future; even in our more aggressive moods we are "no longer like Cortés." Thus, history is still *magistra vitae,* not in the sense of announcing an inescapable fate but of providing lessons for a learning experience. To conclude with Todorov:

> We are like the conquistadors and we differ from them; their example is instructive, though we shall never be sure that by *not* behaving like them we are not in fact on the way to imitating them, as we adapt ourselves to new circumstances. But their history can be exemplary for us because it permits us to reflect upon ourselves, to discover resemblances as well as differences: once again self-knowledge develops through knowledge of the other.[38]

GADAMER, DERRIDA, AND THE HERMENEUTICS OF DIFFERENCE

Gemeinsam lass uns atmen den Schleier,
der uns voreinander verbirgt.

—Celan, *Fernen*

Philosophy's relation to the world of lived experience—the "life world"—is complex and controverted. In traditional vocabulary, the issue is whether philosophy's habitat resides inside or outside the Platonic cave. The issue has not come to rest in our time. While "analytical" philosophers prefer to externalize or distance their targets of analysis, Continental thinkers (at least since Heidegger) refuse the comforts of this spectatorial stance. Like sensitive seismographs, European thinkers register the subterranean tremors which in our time affect the once solid underpinnings of Western culture: the pillars of subjectivity, of the *cogito,* and of rationality seen as means of mastery over nature. What emerges from these seismographic soundings is an experience of dislocation or ontological decentering: a decentering fudging the boundaries between subject and object, between self and other, and between humans and nature (the former *res extensa).* As it happens, this experiential tremor is accompanied in our time by a broader geopolitical dislocation: the displacement of Europe from center stage and its insertion into a global welter of competing or alternative cultures and counter-cultures. To be sure, Europe and the West still forcefully assert their hegemony; but the self-confidence or self-assurance of this hegemonic position is irremediably lost or at least placed in jeopardy.[1]

The present chapter explores this double move of dislocation by attending to two particularly prominent and reliable seismographs: Hans-Georg Gadamer and Jacques Derrida; although proceeding from different angles and prompted by different motives, the two thinkers have greatly contributed to illuminating the dimly lit landscape of our time. Of the two, Gadamer has the advantage of long-range vision and of a truly "secular" perspective. Born in 1900, he has been a particularly durable, attentive, and astute participant in the agonies and transformations of our century. Throughout his long career, his reflections have continuously concentrated on the porous relations between self and other, between reader and text, and between speaker and language; to this extent, his work has served as a beacon for several generations of students preoccupied with the "end of metaphysics" and the resulting sense of refracted identities and a selfhood infected with otherness. At the same time, his work resonates deeply with larger global and geocultural concerns. As the foremost contemporary representative of European "humanism" and the European "humanities," Gadamer has persistently reflected and commented on the significance of European (or Western) culture, alerting readers both to its intrinsic grandeur and to its tragedy or possible limitations. Moving along different paths—farther removed from traditional humanism—Derrida likewise has focused attention on the issue of "postmetaphysics" and its implications for self-other and cross-cultural relations. Thus, in diverse ways, both thinkers have laid the groundwork for a complex "hermeneutics of difference" beyond traditional conceptions of identity and dialectics, a hermeneutics which can provide an important building block for the emerging global city and a dialogically construed global ecumenicism.

- This chapter proceeds from the issue of interpersonal or self-other relations to broader geocultural concerns and especially to the topic of cross-cultural dialogue. In order to illuminate the first issue, I take as my guide a short book titled *Wer bin Ich und Wer bist Du?* which contains Gadamer's comments on the poetry of Paul Celan and, in this connection, probes the interpenetration of self and other and of identity and difference. The discussion of Celan is supported and fleshed out at this point by references to some of Gadamer's exchanges with Derrida, having to do chiefly with the role of dialogue and the "good will" in dialogue. Attention then shifts to the larger cultural arena, taking as a reference point one of Gadamer's more neglected (though unjustly) writings, *The Legacy of Europe (Das Erbe Europas)*. Again, Gadamer's arguments in this domain are further profiled and (perhaps) delimited by reference to one of Derrida's recent publications: *The Other Heading: Reflections on Today's Europe*. The chapter concludes by focusing on the relevance of a hermeneutics of difference for global cross-cultural encounters in our time, encounters which move beyond the confines of "Orientalism" or traditional Eurocentric modes of discourse.

I

As indicated, Gadamer's work has always revolved around the issue of self-other relations. During the waning years of the Weimar Republic and in the face of Fascist totalitarianism, the young Gadamer sketched the contours of a dialogically interactive republic—an image heavily indebted to the legacy of Platonic dialogues (though minus any resort to a "guardian class" possessed of ultimate wisdom). Steering clear both of utilitarianism and of utopianism, dialogue in this context was the medium of a community constantly in the process of formation, a process in which both the sense of public life and the selfhood or identity of participants are persistently subject to renegotiation.[2] This view of dialogue was deepened and philosophically corroborated in the postwar years as a result of Gadamer's intensified turn to language and hermeneutical understanding, a turn which at least in part was an outgrowth of his prolonged encounter with Heidegger. A magisterial apex of his mature thinking, *Truth and Method* (1960) presented dialogue as the connecting link between reader and text, between present and past, and between indigenous and alien culture. Still, notwithstanding their rich insights and achievements, Gadamer's writings up to this point continued to reflect or reveal a certain kind of idealism: that is, an outlook where difference was somehow attenuated in favor of a nearly preestablished harmony between self and other and of an eventual "fusion of horizons" between reader and text. A combination of factors and subsequent experiences contributed to a progressive modification of this outlook: foremost among them the work of the later Heidegger; the impact of French poststructuralism; and the exposure to the poetry of Paul Celan. Without in any way trying to rank these factors or to privilege one over the other, we begin with the latter experience.

In the decade following *Truth and Method,* Gadamer turned repeatedly to a reading of Celan's poetry, offering lectures and writing papers on the topic. His comments were finally collected in *Wer bin Ich und Wer bist Du? (Who am I and who are you?),* published in 1973. This slender volume offers a probing commentary on Celan's poetic cycle, called "Crystal of Breath" *(Atemkristall).* The accentuated sense of difference and radical otherness is immediately evident in the preface preceding the commentary. As Gadamer notes: "Paul Celan's poems reach us—and we miss their point" *(wir verfehlen sie).* This failure or rupture of communication is by no means haphazard or accidental; after all, it was Celan himself who described his poetry as a "message in the bottle" *(Flaschenpost)*—leaving it entirely up to the reader to decode the message and even to determine whether the bottle contains any message at all. In his preface, Gadamer describes himself simply as a recipient of Celan's bottle and his commentary as "decoding efforts" seeking to decipher "nearly illegible signs." Approaching such bottled or encoded signs, he observes, requires sustained patience, diligence, and attentiveness to the emphatic difference or otherness of the text. Poems trapped in a bottle cannot possibly be expected to yield complete transparency or to be amenable to logical resolution like a mathematical puzzle. Still, recognition of difference is not equivalent to a counsel of despair. As Gadamer writes, pointing to his own endeavor:

> In presenting the outcome of prolonged attentiveness, this reader believes to have detected "sense" in these dark incunables—not always a univocal sense, and surely not always a "complete" (or completely transparent) meaning. In many instances, he has only deciphered some passages and offered vague hunches how the gaps of his understanding (not of the text) could be mended. Whosoever believes to have already "understood" Celan's poems, this person is not my interlocutor and not the addressee of these pages. Such a person does not know what understanding means in this case.[3]

The poems discussed in Gadamer's book are titled "Crystal of Breath" and belong to a larger poetic cycle called "Turning of Breath" (Atemwende). These allusions to breath and its turning and crystallization offer a clue to the coded message in the bottle: what the reader encounters here is a peculiarly ruptured communication or a communication through noncommunication. As Gadamer observes: "In his later poetry, Paul Celan approaches more and more the breathless stillness of silence in the word turned cryptic cipher." To penetrate or make headway into this kind of poetry, the reader must be ready for a long search or for a journey into alien terrain, where readiness does not mean a specially erudite preparation but simply a willingness to listen to the "breathless stillness" of the word. In this journey, some clues or signals may be provided by the poet himself, although these must be treated with great caution and circumspection. Poetry is not simply the expression of the poet's private feelings or a disclosure of his or her inner selfhood (or ego); hence, pondering the sense of a poem cannot simply be replaced by psychic empathy. These caveats are particularly important in the case of the cryptic or "hermetic" poetry of Celan—despite Celan's repeated invocation of personal pronouns (such as I, thou, we, or you). Notwithstanding this invocation, Gadamer notes, the actual reference of

Celan's pronouns remains in every case "profoundly uncertain." Thus, the term *I* frequently employed in the poems does not simply denote the poet's selfhood seen as something distinct from the "selves" of his readers, rather, the term refers to the self in general, to "every one of us." Yet, even this formulation is still precarious—because the self of everyone can likewise not be stabilized or pinpointed with certainty, given its embroilment with a "thou" or other (including its own other). As used by Celan, the term *thou* or *you* means or can mean again anybody: the reader, a friend or neighbor, or perhaps "that closest and most distant thou which is God." According to Gadamer, the precise target of the address "cannot be determined"; in fact, "the thou is an 'I' just as much and as little as the I is a self (or ego)."[4]

These comments are exemplified in the first poem of Celan's cycle which starts immediately with pronouns saying: "You may readily/Welcome me with snow." Subsequent lines of the poem allude to the lushness of summer days and to the restless pace of a life lived "shoulder to shoulder" with the exuberant growth of nature. It is against the backdrop of summer's exuberance that the beginning of the poem welcomes the stillness of snow, but it does so with personal pronouns. Who or what is meant by the opening "you" of the poem, Gadamer asks and responds: "Nothing more specific or determinate than the Other or otherness itself which, after a summer of restless striving, is expected to grant welcome relief." Likewise, the "I" invoked in these lines is not simply the poet's selfhood but any (human) being longing for winter and silence, perhaps even for the withdrawn reticence of death. In Gadamer's words: "What is expressed in these lines is the readiness to accept otherness—whatever it may be." The appeal to winter and snow—it is important to note—involves not merely a reference to a change of seasons or an outward cycle of nature; rather the appeal is manifest in the poem itself, in its subdued brevity and reticent sparseness. To this extent, the lines instantiate poignantly the turning and crystallization of breath. In Gadamer's words, the stillness of the verses is

> the same stillness which prevails at the turning of breath, at the near-inaudible moment of the renewed inhalation of breath. For this is what *"Atemwende"* signifies: the experience of the noiseless, motionless gap between inhaling and exhaling. I would wish to add that Celan connects this turning of breath or this moment of breath reversal not only with a posture of motionless reticence, but also with that subdued kind of hope which is implicit in every reversal or conversion *(Umkehr).*

However, this element of latent hope does not in any way detract from the stark sobriety and hermetic nonexpressiveness of Celan's poems. This nonexpressiveness also undercuts or foils the prospect of semantic transparency based on interpsychic empathy. As Gadamer adds: "The distinction between me and you, between the self of the poet and that of his readers miscarries." To the question: "Who am I and who are you?" Celan's poetry responds "by leaving the question open."[5]

Gadamer's comments on the remainder of Celan's poems are richly nuanced and probing—and completely resist summary in the present context. At the end of his step-by-step exegesis, Gadamer appends an epilogue which usefully highlights the most salient points of his commentary. A central point concerns the character of poetic exegesis or of the interpretation of poetic texts, especially of cryptically encoded texts such as Celan's message in the bottle. According to Gadamer, the interpreter in this case has to proceed in a diligent but cautious manner, avoiding the temptations both of complete appropriation and of renunciation: since Celan's verses hover precariously between speech and silence, disclosure and concealment, exegesis likewise has to steer a middle course between understanding and nonunderstanding, by offering a careful account which yet leaves blank spaces intact. For Gadamer, the endeavor of understanding cannot simply be abandoned—notwithstanding the poet's reticence. As he notes, it is not sufficient merely to register the failure or rupture of understanding; rather, what is needed is an attempt to look for possible points of entry and then to inquire in which manner and how far understanding may be able to penetrate. However, the goal of this interpretive endeavor should not be mistaken: the point is not to render transparent what is (and must remain) concealed, but rather to comprehend and respect the complex interlacing of transparency and nontransparency in poetic texts. In the words of the epilogue:

> The objective is *not* to discern or pinpoint the univocity of the poet's intent; not by any means. Nor is it a matter of determining the univocity of the "meaning" expressed in the poem itself. Rather what is involved is attentiveness to the ambiguity, multivocity and indeterminacy unleashed by the poetic text—a multivocity which does not furnish a blank check to the license of the reader, but rather constitutes the very target of the hermeneutical struggle demanded by the text.[6]

In its stress on interpretive perseverance, Gadamer's epilogue reflects something like a generic disposition or a "good will" to understanding, that is, a disinclination to let rupture or estrangement have the last word. Instead of celebrating the incommensurability of "language games" or "phrase families" (to borrow terms coined by Wittgenstein and Lyotard), Gadamer's account accentuates the open-endedness and at least partial interpenetration of languages and discourses. In lieu of a radical segregation of texts and readers, his hermeneutics tends to underscore their embeddedness in a common world—although this world is not so much a "universe" as a "pluriverse" or a multifaceted fabric of heterogeneous elements. Above all, the epilogue does not grant to poets the refuge of a total exile. Such an exile, in Gadamer's view, would transform the poet's text into the object of an esoteric cult or of academic expertise. For these and other reasons, he considers "sound" the general maxim that poetry should be treated not as a "learned cryptogram for experts" but rather as a text destined for the "members of a language community sharing a common world," a world inhabited by "poets and readers and listeners alike."

Operating in such a multifaceted context, "understanding" *(Verstehen)* cannot mean a process of psychic empathy or a direct grasp of subjective intentionality; given the diversity of outlooks and idioms, exegesis is bound to exhibit the character of struggle or of agonistic engagement, proceeding along the pathway not so much of a pre-established consensus but of something like an "agonistic dialogue." Like every other hermeneutical effort, poetic exegesis has to respect first of all the integrity of the text; that is, it has to be attentive to the "said" (as well as the unsaid) of poetic discourse. To this extent, it is possible to speak of the pure "textuality" of poems quite independently of the poet's particular motivations. Yet, textuality forms part of a broader fabric—the "text" of the world—where readers (successfully or unsuccessfully) seek understanding. To the queries of these readers, the poem responds, even in its cryptic reticence. "Like every word in a dialogue," we read, "the poem too has the character of a response or rejoinder *(Gegenwort),* a rejoinder which intimates also what is not said but what is part of the anticipated sense triggered by the poem— triggered perhaps only in order to be disappointed as expectation. This is true particularly of contemporary lyrical poetry like that of Celan.[7]

Depending on the reader's questions or expectations, a poem will respond differently, that is, in different registers or on diverse levels of sense and significance. Contemporary poetry requires readers to be in a way multilingual or open to a diversity of idioms and discursive modalities. As Celan himself noted at one point, his poems permit "different possible starting points" of interpretation, thus allowing a movement between levels of meaning (and nonmeaning). This allowance— Gadamer is quick to add—should not be equated with randomness or with a disjointedness of the text itself. Here again Celan's own testimony is pertinent to the effect that his poems do not exhibit chasms or rigid disjunctures. Although a complex pluriverse—Gadamer observes—Celan's poetry displays an inner coherence and integrity, an integrity often accomplished through linguistic abbreviation, condensation, and even omission. To this extent, his poems resemble not so much a labyrinth or a magician's box as a polished crystal (a "breath crystal") refracting light in multiple ways. In the words of the epilogue: "What distinguishes a good poem from a stunning magical trick is the fact that its inner precision becomes all the more evident the more deeply one enters into its structure and its modes of efficacy." This aspect has been duly recognized by contemporary "structuralist" analysis, although, by clinging solely to semiotic elements, structuralism fails to correlate linguistic coherence with the broader semantic world context, including the context of readers' expectations. Only attentiveness to this broader context can give room to the poem's semantic plurivocity. Poems, in Gadamer's view, are not simply self-contained art objects but acquire their proper status only through dialogical exchange with readers. What a poem is offering or intimating, he writes, every reader "has to supplement from his/her own experience. This is what 'understanding' a poem means."[8]

As the epilogue emphasizes, supplementation of this kind does not denote a lapse into private idiosyncrasy or arbitrary constructions, a lapse which would ignore or bypass the otherness of the text and its intrinsic demands. Hermeneutics from this angle is not a synonym for subjectivism and willful appropriation, but rather for a sustained, dialogical learning process. Subjective impressions, Gadamer insists, are "no interpretation at all"; they are rather "a betrayal of exegesis as such." The common source of exegetic failure resides in unwillingness (or lack of good will) to face up to the text's appeal, including its possibly encoded message in the bottle; such unwillingness surfaces in the imposition of extrinsic frameworks or criteria and more generally in the obstinate clinging to private feelings: "This kind of understanding remains captive to subjectivism." Preferable to this type of approach would be recognition of the radical otherness of the text and the simple admission of nonunderstanding; in the case of Celan's poetry, the latter admission may actually very often be a sign of "interpretive honesty."

Yet, for Gadamer, nonunderstanding cannot in turn be elevated into a general goal or maxim, which, in practice, would constitute a recipe for indifference or a relaxation of interpretive effort. Textual difficulties or recalcitrance cannot dispense from the rigors of the "hermeneutical circle," the constant alternation between inquiry and textual response. To be sure, hermeneutical endeavor does not yield an "objective" meaning or the invariant "truth" of a poem; both the diversity of readers' expectations and the multivocity of the text itself militate against such a final completion of understanding. Yet, diversity of access and semantic levels does not add up to a simple triumph of relativism, which could readily be a motto of subjective self-indulgence. As the epilogue notes, carefully blending textual demands with exegetic latitude:

> It is not contradictory to accept in one case different possible interpretations which all resonate with the sense of the poetic text, and in other instances to consider one kind of interpretation more precise and hence more "correct." Different things are involved here (and need to be considered): on the one hand, the process of approximation toward "correctness" which is the aim of every interpretation; and on the other, the convergence and equivalence of levels of understanding which all may be "correct" in their way.[9]

The accent on such an interpretive stance—a hermeneutics of difference respecting both the otherness of the text and the endeavor of understanding—was intensified in Gadamer's later work, especially in some writings resulting from the "Gadamer-Derrida encounter" of 1981. In an open letter published a few years after that encounter, Gadamer defended himself vigorously against charges of a certain idealist or metaphysical penchant which had been leveled against him by Derrida and others. "I too affirm," he asserted at the time, "that understanding is always understanding-differently" *(Andersverstehen)*. What is brought to the fore when a "word reaches another person" or a text its reader, can never be stabilized "in a rigid identity" or consensual harmony. Rather, the letter added, encountering a word or a text means always a certain stepping outside oneself, though without relinquishing one's questions and anticipations.

Thus, understanding does not simply amount to consensual convergence or an effort "to repeat something after the other," but rather implies a willingness to enter the border zone or interstices between self and other, thus placing oneself before the open "court" of dialogue and mutual questioning. It was in this light that one also had to assess the meaning of terms such as *self-consciousness* and *self-understanding*—expressions which had been used extensively in *Truth and Method* and which had become a target of criticism (because of their presumed preoccupation with selfhood). According to Gadamer's letter, the terms were not meant to refer to any kind of narrow self-centeredness, but rather to a Socratic process of self-reflection and self-questioning—a reflection that is bound to undermine precisely the assumption of a stable identity or rigid self-certainty. Resuming the central motif of his earlier Celan interpretation— *Wer bin Ich und Wer bist Du?*—Gadamer profiled more sharply the trajectory of his own work. Hermeneutics, he noted (agreeing at least partly with Derrida), involves a decentering—though not an erasure—of selfhood and semantic meaning: "For who we are is something unfulfillable, an ever new undertaking and an ever new defeat."[10]

This line of argument was still further expanded in an essay "Hermeneutics and Logocentrism," written a few years later. Here again, Gadamer countered accusations charging his work with harboring a crypto-idealism and, more specifically, a "logocentrism" hostile to the recognition of difference and bent on incorporating and submerging otherness in the vortex of selfhood. As advanced by Derrida and other recent French thinkers, the accusation had a certain intuitive appeal—its rupturing of self-enclosure—but was ultimately misguided. For, in postulating a radical otherness or alterity, "deconstruction" of hermeneutics was liable to foil or frustrate precisely the concrete encounter or engagement of self and other. In Gadamer's words:

> Now Derrida would object by saying that understanding always turns into appropriation and so involves a denial of otherness. Levinas, too, values this argument highly; so it is definitely an observation that one cannot dismiss lightly. Yet, it seems to me that to assume that such identification occurs within understanding is to impute a position which is indeed idealistic and "logocentric"—but one which we had already left behind after World War I in our revisions and criticisms of idealism. . . . Theologians like Karl Barth and Rudolf Bultmann, the Jewish critique of idealism by Franz Rosenzweig and Martin Buber, as well as Catholic writers like Theodor Haeckel and Ferdinand Ebner served to shape the climate in which our thinking moved at the time.

Notions such as the 'fusion of horizons' discussed in *Truth and Method,* he added, should not be taken in the sense of a complete merger or a Hegelian synthesis but in that of an engaged dialogical encounter: "I am not referring to an abiding or identifiable 'oneness,' but just to what happens in conversation as it proceeds." Dialogical encounter was perhaps less indebted to Hegelian dialectic than to Socrates and to the Socratic method of self-inquiry through interrogation and mutual contestation. According to the essay, it is "in Socrates" that we find an idea or a clue "from which one must start and from which I too have started out as I sought to reach an understanding of and with Derrida." This clue is that "one must seek to understand the other" even at the risk of self-critique and self-decentering, which entails that "one has to believe that one could be in the wrong." Regarding the accent on "différance," Derridean deconstruction contained a valuable insight, but one which was entirely germane to hermeneutics properly understood: "Difference exists within identity; otherwise, identity would not be identity. Thought contains deferral and distance; otherwise, thought would not be thought."[11]

II

Viewed as an agonal engagement, Gadamerian hermeneutics is relevant not only to textual exegesis in the narrow sense, but it also radiates deeply into the broad arena of social and political concerns. Just as his early essays on a dialogical republic were addressed at the political scene in the Weimar (and later Fascist) era, so his later writings on hermeneutical understanding are pertinent to our emerging "global city," that is, to an incipient world order marked by a contestation among cultures and by a growing resistance to one-sided Western hegemony. As it happens, and as I have indicated before, Gadamer has not been an idly detached spectator of the developments of our age; repeatedly, he has voiced his (philosophically seasoned) views on the dilemmas and future prospects of humankind in the evolving global setting. For present purposes, I take as a road marker *The Legacy of Europe,* a study published barely a decade after the encounter with Derrida. In this study, Gadamer showed himself as a concerned European or a conscientious citizen of Europe, but a properly chastised and "decentered" Europe. While pinpointing and commemorating the distinctive features and accomplishments of Europe, the study at no point endorses a supremacist outlook—and certainly not a stance of "Eurocentrism" which has been the target of much worldwide criticism and resentment. Instead of accentuating Western advances in science and technology, the study underscores the internal heterogeneity and diversity of traditions which constitute or shape European culture. It is this intrinsic multiplicity, this unity in and through difference, that for Gadamer marks the genuine "legacy of Europe," a legacy that may serve as an exemplar also to non-Western societies and to an impending ecumenical world culture.

   Gadamer's decentered perspective is evident clearly in the opening essay of the study, "The Multiplicity of Europe: Legacy and Prospect." In the first lines of the essay, the author presents himself not as a neutral onlooker but as a reflectively engaged participant in the unfolding events of our century. He writes: "I have lived through this tumultuous epoch from my childhood on, and hence I may count as a witness"—not as someone claiming a specialist's expertise, but as a philosopher seeking to come to terms with real-life experiences. One of the central experiences of our century, for Gadamer, is the dislocation of Europe from center stage and its insertion into a global network of interactions. In his words: "The epoch of the two World Wars has magnified and projected everything into global dimensions. In politics, the issue is no longer the balance of powers in Europe, that old cornerstone of diplomacy which was intelligible to everyone. Rather, what is at stake today is a global balance or equilibrium, that is, the question of the possible co-existence of immense power constellations."

This profound transformation affects the status and role of Europe in the world today, assigning to it a much reduced position by comparison with the past. As Europeans, Gadamer adds, "we are no longer *chez nous* [amongst ourselves] on our small, divided, rich and diversified continent"; rather, we are intimately inserted and implicated in "world events." Being embroiled in world events, Europe is also haunted and overshadowed by the global threats or dangers facing humanity today: especially the threats of nuclear catastrophe and ecological disaster. For Gadamer, this is the present social-political reality from which thinking has to start: "Europe is intimately enmeshed in the contemporary world crisis—a crisis for which no one can offer a ready-made solution."[12]

What role can and should Europe assume in this precarious situation? To tackle this question requires some reflection on the meaning and distinctive significance of Europe as manifest in the long trajectory of its history. Following in the footsteps of Husserl and Heidegger, Gadamer locates the distinctive trademark of Europe in the penchant for a philosophy which from the beginning is drawn less to meditation than to inquiry and thus bears some intrinsic affinity with science (in the broad sense). In our European or Western culture, Gadamer notes, philosophy "from its inception has been linked with scientific investigation"; this, in fact, is "the novelty or novel feature which profiles and binds Europe together." Over the course of many centuries, the scientific aspect or offshoot of philosophizing came to extricate itself from the broader fabric of European culture, a process which then served as springboard for the ascendancy of Western science and technology to global hegemony. Yet, for Gadamer, this is only part of the story. While friendly to scientific inquiry, philosophy in the West was traditionally also connected with metaphysics, art, literature, the humanities, and theology. In the premodern era, these features formed part of the prevailing cultural framework, a framework whose ingredients were not fused in a bland synthesis but rather stood side by side in tensional and often conflictual relationships. To cite Gadamer again: in Europe culture and philosophy took shape in a

manner which "gave rise to the sharpest tensions and antagonisms between the diverse dimensions of intellectual activity." Still, given the
original conception of philosophical inquiry, the decisive issue in European culture—an issue eventually marking Europe's position in the
world—was bound to be the relation between philosophy and science or that between science and the other ingredients of the cultural
fabric.[13]

The ascendancy of science (meaning empirical science) both in the
European and in the global context was a product of the modern epoch,
particularly of the dismissal of classical and medieval teleology in favor
of the cognitive and technical mastery of nature. Instead of being a
participant in a broader cultural discourse, science emerged as the
dominant idiom due to the scientist's ability to distance the entire surrounding world into a pliant target of analysis and thus to act as a general overseer (or overlord). The modern epoch, Gadamer comments,
heralds a historical period in which human reason or intellect is able
"to transform nature into artificial objects and to reshape the entire
world into one giant workshop of industrial production." The reaction
of traditional philosophy to this upsurge of science was initially purely
defensive; practitioners often retreated into a simple "underlaborer"
position, a stance limiting reflection to the refinement of conceptual
tools and epistemic techniques needed for scientific inquiry.

This retreat was particularly widespread in the nineteenth century,
during the heyday of positivism. In the meantime, however, the situation has dramatically changed. In view of the crisis potential of our
age—triggered in part by the triumph of technology—the issue is no
longer simply to assist science, but to reflect anew on the relation of
science to other dimensions of culture, both in Europe and in the global
arena. According to Gadamer, a major credit for the changed outlook
in the European setting goes to phenomenology and hermeneutics as
inaugurated by Husserl and Heidegger. Particularly crucial in this context is Husserl's notion of the 'life world,' a notion that thematizes the
broad backdrop of lived cultural experience from which science itself
arises and without which its vocabulary would be unintelligible. The
writings of Heidegger and his successors further concretized the notion by linking it with human "praxis" and the basic "worldliness" of
human existence. What comes into view from this vantage is the intrinsic situatedness of human life, signaled by such features as "temporality, finitude, projection, remembrance, forgetfulness and being
forgotten."[14]

Worldly situatedness challenges the prerogative of distantiation, or
at least the presumption of the spectator or overseer to possess a privileged or the only correct slant on reality. Pursuing the insights of

phenomenology and hermeneutics, contemporary philosophy is attentive to the contextuality of human experience, its embeddedness both in historically grown culture and in the natural environment, where nature is no longer seen merely as extended matter. As Gadamer states forcefully: "Nature can no longer be viewed as simple object of exploitation; rather, in all its manifestations it must be experienced as our partner, that is, as the 'other' sharing our habitat." Seen as our partner, nature is intimately entwined with us; far from denoting a radical externality, nature is "our" otherness or the "other of ourselves" (das Andere unserer selbst). And in fact, Gadamer asks, is there a genuine otherness which would not be the other of ourselves?

This consideration is particularly important in the domain of human co-existence, that is, of intersubjective and cross-cultural "co-being" in a shared world—where the issue is neither to distance the other into the indifference of externality nor to absorb or appropriate otherness in an imperialist gesture. On the cross-cultural level, this aspect of self-other entwinement has been one of the profound historical experiences of the European continent, which brings into view the peculiar cultural pertinence of Europe or of the "legacy of Europe" in our time, above and beyond the ongoing Westernization of the globe under the auspices of European science. For Gadamer, it is chiefly the multiplicity (or multiculturalism) of Europe which harbors the continent's legacy and promise for the world. As he writes:

> To live with the other, as the other of the other—this basic human task applies to the micro- as well as to the macro-level. Just as each of us learns to live with the other in the process of individual maturation, a similar learning experience holds for larger human communities, for nations and states. And here it may be one of the special advantages of Europe that—more than elsewhere—her inhabitants have been able or were compelled to learn how to live with others, even if the others are very different.[15]

The multiplicity of Europe, in Gadamer's view, is evident in the diversity of national (and subnational) historical trajectories, in the heterogeneity of literary and religious traditions, and—above all—in the rich profusion of vernacular languages. In the face of ongoing efforts aimed at European unification, this multiplicity for Gadamer cannot and should not be expunged. From a global cultural perspective, the unification of Europe—especially in terms of a geopolitical power constellation—is of relatively minor significance. Unification would be a particularly dubious goal if it entailed the standardization of culture and language, at the expense of historical vernacular idioms. According to the essay, the deeper significance of Europe resides in its multicultural and multilingual character, in the historical "cohabitation with otherness in a narrow space"; experienced as a constant struggle and challenge among European peoples, this cohabitation implies a lesson for humanity at large, for an evolving ecumenical world culture.

The emphasis on indigenous traditions and vernacular idioms may seem to run counter to the prospect of a self-other entwinement or a genuine co-being with otherness. Indeed, concern with cultural distinctness may harbor the danger of a retreat into parochialism or ethnocentrism, but this retreat is not compelling. As Gadamer points out, the role of local traditions is a feature endemic to hermeneutics or the "hermeneutical circle" with its emphasis on "prejudices" or prejudgments seen as corrigible but not expendable starting points of understanding. In exegesis just as in any other form of disciplined inquiry, there must be room for critical alertness to prevent the congealment of preconceived ideas. Yet, Gadamer concludes,

> where the goal is not mastery or control, we are liable to experience the otherness of the other precisely against the backdrop of our own prejudgments. The highest and most elevated aim that we can strive for is to partake in the other, to share the other's alterity. Thus, it may not be too bold to draw as final political consequence of these deliberations the lesson that the future survival of humankind may depend on our readiness not only to utilize our resources of power and (technical) efficiency but to pause in front of the other's otherness—the otherness of nature as well as that of the historically grown cultures of peoples and states; in this way we may learn to experience otherness and human others as the "other of ourselves" in order to partake in one another.[16]

In *The Legacy of Europe,* the discussion of Europe's global significance is continued and fleshed out further in a chapter titled "The Future of European *Geisteswissenschaften"* (humanities). In opposition to the "eternal verities" of traditional metaphysics as well as the universal propositions of modern science, the humanities in Gadamer's view place the accent on historically grown traditions, the rich nuances of vernacular idioms, and the concrete fabric of the human life world. Under the influence of nineteenth-century historicism and twentieth-century phenomenology and existentialism, humanistic inquiry is attentive increasingly to such philosophically charged issues as temporality, historicity, and the finitude of human life. To this extent, although challenging traditional metaphysics, the humanities are heir to Europe's deeper metaphysical concerns. In Gadamer's words, it is

"precisely the humanities" which have "taken over (more or less consciously) the great legacy of ultimate questioning" and which thereby
have given to philosophy a new "historical orientation."[17]

In focusing on historical diversity and contingency, the humanities
bring into view an aspect of Europe's legacy which is often ignored or
bypassed in the face of the steady Westernization of the world, a process
seemingly bent on the relentless standardization and homogenization
of the globe. In opposition to this leveling process, the humanities accentuate the multiplicity of Europe, the fact that Europe is a "multilingual fabric" consisting of the most diverse national and cultural traditions. This historical multiplicity has relevance beyond the borders
of Europe for global development and the emerging world culture.
"What we are witnessing," Gadamer writes,

> is in truth a global process which has been unleashed by the end
> of colonialism and the emancipation of the former members of
> the British Empire [and other empires]. The task encountered is
> everywhere the same: to forge and solidify indigenous identities
> in the search for national [and subnational] autonomy. . . . This
> leads us back to our central theme. What is at stake is the future
> of Europe and the significance of the humanities for the future
> role of Europe in the world. The central issue is no longer Europe
> alone, but the cultural framework produced by the global econ-
> omy and the world-wide network of communications—and thus
> the prospect of cultural multiplicity or diversity as emblem of the
> emerging civilization on our planet.

This issue throws a spotlight on the problem of human and social evolution and especially on the controverted question of social "development." By contrast with an earlier simplistic identification of the latter with Westernization—Gadamer notes—the meaning and direction
of development or modernization have lost their "univocity" or un-
ambiguous character in our time. As a result, many countries today
are engaged in the difficult search for a mode of culture capable of
reconciling "their own traditions and the deeply rooted values of their
life world with European-style economic progress"; "large segments
of humanity" now face this agonizing issue.[18]

In seeking to balance science and technology against indigenous
or native traditions, developing countries implicitly or obliquely pay
tribute to the European legacy of the humanities; thus, anticolonial-
ism and opposition to "Eurocentrism" are not necessarily synonymous
with the obsolescence or irrelevance of European thought. According
to Gadamer's account, attention to local or national life-forms is everywhere in the ascendancy. What preoccupies leading intellectuals in

the third world, he notes, is no longer or not solely the absorption of the European Enlightenment and its offshoots, but rather the question of "how genuine human and social development is possible on the basis of indigenous traditions." This question, however, brings to the fore the teachings of Herder, one of the founders of the European humanities renowned for his concern with "folk spirit" and his collection of the "voices of peoples in song." Following in Herder's footsteps, humanistic inquiry since its inception has tended to concentrate on the diversity of historical traditions and life-forms, and especially on the role of "culture" seen as the development or unfolding of native endowments.

Encapsulated in the humanities or human studies, Herder's legacy— in Gadamer's view—constitutes a bulwark against the relentless standardization of the world, that is, against its one-sided "Westernization" under the auspices of science, industry, and technology. The issue facing humankind today, we read, is whether development is going to reach a grinding halt in the utopia or dystopia of a rationalized "world bureaucracy" *(Weltverwaltung)* or whether, on the contrary, history "will keep on moving" with its intrinsic tensions, conflicts, and diversified strands. The issue cannot be settled in advance, yet present-day societies show powerful tendencies supporting the second alternative. Countering the pull of global standardization and uniformity, our time witnesses a steadily intensifying trend "toward differentiation and the fresh articulation of hitherto hidden distinctions." Opposing the hegemonic claims of some superpowers, and cutting across the fragility of traditional nation-states, "we find everywhere a striving for cultural autonomy—a striving peculiarly at odds with prevailing power constellations."[19]

This striving is evident within the confines of Europe—for example, in the conflict between the Flemish and the Walloons in Belgium and in the secessionist struggles of the Basques in Spain and the Baltic states in the East. However, the deeper implications of this phenomenon are global in scope and concern the character of the emerging world culture. Far from constituting a bland melting pot, Gadamer Europe "exhibits in the smallest space the richest heterogeneity" and a "plurality of linguistic, political, religious, and ethnic traditions which have posed a challenge for many centuries and generations." It is this heterogeneity of cultures and historical trajectories in Europe which provides a lesson for the world today, precisely as an antidote to the leveling thrust of technical and industrial uniformity. As Gadamer adds, cultivation of native traditions is by no means incompatible with cross-cultural tolerance, provided "tolerance" is understood not as outgrowth of neutral indifference but as the appreciation of otherness from the vantage of one's own life world (and its prejudgments). It is a "widespread mistake," he writes, to consider tolerance a virtue requiring the renunciation of indigenous life-forms and beliefs; yet, given that otherness implies selfhood as its correlate, tolerance can only proceed from a concrete dialogical (perhaps agonal) engagement between different perspectives and modes of lived experience. To this extent, the diversity of cultures—inside and outside of Europe's borders—is not so much an obstacle to, but a precondition and enabling warrant for, an ecumenical order. Herein, Gadamer concludes, resides the genuine significance of Europe—a properly decentered and chastised Europe—in our contemporary world: "This appears to me as the most evident mark and the deepest spiritual emblem of European self-consciousness: the ability, in the contest and exchange with different cultures, to preserve the distinctive uniqueness of lived traditions. To support this preserving effort is, in my view, the lasting contribution which the humanities can make not only to the future course of Europe, but to the future of humankind."[20]

Gadamer has not been alone among Continental philosophers in reflecting on the role of Europe or European culture in today's world. As in the case of interpersonal (or self-other) relations, his views on European cultural diversity can be fruitfully juxtaposed to some of Derrida's recent comments on the same topic. Here the comparison can serve both to corroborate Gadamer's general approach and to further sharpen and delimit some of its basic contours. In his *The Other Heading: Reflections on Today's Europe,* Derrida, like Gadamer, underscores the cultural multiplicity or "multiculturalism" of Europe, without renouncing all the same the recollection of a certain cultural identity, that is, the notion of a shared "legacy of Europe." Derrida is reacting obviously against the upsurge of xenophobia and local chauvinism in parts of Europe:

> On the one hand, European cultural identity cannot be dispersed (and when I say "cannot," this should also be taken as "must not"—and this double state of affairs is at the heart of the difficulty). It cannot and must not be dispersed into a myriad of provinces, into a multiplicity of self-enclosed idioms or petty little nationalisms, each one jealous and untranslatable. It cannot and must not renounce places of great circulation or heavy traffic, the great avenues or thoroughfares of translation and communication, and, thus, of mediatization.

Yet, while critiquing insidious fragmentation, Derrida is equally troubled by the specter of uniformity, promoted by public or private engines of standardization and homogenization: *"On the other hand,* [Europe] cannot and must not accept the capital of a centralizing authority that, by means of trans-European cultural mechanisms, by means of publishing, journalistic, and academic concentrations—be they state-run or not—would control and standardize" every facet of life. "Neither monopoly nor dispersion" thus becomes the motto for European culture.[21]

However, the simplicity of this motto is somewhat deceptive; Derrida's observations on the topic can certainly not be confined to a bland 'unity in difference' formula. While seconding and corroborating the notion of European 'cultural diversity,' his comments thematize other forms of difference only obliquely intimated in Gadamer's book: namely, the difference of Europe and non-Europe, and (most important) the difference of Europe from itself. Referring to the traditional self-conception of Europe as the "cape," the headland or "capital" of the world—"capital" here used both in the geographical and in the economic sense—Derrida points to the possibility of another direction in our time, a direction that resolutely transgresses the confines of Eurocentrism (without lapsing into its simple negation). This possible direction is what he calls the "other heading" *(l'autre cap),* a heading which, he says, is "not only ours *(le nôtre)* but the other *(l'autre),"* that is, not only one "which we identify, calculate, and decide upon, but the *heading of the other,* before which we must respond, and which we must *remember,* of which we must *remind ourselves."* Accentuating further the character of this transgression, Derrida notes that it involves not only a change of direction but also a change in the meaning of direction, a turn from purposive-teleological striving to a kind of reciprocal happening or disclosure: "Beyond *our heading,* it is necessary to recall ourselves not only to the *other* heading, and especially to the *heading of the other,* but also perhaps to the *other of the heading,* that is to say, to a relation of identity with the other that no longer obeys the form, the sign, or the logic of the heading, nor even of the *anti-heading."*[22]

Applying these observations to the role of Europe in the world today, Derrida arrives at a double injunction—which may be a double bind——for Europeans or members of Western culture in general. This injunction erects a barrier both against assimilationism or "melting-pot" universalism, on the one hand, and against cultural narcissism, on the other. "It is necessary *(il faut),"* Derrida says, "to make ourselves the guardians of an idea of Europe, of a difference of Europe, *but"*—and here the doubling of obligation occurs— *"but* of a Europe that consists precisely in not closing itself off in its own identity and in advancing itself in an exemplary way toward what it is not, toward the other heading or the heading of the other, indeed—and this is perhaps something else altogether—toward the other *of* the heading, which would be the beyond of this modern tradition, another border structure, another shore." Later on in his remarkable essay, Derrida the deconstructionist (so often accused of nihilism) invokes explicitly the Kantian legacy of practical reason with its focus on moral "duty," although that duty now undergoes a subtle twist or dislocation. What is required of us today, he writes, is "the *duty* to respond to the call of European memory, to recall what has been promised under the name of Europe, to re-identify Europe." Reflecting the double bind of our time, however, the same duty "also dictates opening Europe, from the heading that is divided because it is also a shoreline: opening it onto that which is not, never was, and never will be Europe."[23]

In opening itself to the otherness of another shore, one needs to add, Europe does not only face up to an external other—a geographical or geopolitical difference—but also (and more important) to an internal rift or a kind of self-difference. This encounter further complicates the notion of cultural identity by infecting that notion itself with difference. In Derrida's words, formulated as a basic axiom: *"What is proper to a culture is to not be identical to itself."* This does not simply mean "not to have an identity" (in the sense of pure rejection), but rather "not to be able to identify itself, to be able to say 'me' or 'we'" and thus "to be able to take the form of a subject only in the non-identity to itself or, if you prefer, only in the difference *with itself (avec soi)."* Beyond the issue of the relation of Europe to the world and to itself, this conjunction of identity and difference (or nonidentity) applies for Derrida to every kind of self-conception or self-relation. Self-conception from this angle is not only mediated through the other, but is internally mediated, fractured, and doubled-up. In terms of the double injunction mentioned before, selfhood can be said to obey the "grammar of the double genitive" or else to be caught in a double bind: "There is no culture or cultural identity without this difference *with itself.* . . . This can be said, inversely or reciprocally of all identity or all identification: there is no self-relation, no relation to oneself, no identification with oneself, without culture [i.e. cultural identity], but a culture of oneself *as* a culture *of* the other, a culture of the double genitive and of the *difference to oneself."*[24]

III

Although densely formulated—and sometimes denounced as nearly impenetrable—Derrida's arguments have a clear (and nonenigmatic) relevance for our time; far from reflecting dilemmas of an idly specu-

lative mind, his comments resonate deeply with the secular dislocations and fissures mentioned at the opening of this chapter. To this extent, his writings ably complement and corroborate the seismographic
qualities of Gadamer's work. As it seems to me, the views of both
thinkers on the issue of identity/difference deserve close attention both
for philosophical-theoretical and for political reasons. On a strictly
philosophical plane, both thinkers venture into postmetaphysical terrain, a move which destabilizes and jeopardizes the traditional centrality of the *cogito* (or *ego cogitans)* and whose effects spill over onto
the status of Europe as the traditional headland or "capital" of reason
and enlightened discourse. In terms of social-scientific analysis, their
arguments are at odds with a prominent tendency in contemporary
"culture theory": the tendency to reduce culture (and cultural difference) to a mere outgrowth of sociological determinants or else to an
epiphenomenon of political economy.[25] Most important, however, for
present purposes is the relevance of their work under geopolitical and
geocultural auspices. In a world rent by the competing pulls of Western-style universalism and bellicose modes of ethnocentrism, their accent on interhuman and cross-cultural entwinement opens a hopeful
vista for the future, one pointing beyond the (mutually reinforcing)
dystopias of global bureaucracy and of xenophobic fragmentation or
exclusivism.

The latter claim may not be fully persuasive for a number of reasons. Basically, what has been presented here so far is vulnerable to
at least two main objections: first, that the relation between Gadamer
and Derrida has been left on the level of a vague affinity whose precise contours would have to be further specified; and second (and
more crucially) that the concerns of both thinkers revolve mainly around
Europe or European culture (including internal cultural diversity), which
seems to betray remnants of Eurocentrism. Both objections are complex and involved, too complex to be treated here fully; the response
shall be limited. To a considerable degree, both issues can be clarified or disentangled by shifting the focus back to the common mentor or chief source of inspiration of both thinkers: Martin Heidegger.

In a simplifying fashion, one might say that Gadamer—until *Truth
and Method*—drew support chiefly from Heidegger's early work,
whereas Derrida pursued insights garnered mainly from the later writings. In a more subtle and nuanced way, David Hoy has discussed the
relation between the two thinkers from the angle of a hermeneutics of
recovery and suspicion, respectively. Gadamer's hermeneutics and
Derrida's deconstruction, he writes, seem to "take the Heideggerian
account in different and apparently opposed directions." As seen by
deconstructionists, Gadamer's approach appears to harbor "the hidden

assumption that the text has an internal unity of meaning, and that meaning is a single thing that interpretation must aim at *reconstructing"* (or recovering). In contrast to this recuperative move, Derridean deconstruction is bent on "questioning this faith in the meaning of the text" by finding in the language of the text "moments where the assumption of the unity of meaning fails." As Hoy shows, however, neither approach can be pushed or consistently maintained in isolation: the hermeneutics of recovery finds its limits in the unsaid or undisclosed—and Gadamer's reading of Celan's poetry fully concurs with this fact—while deconstruction cannot simply dispense with meaning, without appearing to "fantasize an escape" from the hermeneutical circle. For Hoy, Heidegger's own account has the advantage of accommodating "central features of both the reconstructive and the deconstructive enterprises."[26]

The second issue is more difficult to resolve—even when attention is turned back on Heidegger. Like Gadamer and Derrida, Heidegger throughout his life was deeply preoccupied with Europe and with the fate of Europe and European culture (what has sometimes been called the "crisis of Europe"). According to some critical observers, Heidegger's entire work was rooted in the premises of Greek or Graeco-European philosophy, to the point of entirely blocking access to non-European modes of thought. Stated in this manner, the charge is certainly misguided and can readily be rebutted. Although treating "philosophy" in the strict sense largely as a European or Western preserve, Heidegger over the years came to equate this kind of philosophy with what later came to be known as "logocentrism," a straight-laced type of rationalism from which he tried to escape in the direction of "another beginning" and a more recollective mode of thinking *(Andenken).*[27] Some of his ventures beyond the confines of Eurocentrism have been mentioned before, especially his serious concern with forms of Asian thought (mainly Taoism and Buddhism). Still, there seems to be a limitation which is particularly important in the context of the present volume, many of whose chapters are devoted to India and Indian thought.

It can hardly be denied that Heidegger never commented explicitly or extensively on Indian tradition and culture. This fact is clearly acknowledged by J. L. Mehta, one of his most attentive Indian students. In Mehta's account, however, Heidegger's distance from India was due not to a lingering Eurocentrism but, on the contrary, to the suspicion (a misplaced suspicion) of a facile congruence of classical Indian thought and Western logocentrism. Since the latter mode of thinking, Mehta writes, had been "fulfilled in its amplest and purest form in the Greek tradition," Heidegger was "not interested in how Sanskrit speaks (in the sense in which, according to Heidegger, it is language that speaks, not man), nor in the tradition that has evolved out of it."[28]

Mehta dedicated much of his lifework to showing the groundlessness of the noted suspicion and the extent to which classical Indian thought in fact transgressed the bounds of logocentrism. The same issue has been addressed by Raimundo Panikkar, in the course of a personal meeting with Heidegger. On that occasion, Heidegger was at least open to the suggestion of a postmetaphysical, nonlogocentric strand in classical Indian thought, although his openness was qualified by an admission of relative unfamiliarity. Specifically, Panikkar during their discussion had raised the question of whether Heidegger's thinking of "being" might not somehow be akin to the notion of 'brahman' as developed in the *Upanishads,* where *brahman,* although omnipresent, can be conceived "neither as the subject nor (even less) as the object of thought." As one should note here, Panikkar in his own lifework has been an important bridge builder and mediator, between East and West as well as between major world religions. As a corollary of his cross-cultural endeavors, Panikkar has also developed a distinctive hermeneutical approach, one that resonates strongly with Heideggerian thought by steering a course between reconstructive and deconstructive modalities. Emphasizing the otherness marking the topography of different cultures, the approach is termed "diatopical hermeneutics," in contradistinction from monocultural and historicist forms of interpretation. Shunning the comfort of a preestablished framework or common denominator, diatopics here relies solely on dialogue and processes of reciprocal learning. In Panikkar's words:

> Diatopical hermeneutics is the required method of interpretation when the distance to overcome, needed for any understanding, is not just a distance within one single culture or a temporal one, but rather the distance between two (or more) cultures, which have independently developed in different spaces *(topoi)* their own modes of philosophizing and ways of reaching intelligibility along with their proper categories.[29]

At this point, and by way of conclusion, I want to descend from the level of hermeneutical and methodological considerations to the plane of actual cross-cultural encounter. In keeping with the India-focus of many subsequent chapters, I wish to highlight a concrete instance of the encounter of Europe and the non-West: the example of European rule in India. In an essay titled "India and Europe: Some Reflections on Self and Other," Nirmal Verma, the noted Indian novelist and poet, has pondered the agonal relations and profound agonies marking the contacts between the two cultures. As Verma points out, the impact of Europe on Indian culture was more far-reaching and disturbing than that of earlier invasions or conquests; for Europe's influence affected not only overt social structures but also unconscious underpinnings of traditional ways of life. Far from being confined to "territorial space," he writes, Europe sought "to colonize India's *sense of time*, its present being merely a corruption of the past, its past, though glorious, believed to be dead and gone." In this scheme, Indian temporality could be rescued only if its past were "transformed into European present," that is, recast "in the ideal image of Europe." This assault on the time frame also involved an attack on traditional identity, for "the idealized image of the European man subverted the Hindu image of his own 'self,' reducing it to a state of 'sub-self'" constantly aspiring toward fulfillment in the European model.

As a result of these developments, Indian culture was internally split, looking like Janus "toward opposite directions at the same time: toward Europe for knowledge and material progress, and toward its own tradition for *moksha* and salvation." As it happened, a similar schism came to afflict European culture or the European psyche as it was exposed to the fissures of the colonized. Despite all her material advancement and prosperity, Verma observes, Europe during the last hundred years came increasingly to be "haunted by a 'wasteland' feeling of inner desolation," thus bearing witness to relational difference: "Was it a nemesis of fate that, through the circuitous path of history, India and Europe had arrived at a point where the face of the colonizer appeared as ravaged and forlorn as that of the colonized?" Regarding the future relations of these cultures, Verma appeals indeed to dialogue, but to a dialogue permeated by agonal respect, reticence, and even silence:

> Two traditions, Indian and European, are seeking a sort of completion in one another, not through a philosophical discourse or mutual cross-questioning, but by creating a "common space" within which the voice of the one evokes a responsive echo in the other, feeling the deprivations of one's own through the longings of the other. . . . After all the utterances have been made by the anthropologists, historians and philosophers on either side, perhaps time has come for both India and Europe to pause a little, listening to one another in silence, which may be as "sound" a method of discourse as any other.[30]

RADHAKRISHNAN ON BEING
AND EXISTENCE

As indicated before, Edward Said linked Orientalism closely with European or Western colonialism and imperialism; in his portrayal, Western discourse about the Orient was basically a monological enterprise
designed to conceptualize, manipulate, and eventually to dominate
the non-West. Although largely accurate as a description of scholarly
practices during the heydays of colonialism, Said's account requires
some modification when applied to our age. At least occasionally or
intermittently, Orientalist monologue in our century has given way to
an incipient dialogue making room for the participation of intellectuals and writers from the (formerly) colonized world. Reflecting on the
story of Western encounters with non-Western modes of thought, Wilfred Cantwell Smith hails this fledgling dialogue as an important new
phase in cultural relations. In comparison with preceding forms of Oriental studies, our age for Smith heralds the emergence of a new "major
stage," different in type from earlier Orientalism. While the nineteenth
century was a time of immense encyclopedic, but one-sided, erudition about other cultures, our century inaugurates a phase where "those
other peoples themselves" are present; thus large-scale compilations
of data are now progressively supplemented by "a living encounter—
a large-scale face-to-face meeting among persons of diverse faith."
Pondering the implications of this change, Smith adds that future historians may well "look back upon the twentieth century not primarily
for its scientific achievements but as the century of the coming together
of peoples, when all mankind for the first time became one community."[1]

To illustrate the described change, Smith refers among others to the
Indian philosopher Sarvepalli Radhakrishnan, especially to the fact
that the latter was appointed in 1936 Spalding Professor of Eastern Religion and Ethics at Oxford University. No better example could have
been chosen for the purpose (although Smith would probably have
been the first to acknowledge that "one sparrow does not make a
spring"). A contemporary and friend of Gandhi, Nehru, and Rabindranath
Tagore, Sarvepalli Radhakrishnan (1888–1975) was no doubt the most
prestigious and widely renowned Indian thinker of his time and generation. Trained at some of the best colleges and universities in India

and embarking on an academic career (which led from the universities of Madras and Mysore to Calcutta and Banares), the fame of his teaching and publications soon spread beyond the boundaries of his native country. In 1927, while teaching in Calcutta, he was invited to present the Upton lectures at Manchester College in Oxford, a distinction which was followed by his Hibbert lectures in Oxford in 1929. Having solidified his reputation through these journeys, Radhakrishnan was invited in 1936 to join the faculty at Oxford University, a position he maintained until 1952. Following the achievement of Indian independence, his academic career was supplemented by numerous public-political engagements and accomplishments. Thus, he served his country as ambassador to the Soviet Union and, somewhat later, as president of the Republic of India from 1962 to 1967 (in this manner coming perhaps closer than any other modern philosopher to the position of a Platonic philosopher-king).

For present purposes, the most pertinent aspect of Radhakrishnan's career was his role as a partner in the dialogue between East and West. This role was indeed one of Radhakrishnan's most cherished aspirations. Throughout his life and in a number of settings, he conceived of himself as a mediator or bridge builder between different worlds and life-forms. Religiously a spokesman of "neo-Hinduism," Radhakrishnan's outlook sought to mediate precariously between India's classical past and the democratic present, between ancient beliefs and contemporary understandings (a procedure that was likely to displease both staunch traditionalists and radical modernizers).² A similar mediating role can be seen in the more strictly philosophical domain. An eminent scholar equally versed in Western and Indian philosophical literature, Radhakrishnan attempted to lay the groundwork for a viable blending of Western learning and Indian insights, and thus for a genuinely cosmopolitan philosophical discourse. It is precisely in this context that critical reservations may be raised about his work. Eagerly pursuing the goal of dialogue and global understanding, Radhakrishnan was perhaps not always careful enough to guard against the pitfalls of syncretism or a facile synthesis. While seeking to arbitrate between diverse life worlds and thought forms, his writings were not always sufficiently sensitive to the difference or otherness of cultural idioms—or not sufficiently patient to allow mutuality to arise out of the agonal relation of different voices.

In the present chapter, the discussion of Radhakrishnan proceeds in several steps. The first section offers an introduction to Radhakrishnan's general frame of reference, focusing on his metaphysical ontology and relying for this purpose chiefly on his own quasi-autobiographical account. The second step endeavors to illustrate some key features of his philosophical outlook by turning to his interpretation of such classical texts as the *Brahma Sutra* and the *Bhagavad Gita*. The conclusion gives a tentative assessment of his contributions by placing them in the context of current Western philosophical trends in an effort to remove obstacles to fruitful discussion.

I

Radhakrishnan's work is not available in a handy format or in a neatly synoptic system; but it is by no means esoteric or inaccessible to Western readers. On repeated occasions, Radhakrishnan outlined and summarized key facets of his outlook, as, for instance, in his Upton lectures of 1927 *(The Hindu View of Life)* or his Hibbert lectures of 1929 *(An Idealist View of Life)*. Over the years, formulations of his outlook showed a steady evolution or growth, in terms of circumspection and maturity of insights, as befits a reflectively engaged pursuit. For present purposes an access route to his thought is an account written relatively late in his life (1950), namely, his introduction to the volume devoted to his work in the "Library of Living Philosophers" (edited by Paul Schilpp).[3]

The essay is in part autobiographical in character, and in part offers an overview of philosophical themes recurrent in Radhakrishnan's work. Regarding the former aspect, one may note the author's reticence in providing details and indulging the reader's curiosity. As he observed in a letter addressed to the editor, he was not persuaded "that the events of my life are of much interest to the readers of this volume. Besides, there is a sense in which our writings, though born out of ourselves, are worth more than what we are." These lines are illustrative of the general tenor of Radhakrishnan's work: his tendency to deflate subjective intentions and to debunk authorial conceit. As one may recall, Michel Foucault at one point termed Western man a "confessing animal," arguing that the impulse to confess has been ingrained in Western life-forms at least since the early Middle Ages. If this argument is correct, Radhakrishnan is not a typically or fully Western thinker: his introductory essay bears the telling subtitle "Fragments of a Confession."[4]

Heeding the author's counsel, I shall not dwell here on biographical data, except to lift up a few observations of a more general import. Commenting on his student days at Madras Christian College, Radhakrishnan recalls that he initially vacillated about his program of studies but then stumbled on some philosophy books which decided his future career. To all appearances, he notes, this was a "mere accident. But when I look at the series of accidents that have shaped my life,

I am persuaded that there is more in this life than meets the eye. . . .
Chance seems to form the surface of reality, but deep down other forces
are at work." Although casually stated, these sentences can readily be
linked up with the author's persistent correlation of surface and depth
phenomena, of appearance and reality or—in Indian terms—of *maya*
and *sat* (or being). Equally casual but revealing are the remarks which
follow almost on the heel of the preceding passage. "My conception
of a philosopher," we read, "was in some ways similar to that of Marx,
who proclaimed in his famous *Theses on Feuerbach* that philosophy
had hitherto been concerned with *interpreting* life, but that the time
had come for it to *change* life." The relevant point for Radhakrishnan
was that philosophy must be seen as a "creative task" and that—although involving on one level a "lonely pilgrimage of the spirit"—on
another level it is a "function of life" or a committed service to others.

Clearly, Radhakrishnan's career amply reflects this basic conviction of the need to balance or combine theory and praxis, theoretical
reflection and political engagement, the role of the philosopher and
that of the statesman. Probably the most important nexus stressed in
his work, however, is the correlation of reason and faith, of secular
and spiritual life—an aspect underscored in the opening pages of
"Fragments." Pointing to the growing interaction or interpenetration
of cultures in our time, the essay states: "With its profound sense of
spiritual reality brooding over the world of our ordinary experience,
with its lofty insights and immortal aspirations, Indian thought may
perhaps wean us moderns from a too close occupation with secular
life or with the temporary formulations in which logical thought has
too often sought to imprison spiritual aspiration." While the world
today may be drawn together by economic and technological forces,
our moral and reflective sensibility is still struggling to keep abreast:
"The world which has found itself as a single body is feeling for its
soul."[5]

Closely allied with the linkage of Western and Indian culture, in
Radhakrishnan's presentation, is the issue of the relationship between
tradition and modernity, between past, present, and future. No doubt,
this issue (more than any other) is the one he himself had to wrestle
with intensively following his early student days. As the essay observes
candidly, India has had a long tradition, "and I grew up in it; I started
therefore with a prejudice in its favor." Going to Christian missionary
schools was both an enlightening and a deeply charring experience
since his teachers (on the whole) were not favorably inclined to his
childhood beliefs: "By their criticism of Indian thought they disturbed
my faith and shook the traditional props on which I leaned." Over
time, Radhakrishnan came to appreciate this disturbance as a salutary

occurrence, one which awakened him from his dogmatic slumber (but without ultimately destroying his moorings). As he adds in a genuinely Socratic vein: "There cannot be an authentic philosophical situation unless there is uneasiness about prevalent opinions. If we lose the capacity to doubt we cannot get into the mood of philosophic thought."

In our age, the need for critical doubt or reflection is enhanced and even dictated by the growing interaction of cultures on a shrinking globe. In the words of the essay, "We live in a time when we have become the inheritors of the world's thought," having accumulated "much historical knowledge about religions and philosophies." In this situation, the exclusive claims of any particular life-form or tradition are bound to erode. In fact, exposure to the multitude of available perspectives may be conducive to a thoroughgoing skepticism or relativism, or else to an unreflective and authoritarian traditionalism— neither of which appealed to Radhakrishnan. Faced with competing models or paradigms, he writes, "we become either traditionalists or skeptics. A critical study of the Hindu religion was thus forced on me." Basically, his solution to the conflicting demands of past and present was a recourse to interpretive mediation, one closely resembling Gadamer's notion of 'hermeneutics' and the 'hermeneutical circle': "Philosophic experiments of the past have entered into the living mind of the present. . . . Life goes on not by repudiating the past but by accepting it and weaving it into the future in which the past undergoes a rebirth. The main thing is to remember and create anew."[6]

Radhakrishnan's own work shows both continuity with and a creative rethinking of philosophical and religious traditions. "Fragments of a Confession" is forthright in disclosing some of the antecedents or inspirations of his work, both in the East and in the West. Regarding Indian culture, the central influence comes from Vedic or Vedantic teachings as filtered through later interpretations, particularly through Shankara's transcendental monism *(Advaita Vedanta)* and Ramanuja's personal theism; these precedents are enriched through later accretions and reformulations reaching from Ram Mohan Roy to Vivekananda and Tagore. Regarding Western thinkers, Radhakrishnan cites the writings of "Plato, Plotinus and Kant, and those of Bradley and Bergson" as having influenced him "a great deal"; but his list probably needs to be expanded. Some of his views on historical or cultural development show an affinity with Hegelian teleology. In addition, "Fragments" gives ample room to a discussion of Whitehead's metaphysics as well as European existentialism from Kierkegaard to Heidegger and Jaspers.

However, there is a further dimension or intellectual resource which eludes mere discipleship and on which Radhakrishnan insists with particular eloquence: the dimension of lived experience and autonomous reflection. Although greatly indebted to teachings of the past, he writes, "My thought does not comply with any fixed traditional pattern. For my thinking had another source and proceeded from my own experience, which is not quite the same as what is acquired by mere study and reading." Philosophical learning and insight, he adds, is more the result of "our encounters with reality" than of the mere "historical study of such encounters." In this insistence on personal experience one may detect echoes of Hegel's *Phenomenology of Spirit* or else of Bradley's concern with immediacy. However, the emphasis resonates probably most strongly with Bergsonian life philosophy and with twentieth-century phenomenology and existentialism, movements marked by their stress on perceptual or experiential "evidence" and on the nonsegregation of thought and life conduct. No doubt, this accent is not neatly or patently congruent with the simultaneous acceptance of metaphysics and transcendental monism. Yet, however this issue may be resolved, experimentalism clearly stands as a powerful antidote to any kind of scholasticism or the mindless repetition of dogmas.[7]

The discussed essay devotes careful attention both to metaphysical teachings, broadly conceived, and to the role of human experience as reflected in European existentialism. On the plane of metaphysics, Radhakrishnan asserts that the world is not an aimless chaos but a purposive fabric organized or generated by "spirit" and aiming toward the latter's progressive manifestation and actualization. Though supported by some Western views, this assertion is ultimately traced to classical Indian, especially Vedantic, sources. "The *Upanishads,*" we read, "believe that the principle of spirit is at work at all levels of existence, molding the lower forms into expressions of the higher. . . . The highest product of cosmic evolution, *ananda* or spiritual freedom, must also be the hidden principle at work, slowly disclosing itself." If spirit is to be a generative and sustaining force, there must be a medium of otherness on which it works and *through* which it achieves self-actualization. This means that spirit in some way presupposes nonspirit just as "being" (another word for spirit) presupposes nonbeing. In Platonic language, the distinction is between the terms *form* and *matter,* while Indian terminology differentiates between *purusha* and *prakriti.*

The relationship between the two sides is complex and difficult to pinpoint, mainly because nonbeing is not simply synonymous with nothingness and matter or nonspirit not simply the antithesis of spirit, although the temptation to lapse into antithetical construals is powerful. Radhakrishnan's account here steers a precarious path between monism and dualism. "The world process," he writes, "can only be conceived as a struggle between two antagonistic but indispensable principles of being and non-being. What is called non-being is the limiting concept on the object side, the name for the unknown, the hypothetical cause of the object world." In a way, he adds, nonbeing is only "an abstraction," namely, that which remains "when we abstract from the world all that gives it existence, form and meaning"; although it denotes "absence of form," there is actually nothing in the world which is "completely devoid of form." While endorsing the supervenience of spirit over matter, or being over nonbeing, the essay carefully seeks to bypass metaphysical dualism: "The two, spirit and nature, *purusha* and *prakriti,* are not two ultimate principles. They are parts of one World-Spirit which divided into two, *dvedha apatayat,* for the sake of cosmic development. The two are opposite, yet complementary poles of all existence."[8]

In light of these metaphysical premises, Radhakrishnan is firmly opposed to naturalistic or materialistic doctrines which deny the emergent or supervenient character of spirit over nature or reduce the former to the latter. The same premises prompt him to sympathize with aspects of Bergson's evolutionary theory where he *"élan vital"* is assumed to overreach processes of natural selection and adaptation. What he finds troublesome in this scheme is the absence of an orderly teleology and also the inadequate account of the status and role of material conditions. "Bergson," he writes, "speaks of an interruption in the forward progress of the spiritual principle, a falling away in the opposite direction which is matter." But there is "no satisfactory account in Bergson of the rise of matter, of the accident of interruption." Some of these defects are corrected in Samuel Alexander's evolutionism or his incipient "process theology" where God (as highest reality) is seen not so much as the creative beginning or a finished presence but as the goal or culmination emerging from a steadily progressing "space-time" matrix.

While approving the orderly pattern of development as postulated by Alexander, Radhakrishnan objects to its historicism and radically futurist quality: "Unless we posit an absolute, perfect and changeless and outside time and so outside the evolutionary process, we cannot be sure of the direction of the evolution or the accomplishment of its purpose." Whitehead's philosophy is invoked at this point as the closest approximation to an appropriate metaphysical framework. In Whitehead's formulation, God or the eternal is a realm of infinite possibilities, while nature or empirical reality is the domain of actuality involved in a steady process of transformation. Prior to the creation of the natural world, God exists as "absolute wealth of potentiality," but only on the level of conceptual abstraction. Only by passing through nature and the world can God's potentiality (or at least a set of primordial possibilities) reach actuality and thus completion. The essay notes, quoting from *Process and Reality:* "The consequent nature of God . . . is the realization of the actual world in the unity of his nature and through the transformation of his wisdom. The primordial nature (of God) is conceptual, the consequent nature is the weaving of God's physical feelings upon his primordial concepts."[9]

Elaborating on these insights and translating them into his own idiom, Radhakrishnan proceeds to formulate a metaphysical conception relying on the distinction and complex relationship of "being" and "world." In this conception, being occupies a foundational status with regard to the world, in the sense of both transcending and comprising the latter. "The very existence of this world," we read, "implies the existence of Being from which the world derives. Being is the foundation of all existence, though it is not itself anything existent." Thus, "whenever we say that anything is, we make use of the concept of Being; it is therefore the most universal and the most comprehensive concept." Being in this universal sense is not a thing or one of the empirical "beings" or objects; for this reason, it cannot be empirically demonstrated but must be accepted as "self-evident"—for if it were not, "nothing can possibly exist." For the same reason, being is a category of metaphysics in a strict or literal sense, by being located beyond the physical or mundane and thus radically transcending the world. In Radhakrishnan's words: Being "forms an absolute contrast to and is fundamentally different from all that is." The notion of *'aseitas'* means "the power of Being to exist absolutely in virtue of itself, requiring no cause, no other justification for its existence except that its very nature is to be." There can be "only one such Being and that is the divine spirit." In Indian tradition the term for this spirit is *brahman* as articulated in the *Upanishads.* A similar view is present in the "I am that I am" of scriptures and in Thomas Aquinas's description of God as *Esse* pure and simple. What is common to these formulations is the notion that "God is absolute as distinct from dependent and conditioned being; as the ground of an ordered multiplicity He is one and not multiple."[10]

The question that arises at this point is that of the relation between being and world and, more specifically, of the reason or motivation of the latter's existence. Following idealist teachings, Radhakrishnan here takes recourse to the absolute freedom of spirit, that is, its ability to create (or not create) the world: "To the question why should such an order (as the actual world) exist at all, the only answer is because the absolute is both Being and freedom; He is *actus purus,* unconditional activity. All the worlds would collapse into nothingness if He were not active; His will prevents Being from being the abyss of nothingness." Turning again to Vedantic sources, Radhakrishnan identifies

God's primordial essence with *brahman* and the aspect of creative freedom with Ishvara: "There are two sides of the supreme: essential transcendent Being which we call Brahman, free activity which we call Ishvara: the timeless, spaceless reality and the conscious active delight creatively pouring out its powers and qualities." In terms of the essay, creative activity is a synonym for the "divine *logos*" which shapes the world and forms it into a cosmos. On this level, according to Hindu thought, divine potency is not completely absolute or free from contingency but rather a "personal being who shares in the life of his finite creatures" bearing in them and with them "the whole burden of their finitude."

Amplifying further on the relation of being and world, the essay invokes the distinction found in the *Upanishads* between *brahman* as absolute being, Ishvara as unconditional activity, and "world-spirit" (in its subtle or less subtle forms); on the last level, an additional distinction can be made between the spirit's creating, sustaining, and dissolving capacities (Brahma, Vishnu, Shiva). The world itself, from this perspective, has the status of an appearance, in the complicated sense of being both a manifestation and a dependent or apparent—though not simply illusory—reality; these diverse shadings of meaning coalesce in the traditional concept of '*maya*.' In Radhakrishnan's words: "This world is not an illusion; it is not nothingness, for it is willed by God and therefore is real. . . . The absolute alone has non-created divine reality; all else is dependent, created reality. This is the significance of the doctrine of *maya*."[11]

Against the background of these metaphysical conceptions, the essay turns to a consideration of the "human condition," that is, the status of human life in the context of *maya*. As Radhakrishnan recognizes, this condition has been explored in recent times particularly by European existentialism, although there are numerous precedents to the existentialist approach. Thus, the *Upanishads* are said to contain "frequent psychological analyses of the human individual" which resemble existentialist insights; similarly, the Buddha and other Indian thinkers viewed life as a transitional stage and the human being as "a *samsarin*, a perpetual wanderer, a tramp on the road" moving toward a higher metamorphosis. The emphasis of European existentialism has been on man as a nonthing or nonobject, that is, as a creature standing out (ek-statically) from the realm of *maya*. The human self in this view, Radhakrishnan comments, "is not an object of scientific knowledge. It is immersed in being; it participates in the creative intention of the cosmos."

With its accent on human freedom, existentialism signals a protest against the reduction of existence to material forces and also to mere "forms of thought or universal relations" or categories which deny the "incommunicable uniqueness" of individual life; it even involves a protest against Platonic essentialism where the universal is merely "differentiated by the presence of accidental forms." This emphasis was particularly strong in Kierkegaard who asserted that "man is not an object to be known but a subject with a self to acquire" and with the capacity for free individual self-formation. In Heidegger's *Being and Time,* human existence is differentiated from subhuman entities (like stones, plants, or animals) which subsist "without consciousness of their existence." Human being or *Dasein,* in Heidegger's view, includes "the power, the determination to stand out of existence and in the truth of being. If man fails to transcend his existential limits, he too would be condemned to death and nothingness."[12]

To be sure, as Radhakrishnan realizes, human existence in Heidegger's treatment (and in that of other existentialists) is marked not only by freedom but also by finitude, by embeddedness in temporality and worldliness. In Heidegger's case, he notes, "existence is threatened with two dreadful convictions, that of death and transitoriness and the dread of death." Man, Heidegger says, is aware of the "intense actuality of life at the moment life is ebbing away." In being exposed to this dread, human *Dasein* experiences the "radical insecurity of being" and finds itself hovering at the brink of nothingness. In Radhakrishnan's view, however, this experience is not a terminal point but only a stepping-stone or a gateway toward a higher mode of self-awareness. By itself, the focus on dread and existential brokenness is likely to have a demoralizing effect; as such, it is not congruent with classical Hindu teachings. "Indian thinkers," we read,

> will not view with sympathy the tendency which we find among a few existentialists to accept the human predicament of distress and crisis as final and even find satisfaction in it. The delight of some existentialists in anguish, their acceptance of anarchy as destiny, their contented contemplation of man's disaster and nothingness, their preoccupation with the morbid and the perverse, their rejection of absolute and universal values—will not find much support in the writings of the ancient Indian thinkers.

Although tension, anxiety, and suffering cannot be denied in human life, they have to be seen as serving a dialectical and teleological purpose; for, without these factors, man "would not become aware of his utter nothingness, his forlornness, his insufficiency, his dependence, his weakness, his emptiness." Thus, human suffering constitutes a passageway to deeper insight—in metaphysical language, to the transition from existence to being. Man, Radhakrishnan comments, "must first experience the void, the nothingness, the *sunya* of the Madhyakama Buddhist, not for its own sake but for transcending it, for getting beyond the world of *samsara* to the other shore of being." In Heideggerian philosophy, the experience of dread raises the issue "whether man shall attain to being or shall not, whether he shall annihilate nothingness and get beyond it." What the overcoming of nihilism yields is an ascent to a "reality which is different from existence," to a spiritual center transcending temporality or to a "time-transcending element."[13]

Ascent to transcendence or trans-temporality for Radhakrishnan is basically a religious experience, an itinerary of the self toward God. Some of the most captivating passages in the "Fragments" have to do with this itinerary. Pointing to the effects of technological society on attitudes both in the East and in the West, the essay states: "Almost all of us are atheists in practice, though we may profess belief in God. We may visit temples, attend services, repeat prayers; but we do all this with a kind of reverent inattention, or sacred negligence." What this negligence points to is lack of a lived faith. To be sure, there are exceptions to inattention: for some, religion offers a refuge or escape from a hostile world; for others, it provides a means to legitimate or justify the status quo. Honest people concerned with social ills are likely to be repelled by these examples; in this sense, "militant atheism is the answer to dishonest religion."

For Radhakrishnan, religion should be an enticement both to personal self-transcendence and to a concrete engagement with the sufferings of the world. "Our religion," he writes, "must give us an energy of thought which does not try to use evasions with itself, which dares to be sincere, an energy of will which gives us the strength to say what we believe and do what we say." If the world is today passing through a mood of atheism, it is because "a higher religion is in process of emergence." In the essay, reflection on this process elicits eloquent and inspiring formulations. "The meaning of history," we read, "is to make all men prophets, to establish a kingdom of free spirits. The infinitely rich and spiritually impregnated future, this drama of the gradual transmutation of intellect into spirit, of the son of man into the son of God, is the goal of history." In classical Hindu terminology, the culmination or final aim of history is *"brahmaloka,"* or the kingdom of God, a point where divine potentiality merges with actuality. As Radhakrishnan notes, using Whiteheadian language: "When the kingdom of spirit is established on earth as it is in heaven above, God the antecedent becomes God the consequent. There is coincidence of the beginning and the end. . . . The truth about the earth is the *brahmaloka,* the transfiguration of the cosmos, the revolutionary change in men's consciousness, or new relationships among them, an assimilation to God."[14]

II

When writing "Fragments of a Confession," Radhakrishnan had already completed his commentary on the *Bhagavad Gita* and was just beginning to embark on a similar labor of interpretation devoted to the principal *Upanishads*—a work to be followed later by an equally painstaking treatise on the *Brahma Sutra*. As students of Indian culture will realize, the three classical texts combined constitute the "triple canon" *(prasthana-traya)* which forms an important pillar of Hindu religion and philosophy.[15] In his studies on each of these texts, Radhakrishnan offers a careful translation with numerous annotations and clarifications, preceded by a lengthy introduction detailing the background of the text, its interpretive history, and its general significance. For present purposes, the focus shall turn briefly to his commentaries on the *Brahma Sutra* and the *Bhagavad Gita,* mainly because of the complementary character of the two works. Composed roughly in the second century B.C., the former text provides an interpretive synopsis or summation of the principal teachings of the *Upanishads* and thus of the Vedic tradition; by contrast, the second text (dating roughly from the fifth century B.C.) delineates more the practical implications of these teachings for the "human condition" or for concrete human life in the world. Differently phrased, while the *Brahma Sutra* thematizes issues on the level of metaphysics or a metaphysical ontology, the *Bhagavad Gita* points in the direction of a practical ontology.

After briefly situating the *Brahma Sutra* in its cultural context, Radhakrishnan proceeds to recount its interpretive or "effective" history *(Wirkungsgeschichte)* from Shankara over Ramanuja to Baladera. To a large extent, his interpretation of the text follows the lead given by Shankara and *Advaita Vedanta,* but without any trace of scholasticism or narrow discipleship. For Radhakrishnan, exegesis involves not merely the mindless repetition of ancient phrases but rather an act of creative application, that is, an endeavor to bring a text to life in the changed circumstances of the present. As he states in the preface to his study: "While taking note of the traditional interpretations, I have also in mind the problems of our age. It is my endeavor to present a reasoned faith which deals justly with the old Indian tradition and the demands of modern thought." These comments apply with special force to the *Brahma Sutra,* which in its own time was the outcome of reflective-interpretive recuperation; but they can be extended to classical teachings in general, provided they are assumed to have continuing relevance. In Radhakrishnan's words: "The classics should be not only guardians of the past but heralds of the future. They are dead if they are mechanically and unthinkingly accepted; they are alive if each generation consciously decides to receive them." Every interpretation, he adds in a quasi-Gadamerian vein, proceeds from the interpreter's own life-situation, his or her particular judgments or prejudgments, which are not incorrigible given further study and thought: "My views are based on experience, authority and reflection."[16]

What leads Radhakrishnan to the *Brahma Sutra* is basically the spiritual emptiness of our time, induced by technological civilization; Vedic insights are invoked as (at least) partial remedy for this situation. The *Brahma Sutra* opens with the words "Now therefore an inquiry into (or a desire to know) *brahman*," which Radhakrishnan interprets to mean an inquiry into "ultimate reality" or the dimension of transcendent being. The question is how this reality permits inquiry or how it can be "known" or apprehended (in a loose sense of these terms). According to the commentary, *brahman* is basically a plenary being or substance which is the source of all beings or substances in the world; at the same time, it is a nonthing or nonobject which radically eludes or transcends finite objects or beings. In the words of Radhakrishnan, (who largely echoes Shankara's exegesis): "There is ontological otherness, the otherness of the transcendent absolute, source of all existent things, the perfect being from which all existent things derive their being and nature. Apart from this transcendent reality existent things neither exist nor persist."

While being the source of beings, *brahman* in another sense is entirely beyond, or extricated from, worldly phenomena: "The supreme is completely different from the contingent things of the world; it is the presence behind the phenomena and transcendent to them." As a corollary, the supreme is "non-dual, free from the distinctions of subject and object." On this level, *brahman* is not simply plenary being, but a paradoxical blending of positive and negative features, a coincidence of opposites: "It is all and nothing, self and non-self, activity and rest, formlessness and form, the unknown knower in which all things are known, the void from which all fullness flows." When viewed on this plane, *brahman* can best be approached negatively or through *via negativa*. "We teach Brahman without speaking about it," Radhakrishnan comments, since "every spoken word narrows down being." We may at most say or affirm that "being is itself"; but "beginningless, absolute Brahman is not known by gods or sages." According to the *Upanishads,* transcendent being can be described only as "not this, not that" *(neti, neti).* In the words of another Vedic text: "Some prefer non-duality; others prefer duality.

They do not understand the truth which is the same, free from duality and non-duality."[17]

Although radically transcendent and eluding positive description, *brahman* at the same time sustains and permeates the world, preventing the latter from lapsing into nonbeing. In a certain sense, *brahman* even merges with the innermost self or soul of human beings (not to be confused with the empirical self or psychological ego). "The supreme reality," we read, "is not out there but is one with our deepest self. Brahman is *Atman,* the universal spirit: *tat tvam asi."* When approached in this function as world-spirit, absolute being is not merely a transcendent principle but a creative urge molding and sustaining the world; *brahman* shades over into the personal God Ishvara. While the former is the "transpersonal ground and abyss of everything personal," Ishvara is a personal deity accessible through prayer and worship. Yet, ground and personal deity should not be viewed as distinct entities, but rather as different aspects of the same ultimate reality viewed in diverse guises.

In the role of divine spirit, Ishvara creates and molds everything that is unformed or formless and guides the world to its spiritual goal. In this respect, Ishvara is creative spirit *(purusha)* supervening on matter or nature *(prakriti).* In Radhakrishnan's words: "The cosmic process is the interaction between the two principles: it is the supreme *purusha* or God working on *prakriti* or matter." Although seemingly antagonistic, the two principles are actually "complementary aspects" of absolute reality, for the simple reason that "the principle of nonbeing is dependent on being." In its relation to the world, divine spirit can be further differentiated into its creative, sustaining and dissolving powers or capacities—or, on the level of deities, into the triad of Brahma, Vishnu, and Shiva (or else of Vishnu, Shiva, and Shakti). This differentiation, to be sure, should not be construed along polytheistic lines; in their anthropomorphic garb, Radhakrishnan notes, deities are merely meant "to assist the mind" in its attempt to comprehend what is manifested through them. Even when theologically sublimated, a personal God is "only a realization of that which is beyond both being and its opposite non-being. . . . We try to naturalize what is beyond nature."[18]

In terms of classical Vedic teachings, the world itself is a domain of flux and ceaseless change *(samsara),* but it is not entirely cut adrift from permanence and transcendent being. To treat it as self-subsistent or cut adrift means to succumb to illusion or ignorance *(avidya).* Actually, the world is neither self-contained nor simply illusory or deceptive; as an outgrowth or appendage of transcendent being, it possesses its own kind of reality, that is, a partial reality dependent on being. In Radhakrishnan's words: "The world is not a deceptive façade of something underlying it; it is real though imperfect. Since the supreme is the basis of the world, the world cannot be unreal: *maya* has a standing in the world of reality." In Shankara's exegesis, it was a mistake to regard the world as illusion or a mere figment of the human mind; more generally, reality could not be reduced to objects of consciousness. Although imagination may be involved in shaping the world, it is divine or "cosmic imagination" and not subjective or private fancy.

While linked on a depth level with *brahman*, finite beings or things by themselves inevitably inhabit a twilight zone of being and nonbeing, a state from which they can only emerge through the intervention of spirit, as symbolized chiefly by Ishvara. "All forms of evolving life," the commentary states, "are born and grow in the marriages of the prime mover and the primal darkness. Nothingness is the veil of being according to Heidegger; being conceals itself behind nothingness." The goal of evolving life is to reach perfection by merging with absolute being. On an individual level, this evolution means the movement from the psychological or contingent ego to the universal self or *atman* in its unity with the world-spirit: "The whole attempt of creation is to lift up the phenomenon to the level of the subject, to divinize the empirical ego." However, the movement cannot be restricted to individual endeavors, for every individual lives in solidarity with fellow human beings and the rest of creation: "The destiny of the world is to be transformed into the perfect state of the kingdom of God. The concept of *brahma-loka*, the kingdom of God, is known to Vedic seers, the Hebrew prophets and Zarathustra."[19]

Radhakrishnan's study also comments on specific paths or methods for reaching perfection and thus enhancing the goal state of the world; however, these themes are best discussed in the context of the *Bhagavad Gita* where they occupy center stage. Although officially called an "upanishad," the *Gita* offers not so much a metaphysical doctrine or theory about *brahman* and ultimate being as reflections on the proper conduct of life in the light of transcendent guideposts; broadly stated, it bridges theory and praxis, meditative insight and worldly activity. As Radhakrishnan notes in his commentary on the text: "The *Bhagavad Gita* is both metaphysics and ethics, *brahmavidya* and *yogashastra* . . . ; the truths of spirit can be apprehended only by those who prepare themselves for their reception by rigorous discipline." As in the case of the *Brahma Sutra,* Radhakrishnan first recounts the interpretive history of the *Gita,* ranging from Shankara and Ramanuja to Vallabha and, in our century, to Gandhi and Sri Aurobindo. Next, he sketches the metaphysical assumptions which are not so much developed as simply stated or presupposed in the text.

In the *Upanishads,* he recalls, supreme being is presented both as immutable and transcendent ground and as personal lord of the universe: "The eternal reality not only supports existence but is also the active power in the world." Thus, God is "both transcendent, dwelling in light inaccessible, and yet in Augustine's phrase 'more intimate to the soul than the soul to itself.'" The *Gita* is said to support the view of the *Upanishads* in many passages. "Contradictory predicates," we read, "are attributed to the supreme to indicate the inapplicability of empirical determinations: 'It does not move and yet it moves; it is far away and yet it is near.' These predicates bring out the twofold nature of the supreme as being and becoming; He is *para* or transcendent and *apara* or immanent, both inside and outside the world." However, the chief emphasis of the *Gita* is on supreme being seen as the personal God who creates the world out of nature *(prakriti)* and sustains it in being. This God, Radhakrishnan writes, is "the enjoyer and lord of all sacrifices"; He is "the source and sustainer of values" and "enters into personal relations with us in worship and prayer."[20]

In the *Bhagavad Gita,* the central deity is Vishnu who, in the triad of Brahma, Vishnu, and Shiva, represents the saving and sustaining potency. Vishnu, in turn, is represented by or manifested in Krishna, the teacher-god, who acts as an *avatara* of the deity. The term *avatara* here means both the embodiment or incarnation of the divine in human form and the elevation of the human self to the level of divine spirituality. As Radhakrishnan explains, *avatara* involves not only or not so much "the contraction of divine majesty into the limits of the human frame as the exaltation of human nature to the level of godhead by its union with the divine." Although the *Gita,* he adds, "accepts the belief in *avatara* as the divine limiting Himself for some purposes on earth," it also lays stress "on the eternal *avatara,* the God in man, the divine consciousness always present in the human being." In the *Gita,* Krishna is not a stand-in or inferior place holder for the divine. Rather, he is identified with supreme being, with the changeless truth behind all appearances. More important, however, he is the loving and saving lord making it easy for mortals to understand and follow him; for, "those who seek the imperishable *brahman* reach Him no doubt, but after great toil." The human being to whom Krishna devotes his care and instruction is Arjuna, a leader of the clan of the Pandavas, who was seeking guidance and illumination on the eve of a battle. In Radhakrishnan's words:

> The pupil, Arjuna, is the type of the struggling soul who has not yet reached the saving truth; he is fighting the forces of darkness, falsehood, limitation, and mortality which bar the way to the

higher world. When his whole being is bewildered, when he does not know the valid law of action, he takes refuge in his higher self, typified as Krishna, the world teacher, *jagadguru,* and appeals for the grace of enlightenment.[21]

As teacher of human conduct, Krishna bridges transcendent being and the human condition, the realm of divine permanence and the world of temporal flux, of human struggle and endeavor. In the figure of this teacher, Radhakrishnan notes, "the unity between the eternal and the historical is indicated; the temporal movement is related to the inmost depths of eternity." The lesson imparted by the teacher to Arjuna concerns basically the ascent of the contingent or empirical self toward *atman,* that is, toward union with the divine through self-transcendence. In its successive parts or chapters, the *Gita* delineates several paths or types of discipline *(yoga)* needed for accomplishing this ascent. The goal is in each case the same: purification and liberation from ignorance as well as from desire or attachment *(kama);* phrased differently, the goal is insight or saving wisdom, though wisdom not merely of a theoretical or cognitive but of an existential and ontological sort.

Congruent with Vedic sources, three main paths or forms of discipline are emphasized: namely, *jñana yoga* or the way of knowledge, *bhakti yoga* or the way of devotion, and *karma yoga* or the way of action. In Radhakrishnan's account: "We can reach the goal of perfection, attain the saving truth in three different ways: by a knowledge of reality *(jñana)* or adoration and love *(bhakti)* of the supreme person or by the subjection of the will to the divine purpose *(karma)."* The three paths are distinguished by their different emphasis on "the theoretical, emotional and practical aspects." These aspects, in turn, correspond to the dimensions of being, goodness, and bliss which are unified in God or the divine: "To those seeking knowledge, He is eternal light, clear and radiant as the sun at noonday; to those struggling for virtue, He is eternal righteousness, steadfast and impartial; and to those emotionally inclined, He is eternal love and beauty of holiness." Regarding *jñana,* the *Gita* details ways of avoiding bodily excesses and of training the mind through meditation to focus on being and thus reaching harmony with the divine. *Bhakti* involves in essence a sense of humility, devotion, and tenderness, and a readiness to surrender the will to divine grace. As Krishna states: "This is my promise that he who loves me shall not perish."[22]

The chief accent of the *Gita* for Radhakrishnan is on the path of action or *karma yoga.* At the beginning of the text, anticipating the unfolding drama, Arjuna actually seeks to extricate himself from involvement, preferring simple abstention or retreat from the world. However, his teacher counsels strongly against it. As Radhakrishnan comments: Krishna "does not adopt the solution of dismissing the world as an illusion and action as a snare." He recommends "the full active life of man in the world with the inner life anchored in the eternal spirit; the *Gita* is therefore a mandate for action." In endorsing the path of karma yoga, the *Gita* opposes the notion of a 'radical dualism' (supported by the Samkhya school) between God and world, transcendent being and *maya*, a dualism that tends to downgrade active involvement as pointless in favor of knowledge and meditative liberation. On this point, Radhakrishnan even departs from the teachings of Shankara, who, while clinging to metaphysical monism, clearly subordinated action to contemplation. Countering this stance, the commentary insists on the possibility of pursuing spiritual release while acting or working in the world. The chief target of this insistence is the prevalent Western view—first formulated by Hegel and then popularized by Schopenhauer—that Hinduism and Eastern religion in general are synonyms for world denial or world renunciation. "It is incorrect to assume," Radhakrishnan asserts, "that Hindu thought strained excessively after the unattainable and was guilty of indifference to the problems of the world. We cannot lose ourselves in inner piety when the poor die at our doors, naked and hungry; the *Gita* asks us to live in the world and save it." Emancipation or liberation from this perspective is not simply a matter of withdrawal or retreat but involves the task of transformation or transfiguration affecting human life as a whole: "Liberation is not the isolation of the immortal spirit from the mortal human life but is the transfiguration of the whole man; it is attained not by destroying but by transfiguring the tension of human life."[23]

To be sure, action performed in the spirit of karma yoga does not coincide with activism or the busy pursuit of success and self-importance. As a form of discipline, Radhakrishnan notes, karma yoga clearly involves a mode of renunciation and self-denial, but renunciation not so much of action itself but of the fruits or rewards of action. In the words of the commentary: "Renunciation refers not to the act itself but to the frame of mind behind the act: renunciation means absence of desire." Accordingly, the *Gita* or Krishna as teacher advocates "detachment from desires and not cessation from work." In doing so, the *Gita* steers a course between and beyond the alternatives of worldly busy-ness and simple passivity: "The ideal man of the *Gita* goes beyond these two extremes and works like Purushottama who reconciles all possibilities in the world without getting involved in it." He is "the doer of works who yet is not the doer, *kartaram akartaram.*"

The goal of disciplined action in the *Gita*, as in classical Hindu thought in general, is *brahmaloka* or the world of God, which is seen to loom on the furthest horizon of all endeavors. In pursuit of this goal, liberated spirits, though freed from personal desires, work actively on the task of saving and holding the world together and thus on practicing world-solidarity *(lokasamgraha)*. Although enlightened or emancipated individuals are detached from personal gain and have no selfish desire to act, they undergo the discipline of action for the sake of solidarity with fellow beings and the world at large. To quote Radhakrishnan again: "Though, strictly speaking, there is nothing that remains to be done by the wise sage as by God, yet both of them act in the world, for the sake of world-maintenance and progress, *lokasamgraha*. We may even say that God is the doer, as the individual has emptied himself of all desires." This is the lesson learned by Arjuna at the end of the *Gita* when he agrees to act out the part allotted to him in the world. In this manner he implements the advice of his teacher, Krishna: "As the unlearned act from attachment to their work, so should the learned also act but without any attachment, with the aim to maintain the world-order."[24]

III

As summarized so far, Radhakrishnan's work clearly offers an impressive array of insights deserving careful consideration; his comments on the *Bhagavad Gita*, in particular, exude an exhilarating and contagiously uplifting quality. The reader—especially the Western reader—is likely to find herself often in the position of a groping Arjuna eagerly attentive to the teacher's instructions. The critical questions raised here are in no way prompted by a lack of appreciation of the discussed opus but rather by the desire to reach better insight and understanding and ultimately by the desire to facilitate cross-cultural dialogue. The main question concerns the status of metaphysics or metaphysical ontology as reflected in Radhakrishnan's work; also of concern is the relation between this metaphysics and karma yoga or between transcendent being and the human condition.

It is chiefly on the level of metaphysics, I believe, that difficulties are prone to arise for cross-cultural understanding—particularly in a time when Western thought is moving toward the "end" or "overcoming" of metaphysics. Basically, this move is prompted by the incongruities of traditional metaphysical accounts and their inability to come to grips with temporality and human finitude. These incongruities are amply evident in Radhakrishnan's writings. Thus, transcendent being is variously described as plenary being, as nobeing or nothing, or else as a mixture of being and nonbeing. Simultaneously, *brahman* is said to be located beyond the subject-object bifurcation; but *atman* (in its unity with *brahman)* is also presented as the highest mode of subjectivity or subjective consciousness. Divine spirit or *purusha* is claimed to be radically different from, and superior to, the realm of matter or nature, but its effects are also seen as immanently pervading the world. A few examples to illustrate these quandaries must suffice.

In the introduction to the *Brahma Sutra,* ultimate reality is described as "perfect being from which all existent things derive their being and nature" or else as "the presence behind the phenomena and transcendent to them"; this view is said to point to the fact "that there is something and not nothing" and to the "power of that which resists non-being." At the same time, however, transcendent being is also portrayed as the coincidence of opposites in which sense it signifies "all and nothing, self and not-self, activity and rest, formlessness and form, the unknown knower in which all things are known, the void from which all fullness flows." Emphasizing the negative or nonsubstantive side of *brahman,* the same study counsels the *via negativa* or the path of a negative ontology. "The supreme principle," we are told, "is conceived in the *Vedas* not only as the substance of the world and of all beings but also as that which transcends them 'by three quarters' existing as the 'immortal in the heavens.'"

Dualism and nondualism *(advaita)* are embroiled in a similar ambivalence or undecidability. On the one hand, supreme reality is depicted as "non-dual, free from the distinctions of subject and object"; on the other hand, Vedic teachings are invoked to the effect that *brahman* is beyond otherness and nonotherness and "free from duality and non-duality." The commentary on the *Gita* is instructive in pointing up the ambiguity affecting the human condition, especially the relation between mind and body, spirit and nature. "The life of the soul," Radhakrishnan affirms, in a passage critically responding to Descartes, "permeates the life of the body, even as the bodily life has its effect on the soul." In this sense, there is a "vital unity of soul and body in man; the real dualism is between spirit and nature, between freedom and necessity." Although generally opposed to the Samkhya school and its bifurcation between spirit and matter, subject and object, the same commentary states: "Liberation is a return to inward being, to subjectivity; bondage is enslavement to the objective world, to necessity, to dependence."[25]

Similar quandaries can easily be detected in "Fragments of a Confession." As previously indicated, absolute being is described there as "the foundation of all existence, though it is not itself anything existent"; as transcendent reality it "forms an absolute contrast to and is fundamentally different from all that is." Underscoring these qualities, another passage portrays this reality as "supreme plenitude" or else as "being without nothingness, being by itself, being which transcends the time order, the totality of nature." At the same time, however, absolute being also sustains and pervades the world, lending life to every mode of existence: "If the supreme is one and many, if He is being and activity, if He is transcendent and immanent, then the spirit lives in the world, being is in existence." Yet, given the entanglement of existence in nature *(prakriti)* and thus in death and nothingness, being on this account cannot be entirely free or removed from nonbeing—a consideration which again lends credence to the *via negativa.*

The relation of being and nonbeing is symptomatic for other metaphysical dualisms or dichotomies, including the subject-object distinction. "In integral insight," the essay states, "we are put in touch with actual being; this highest knowledge transcends the distinction of subject and object." At other points in the essay, however, this insight is bracketed or revoked. "The supreme is not an object but the absolute subject," we are told, "and we cannot apprehend it by either sense-perception or logical inference. Kant was right in denying that being was a predicate." Referring to absolute reality or to being "which is not existence," another statement affirms: "This being, subject, spirit is not an object presented to thought; it is the basis and source of thought." Following in the footsteps of some existentialists, "Fragments" tends to locate the distinctive quality of human existence in internal consciousness (which is another term for subjectivity): "Man, a product of nature, subject to its necessities, compelled by its laws, driven by its impulses, is yet a non-nature, a spirit who stands outside of nature, outside of his 'given' nature."[26]

The point here is not to chalk up some mental lapses or inconsistencies (which would be pedantic); nor am I centrally troubled by the status of "integral insight" or intellectual "intuition" as applied to transcendent being—an issue which has been frequently and thoroughly discussed. The concern is rather with metaphysics itself. In many of his formulations, Radhakrishnan shows himself indebted to Western metaphysics as it has developed since Plato's time—albeit with some reservations. On several occasions he asserts that knowledge of being must be "accepted as foundational" or that being is the "foundation of all existence"; he also equates *brahman* with the Thomistic *"Esse* or being, pure and simple," but simultaneously cautions that being is "not a Platonic essence or a pale abstraction."[27]

As it happens, "foundational" metaphysics, with its focus on being as primordial substance, has been beleaguered in Western thought for

some time. An initial foray was undertaken by Hegel with his relega-
tion of "being" as such to a preconceptual and thus basically prephilo-
sophical level. Viewing preconceptual or indeterminate being as synonymous with emptiness and nothingness, Hegel shifted the accent
resolutely to "becoming" and thus to a historical teleology culminating in the triumph of the "idea," "spirit," or "subjectivity" on a conceptual and wholly intelligible level. The same accent also shaped his
assessment of Hinduism and Eastern thought in general, namely, as a
thought hovering on the level of negativity and indeterminacy. Given
this background, any borrowing done by Hinduism from Hegelian teleology and vocabulary (including the modified Whiteheadian variant)
is bound to be deeply problematical and hazardous—which does not
necessarily vindicate the correctness of Hegel's assessment; for clearly,
even under teleological auspices, being does not simply vanish without a trace. Notwithstanding his dialectical acumen and his notion of
'Aufhebung,' Hegel regarded being as completely absorbed in becoming, to the point of asserting the identity of concept and reality,
spirit and world. (It is this identitarian view which in recent times has
been radically challenged.)

Hegel's assessment of Indian thought was continued and further
solidified by Schopenhauer, albeit under radically different auspices.
While for Hegel preconceptual indeterminacy was a mark of insufficiency and nondevelopment, Schopenhauer extolled the same feature as a sign of profundity and as exit route from the realm of willing and representational thinking. Despite its antithetical posture to
German idealism, Schopenhauerian "pessimism" thus left intact central premises of Hegel's metaphysics and especially his construal of
being (as indeterminate emptiness). With some modifications, the
same might be said of Nietzsche's philosophy, notwithstanding his
more relentless anti-idealism. In large measure, Nietzsche accepted
the portrayal of Eastern thought as negative or world denying; but he
proceeded to treat negativity or "nihilism" as a precondition and a
gateway to a new world affirmation. While shunning idealist terminology, this stress on world affirmation recaptured the Hegelian focus
on "becoming," though it shifted the accent from "idea" or "spirit" to
willing or the "will to power." The central target of Nietzsche's critique was "Platonism" or what he took to be the core of Plato's teachings, namely, the "two-world" doctrine or the radical bifurcation of
essence and appearance, form (or spirit) and matter. World affirmation through will to power was meant to serve as remedy for these bifurcations and for related pitfalls and antinomies of traditional metaphysics. Dispute rages over the relationship or compatibility between
affirmative practice and "overcoming" (particularly Zarathustra's mode

of self-overcoming). In light of many Nietzschean passages, however, there is reason to doubt that world affirmation in his account was sufficiently imbued with the sense of detachment or nonattachment counseled by Krishna as the proper mark of a *sannyasin* and practitioner of karma yoga.

In a new guise, the question of being was taken up again in our century by Heidegger. Departing from Hegel, Heidegger refused to treat being simply as indeterminacy; questioning the supremacy and exhaustiveness of the "concept," he opened the road to a renewed interchange between the conceptual and the preconceptual, between spirit and its worldly underpinnings. Yet, this turn to being was not designed as a simple retrieval of (Western) metaphysics, but rather as a stepping stone to the "overcoming" *(Überwindung* as *Verwindung)* of metaphysics construed as a substantive or foundational doctrine of being. Together with Nietzsche, Heidegger attacked the traditional two-world conception—the opposition of essence and appearances— as incompatible with the finitude and worldliness of human existence. In *Being and Time,* being was presented not so much as the ideal essence nor as the teleological goal of existence but rather as the open arena in which existence or *Dasein* as a temporal creature has to find its way.

The close linkage or intertwining of being and existence was also underscored in the notion of 'ontological difference' according to which being is both present in and absent (or different) from beings. In his later writings, Heidegger became progressively disenchanted with metaphysical and ontological vocabulary—a development which led him steadily to place being under "erasure," that is, to treat is as a mere trace on a palimpsest on which contingent worldly experiences or narratives have been superimposed. The same erasure is also evident in the accent on the withdrawal or retreat of being as a mode of ontological disclosure and also in the notion of 'appropriation' or *Ereignis* where being and time emerge as the outcome of a nonfoundational event or "giving" *(es gibt).* The movement to erasure and postmetaphysics has been intensified in recent French thought, particularly in Derrida's "deconstruction" of traditional philosophy. The point of human existence, on this deconstructive reading, is not to blend with being but at most to participate in ongoing and unfounded "worldplay" (which is perhaps akin to the Indian notion of *'lila').*[28]

The point here is not to vindicate deconstructive arguments in their more extreme form. What is important is the steadily intensified endeavors in recent Western thought to overcome or transgress metaphysics with its ingrained bifurcations. To be sure, transgression or erasure here does not simply mean elimination, but rather an attempt at a different and more nuanced reading. In large measure, what such a new reading involves is a transplantation of metaphysical teachings from the level of knowledge or epistemology to the domain of metaphor and other literary or rhetorical tropes. Seen from this angle, meta-physical concepts are not so much the result of a cognition of essences as the outcome of transcendental-poetic imagination, of the ongoing labor of creative world and meaning constitution. To this extent, terms such as *brahman, Ishvara,* or the *world-spirit* are not so much cogni-tive essences as poetic or "imaginative universals" (in Vico's sense). Heidegger's later turn to poetic language appears as a necessary corol-lary of his intense preoccupation with being (especially when the lat-ter was placed under erasure). There is some support for this view by an eminent student both of Western and of Indian thought, J. L. Mehta. The latter observes at one point:

> Concern for the "philosophy" of the Upanishads and the Vedanta, for their content, has stood in the way of sufficient attention being paid to the medium: the literary structure and style; the poetry and not just the prose of these writings; the rhetoric and what ap-pear to be minor embellishments; the magico-mythic elements still clinging to an endeavor where they do not seem rightfully to belong . . . ; above all, the verses of obeisance and praise to be found at the beginning and conclusion of most Vedanta works.[29]

To be sure, neither Heidegger nor Mehta counsel a simple merger or indiscriminate fusion of philosophy and poetry. Leaving open their precise correlation, one may note the following: Given the importance of poetic language, imaginative world disclosure (in a postmetaphys-ical sense) can never be completely replaced or superseded by ad-vances in rational-cognitive or scientific knowledge; contrary to Hegel's assumption, the movement of the world spirit does not simply pursue a unidirectional path (from metaphor to concept). If this is so, how-ever, the dialogue between East and West can still be nourished by the imaginative or metaphysical-ontological teachings of the past; in fact, these teachings gain added significance in the context of tech-nological civilization. This aspect is accurately stressed in Wilhelm Halbfass's study *India and Europe.* Pointing to the possibility of a re-cessed dialogue behind the glare of technical information exchanges the study concludes: "For Indians as well as Europeans, the 'Euro-peanization (or Westernization) of the earth' continues to be inescapable and irreversible. For this very reason, ancient Indian thought, in its unassimilable, non-actualizable, yet intensely meaningful distance and otherness, is *not* obsolete."[30]

There is another sense or context in which Indian teachings, in my view, are by no means obsolete (and perhaps more actualizable), namely, the domain of practical life, that is, of karma yoga construed as a nonattached or nonpossessive mode of action. In this domain, too, recent Western thought has initiated a tentative rapprochement as is evident, for example, in Heidegger's study on *Gelassenheit* ("serenity" or "releasement," but awkwardly translated as "Discourse on Thinking"). Yet, Heidegger's lead or initiative in this field is probably more halting and limited than on the meditative plane, which lends added weight to Indian insights, particularly as reformulated by neo-Hinduism. In this respect, Radhakrishnan can serve as a reliable guide and mentor, given his life-long combination of thinking and political practice. His "Fragments of a Confession" contains captivating passages on the role of karma yogins or detached agents in the world. "These free spirits," he writes, "reach out their hands towards the warmth in all things. They have that rarest quality in the world: simple goodness, beside which all the intellectual gifts seem a little trivial. They are meek, patient, long-suffering; they do not judge others because they do not pretend to understand them." Turning to Indian history, Radhakrishnan finds outstanding exemplars of this mode of life: "After years of solitary contemplation the Buddha attained enlightenment; the rest of his life was devoted to intense social and cultural work. According to Mahayana Buddhism, the released spirits retain their compassion for suffering humanity."

In our own century, Mahatma Gandhi, "well known as a religious man," did not seek to "escape from the human scene" in order to cultivate a solitary destiny; rather, "he reckoned social reform and political action among his religious duties." Active engagement on the side of the oppressed and underprivileged was, in his view, "a part of spiritual life." Gandhi's conduct—and that of karma yogins like him—is not narrowly centered on selfhood, nor does it proceed from condescension or patronizing pity. Instead, it is anchored in "the conviction of the solidarity of the world, *lokasamgraha,*" the conviction that "vicarious suffering, not vicarious punishment, is a law of spiritual life." In general terms, karma yogins preserve and redeem the promises of the past in their own age and with an eye to the future: they "bend to the very level of the enslaved to emancipate their minds and hearts; they inspire, revive and strengthen the life of their generation."[31]

HEIDEGGER, BHAKTI, AND VEDANTA

A Tribute to J. L. Mehta

Lord, my heart is full
of your footprints.

—Tukaram, *For Vithoba*

The broader theme of this study is the relation of self and other. Viewed on a sufficiently abstract level, the relation appears simple and unproblematical: self and other presuppose each other, one may glibly say, in the same way as identity and difference are correlated. However, the simplicity vanishes as soon as one descends to a more concrete or practical level. For, how can we or should we approach the other, especially an other belonging to a distant world, to a radically different culture? Are we always condemned to misunderstand, seeing that our approach necessarily departs from our own life world and our taken-for-granted assumptions and prejudgments? Perhaps, given the danger of misconstrual, we should abandon the effort altogether, retreating instead into our familiar habitat and the safety of time-worn traditions. But then how should we even come to understand ourselves, bereft as we would be of a responsive foil or counter-image? Moreover, retreat is no longer really a viable option in our present world situation, a situation marked by the growing interpenetration of cultures and the steady globalization of markets, media, and technology.

Thus, to return to the initial question: How can we properly gain understanding? Proceeding from our own assumptions, are we constrained to incorporate alien life-forms by assimilating them into our categories and beliefs? Perhaps, to avoid blatant cultural imperialism, we want to construct a neutral framework generally applicable to all cultures alike. But in constructing and applying this framework, are we not again trying to dominate and domesticate the world by excising precisely the difference or "otherness" of the other's culture? As Jitendra Mohanty has noted, in proceeding from a Western cognitive framework, even a traditional-hermeneutical framework, and seeking to extend the latter to non-Western life-forms, are we not embroiled or participating in "that cultural violence which a good interpreter should seek to avoid?"[1]

Mohanty's comments appear in an introductory essay he wrote for a volume of posthumously collected papers by his friend and compatriot, the Indian philosopher J. L. Mehta. Sensitively formulated, Mohanty's question touches on a central nerve string of Mehta's life and work, by pinpointing a crucial issue with which he wrestled throughout his long and productive career. More perhaps than most non-Western intellectuals in our time, Mehta was genuinely a citizen of two cultural worlds, carefully seeking to explore the precarious pathways between the two without lapsing into a bland syncretism. Born in 1912 in Calcutta, the young Mehta grew up and studied mainly in Banares where in due course he became a teacher of psychology and philosophy—in an ambiance deeply saturated with Brahmanic and Sanskrit learning. While still fully immersed in this ambiance, he steadily underwent the influence of "winds blowing from the West" (as he noted later), especially in the form of Western literature (Proust, Joyce, Thomas Mann), Western psychology (Freud, Jung), and Western philosophy (initially mainly Wittgenstein).

These initial contacts soon prompted him to concentrate his attention more thoroughly on Western thought, an endeavor that led him from the study of Husserl and Jaspers progressively in the direction of Heidegger's hermeneutical phenomenology (which became the topic of his first major publication). Having gained a solid textual grounding, Mehta around 1957 left India for an extended sojourn in the West, a sojourn whose way stations included a year of study in Germany (Cologne and Freiburg), a longer affiliation with the East-West Center at the University of Hawaii, and finally a regular faculty position at the Center for the Study of World Religions at Harvard University. After his retirement from Harvard in 1979, Mehta returned to India—a return that for him was also in many ways an intellectual homecoming, for it allowed him to probe more deeply into his own Hindu heritage. He stated in an essay written shortly before his death:

> My life-work has been too intimately visited by "modern" secular winds for me to be able to take unquestioningly for granted my inherited modes of thought and living. But I am also unable, because my bond with tradition is not wholly broken, to take the modern present as normative or as giving me a right to sit in judgment on those traditional norms which still reach down to me with magisterial authority.[2]

These pages are meant as a posthumous tribute to Mehta whom I
never had the good fortune to meet (he died in 1988). Those who knew
him are unanimous in their praise for his scholarship, his equanimity,
and his gentle humanity. Speaking for many, Mohanty in his introductory comments says that "he bore his scholarship lightly" and that,
when recognition and honors came to him late in his life, "this did not
change him. There was a sweet simplicity about him which concealed
the enormous scholarship that he had acquired." Regarding Mehta's
writings, and especially the essays collected in his volume, Mohanty
remarks that they show "the instincts of a discoverer and the sensibil-
ities of a poet, the attachment of a lover and the distancing of a thinker"—
high praise indeed from a renowned fellow philosopher. Among all
of Mehta's writings, none received more widespread and deserved acclaim than his study of Heidegger (which was first published in 1967
in Banares as *The Philosophy of Martin Heidegger* and later, in 1976,
in revised form at the University Press of Hawaii as *Martin Heidegger:
The Way and the Vision*). As Mohanty reports, it was Hannah Arendt
who, during a conversation at the New School for Social Research,
offered this testimony: "Do you know that the best book on Heidegger, in any language, is written by an Indian?"[3]

The following cannot possibly provide a full review of Mehta's multifaceted opus. For the present purpose—which is geared toward the
issue of a nonviolent hermeneutics—these pages are limited to three
aspects or dimensions of Mehta's work. Turning in a first step to the
general problem of understanding, I explore Mehta's relation to Heidegger's and Gadamer's teachings and the lessons he drew from these
teachings for cross-cultural dialogue and self-other engagement. Next,
attention shifts to Mehta's endeavor to apply hermeneutical exegesis
to India's classical heritage, as manifest in the Vedas and Vedanta. The
conclusion probes Mehta's attachment to postclassical forms of Hindu
religiosity, that is, to the legacy of popular faith and devotion as recorded
in the *Bhagavad Gita* as well as later Puranic literature and *bhakti*
poetry.

I

Intellectually, the deepest Western source of inspiration for Mehta has
been Martin Heidegger, although his approach to that thinker was circuitous and halting and his knowledge of the latter's work almost entirely self-taught. As he wrote late in his life (in a memorial paper dedicated to his mentor), nobody had "told" him about Heidegger during
his student days or during his early years as a teacher in Banares. It
was almost by accident that, in the decade after the war, he stumbled

on some writings of the German thinker—especially his *What is Meta-physics?*—and underwent a kind of "heureka experience" as a result. From there he moved on to his study year in Germany where he met with Heidegger in Freiburg, an encounter which encouraged him to write his lengthy study on the latter's "philosophy" (later more aptly restyled as his "way and vision"). It was in this circuitous manner, Mehta comments, that he eventually "found 'my' Heidegger—the Heidegger of a lone Indian, all by myself."

Yet, what he found was not just an idiosyncratic experience, a private insight tailored to a lonely sojourner between two worlds. Probing into Heidegger's work, he discovered in the attempted "overcoming" of metaphysics a pathway to a new encounter of East and West, Orient and Occident, a pathway liberating the East from subservience to Western categories while simultaneously enabling the West to retrieve hidden (pre-Socratic) resources for a "new beginning." From the vantage of Heidegger's "no-longer metaphysical thinking," East and West were no longer opposed as the rational to the "mythic," with the result that the Asiatic East was no longer simply the adversary to be negated; conversely, the same vantage allowed the East to "accept the West in its otherness, without being swallowed by the history that has emanated from it." In another memorial paper for Heidegger, Mehta described his mentor as a "Western kind of *Rishi*"—that is, a Western thinker who was also an "untimely *Rishi* in this time of need." He added:

> For all non-Western civilizations, however decrepit or wounded, Heidegger's thinking brings hope, at this moment of world history, by making them see that, though in one sense (and precisely in what sense) they are inextricably involved in Western metaphysical history in the form of "world civilization" (as Heidegger has called it), in another sense they are now free to think for themselves, in their own fashion.[4]

In his writings, Mehta recurrently invokes Heidegger's teachings, as well as those of his foremost student, Hans-Georg Gadamer, with the intent not of recapitulating these teachings but of deriving lessons for our present context of an emerging "world civilization." Without being overly schematic, one can arrange these lessons under three main rubrics or thematic headings: first, the overcoming of metaphysics, especially the modern metaphysics of the *cogito;* next, the issue of historical development with particular attention to the Western idea of "progress"; and finally, the problem of hermeneutical understanding with a focus on cross-cultural dialogue or engagement. In all three areas, unsurprisingly, Hegel emerges as a crucial foil or backdrop for

Heideggerian initiatives. With regard to modern metaphysics, Mehta pointedly refers to Hegel's *Lectures on the History of Philosophy* as a telling gauge of the self-consciousness of the modern age; for it was in these *Lectures* that Hegel celebrated Descartes' discovery of the *cogito* as the inauguration of modernity, noting that, in encountering Descartes, the historian of philosophy (like a sailor "after a long voyage upon stormy seas") finally reaches *terra firma*.

Following Descartes, the notion of the *'cogito'* was refined and deepened by a string of thinkers in various guises—those of the Leibnizian "monad," Kant's transcendental consciousness, Fichte's infinite ego, Hegel's absolute spirit, and Schelling's primordial freedom. Surveying this trajectory of formulations, Mehta concludes that the entire history of modern Western philosophy can indeed be described as the "history of the explication and development of a theory of subjectivity." However, this trajectory was deflected in our century both by the "linguistic turn" and by the existentialist stress on finitude and worldliness (being-in-the-world). Heidegger's *Being and Time,* in particular, was at pains to show that human existence or *Dasein* does not fit into the schema of modern epistemology with its stress on the distinction between subject and object, knower and known. Instead of privileging consciousness or self-consciousness, Heidegger centerstaged *Dasein's* openness to being; and once this shift is properly taken into account, "the representation of man as subject is, to speak with Hegel, brushed aside."[5]

Overcoming metaphysics, to be sure, was not narrowly confined to a transgression of the Cartesian *cogito.* In Heidegger's work, the term *metaphysics* stands for the long and sustained project of Western philosophy from Plato to the present; to this extent, it is another name for "Occidental thought in the entirety of its essence." Seen from this angle, the attempt to overcome metaphysics—or rather to transcend metaphysical reasoning by finding the way back into the buried ground of that reasoning—signaled an effort to expose the historicity or historical particularism of Western thought and thus to make room for a new and different beginning. In Mehta's words, Heidegger's wrestling with metaphysics—which never amounted to a simple reversal or denial—involved a critical engagement with the Western philosophical tradition in such a way that this tradition would yield fresh resources and provide "a liberative rather than a restrictive basis for future planetary thought." Construed in this manner, Heidegger's engagement was bound to run head-on into Hegel's metaphysics and especially into Hegel's conception of human history.

In Hegel's view, the earliest phase of history is basically a phase of backwardness and inchoate mumbling, a condition which needs to be transcended or "sublated" in subsequent stages through the progressive labor of thought. This view was radically challenged and unhinged by Heidegger's critique of metaphysics. In contrast to Hegel's reliance on dialectics leading from obscurity to ever-higher levels of insight and clarity, Heidegger concentrated attention on what remains still "unthought" in every thought, that is, on what is held back in past modes of thought and experience. As Mehta comments, Hegel's basic error from Heidegger's perspective was to assume that "philosophical thought is at its purest and most abstract in its historical beginning" and that "history begins with the primitive and the backward, the clumsy and the weak." To counter this assumption, he cites from *An Introduction to Metaphysics:* "Just the opposite is true. The beginning is the uncanniest and mightiest. What comes after is not development but shallowness and diffusion." The same *Introduction* places the overcoming of metaphysics and the resumed accent on being precisely in the context of a historical recovery and renewal. To ask again the question of being, we read there,

> means nothing less than to recapitulate the beginning of our [i.e., Occidental] historical-spiritual existence, in order to transform it into a new beginning. This is possible; it is in fact the authentic pattern of historicity, for all history takes its start in a fundamental happening. But we do not repeat a beginning by reducing it to something past and already known, which we may simply observe and ape. The beginning must be begun again, *more radically,* with all the strangeness, the darkness, the insecurity that attend a true beginning.[6]

This emphasis on renewal or "repetition" has distinct relevance for the history of philosophy and religion. In his history of philosophy, Hegel portrayed Indian and Asiatic thought simply as an amorphous embryo, as an outlook lacking conceptual clarity and determinate shape. Similarly, in his philosophy of religion, he described India as a "land of imaginative inspiration," a "fairy region, an enchanted world," a "region of phantasy and sensibility," but in any case a world incapable of producing genuine philosophy. Under the influence of German romanticism, India represented for him "the character of spirit in a state of dream," a character in which he detected "the generic principle of Hindu nature." Needless to say, the task of spirit for Hegel was to awaken from this dream state—from the state of the "dreaming Indian"—in order to assume its role as self-conscious reason and subjectivity in the world. This process of awakening forms the inner heartspring of the Hegelian dialectic and, more generally, of the West-

ern theory of "progress" in its various formulations; whether under
Hegelian, Marxist, or empirical-evolutionary auspices, historical development since Hegel is seen as the progressive self-realization of
human reason, will, or other capacities.

As Mehta notes, however, this process of realization is not innocently spiritual, but involves the growing ascendancy of reason over
imagination, of Occident over Orient, what Husserl and (following
him) Heidegger called the progressive "Europeanization of the world."
The latter ascendancy was clearly accepted by Hegel in his philosophy of history when he anticipated that India's dream state would be
disrupted and transformed by Western colonialism—as was happening already in his time under British control. As Mehta comments wryly:
"Is it not indeed the privilege of the spirit in the waking state, as represented by the modern Hegel-speaking Western consciousness, to be
master of its dreams?" From this vantage, he adds, Hegel

> said something profoundly true, unbeknownst to himself, when
> he prognosticated, continuing his sentence on the English lord-
> ship over India: "for it is the necessary fate of Asiatic empires to
> be subjected to Europeans; and China will, someday or other, be
> obliged to submit to this fate." For the spirit which woke up, or
> dreamt that it did, after Socrates in the history of Western thought,
> *has* conquered the world and incorporated it into its own big
> dream.[7]

Fueled by the dialectic of reason, Western ascendancy has an important—and deleterious—impact on the project of cross-cultural understanding. Paralleling the advance of colonial expansion, it is the
privilege of the West to comprehend Asia or the East, not vice versa—
and this by virtue of its higher conceptual maturity. Endowed with the
power of negation or negative determination, Western reason according
to Hegel had the capacity of distancing and analyzing or dissecting
the world, thereby rendering it amenable to rational control. Willing
to undergo the labor of negation and alienation, Western spirit first of
all retreats or emancipates itself from the world, thereby gaining the
freedom (in a next step) to objectify the contents of the world in order
finally to integrate or absorb the latter into its conceptual framework.
Understanding from this dialectical vantage amounts largely to an effort of incorporation, assimilation, and self-aggrandizement.

Mehta speaks in this respect of hermeneutics construed not as an
opening of horizons but as "a weapon directed against the other."
From Hegel's interpretive strategy, he notes, "the being of the other,
far from being acknowledged in its otherness and as a voice trying to

reach me with its truth," can only appear as "spirit in a state of dream" and as an element assimilable in the vast drama of the unfolding dialectic; whatever exegetic "charity" may be operative in this process is "stifled by the metaphysics of *Geist.*" Just as in the case of the theory of progress, however, Mehta finds in our age a promising departure from the Hegelian strategy, in fact, a "breakthrough" or breaking away from the tradition of Western speculative thought. Nietzsche's *Birth of Tragedy,* Heidegger's *Being and Time,* and Gadamer's *Truth and Method* are in his view the crucial "landmarks" of this departure which opens the path to a new mode of hermeneutical understanding: a hermeneutics of "letting-be," one that "does not turn the past or the other into a dream image, an unreality, by the adoption of the *Aufhebung* principle of Hegel, but lets them be, real and speaking in their own right."[8]

Throughout Mehta's writings, hermeneutics forms a crucial topic whose meaning and implications are examined with steadily deepening rigor and intensity. Several of his essays give an overview of the development of modern hermeneutics—from Schleiermacher's theological exegesis over Dilthey's historicist brand of inquiry to Gadamer's philosophical (or philosophical-ontological) mode of interpretation. As he repeatedly emphasizes, it was chiefly Heidegger's *Being and Time* that laid the groundwork for a radical reformulation of hermeneutics: its transformation from a specialized type of inquiry, based on introspective empathy, into a constitutive feature of *Dasein* or human existence as such. Seen as "being-in-the-world," *Dasein* for Heidegger was thrown into a situation and at the same time constrained to project itself into the future—a condition that requires a constant interpretive effort geared both toward self-understanding and toward an understanding of others and the world. In his "existential analytic," Mehta comments, Heidegger has "laid bare the ontological structure of man, and this includes understanding as an intrinsic constituent of man's being-in-the-world."

Conceived in this manner, hermeneutical understanding is no longer a mere act of empathy extending from an inner self (or subject) to another self (or the world of objects) but rather a basic mode of human "being-there," that is, an emblem of *Dasein's* "primordial openness" to other beings and the ground of being as such. Far from reflecting a subjective-intentional design, understanding always has the character of mutuality or of an experience one undergoes with others and the world, with the result that the attainment of a new level of understanding of others also implies a new kind of self-understanding and thus a process of self-transformation. Most important, given this aspect of mutuality, understanding can no longer be construed in terms of a dialectic bent on rational appropriation and assimilation; instead, its proper goal is that of a concerned "letting-be" *(Seinlassen)*. In Mehta's words, paraphrasing Heidegger: "The happening of understanding, and of a tradition as its cumulative result, is itself an ontological process, a continuous language event and an event of truth, rather than a series of operations performed by a subject upon something objectively given; [it involves] remembrance of what has been and an anticipative reaching out to the future and openness to it."[9]

Building upon the insights of *Being and Time,* Gadamer's *Truth and Method* fleshed out and further developed this view of understanding in the direction of a dialogical engagement between self and other, between reader and text. In accord with the notion of 'existential thrownness,' understanding for Gadamer always proceeds from existing preunderstandings and prejudgments (including prior self-understandings) which are nourished by a particular history or tradition — although a tradition which needs to be constantly recuperated (once its taken-for-grantedness has vanished). These prejudgments may seem at a first glance distorting, and they *are* distorting if they are stubbornly maintained in full awareness of the distortion; yet they are also conditions of possibility or enabling premises of understanding by providing a starting point for reciprocal questioning. Deviating from Dilthey and the older exegetic tradition, Gadamer's hermeneutics does not rely on empathy or an effort to gain access to the other's psyche or the mind of the author *(mens auctoris);* instead, the accent is placed on understanding the meaning of an experience, text, or tradition, an understanding that can arise only out of a concrete engagement in which existing modes of self-perception or identity are tested and possibly transformed.

Such testing can occur between individuals, between reader and text, but also between different cultures. "No culture," Mehta notes, "is an island enclosed within its own horizon, though all cultures and traditions have their being within such horizons"; it belongs to the very essence of the "hermeneutic experience" that through it these horizons "open out, move towards and fuse with each other, in however small degree." Placed in a historical framework, the encounter of perspectives is at the heart of what Gadamer calls "effective historical consciousness" *(wirkungsgeschichtliches Bewusstsein)* whereby past meanings are retrieved, mediated, and recast in the light of new concerns. What is crucial—for Gadamer as it was for Heidegger—is that understanding involves not an intentional strategy but rather participation in an ongoing interplay of questioning, an interplay which implies not an attempt at mastery but a willingness to give oneself over "to the *Sache.*" Participants in this process are not bystanders but are inserted into a "happening of truth"; in this sense, we always "come as it were too late, as Gadamer puts it, when we want to know what we should believe."[10]

Together with Gadamer, Mehta opposes the "happening of truth" to the infatuation with "method," especially if methodology is expected to yield a neutral, scientific access to meaning. As a movement of living thought, he writes, cross-cultural understanding is concerned with a "mutual sharing of horizons," not with "discovering a formula for the 'other' culture" or "grasping it in a concept." From a Gadamerian vantage, the notion of 'neutral exegesis' and a scientific history is largely a chimera. Following in the footsteps of Enlightenment rationalism, historicism and evolutionary theory tend to rob the past of effective potency while holding up "the image of a disenchanted, demystified, and rationalized world" neglectful of human temporality. Under the impact of positivism, even hermeneutics is sometimes styled as a "science of interpretation" designed to offer objective, universally accessible knowledge. Where this model prevails—as happens in some versions of psychoanalysis, anthropology, and cultural analysis—understanding is transformed into a method for ordering, managing, or streamlining the world or else into an instrument for "decoding, unmasking, and mastering" an unconscious or repressed experience. "Strange hermeneutics," Mehta observes, "in which a valid dialogue can begin only after [cognitive] understanding has first been achieved, rather than being itself the locus or the playground in which understanding has its very being."

A similar objectivism can sometimes even be found in the comparative study of religions, especially where the latter is erected into a "science of religion" (Religionswissenschaft). Mehta finds it strange that positivism should continue to linger in a discipline ostensibly so far removed from its premises and that its scholars should have remained largely cut off from the "liberating contemporaneous developments" in philosophy, literature, and literary theory. "May it be," he asks,

> that the very starting point, the conception of the study of religion as the study of "other religions" has resulted in an exaggerated concern with methodology, in an admirable openness to social science and anthropology, but in too little regard for the task of religious *thinking*, of finding an appropriate way of talking about *all* religious traditions and about the history of religion (in the singular) in their global togetherness?

Taking his cues from Wilfred Cantwell Smith, Mehta insists that religious studies can proceed not from neutral curiosity but only from a genuine religious interest, one "no longer tied to specific theologies, and yet religious, pushing towards an integral, universal way of thinking about *homo religiosus*."[11]

Although critical of objectivism and the fascination with method, Mehta does not simply reject science or the endeavor of rigorous scholarship, provided they are not presented as substitutes for understanding. His endorsement of scholarship extends even to the discipline of Indological studies, which, over the past two hundred years, has emerged as an integral part of Western academia. Although appreciating Edward Said's critique of "Orientalism" as a corollary of Western colonialism and imperialism, Mehta is unwilling to discard the fruits of Western-style learning wherever they promote a broadening of horizons. The problem for the Indian, he writes, is not "finding out strategies for discrediting this scholarship" but rather discovering how to share in Western learning "without having to surrender his personal relationship to his own tradition."

Faithful to the demands of hermeneutical engagement, the alternatives for Mehta are not adoption of Western science and secularism versus their rejection in favor of a native traditionalism. Given the growing interpenetration of cultures, Indians have no longer the option either to embrace Western reason as the "inner telos" of humankind or to "entrench ourselves into a specifically Indian philosophizing." Instead, the only viable pathway is to try to *"understand both [cultures] in their mutual otherness,"* to "learn the language of each" and thus to "evolve ways of thinking and talking which will be truly appropriate to our membership of both worlds." The goal of such hermeneutical engagement for Mehta is not a bland universalism or homogenizing syncretism but rather the cultivation of respect for difference fostered by inobtrusive understanding: "No facile compromise or reconciliation, miscalled 'synthesis,' but a relentless exposure to the tension between the scientific consciousness and the legacy of the past is the way we can learn to address the right questions to our religious tradition and be rewarded by answers truly adequate to our present situation."[12]

II

Mehta's comments were not empty phrases but fully backed up by his life experience. During many years of study and then during his prolonged stay abroad he thoroughly "exposed" himself to Western culture and scholarship, though not simply for the sake of idle curiosity. As in the case of Hölderlin (as read by Heidegger), venturing abroad was for Mehta only a sustained preparation for an eventual homecoming, a return that would enable him to "address the right questions" to his own tradition, especially the tradition of classical India. In this respect, the road was partially cleared but at points also made nearly impassable by Western Indological scholarship. As Mehta observes, leading Western thinkers on India—such as Hegel, Schelling, and Schopenhauer—clearly had only a secondhand knowledge of the Indian world, based on "secondary sources and inadequate research"; moreover, despite good intentions, their approach tended to remain thoroughly mired in Western metaphysical assumptions. Even a leading German Indologist such as Paul Deussen (a friend of Nietzsche) could not see—despite resolute efforts—to what extent his understanding of India was still governed by "the very Kantian presuppositions on which he took his stand as on unshakable ground."

Elsewhere, scruples about philosophical presuppositions were even less developed; especially in England, the "unshakable ground" of Indology frequently coincided with colonial expansion. Thus, when the Boden chair for Sanskrit was established at Oxford in the latter part of the last century, the specified task of the chairholder was the translation of the Bible into Sanskrit so as "to enable his countrymen to proceed in the conversion of India to the Christian religion." The linkage of Indology to imperial interests was perhaps most openly articulated by Lord Curzon in 1909 when, speaking to the House of Lords, he stated, "Our capacity to understand what may be called the genius of the East is the sole basis upon which we are likely to be able to maintain in the future the position we have won." He also said, "No step that can be taken to strengthen that position can be considered undeserving of the attention of His Majesty's Government." Pleading for the creation of a school of Oriental Studies in London, Curzon bluntly declared that "such studies are an imperial obligation . . . part of the necessary furniture of Empire."[13]

Undaunted by these "Orientalist" obstacles, Mehta in his later life sought to find his way back into the classical sources of Indian thought, particularly the treasures of the *Rigveda* and other *Vedas*. Perhaps more than elsewhere, access to these treasures was facilitated but also obstructed by Western Indology. (One may recall Max Müller's famous description of the *Rigveda* as "crude, childish, unscientific," reflecting the character of an "ancient and simple-minded race of men.") Mehta manages both to pay tribute to and disassociate himself gently from Indological scholarship. It would be "churlish," he writes, to deny the "new illumination and breath of fresh air" offered by modern *Rigveda* philology. Still, it is obvious that Western learning comes to the subject "from outside" and often treats the *Veda* as an "object" rather than as a living reality; typically, it is more concerned with historical antecedents of the text than with "what it has meant to the people whose faith it has nourished" over long periods of time.

From the angle of Indian lived reality, the *Rigveda,* however, has functioned as "a founding origin and source," with the result that most subsequent religious literature is in the nature of a "series of footnotes" or a "massive commentary" on it. Thus, there is here a clear instance of that tension between Western knowledge and indigenous experience mentioned above. While the Western scholar seeks to understand Vedic texts "without being religiously involved" and armed with "extraneous" prepossessions, the Indian lives within a "cumulative tradition" of which the roots are in the *Veda* and seeks to re-experience the latter in light of "all that has emerged from it in a time of present need." What the contemporary Indian reader of the *Veda* seeks, Mehta observes (speaking in his own behalf), if that reader is "modern and not untouched by a sense of historical distance" generated by modernity,

> is both to understand this text and to experience an epiphany. He must live, truthfully, suffering in full awareness the "darkness of these times" and with hope in the coming dawn, and assist in its emergence by the only act of worship appropriate to the goddess *Vac* (Word, Logos): a prior dedication to the *Sabda-Brahman* (reality as word) that the *Veda* is, to which no word of whatever provenance can be alien.[14]

Mehta's comments on the *Rigveda,* and the Vedic tradition in general, are fascinating and revealing of his distanced yet deeply engaged reading. Heeding Heidegger's view of the uncanny night of beginnings, he regards the *Rigveda* not only as the *"arche*-text" of the Hindu tradition but as "the *arche,* the animating source of the religiousness" which generated and sustained that tradition. As a kind of *Ur-Dichtung* this *Veda* is for Mehta not simply a collection of meanings. Rather it signals "the very opening up of a horizon of meaning" out of which subsequent ages were able to construct a whole stream of sacred texts and insights. Focusing on the *Rigveda* and its legacy, Mehta singles out a number of key features for closer consideration. First of all, there is the "sacredness and all-pervasive reality of the word *(vac, brahman)"* which constitutes a focal point in Rigvedic experience (Mehta follows here Indologist Paul Thieme in rendering the term *brahman* as sacred word or utterance). As he notes, *brahman* basically means "giving poetic form, a verbal formulation," though not for the sake of human self-expression but in response to a divine call or inspiration. The *rishi* or poet fashions a *brahman,* but not as its originator or creator; for the latter is god given *(devattam).* It was the centrality of the sacred word that generated among the heirs of the Vedic legacy that "sensitivity to language" that resulted later in the grammar of Panini and the transformation of Vedic into classical Sanskrit.

A second feature of the *Rigveda* is its wisdom and even its "speculative passion" that "breaks out once in a while" (though it is mostly restrained). From this, Mehta says, flows "the mighty torrent, swirling and surging, of Upanishadic thought" that later gives way to the "ceaseless creativity" of the philosophical systems *(darshanas),* above all the *Vedanta.* Third, the Vedic hymns contain a narrative and "mythopoeic" strand, although it surfaces often tangentially; this strand is elaborated in later hymns but finally "bears rich fruit" in the massive epic and Puranic literature of later centuries. Next, there is the central importance of *rita* in the *Rigveda* and the entire Vedic religion—a term that Mehta, following Heinrich Lüders, translates as "truth." (It was Lüders who asserted: "To have made Truth the highest principle of life, that is a deed for which perhaps even modern peoples might envy those ancients.") However, truth here does not simply denote a correspondence or adequation to external facts (which is its preferred meaning in Western metaphysics); instead, it designates the largely concealed "sacred origin and goal" of all thought and activity (in a manner akin to the preSocratic *aletheia* discussed by Heidegger). Between *rita* as truth and the world of gods, as well as between gods and humans, there prevails a convenantal bond or a relation of friendship, which is the final point highlighted by Mehta. Friendship, we read,

> is the commonest name in the *Rigveda* of the bond between men and the gods, and so of the bond between man and truth. The lordship of transcendent truth and the ultimate sacredness and sanctifying nature of the "region of truth" make it the relationship of all relationships, so that "being true to" is the common sacred measure and norm for man's relationship to the gods, to nature, to other men, and to himself.[15]

While honoring the work of noted Indologists, Mehta does not follow their arguments completely or without reservations. One point of disagreement has to do with the status of the world or "cosmos" opened up by Vedic religion. In their interpretation of Vedic texts, both Thieme and Lüders spoke repeatedly about "Vedic cosmology" or the "worldpicture of Vedic Aryans." Mindful of Heidegger's caveats, Mehta objects to this description. Both Vedic scholars, he says, "speak in terms of *Weltbild* and *Weltanschauung,* as though the Vedic *rishis* were talking about nature in the modern sense, as an object confronting the human subject" and amenable to observation *(Anschauung).* In light of recent hermeneutical teachings, however, "can we afford to ignore the philosophical critique of the concept of world and the idea of a world-picture by Heidegger or by Wittgenstein and, more recently, Richard Rorty?" From the angle of *Being and Time,* the term *world* must be seen as an *"existentiale"* or an "aspect of man's mode of being," while in Heidegger's later work it refers to "the unified play of the four-fold of earth and heaven, gods and mortals, in which man dwells on earth as his home, under the heavens."

Such a view is completely blocked by observational language, just as is the spirit of Vedic religion. Under the rubric of *Weltanschauung,* we read, there clearly cannot be "any *sacred* fire (Agni), or the *sacred* waters here below, or a *sacred* plant (Soma)." Yet, for the Vedic seers Agni was not just an observable fire but rather "the burning flame of longing for self-transcendence, the vehicle which carries man's message to the gods," while Soma represented "the ultimate end of human spiritual endeavor, the fullness of awareness, potency and joy, in short, immortality." Another reservation concerns the status of Vedic gods, such as Agni, Rudra or Varuna. For Thieme and other Indologists, these gods were either personifications of forces of nature or else embodiments of abstract concepts. What these scholars failed to take into account, Mehta comments, is that the Vedic seers may have used traditional nature imagery "for their own purposes and novel ends." The notion of 'embodied abstractions' was particularly misleading. "Do we see here a process," Mehta asks, "of moving from *logos* to *mythos* rather than the other way round?" If Vedic seers had ascended to the level of abstractions, "why would they go about re-entering the deifying, mythic darkness again?" For Mehta, neither the Vedic gods nor *rita* or *vac* were deified abstractions—just as little as Heidegger's 'being' is an abstract concept. Instead, they formed part of a poetic world disclosure, an inspired *'aletheio-poiesis'* (which becomes intelligible from the vantage of Heidegger's remarks on language).[16]

The same kind of poetic world disclosure can be found in later classical literature, especially in the "mighty torrent, swirling and surging" of Upanishadic texts. In commenting on Far Eastern thought, Heidegger at one point had portrayed Lao-tzu's *Tao Te Ching* as a form of "poetic thinking," as a meeting ground of reflective thinking and poetry. Turning to the Indian context, Mehta asks, may we not see the Upanishadic utterance as inhabiting a similar sphere, as moving in "this region where 'poetizing' and thinking are neighbors"—and not only moving in it but opening it up first of all as a "foundation and fountainhead for Indian thought?" Actually, it was with reference to (one aspect of) the *Upanishads,* that Heidegger made one of very few recorded comments on India. In the course of a seminar on Heraclitus

(conducted jointly with Eugen Fink in 1966 and 1967), Heidegger remarked in an almost offhand fashion: "For Indians sleep is the highest life." What sense can one make, Mehta asks, of Heidegger's provocative and seemingly quite misleading statement? To elucidate this possible
meaning, he turns to Upanishadic texts—especially the *Brihadaranyaka*
and the *Manduka Upanishad*—where the states of human being or
the stages of human selfhood are discussed (as an elaboration of the
sacred syllable *OM*). According to these texts, human selfhood can be
traced from a "waking" state immersed in everyday awareness to the
stages of light dream and deep sleep where subject-object divisions
progressively drop away, until finally a fourth stage *(turiya)* comes into
view, a condition of authentic selfhood or pure being where *atman*
and *brahman* are able to coalesce.

   Why, Mehta asks, does Heidegger "stop short with sleep as the highest," while failing to mention this fourth stage beyond waking from
which the other three derive their meaning? Perhaps, he speculates, it
was Heidegger's concern with finitude that held him back from taking a metaphysical leap (into an ideal world) and thus prevented him
from seeing that "even for Indians sleep is not and cannot be the highest life." Yet the situation was probably more complicated and had to
do (again) with the problem of language and cross-cultural translation.
In Western Indology, the fourth state—especially in its connection
with *chit*—was commonly rendered as the abode of absolute *selfhood*
or *pure consciousness,* terms which from Heidegger's perspective are
emblems of Western metaphysics and "modern subjectivism." Things
might be different, Mehta suggests, if *chit* were seen as relating to
human consciousness in the same way as the term *being* relates to *beings* in the Western ontological tradition. Thus, it is this "linguistic
problem"—which already "caused no end of trouble to Hegel"—that
may have prevented Heidegger from "taking the step from sleep to the
fourth state."[17]

   By way of the *Upanishads,* Vedic insights subsequently infiltrated
the diverse philosophical systems or schools of thought—among which
Mehta pays special attention to *Vedanta.* Here again it was a matter
of disengaging himself from Western scholarship while still respecting some of its findings. A case in point is Indologist Deussen who expertly translated and interpreted important *Vedanta* texts without re-
alizing his continued indebtedness to Kantian and Schopenhauerian
presuppositions. Even distinguished Indian philosopher K. C. Bhattacharya, in his studies devoted to *Advaita Vedanta,* was insufficiently
sensitive to the persistent legacy of (German) idealism in his thought.
In an attempt to extricate himself from this predicament and make a
fresh start, Mehta turns simultaneously to some of the classical spokes-

men of *Vedanta*—such as Shankara and Sureshwara—and to Heidegger's work, *not* with the aim of finding in the latter the key for unlocking classical texts but of initiating a kind of dialogue in which the two perspectives could interrogate each other.

The difficulties of this undertaking are obvious on several levels. For one thing, Shankara lived and wrote standing in the relatively unbroken tradition of classical Hinduism, while Heidegger inherited Nietzsche's rupture with the past. Still, Mehta notes, Shankara too was "not just a traditionalist intent on restoring the Vedic tradition" but an original thinker "moved by the experience of his age as destitute, pervaded by an absence and hanging in the abyss" (occasioned by the long period of Buddhist dominance). Next, there is the problem of cultural and temporal distance, especially the fact of Heidegger's relative aloofness from classical Indian thought—more specifically his tendency to lump the latter together with Western-Platonic metaphysics (a tendency that explains his preference for Far Eastern culture as holding greater promise for "nonrepresentational" thinking). In a modest but important footnote, Mehta seeks to correct or counterbalance this metaphysical construal of Sanskrit literature. Granting the metaphysical component in Sanskrit, he writes,

> It may be instructive to investigate the correctives it has developed against this representational or objectifying element, thus exhibiting its own genius: a mode of utterance in which representation and the cancellation of the representative force are held in tension and balance. Perhaps the uniqueness of Indian philosophy and religion lies in the simultaneous deobjectification of the objectified, in the iconoclastic moment which is never long absent from its iconism.[18]

The encounter of Heidegger and *Vedanta,* in Mehta's view, offers clues for a fruitful pursuit of comparative cultural and philosophical studies beyond the pitfalls of one-sided assimilation or shallow synthesis. In the past, he notes, comparative philosophy has proceeded largely on the basis of an uncritical employment of metaphysical ideas, assumed to be "obviously and eternally valid" and hence indiscriminately applied to non-Western cultures and traditions (such as those of India). Yet, something remarkable is likely to happen if we take seriously Heidegger's talk of the "end of philosophy" and the "overcoming of metaphysics," for what these notions herald is a new freedom from metaphysical biases, a "loosening of the hold of the 'concept' on thinking," and a fresh openness to the "matter of thinking, wherever going on, East or West." From Heidegger's perspective, the end

of philosophy as metaphysical reasoning does not mean its termina-
tion but rather its consummation and completion, the fact that it has
reached its extreme fulfillment in the emerging "world civilization"
predicated on the triumph of Western scientific-technological reason.

Are we to think of comparative philosophy, Mehta asks, as a "continuation of this consummation," as a contribution to this world civilization and in its service? Or should we not rather think of it in terms
of the "task of thinking" which, according to Heidegger, still remains
reserved for us at the end of metaphysics: namely, the task of retriev-
ing beginnings in order to explore the untapped future potential in past
thought? Mehta's own preferences clearly point in the second direction. If we wish to retain the term, he writes, comparative philosophy
would then be "a name for the task, infinitely open, of setting free" the
promise of the past, the task of "bringing into view and articulating in
contemporary ways of speaking, in new ways of speaking, the matter
of thinking which, in what has actually been realized in thought, still
remains unsaid and so unthought in the traditions of the East."[19]

With specific reference to *Vedanta,* this approach signals the need
for a re-interpretation of classical texts and their guiding ideas. A case
in point is the term *brahman,* whose Vedic meaning had already been
recast by some Indologists as "sacred utterance," as opposed to a metaphysical essentialism. In Mehta's view, this rethinking of the term needs
to be carried forward into post-Vedic literature. As he writes, neither
the *Upanishads* nor Shankara were concerned with epistemology in
the Western sense, with the result that the term *brahman* for them was
not equivalent to Aristotle's *being (to on),* just as little as *brahman-
vidya* corresponded to a *legein* or *theorein* in the Greek sense. Taking
some cues from the later Heidegger, Mehta prefers to associate *brahman* with world disclosure or a kind of happening in which everything
participates (without resort to metaphysical essences). Seen from this
angle, *brahman* is indeed being, but *not* in the sense "in which it is
other than what it is being for or to," not in the sense of "what knowing, thinking and speaking are about, other than them, as a reality confronting them," but rather "inclusive of these as themselves modes of
being." To this extent, *brahman* is *"sat, chit* and *ananda* in one and as
one, and my being is one with it."

This view finds support in some of Shankara's writings (especially
his commentary on the *Brahma Sutra)* which completely reject the
identification of *brahman* with an (ideal) object of knowledge, predicating any understanding of *brahman* instead on the removal of "the
distinction of objects known, knowers, acts of knowledge etc., which
is fictitiously created by nescience *(avidya)."* Despite their monumental
stature, however, even Shankara's texts cannot simply be taken as fixed

entities or finished structures. Insofar as it is a way of thinking, Mehta insists, Vedantic thought or Vedantism has been and will remain "a thinking of the unthought in what has been thought" and thus "a perpetually novel start." This vantage point bestows a continual freshness and youthfulness on *Vedanta* and on the work of Shankara as its foremost proponent. Perhaps, the beginning of *Vedanta*, we read, "still hides a secret for future thinking and saying; perhaps Shankara's thinking still contains a meaning, still awaiting the work of thought to be clearly seen, from which his school itself was side-tracked, even while bringing it to *one* consummation. . . . If so *Vedanta* thinking, far from being a closed and completed whole, remains a task for the open future."[20]

III

Mehta's observations on classical texts are penetrating and important; but they do not exhaust his engagement with India and Indian traditions. A tribute to his work would be entirely inept and inadequate if it failed to mention another dimension: his involvement with the legacy of popular and devotional Hinduism as nourished by epic and Puranic literature. In this respect, Western Indology has probably been on the whole more a hindrance than a support. In preparing his magisterial edition and translation of the *Rigveda*, Max Müller wrote in a letter about its importance for Indians: "It is the root of their religion, and to show what that root is (no temples, no idols), is I feel sure, the only way of uprooting all that has sprung from it during the last 3,000 years." Subsequent scholarship in the West has in large part shared in this downgrading of popular Hinduism in favor of classical "roots." Mehta's work is completely untouched by this bias. In his discussion of *Vedanta* thinkers, he refers approvingly to Sureshwara's description of *Vedanta* as "a science flowing out from the holy foot of Vishnu," adding that this is "no figure of speech only."

For Mehta, one of the most remarkable aspects of Indian history is the continuity of religious faith and devotion throughout the centuries. In the midst of the "most dramatic changes and ruptures" in their history, and despite "so many broken threads," he observes, the one thing "to which Hindus clung and never let go, to which they tenaciously held on by dint of continued creative transformation," was their "immediate, living relationship with the sacred." This clinging is sometimes chided or condescendingly mocked by Western scholarship as a failure to rise from *mythos* to *logos* or from magic to reason. But from the vantage of our own time, the time of an emergent world civilization, the situation may appear in a different light. For, in our age of

"consummated desacralization" of all aspects of life and of a deepening insight into the effects of secularization, it may be possible to
perceive the phenomenon of Indian religiosity for the "wonder that it
was" and continues to be. "The question today and at this hour in the
religious history of mankind, as in reality always," Mehta states, "is
not whether there are many gods, or two, or the one and only, or
whether this religion or that is 'true,' but whether human living is not
to be irretrievably banished from the dimension of the holy, within
which all talk of God and the gods, near or remote, present or absent,
transcendent wholly or also immanent, has any meaning."[21]

In referring to Indian religion or religiosity, Mehta does not mean
to subscribe or lend support to the Western bifurcation of faith and
reason or theology and philosophy. A central aim and ambition of his
work is precisely to move beyond this division of domains and thus
"beyond believing and knowing" in the direction of a thinking or
thoughtful faith where mind and heart are joined. The preeminent
place of this joining is the sphere of the "holy," a sphere inhabited by
homo religiosus who is a bridge between the visible and the invisible
or *"ein Pfeil der Sehnsucht nach dem andern Ufer"* (in Nietzsche's
terms). In clinging to the sacred and making room for the dimension
of the holy, Indian tradition in Mehta's view gives evidence of the persistence of thoughtful faith or a faithful mode of knowing, a mode that
allows us to think "the holy and the true in their intrinsic, indivisible
unity" and thus to experience "that integral plenitude, in that highest
abode of Vishnu and seat of *rita.*"

To be sure, this tradition is today under siege and exposed to a
steady process of erosion. Humankind, Mehta comments, lives today
in a "disenchanted world," and religion is no longer the "central, integrating and historically effective force" that it was in the past. To the
extent that it is embroiled in the process of modernization, India too
has become nilly-willy a participant in the "worldwide phenomenon
of secularization." Yet the issue for Indian intellectuals is whether to
be simply pliant tools of disenchantment or else to engage in cultural
resistance by bearing witness to an older promise. Before we advance
"from a 'developing' to a 'developed' status" and banish all "so-called
superstition," Mehta asks, is it not important and timely "to keep the
'rumor of angels' alive" and, in doing so, to grant a human abode to
the sacred? In large measure, he perceives his own life work in terms
of such an engagement. As he noted in one of his last essays, his life
world at that time was surely no longer fully inhabited by "the ethos
of the community in which I was born and raised," although traces of
it remained a "cherished element in the very core of my being." In the
meantime, he had also become a participant in "the life world of the

India of today" and even in "the Western worldwide phenomenon of technicity" (Heidegger's world civilization). His essay queries, "What, in such a situation, is there left for me to do than go questing after the traces of sacrality, go back to the sacred texts of my tradition and try to find a language in which they may be made to speak meaningfully today?"[22]

Mehta's sustained "questing" after these traces is exemplified in his comments on epic and Puranic literature. His final lecture at the Harvard Center for the Study of World Religions concluded with a section titled "Considerations on the *Ramayana.*" These considerations are learned and scholarly; but they are by no means a mere exercise in *Religionswissenschaft.* As he notes, he himself grew up in a section of Banares called "Ramghat," near the place where Tulsidas is said to have composed his "Petition to Rama"; and in a neighboring house, weekly group recitals of Tulsidas's *Ramayana,* accompanied by music, "formed the ambience of my life for twenty years." These and other reminiscences form the backdrop for his intent, at the end of a long career, to "bring the beginning and the end together" by concluding with "a few words in praise of Rama." On Mehta's reading, the *Ramayana* is an epic tale about human deeds, but it is also a sacred story. More precisely, it is a story about the transfiguration of the human into the divine.

At the beginning and in the foreground of the story we find a struggle between humans and demons, with the gods simply "looking down from heaven, keenly watching the fortunes of battle." At this point, Rama, the hero of the story, is entirely and preeminently human. But, Mehta asks, "what is it to be human? What is man that he should serve the gods and battle against demons, that in doing so he may shine forth in a light beyond him and fulfill and manifest the divinity in him?" Born a *kshatriya* prince, Rama is driven into exile and challenged by demons who rob him of what is dearest to him (his wife Sita), experiences which set the stage for a profound seasoning and transformation. "What goes on in the pages of Valmiki, as we move from book to book," we read,

> is a gradual revelation and unfolding of the true nature of Rama, of the more than human in this very human prince, as in a photographic film from a Polaroid camera. So far as I know, neither the progressive changes in landscape and geography, the crossing and descent, nor the change in Rama, not into something other than human, but in respect to the suprahuman light that shines through him with ever-growing intensity; none of this has been noticed by scholars. Not once is he identified by the poet with

Vishnu, nor is there a suggestion that he thinks of himself as such. And yet, the picture on the photographic plate keeps on developing.

In the end, on the invitation of Brahma, Rama is able to return to his divine abode. The interpreter of the later age, Mehta adds, of "our age in which *dharma* stands on one leg," may wish to read the *Ramayana* as a purely human tale or adventure. But he can also read it and retell it as "the story of the highest repository of human devotion, if his concern is with *dharma* and *moksha.*" Pure devotion, however, leads to that "serenity from which flows all compassion. That is Rama."[23]

Five years after his return to India, Mehta presented a lecture on the *Mahabharata* in Delhi. There, after acknowledging the great distance separating modernizing or "developing" India from its epic past, Mehta with quiet intensity evokes the memory of *kurukshetra,* speaking of the "vital force" with which the epic tale inhabits "our imagination even today." In his account, there are several reasons for this continued vitality. For one thing, the *Mahabharata* is simply "a rattling good yarn and a mine of minor stories" which have served as source and inspiration for a good deal of subsequent literature. Above and beyond this, the epic is for Mehta "a work of superb poetic craftsmanship and imaginative vigor, not yet fully explored," a work that has the continuing power to enlarge our understanding "because the story it tells and the realm of meanings it opens up can give us a glimpse of our human situation, of the reality of what *is.*" As he recognizes, the *Mahabharata* is a tale of dramatic turbulence and unmitigated violence, but it does not glorify the latter. Its central message, "repeated again and again," he writes, is "that nonviolence *(ahmisa)* and compassion *(anrisamsya)* are the highest duties of man, states of being without which we fail to be completely human."

According to Mehta, the story revolves around the relation between *"kshattra"* and *"brahma,"* the former denoting physical prowess and strength, the latter the power of reflective insight and wisdom. It is the uprising of a quasi-demonic *kshattra* against a wisdom faithful to divine *dharma* that causes the banishment and suffering of the Pandavas, triggering again a process of transformation and transfiguration. Far from merely recounting the story of an "internecine conflict between two groups of blood-relatives," the *Mahabharata* for Mehta reports the Pandavas's agonizing struggle against, and final victory over, a rebellious *kshattra* force, demonstrating in the end that *kshattra* divorced from *brahma* is "ruinous" while in the service of *brahma* it may guide to peace. This lesson is underscored in the final encounter of the Pandavas with Ashvatthama, when Krishna orders the former to put away their arms, an order only Bhima disobeyed:

> Then Krishna and Arjuna step down from their chariot, throw
> away their arms, walk into the fiery circle of that ultimate weapon
> [of Ashvatthama] and forcibly make Bhima obey and stop fight-
> ing. Then the weapon became quiescent and inactive. In the very
> midst of the discourse of violence, what more eloquent testimony
> could there be to the power of nonresistance, or nonviolent re-
> sistance, which is the quintessence of Gandhi's philosophy of
> nonviolence.[24]

Underscoring the human-more-than-human character of the epic
poem, Mehta's lecture contains intriguing comments on Krishna/Vishnu
and Shiva, that is, on the most popular deities of devotional Hinduism.
Despite the accent on human exploits and interclan rivalries, he notes,
what happens in the *Mahabharata* seen in its narrative structure, "cannot be understood unless the crucial roles played in the drama by Krishna and Shiva are understood." Drawing some inspiration from Heidegger's discussion of temporality and being toward death (as well as
his remarks on the "passing while"), Mehta presents Krishna/Vishnu
as the very source of time or, more precisely, as the sustainer and pre-
server of temporal human being in the world. As the ultimate divinity
and absolute reality, he writes, Vishnu is "the origin of time itself" or
of human temporality; under his auspices, everything that comes into
being "endures for a while and then passes away, including individual mortals and entire civilizations."

During its life span, every living being is backed up by a divine
power; the potency granting or allotting time to each being (including each individual *Dasein)* is "mythically speaking, Vishnu or Narayana
incarnate as Krishna in human form." To this extent, Krishna is the
supporting, beneficial, strength-giving agency in human life within a
temporal frame "where *dharma* in conjunction with the other *pu-
rusharthas* holds sway." Yet time in this context (and in a Heideggerian sense) is not clock time but rather a temporality poised in the precarious balance of life and death, presence and absence, arrival and
departure. At the outskirts of an allotted time span, temporality itself
takes on the character of evanescence, dissolution, and even death —
a power that is "mythically named Rudra or Shiva." In the *Mahabharata,* Mehta observes, Shiva is not directly a player or agent in the
story, but an "outsider," a "strange, uncanny figure" at the outskirts
of human activities. Still, from behind the scene (as it were), he takes
a hand in "structuring the plot of the narrative." Thus, throughout the
unfolding events of the epic story, "Rudra's shadowy presence haunts
the realm of the living." Though absent in person, Shiva is present:
"Through his signs and symbols, hints of his actuality are there

throughout the narration and they surface clearly at crucial points in the narrative."[25]

Mehta's relation to Hindu deities was not confined to the level of speculative observations. Honoring the yardstick of a faithful wisdom or thinking, his work was also saturated with genuine devotion and a deeply rooted *bhakti* religiosity, especially as cultivated in the Vaishnava tradition. Some of his finest and most moving writings deal precisely with this tradition which stretches from the *Bhagavad Gita*, focused on Krishna, to the later *Vishnu Purana* and *Bhagavata Purana* and finally to the lyrical *bhakti* of Chaitanya Mahaprabhu and his heirs. In Mehta's account, the *Bhagavad Gita* can be regarded as the *"archetext of Ekanti* Vaishnavism," a text in which devotional surrender or *bhakti* is taught as the highest mode of *yoga* or of the joining of humans with the divine. Far from counseling a simple emotionalism, *bhakti* in the *Gita* is presented as a "gathering together of mind, intellect and heart in their unity," a form of relationship with the highest in which "man's whole being" is concentrated on this outreach or self-transgression. Replicating the ancient relation between Nara and Narayana, Arjuna in the *Gita* is "Krishna's *bhakta,"* that is, his "dear friend" patterning himself completely on his beloved mentor. With an accent more on intellectual and ethical commitment, the *Vishnu Purana* portrays the demon-born Prahlada as the "prince of *bhaktas"* completely devoted to Vishnu/Krishna. It is through intense meditation that Prahlada is shown here to achieve juncture *(yoga)* with the divine. In Mehta's words: *"Bhakti* here is meditative insight risen to the pitch of ecstasy." Because Prahlada knows that Vishnu abides everywhere and in everything, "he looks upon everyone as equal, without distinction of friend and foe"; in his view, we should have *bhakti* toward every creature, "because the Lord dwells in all beings."[26]

According to Mehta, however, the preceding texts offer only faint glimpses of *bhakti*—whose full depth or strength is revealed in the *Bhagavata Purana*. While in the *Gita bhakti* was more proclaimed than illustrated, and while the *Vishnu Purana* concentrated on an ideal meditative mode, the *Bhagavata Purana* offers a sustained paean to the "love of God." In that Purana, the wise intellectual Uddhava travels as a messenger of his friend, Krishna, to the *gopis* in Vrindaban to persuade them to be content with mental exercises and meditation. But, Mehta notes, his message has little or no effect on the *gopis* whose "minds and thoughts are already in Krishna's keeping" and whose aching hearts remain "utterly absorbed in their beloved" who has parted from them and yet is with them "in the mode of absence, as a trace of his presence." At this point, Uddhava the messenger becomes himself the recipient of a message or a truth which had been hidden from him before: for he comes to realize that loving Krishna as the *gopis* do is "the real thing," the ultimate goal to be pursued even by sages and saints. What Uddhava experiences "in the depth of his being," goes beyond his cognitive awareness, for now "he longs to kiss the dust under the feet of the *gopis* of the Braja and wishes it were possible for him to live in Vrindaban even as a plant in the vicinity of the *gopis.*"

What the Purana here intimates is a blending of mind and heart, a faithful-thoughtful kind of devotion; for Uddhava now is "both a *bhakta,* solely devoted to Krishna as his friend and confidant, and a *muni* or a thinker." As before, Mehta is firm in dissociating *bhakti* from sentimentalism or a subjective-emotive state of mind. Remembering Heidegger's notion of 'mood' *(Stimmung)* seen as a basic tuning, he insists that *bhakti* "involves the total human being" and is "not confined to having feelings of a specific kind." Seen as a generative tuning of the whole of *Dasein, bhakti* transcends the traditional distinction between the three mental faculties of knowing, willing, and feeling; to this extent, it even transgresses the differentiation between three distinct types of *yoga* (with *bhakti* being one of them). As he writes in a Heideggerian vein:

> Contrary to the modern, Western, subjectivistic and man-centered philosophies of life, feeling (as also knowing and willing) must be understood not in the psychological sense of inner commotions and agitations but ontologically as a mode of man's relationship to being. . . . Understood in this metaphysical, non-psychological sense of feeling, *bhakti* represents man's primordial relationship to being, . . . the supreme privilege of man's mortal estate and the ultimate refuge in his search for wholeness and for being healed.[27]

In celebrating *bhakti* and whole-hearted devotion, one should note, Mehta never gave aid and comfort to any sort of religious fundamentalism or a narrow-xenophobic revivalism. Loyal to the teachings of his European mentors, he never forgot that self-understanding of any kind presupposes "going out of oneself" and that "the way to what is closest to ourselves is the longest way back." For Mehta, the encounter of self and other necessarily had the character of mutual interrogation, which implies "mutual openness and so an acknowledgment of the other as question-worthy." Such questioning and mutual recognition held for him also the key not to "world civilization" but to a genuine global community free of domination. The goal of such a global community, he wrote, cannot be achieved "through any sort of *Herrschaftswissen,* or any sort of cultural and conceptual conquest" but only through "this reaching out to the other in active understanding."

These considerations also apply to the situation in India and to the relations between India and the West. The religious tradition of India, Mehta affirms, has been in the past an "open temple" which allowed itself to be touched by "Greek power and beauty," by the thought currents of neighboring China, as well as the divergent influences of Buddhism, Islam, and Christianity. The present encounter with the West, while wrenching in many ways, also allows Indians to distance themselves from tradition and thus to recapture the past freely and with renewed vigor. Now, we read, the Indian

> can joyfully let his religious imagination be enlarged and vivified by the heritage of the Greeks, by the vision of Christianity, and the message of Islam, and he can freely seek to appropriate through creative reinterpretation the tradition of which he is both a product and a trustee. He can accomplish this, but only to the extent that he can see himself and his tradition in the wider inter-religious context of world history.

Thus, faithfulness to tradition and openness to the other, the unfamiliar, perhaps even the threatening, here go hand in hand. In this respect, Mehta's outlook is thoroughly supported by the *Bhagavad Gita* of which he was so fond. There, Krishna instructs Arjuna: "In any way that humans love me in that same way they find my love; for many are the human paths, but they all in the end come to me." And again: "The human whose love is the same for enemies or friends, whose soul is the same in honor or disgrace . . . this human is dear to me."[28]

EXIT FROM ORIENTALISM

Comments on Halbfass

Then there was not being nor non-being. . . .
Death was not, not was immortality. . . .
But the breathless one breathed by itself.
—*Rigveda*, Mandala 10

There was a time when cross-cultural understanding was largely a matter of expertise. Study and comprehension of non-Western cultures, including the "Orient," was consigned to an array of area specialists ranging from philologians to historians and cultural anthropologists. Armed with the arsenal of Western philosophical and scientific categories, area studies pursued a somewhat predatory aim, that of incorporating or assimilating non-Western life-forms into preestablished frames of reference (unless they were relegated to a mysterious otherness beyond the pale of knowledge). To be sure, incorporation of this kind was not a purely academic exercise, but was buttressed and fueled by concrete political and economic ventures of that time, especially the administrative needs of colonial empires. In Edward Said's formulation, this constellation of factors formed the backdrop of Western "Orientalism," a label highlighting the collusion of scholarship with the imperatives of colonial domination.[1] In its distilled form, this kind of constellation is no longer prevalent today. Our age of postcolonialism has also given rise to forms of "post-Orientalism," that is, endeavors to rupture or transgress the traditional Orientalist paradigm. To the extent that Orientalist discourse was part and parcel of a "Eurocentric" world view, transgression sometimes heralds a radical anti-Eurocentrism, perhaps even a dismissal of European scholarship as such; to the degree that the latter was tied also to "logocentrism" (or a "foundational" metaphysics), cognitive understanding tends to give way to constructivism, that is, the imaginative invention of traditions and life-forms. All along this trend is corroborated by the ongoing processes of globalization, processes which, in their pervasive effects, undermine the prerogatives of area specialists.

Clearly, the demise of Orientalism cannot be cause for lament. Still, even while welcoming new departures, one may plausibly be concerned about the manner of the demise, that is, the way in which the exit from Orientalism is sought and performed. Is it really possible to move briskly from Eurocentrism to anti-Eurocentrism (and from logos to antilogos)? Is it sensible to equate traditional learning—however flawed—simply with colonial oppression? Does the critique of cultural "essences" and stable identities really warrant the claim that traditions and life-forms are "up for grabs" and can be constructed *ad libidum?* In our globalizing context, is there not still room and need for cross-cultural understanding—beyond the confines of Eurocentrism and logocentrism? And does such understanding not involve or presuppose a patient learning process, a sustained effort of reciprocal interrogation, which, in turn, can hardly disdain some of the resources (philological, historical, anthropological) of traditional scholarship?

As it happens, the groundwork for such a post-Orientalist inquiry has already been laid in our time by a group of scholars from the West and the non-West, including such distinguished names as Wilfred Cantwell Smith, J. L. Mehta, and Raimundo Panikkar.[2] A younger member of this group—but by no means "junior" in terms of insights and achievements—is Wilhelm Halbfass whose work is the topic of the present chapter. In his outlook and background, Halbfass illustrates and exemplifies some of the important ingredients of the emergent post-Orientalist discourse. Thoroughly trained both in Western philosophy and in the specialized research tradition of Indology, Halbfass stands at the crossroads of interacting (sometimes conflicting) life-forms and language games, a position that enables him to act (at least in some respects) as a mediator or honest broker. While immersed in academic pursuits, Halbfass is also a clearheaded citizen of the world, completely attentive to the complexities of globalization, and especially to the persisting political and economic asymmetries between West and non-West (asymmetries which render the term *post-Orientalism* intrinsically ambivalent).

As it stands today, Halbfass's opus is already impressive by its range and subtlety; apart from a long string of journal articles, his scholarly reputation is particularly tied to three successive publications: *India and Europe: An Essay in Understanding* (1988); *Tradition and Reflection: Explorations in Indian Thought* (1991); and *On Being and What There Is: Classical Vaisesika and the History of Indian Ontology* (1992).[3] Limitations of space as well as (more crucially) limits of my Indological competence militate against any attempt at surveying this vast field of scholarship. The following shall focus on three topical areas which appear to be particularly salient. First is Halbfass's approach to cross-cultural understanding and particularly to Indian culture and traditions. Next, attention shifts to one of the central concerns of traditional Indian thought: the status and meaning of being as articulated in Vedic and post-Vedic texts as well as in philosophical literature. Finally discussion turns to some political problems besetting the relation of India and the West: in particular the compatibility of *homo hierarchicus* with modern democracy and the role and prospects of Indian culture in the context of Western hegemony. These comments will lead me to some concluding remarks on the viability of cross-cultural scholarship, as epitomized by Halbfass's work, in a time of rapid globalization.

I

In his explorations of Indian culture and traditions, Halbfass is keenly aware of the formidable obstacles and complications besetting such an inquiry. These obstacles are due not only to the temporal distance of classical scriptures and their textual complexity but also—and perhaps chiefly—to the role of Western Indological scholarship itself and its bent to compress Indian culture into Western categorial frameworks (or else to treat it as an essentialized counter-image of the West). In his introductory essay to *Tradition and Reflection*, Halbfass comments specifically on recent discussions surrounding "Orientalism" and Eurocentrism as they have emerged in the wake of Said's famous study. As he notes, the basic aim of the assault on Orientalism has been to expose "links between the scholarly exploration and the political subjugation of India and the 'Orient,'" that is, to lay bare the extent to which Western Orientalists have tried to "'represent' the Orient," to "project it as a sphere of 'otherness,'" and in general to "objectify, categorize, and classify it in accordance with European interests of domination." Said's own study, in particular, endeavored to show that Orientalism as an academic discipline has always been "tinged and impressed with, violated by, the gross political fact": namely, its complicity with the "Western projection onto and will to govern over the Orient." While Said himself was primarily concerned with the Western treatment of Islam, his arguments have been extended to India by numerous scholars, including Ronald Inden in his *Imagining India* and other writings. Emulating the deconstructive attacks on Orientalism, Inden charges Indological scholarship with harboring hidden imperialist designs, designs evident in the imposition of "reified" and "essentialized" images on Indian culture and in the attempt to appropriate "the power to represent the Oriental, to translate and explain his (and her) thoughts and acts not only to Europeans and Americans but also to the Orientals themselves."[4]

For Halbfass, deconstructive efforts of this kind cannot be lightly dismissed given the stark background of European colonialism and its pervasive effects. As he writes, there can be "no doubt" that the time for a critical reassessment of Oriental scholarship has arrived. Yet he also cautions against a facile debunking rhetoric which may run afoul of the demands of scholarly integrity. Above all, Said's conception of Orientalism—in Halbfass's view—can itself be seen as a reifying and essentializing construct whose theoretical premises call for critical, perhaps deconstructive, scrutiny. One of the main problems of Said's conception is the blending of "highly selective historical observations" with broad philosophical and metaphysical "generalizations," with the latter often riding roughshod over the task of concrete historical interpretation. Resulting from the merger of "very specific and very general traits," Orientalism is in danger of appearing as a "historical and conceptual hybridization that is no less a construct and projection than the so-called Orient itself."

Similar considerations apply to the arguments of Inden which, again, are marked by a somewhat indiscriminate fusion of concrete historical observations with "fundamental epistemological and metaphysical" claims regarding the status of knowledge as such. To disentangle this (con-)fusion, more sustained efforts of critical exegesis are again called for, efforts that would address such questions as: "What is the role of essentialization and representation in the critical process itself? What are the standards to expose false constructs and super-impositions?" For Halbfass, one of the chief defects of summary pronouncements is the danger of a surface reversal which leaves untouched perceived abuses. With regard to Eurocentrism, the remedy is sometimes sought in the simple cancellation of Western categories; but in this case the recovery of indigenous authenticity is still ascribed to Western largesse (now in the mode of self-denial): "The attempt to eliminate *all* Western constructs and preconceptions and to liberate the Indian tradition from all non-Indian categories of understanding would not only be impractical, but also presumptuous in its own way. . . . This self-abrogation of Eurocentrism is at the same time its ultimate affirmation."[5]

The main lesson Halbfass derives from the preceding comments is the need for patient and sustained cross-cultural inquiry which yet remains fully conscious of the pitfalls of Orientalism. Such an approach entails the endeavor to steer clear both of essentialized constructions of India (as Europe's other) and of a simple deconstructive denial of

Indian culture and traditions. Put differently, Halbfass's critique of Eurocentrism consigns him to a path that moves—however cautiously—beyond the Scylla of a homogenized Indian identity (exploitable by colonial administrators and fundamentalist Hindu movements alike) and the Charybdis of a complete lack of cultural distinctiveness (which would leave India at the mercy of Western-style globalization). Several chapters in *Tradition and Reflection* center on possible strands or dimensions of Indian cultural distinctiveness—beyond the pale of a compact essentialism.

One such strand running through many centuries and surfacing in varying guises and formulations is the "concept of *dharma*." Despite the immense diversity of accents among orthodox and heterodox brands of Hinduism, the concept for Halbfass functioned as a broadly shared, though somewhat inchoate frame of reference over long stretches of time. In his words: "There is coherence in this variety," one that reflects "the elusive, yet undeniable coherence of Hinduism itself, its peculiar unity-in-diversity." Although there was never *"one* system" of understanding *dharma* but only a tensional network of usages, the concept provided a kind of "contextuality" which lent coherence to the "luxuriant welter" of traditional Hindu life. On the one hand, Hindu life was never the "dogmatic and institutional identity of an 'organized religion,'" but on the other hand, it is "neither an 'Orientalist construction,' nor can it be reduced to a brahminical fiction or projection." This broad contextuality was shared both by "sectarian" movements like Shaivism and Vaishnavism with their specific theistic assumptions and by such "supra-sectarian" thinkers as Bhartrhari, Kumarila, and Shankara. In all these cases, understanding *dharma* requires a step beyond Orientalism and anti-Orientalism. To quote Halbfass:

> The modern idea of "Hinduism," or of the "Hindu religion," is a reinterpretation of the traditional ideas and, in a sense, a hybridization of the traditional self-understanding. Yet it is by no means a mere adaptation of Western superimpositions. It is also a continuation of the tradition, an expression and transformation of that self-understanding which articulates itself in its commitment to the Vedic revelation.[6]

Another, still more pervasive strand in Indian tradition is the legacy of the *Vedas* in which *dharma* is one ingredient. Here the contextuality is even more elusive given the factual neglect of the Vedas by broad segments of Hindu life and the distance of Vedic rituals from the popular Hindu pantheon. Even among traditional thinkers formally attached to the Vedas there is wide disparity regarding their status and meaning. Thus, while orthodox spokesmen of the *Mimamsa* regarded the Vedas as timeless texts without author and beyond the range of error, representatives of theistic traditions viewed the same texts as the word of God, but only as one stage in an open-ended process of revelation. Surveying this field, Halbfass agrees that the Vedas contain "no Hindu dogma, no basis for a 'creed' of Hinduism, no clear guidelines for the Hindu way of life.'" Yet, reflecting on Louis Renou's notion of *'prolongements réels,'* he also sees a discontinuous continuity at the heart of Indian culture. Despite the enormous heterogeneity of that culture, he notes, "an idea and vision of the Veda emerges not only as a focal point of Hindu self-understanding, and a center for the precarious unity and identity of the tradition, but also as a prototype for its inner variety and potential universality." Probing more deeply this prototype, Halbfass presents the Vedas not only as a text but as an *"Ereignis"* of world disclosure (in the Heideggerian sense), which implies that Vedic exegesis involves not only a "textual hermeneutics" but a "hermeneutics of the event." In the traditional view, the Veda is the primary or "originary word" *(sabdapradhana),* signaling a beginning where text and world, language and reality are still unseparated and where the text itself "opens and sustains the 'world.'"[7] Although disseminated, deflected, and corrupted in the tortuous course of Indian history, this Vedic insight was never completely abandoned, remaining active as a trace of the past. In a sense, Halbfass notes, "it is this internal multiplicity and variety itself, this challenging and suggestive chaos, that accounts for the significance of the Veda in Hindu philosophy. It provides an elusive and ambiguous guidance, an open, yet authoritative framework, with suggestive hermeneutic patterns and precedents and inherent appeals to human reflectivity." In functioning as a prototype, the Veda harbors an "orientation towards unity and identity" as well as an "inherent tendency to transcend and supersede itself."[8]

In discussing *dharma* and the Vedic tradition, Halbfass also discloses his own preferred approach which can serve as an antidote to Orientalist constructions. Whereas Orientalism objectifies and reifies its target by retaining an external spectator's stance, Halbfass's invocation of hermeneutics implies a dialogical engagement between reader and text, interpreter and *interpretandum,* an engagement through which both partners are potentially transformed (without necessarily entailing an ultimate convergence). As an attentive student of Western, especially Continental, philosophy, Halbfass is thoroughly familiar with the hermeneutical model as developed from Dilthey to Gadamer. Commenting specifically on Gadamer's work, he credits the latter with predicating understanding on the dialogical "recognition of the other, the foreign as such"—beyond the conundrums of total incorporation or expulsion. Objectification in this model is obviated by the participatory involvement of the interpreter who necessarily starts from his own "prejudices" (and not from a clean slate) and for whom the target of interrogation always remains an interpreted other (rather than a reified thing in itself). In his own writings, it is true, Gadamer has tended to confine himself to the Western tradition; but, as Halbfass notes, there is "no compelling reason" why his perspective should not be "applicable in a wider, trans-cultural context." Gadamer's emphasis on the productive role of prejudice, in particular, can help us realize "that, in approaching Indian thought, we carry with us our Western perspectives and presuppositions not merely as an impediment and aggravation, but as a necessary and positive ingredient of understanding itself." Gadamer's approach has been complemented and radicalized by Heidegger, though with greater attention to the perils of Orientalism (seen as a corollary of the Westernization or "Europeanization" of the world) and its deleterious effects on cultural dialogue. According to Halbfass, Heidegger's thesis regarding the Greek origin of Western philosophy and science was no longer a "self-confident proclamation of the uniqueness of Europe," but rather "a statement concerning a global predicament. Europeanization 'eats away all substance from things.'"[9]

In light of these perceptive hermeneutical insights, the reader is bound to be disoriented by a certain tendency in Halbfass's more recent writings which jeopardizes or calls seriously into question the entire enterprise of cross-cultural understanding. "Over the years," we learn in the preface to *On Being and What There Is*, "my methodological positions and philosophical allegiances have changed. The result has been a certain eclecticism and growing doubts concerning the meaning and relevance of the topic itself. We do not know whether the 'question of being' is a meaningful question." After surveying the history of ontological reflection from Plato to the present, the introductory chapter in the same volume turns to recent Anglo-American analytical philosophy as providing a new slant on age-old quandaries. In the new milieu, Halbfass observes, "the focus shifts from the question 'what being is' to the conditions of speaking about it and the confusions in what others have said about it." More specifically, the "methods of modern conceptual and linguistic analysis" and the "tools of symbolic logic" are used "to articulate semantic distinctions, to resolve traditional ontological difficulties by uncovering underlying grammatical and conceptual confusions and to eliminate meaningless questions concerning 'being.'"[10]

At this point, W. V. Quine is invoked and credited with offering a deft resolution of the "ontological problem " by reducing it to "three Anglo-Saxon monosyllables: 'What is there?'" From the analytical vantage, the role of "being" as a noun and of being or "reality" as subjects of statements must be criticized as prime examples of Gilbert Ryle's notion of 'systematically misleading expressions,' distortions which can only be corrected through "empirical research in linguistics." Seen against this backdrop, Heideggerian thought now appears in a new, and by no means favorable, light. Heidegger's insistence on the "question of being" is said to have been "stubborn, almost obsessive, and highly idiosyncratic." His later reflections on the history of being are portrayed as largely fruitless, empty speculations—"Such thought is not committed to tangible results and applicable methods." As a mere reaction against calculative reasoning and conceptual precision, it signals "a withdrawal into poetry, myth, and capricious etymologies. Its aimlessness and futility are deliberate." By indulging freely in "systematically misleading questions," Heidegger's entire work appears dubious and/or misleading: "He seems to represent the consummation of all that is questionable in Western ontology."[11]

Strictures of this kind, in my view, impinge not only on the "ontological problem" and its relevance, but more generally on the role of hermeneutical understanding in Oriental studies. To be sure, Halbfass is not quite ready to dismiss hermeneutics entirely. As he still insists, it is "our first responsibility to understand the Indian statements," which means that we have to be willing to "listen to them as carefully and patiently as possible" and to "be aware of their traditional cultural context and background." Yet understanding alone is no longer seen as adequate in the absence of critical distantiation and analysis; mere familiarization with Indian culture and traditions is said to be deficient unless it is "supplemented by conceptual analysis and clarification." Such clarification and analysis, however, require a turn to resources beyond the pale of hermeneutical or dialogical inquiry: "Clarification implies a commitment to objective standards of precision and analysis." Ultimately, this commitment leads to the demand for a neutral and universal standpoint from which all traditions can be objectively assessed without bias (or a Gadamerian "prejudice").

In our century, this demand has been raised most emphatically by logical positivism and the "unified science" movement, some of whose axioms were later continued by analytical philosophy. "Is there," Halbfass asks, "a truly common ground for a comparison of different traditions of thought and a neutral, universal medium through which they can communicate?" And he replies: "One important recent suggestion is that such a common basis is provided by logical and linguistic analysis and exemplified by the methods of modern analytical philosophy of the Anglo-Saxon type." It is in the context of linguistic analysis that the claim has been advanced that analytical methods (especially the use of symbolic logic) are "separated from the restrictions of the various existing languages" and their particular milieux and hence conducive to "a truly universal understanding of the different philosophical traditions."[12]

One of the chief problems of these passages is the return of supposedly banished ghosts. Above all, the invocation of analysis "of the Anglo-Saxon type" tends to jeopardize the exit from Orientalism and Eurocentrism which Halbfass's earlier studies had so diligently pursued. For clearly, the ascent to analytical objectivity implies again the objectification and reification of cultural traditions and their submission to the categorial frames of an external spectator; moreover, the same ascent vindicates the intellectual superiority of the neutral analyst over the array of cultural and historical contingencies. Halbfass is not unaware of these implications; in light of the long-standing association of universalism and Eurocentrism, students of non-Western cultures surely have to be on their guard. Implicitly or explicitly, he writes, universalism "entails the idea of a privileged viewpoint, a higher level or more comprehensive horizon of awareness and reflection." While we cannot simply discard this universalizing perspective, we also have to be "aware of its background and historical ramifications."

Unable to resolve this dilemma, Halbfass's argument finally ends in a halfhearted eclecticism. On the one hand, he strongly defends the "merits" of Anglo-American analysis. In the pursuit of objectivity, he notes, we should not underrate "the extraordinary instrumental value of modern formal and analytical models, including symbolic logic, in the interpretation of philosophical texts and traditions"; we should also acknowledge "the potential of orderly scientific progress" and thus be willing to face non-Western phenomena from the vantage point of "latest research." On the other hand, objectivity may well be an elusive and perhaps even deceptive standard; we certainly should not construe the perfection of formal methods as "the implicit telos of Indian philosophy or as the goal and essence of philosophy in general." In fact, analysis and the search for conceptual precision can be obtrusive and "interfere with the task of translating and understanding, and with our obligation to respect the Indian tradition in its own context and dimensions." The upshot of these divergent instructions is an agnostic compromise: "At the end, we do not have a well-defined method, and perhaps not even a definite perspective, for our exploration of the Indian texts and teachings. Our procedure will be eclectic."[13]

II

The ambivalence regarding method cannot fail to have obtrusive effects also on substantive topics of inquiry—although these effects are more noticeable in Halbfass's more recent writings. At this point, I choose for purposes of illustration a topic that is crucial in traditional Indian culture and philosophy and which also plays a prominent role in Halbfass's work: that of the status and meaning of being. In a way, the topic has always been one of Halbfass's central preoccupations. In the preface to *On Being and What There Is,* he informs us that the chapters collected in that volume are only fragments of a much larger project: namely, "a comprehensive history of Indian thinking about 'being' and 'what there is.'" The same preface also promises a future volume on the notion of being in *Advaita Vedanta.*[14]

Reflections on the topic, however, antedate the *Vaisesika* study by several years. While devoted chiefly to the role of Indian culture in European self-understanding, *India and Europe* contains important chapters on such concepts as *dharma* and *darshana* which bear at least an oblique relation to being. As indicated before, the study also comments on Heidegger's radicalization of hermeneutics, and especially on his critique of the "Europeanization of the earth" under the auspices of Western science and technology. For Heidegger, Halbfass correctly notes, this development was also a disturbing ontological happening, by promoting the progressive concealment and oblivion of being in favor of calculative rationality: "Philosophy in this sense, which implies a deep 'forgetfulness of being' ('Seinsvergessenheit'), is the mother of science and technology, and of the Atomic Age."[15]

More sustained soundings of the topic in the context of Indian culture can be found in *Tradition and Reflection,* especially in the chapter "Human Reason and Vedic Revelation in *Advaita Vedanta."* Among all the "schools" of classical Indian philosophy, Advaita Vedanta was most closely tied to the Vedic legacy, and this on philosophical and not merely "traditionalist" grounds. While other schools, such as *Nyaya* or *Vaisesika,* paid lip service to the Vedas, and while proponents of *Mimamsa* recognized only the ethical *(dharma)* dimension of scriptures, Advaita Vedanta took seriously the character of the Vedas as "originary word" *(sabdapradhana),* as a world-disclosing event without which human rationality is bound to be left astrand. For Shankara— the foremost spokesman of Advaita Vedanta—human reason was by no means a negligible faculty, but one that was circumscribed by broader contexts (or what one might call "ontological conditions of possibility"). Left entirely to its own devices, human reason—especially calculative rationality—is bound to lead to oblivion or "forgetfulness of being" in a dual sense: forgetfulness of the being of self *(atman)* and of being as such *(brahman)*. To overcome this oblivion, reason has to remember or recall its own rootedness in the "originary word," that is, in the "revealed" sayings of the Vedas which alone can liberate thought from its egocentrism or anthropocentrism. As Halbfass perceptively elucidates this point:

> In claiming its own methods and criteria, human reason displays an anthropocentric attitude of self-confidence and arrogance that is incompatible with that receptivity and openness which is a condition of liberating knowledge. Relying on his own "worldly potential" *(samarthyam laukikam)* of intelligence and reasoning alone, man remains attached to that very world from which he seeks final liberation. No effort of "worldly" reflection by the ego upon itself will yield the liberating insight into the reality of the *atman* as the one absolute witness.[16]

As needs to be stressed again, Shankara's outlook did not imply a simple rejection of reason or a resort to an antirational or irrational intuitionism; on the contrary, his writings are in large measure a model of lucid reasoning. As Halbfass observes, especially the *Upanishads*— the "knowledge portion" of the Vedas—in Shankara's view "respond to human reason, appeal to it, provide it with a context, goal, and basis"; they also contain "so many hints and implicit patterns of reasoning that they seem to anticipate all merely human intellectual efforts." Yet, reason *(yukti, tarka)* for Shankara cannot be entirely self-sufficient; proceeding from an agent "within" the world, reason cannot at the same time survey or thematize the boundaries of that world or the conditions of its own existence. To gain insight on that level, reason has to remember its embeddedness in being, which means it has to be attentive to what is "heard" or disclosed *(shruti)* in the "great sayings" of the Vedas. Unguided by such hearing, reasoning may lead to worldly cleverness, but a cleverness which gets entangled in its own confusions and contradictions. As Shankara repeatedly emphasized—especially in critiquing other schools—unguided reasoning is "dried up" *(suska)*, that is, fruitless and groundless. Although useful for certain limited purposes, human reason is inherently unstable and unfounded, and ultimately even liable to refute and supersede itself, thus showing its incapacity to provide a "foundational" metaphysical grounding. To quote a passage from Shankara's *Brahmasutrabhasya:* "Conclusions which are based on human reflection alone are unfounded. . . . Conclusions at which expert reasoners have arrived with great effort of reflection are viewed as spurious by others, even more expert ones. . . . In this way, it is impossible to find a foundation for the conclusions of reasoning, because of the variety of human ways of understanding."[17]

The inherently unstable character of human reasoning is illustrated in *anvayavyatireka* or the method of affirmation and denial ("positive and negative concomitance," "continuity-and-discontinuity") variously practiced by classical Indian schools. As Halbfass elaborates, the method was chiefly used for clarifying the meaning or great Vedic sayings, such as the famous *tat tvam asi* (thou art that), which requires reflection on the self's simultaneous identity with and difference from itself, that is, on the conjunction of presence and absence or the discontinuous continuity of the self with itself (and of *atman* and *brahman*). According to one interpreter, the method was generally employed in Advaita Vedanta in order "to discriminate between what is and is not the self as well as to show what meanings may be attributed to given terms."[18] This statement, however, is possibly misleading as it seems to reduce *anvayavyatireka* to a simple process of conceptual (perhaps dialectical) definition and determination, a process that might readily be productive of stable identities. This ambiguity is perhaps not entirely avoided in Shankara's writings—or at least in Halbfass's portrayal—where the method often seems to boil down simply to a discrimination between essence and appearance or between the essential and the "accidental" features of an entity. This outcome, however, is foiled by the interpenetration of essence and appearance, and especially by Shankara's association of *anvayavyatireka* with merely human reasoning *(yukti, tarka).* As soon as attention is shifted to the great Vedic sayings, the method reveals its self-destabilizing (or deconstructive) quality. To quote Halbfass on this important point:

> The discriminative knowledge achieved through the method of "continuity and discontinuity" does not anticipate the liberating insight which comes from the Vedic word, nor is there a gradual transition from one to the other. In a sense, reasoning in terms of *anvayavyatireka* produces only an openness which has to be filled, or perhaps even a confusion which has to be eliminated, by the Vedic revelation. To him who has freed himself from false superimpositions by reasoning in this way, who has discarded the whole sphere of objects, who asks in bewilderment *(viksapanna)* "who am I?" *(ko 'smi),* who may even think that he himself has been discarded *(tyakto 'ham)* in this process: to him the Veda speaks in a meaningful and soteriologically effective manner when it says: *tat twam asi.*[19]

In Halbfass's study, the discussion of Advaita Vedanta serves a polemical aim: namely, to oppose the conjunction of reason/revelation in Shankara's thought to the worldly rationalism espoused by many latter-day spokesmen of Vedanta (or neo-Vedanta). In a free variation on John Locke's precedent, prominent Indian thinkers in recent times have advocated the basic "reasonableness of Hinduism," mainly in an effort to render the latter more palatable to Western intellectuals. As Halbfass curtly observes, such portrayals "should not primarily be seen as contributions to historical and philosophical research"; bent on adjusting Advaita Vedanta to the demands of the modern world, their scholarship is overshadowed by their "apologetic goal." Unfortunately, Halbfass's own position is not very distant from, and often stands in close proximity to, the neo-Vedantins. Repeatedly he expresses his inability to embrace or share Shankara's conception. "It is obviously impossible for a modern Western reader," he states, "to follow Shankara into all the details of his Vedic exegesis." Elsewhere he chides Shankara precisely for his truncated rationalism: "With this radical commitment to Vedic revelation, Shankara withdraws ultimately from the open arena of philosophical debate, which the philosophers of the Purvamimamsa, in particular Kumarila, had entered so resolutely."

Statements of this kind in a sense anticipate or foreshadow Halbfass's more recent turn to conceptual analysis. As mentioned before, his *On Being* distances itself from classical ontology or at least deprecates the "question of being" as a mode of rational inquiry. There are, no doubt, different ways to account for the more "rationalist" tone of that study. To some extent, the shift may be due to the focus on the *Vaisesika* school, which respected the authority of the Vedas provided it did not interfere with rational argument. However, the change can surely also be traced to the noted methodological quandaries. To recall again the gist of these quandaries: "Conceptual devices that have been developed by Western philosophical thought will be indispensable tools of translation, interpretation, and analysis; but we will have to use them cautiously."[20]

Despite this methodological shift, one should note, *On Being* is by no means devoid of fascinating ontological vistas which entirely transcend the "Anglo-Saxon" paradigm. The chapter "The Question of Being in India" presents a stunning panorama of classical perspectives, among which *Vaisesika* is only a late and relatively subordinate position. As Halbfass points out, being in classical times was thematized in different contexts, including debates on the status of certain entities (such as soul, God, or universals), but also broader ruminations on the origin of the world. In the Vedas and older *Upanishads*, statements on being and nonbeing were closely linked with reflections on

cosmogony and hence often couched in the language of myth or mythological narrative. Whether privileging being over nonbeing or nonbeing over being, cosmogony at this point was not simply equivalent to
a chain of causation launched by a "prime mover," but was more akin
to an opening and disclosure of the world (or in Heideggerian terms,
a "worlding of the world"). "What is decisive," Halbfass insists, "is the
opening, the separation [of heaven and earth] as such, a separation
that implies not only the creation of free space, but also the establishment of firm boundaries, of distinguishability and bipolarity." Hence,
the fascination was not simply with an "amorphous primeval substance
or substrate as such" but rather with the "open space that is its negation"; using a contemporary phrase, the Vedic sense of the openness
of space and world might be called a "primeval metaphysical *clearing.*"[21]

What emerges from these considerations is that the popular characterization of classical Indian thought as "fundamentally substantial-
ist and cyclical" is basically mistaken or at least badly misleading or
lopsided. According to Halbfass, it may be possible to speak of "two
different Vedic 'ontologies'" or, more cautiously, of "different, though
perhaps supplementary, perspectives on the reality of the world":
whereas the "ontology of substance" plays a more conspicuous role in
"later, Indian, specifically Hindu, philosophy" (including the *Vaisesika*
school), the mythology and "ontology of openness" carries a philosophical weight which "should by no means be underestimated." In
Vedic-Upanishadic texts, being and nonbeing tend to be inserted in a
more primordial "world frame" which is often signified by such terms
as *atman* or *brahman; brahman* in particular is often said to transcend
both *sat* (what is) and *asat* (what is not). In Halbfass's lucid commentary:

> It would not be appropriate to describe such transcendence of all
> polarities as the inclusion and disappearance of all distinctions
> in an undifferentiated primeval substance. We are dealing here
> with a transcendence of a higher conceptual order; it includes
> and supersedes the polarity between distinction and nondistinc-
> tion, differentiation and nondifferentiation itself, and provides im-
> portant suggestions for later conceptual thought and systematic
> philosophy.[22]

In post-Vedic Indian thought, the "ontology of substance" gathered
momentum chiefly as a consequence of the Buddhist assault on essences
and the concomitant ascent of "negative ontology." In reaction against
this Buddhist challenge, several philosophical schools—including
Vaisesika, Nyaya, and *Purvamimamsa*—rose in defense of a kind of
ontological realism: "The concept of substance, the doctrine of uni-

versals and the assumption of a well-structured universe of durable and identifiable entities, and clearly distinguishable categories, are at the heart of this defense." Halbfass's *On Being* is basically devoted to an explanation of the *Vaisesika* version of ontological realism. As he shows, the school was centrally concerned with the "horizontal" enumeration and classification of "world constituents" or entities—an effort which seems to concur with Quine's resolution of the "ontological problem" and with Gustav Bergmann's definition of ontology as "an inventory of what exists (is there)." Proceeding along these lines, *Vaisesika* thinkers listed six fundamental categories or divisions of reality, including substance, quality, motion, and the like. The first rubric was said to comprise nine classes of substances—earth, water, fire, air, ether, space, time, mental organs, and even the soul *(atman)*—in a veritable orgy of ontological positivism. Being itself *(bhava/satta)* was simply viewed as the "common denominator" or the "one universal ingredient of all concrete and particular entities."[23]

While offering a sympathetic account of this philosophical system, Halbfass cannot quite refrain from casting a sideways glance at other alternatives, especially at the legacy of the "ontology of openness" which continued, in modified form, in Shankara's Advaita Vedanta, which Halbfass characterizes by the fitting term *soteriontology* (liberation in and through *brahman*). The epilogue to the study broaches themes for which the reader has been scarcely prepared, except through the initial confession of eclecticism. Borrowing a suggestion of J. L. Mehta, Halbfass admits that "representational" or "objectifying" thinking is "fully present in the Vaisesika system of categories." While this may not be a "Cartesian attempt to establish man as the master and owner of nature," it does constitute an effort "to put the world at our intellectual and conceptual disposal, to explain it once and for all through a process of comprehensive enumeration and classification." This admission is followed, in the concluding paragraph, by an even more startling bow to "soteriontology" and even "negative ontology," that is, to the "search for nonrepresentational, nonconceptual, nonpossessive ways of thinking," although this bow is immediately qualified by endorsement of the "stubborn, though perhaps futile, conceptualization" that is exemplified by *Vaisesika* ontology.[24]

III

The final ambivalence marking *On Being* is not simply an ambivalence concerning two ancient schools of thought—about which one might plausibly remain undecided; in its implications, the ambivalence raises again the specter of Orientalism from which these pages began. As indicated earlier, one of the central features of Orientalism was its resort to "objectifying" or "representational" reasoning in an effort to grasp or intellectually conquer alien life-forms from an external (European) spectator's perspective. To the extent that this is the case, an exit from Orientalism in our time seems to accord a certain privilege to an "ontology of openness" over an "ontology of (objectified) substances"; whatever its other corollaries may be, openness implies at least a certain willingness to transcend established categories in favor of a freer recognition of alien life-forms, thus permitting otherness "to be" in a nonpossessive way. The dangers of predatory modes of cognitive incorporation are by no means slighted by Halbfass. As he notes in *India and Europe,* cross-cultural understanding or dialogue today is complicated by Western hegemony and the ongoing process of Westernization of the globe. "The conditions and perspectives of the two sides of the encounter are fundamentally different," he writes pointedly; "the relationship is an asymmetrical one." Basically, modern India "finds itself in a historical situation created by Europe [or the West], and it has difficulties speaking for itself." As a result, understanding under present conditions requires a special effort to transcend Eurocentrism or "what is European" *(das Europäische)* in the direction of greater reciprocal openness. For "in the modern planetary situation, Eastern and Western 'cultures' can no longer meet one another as equal partners. They meet *in* a Westernized world, under conditions shaped by Western ways of thinking."[25]

Comments of this kind bring into view broader social and political issues, which are the final topic of these pages. Under present conditions of Westernization, cross-cultural understanding is liable to be an intensely agonizing, perhaps agonistic, enterprise. Moreover, Western students of the East are quickly faced with complex questions. How far can openness to the other extend? Are there perhaps (normative) limits to understanding? To put it more provocatively: Are there perhaps legitimate aspects of "Europeanization"—beyond the pale of colonial domination and technological or economic supremacy? For present purposes attention is focused here on an aspect which has tended to dominate or afflict comparisons of East and West: the issue of equality and inequality.

Since the time of Thomas Hobbes, human equality and equal liberty have been the basic premise of Western political philosophy or discourse about politics. Initially formulated only as an axiom (applicable in a hypothetical "state of nature"), the principle of equality and equal liberty in due course came to function as the launching pad for a process of progressive equalization and liberalization of all social conditions, a process that culminated in the establishment of Western democracy. Despite many flawed practices, supporters of Western democracy are commonly agreed on the centrality of equal liberty, irrespective of differences of creed, race, color, or sex. By contrast, Eastern society has traditionally been charged with harboring despotism (a portrayal persisting from the ancient Greeks to Hegel and beyond). Even if the latter charge can readily be unmasked as a blatant form of Eurocentrism, some concerns are bound to linger.[26] In the case of India, one can hardly ignore the long tradition of social stratification and inequality as manifest in the caste structure and in the elaborative differentiation of forms and stages of life *(varnashramadharma)*. How is one to assess this age-old legacy? Is one ultimately forced to choose coldly between Western democracy and Indian culture?

Halbfass's *Tradition and Reflection* contains many suggestive insights on these themes, which can serve as guideposts for further discussion. It is clear that much depends on the meaning of terms such as *liberty* and *equality,* which cannot simply be left to Eurocentric preferences. In modern Western thought, liberty and equality are commonly treated as qualities of individual agents, that is, of autonomous egos seen as constitutive building blocks of social life; as a corollary, social distinctions or differentiations have to be justified or legitimated against the benchmark of uniformity or equal liberty. Apart from some notable exceptions (such as versions of Buddhism), Indian culture on the whole is far removed from this kind of egalitarian individualism; in fact, there is even little corresponding to the Western centerstaging of the human species or "homo sapiens" as predestined master of the world. In his chapter "Man and Self in Traditional Indian Thought," Halbfass elaborates perceptively on this point. He writes, "There is no tradition of explicit and thematic thought about man as man in India, no tradition of trying to define his essence and to distinguish it from other forms of life." Referring to formulas such as "homo sapiens" or "rational animal," he finds in India "nothing comparable to that tradition in the West which has its roots in ancient Greek as well as Biblical sources and leads through the Renaissance and Enlightenment periods to the growing anthropocentrism of Western thought."[27]

The contrast here is striking and pregnant with important consequences. In reflecting on "man" *(purusha)* or human life, traditional Indian thought places the accent not on a Western-style "species equality," but rather on something like a fraternal contextuality, that is, the embeddedness of humans in a rich and "luxuriant" fabric of life reaching from the animal kingdom all the way up to the Gods and *brahman*. In Halbfass's words, in the Indian context "the tendency to keep the borderline between men and animals permeable at least to some extent is not surprising. No rigorous anthropocentrism or human self-elevation, even of a soteriological type, can develop in a tradition of thought that takes the idea of *samsara* and the unity of life for granted." While subordinating equality to contextuality, Indian thought also recasts the notion of liberty by severing it from all individualistic, egocentric, or anthropocentric designs. Ultimately, especially in Shankara's "soteriontology," freedom means liberation from separation and self-centeredness and hence release into the "world frame" of *brahman.* To quote Halbfass again:

> The true privilege of man is not to be the master of his world, but to be liberated from it; his mandate is not to employ other creatures as instruments for his own needs and desires, but to use himself, his own human existence, as a vehicle of self-transcendence. . . . It is not man as man, as *animal rationale,* who ought to be liberated, but the self *in* man; and liberation of the self is liberation from being human as well as from any other limiting worldly condition.[28]

Deep in their implications, these comments surely need to be pondered carefully and cautiously. As one should note immediately, phrases such as *liberation from the world* or *from being human* cannot and must not be misconstrued as a retreat into a Western-style essentialism or universalism; nor should the expression *unity of life* be misread in the sense of a *melting-pot* uniformity. (It may well be that Shankara's opposition to Buddhism was derived from his fear—perhaps misdirected—of such a melting-pot ideology.) In traditional Indian thought, both the notion of fraternal contextuality and the idea of soteriological liberation were closely linked with and even predicated on the assumption of an all-pervasive differentiation and distinctness of world elements.[29] This emphasis on differentiation can ultimately be seen as the legitimating underpinning of the Indian caste system and of the theory of *varnashramadharma;* in recent time, it has buttressed the formulation of *"homo hierarchicus"* as the character type marking Indian culture.

As Halbfass notes, commenting on Indian inegalitarianism (and countering again the democratic claims of neo-Vedanta): "Traditional Hinduism develops a whole complex system of formalistic and legalistic restrictions, of rules of ritualistic qualification *(adhikara),* which divide mankind into fundamentally different groups and also determine their access to sacred knowledge and final liberation." In orthodox Hinduism, it is not simply "man as man" who is eligible for liberation; numerous restrictions limit the soteriological privilege "not to man in general, but to specific classes of human beings." This stress on differentiation also marked Advaita Vedanta. For Shankara, human "worldly competence" *(samarthyam laukikam)*—which may be equally or inequally distributed—was not sufficient to account for liberating insight. To attain liberation meant "to discover one's own true identity"; but human identity was not the self-constituting ego, but the self-transcending *atman* (in the direction of *brahman).*[30]

The concluding chapter in *Tradition and Reflection* is specifically devoted to *homo hierarchicus* as initially formulated by Louis Dumont; although not narrowly exegetic, the chapter is said to "support in its own way what Dumont calls 'the main idea' of his book." As Halbfass shows, homo hierarchicus was not an isolated feature but part of a more pervasive rank order or hierarchy of living beings which extended "from Brahma to the tufts of grass." The chapter discusses in detail the various ways in which classical Indian thought justified or legitimated social hierarchy, including the *varna* system: ways that ranged from the simple endorsement of Vedic injunctions to biological-hereditary explanations, reliance on character types or inherent "qualities" *(gunas),* and sometimes even to the invocation of metaphysical "caste universals." There was persistent controversy and contestation among these diverse forms of legitimation, punctuated by occasional attacks on the entire hierarchical system (especially from the side of Buddhism and Jainism).

Yet, despite these disagreements, the mainstream Indian view in classical times solidly favored stratification. This was also true of Advaita Vedanta (despite recent liberal construals, which are historically dubious). For Shankara, it is true, all caste barriers and social distinctions were ultimately rooted in *maya* or *samsara* which the self was meant to transcend; but again, transcendence here did not signal dissolution into sameness, but freedom in the midst of difference. As Halbfass observes (somewhat misleadingly), caste differences here are "irrelevant only in the light of the absolute unity of the absolute, but not with respect to interpersonal relationships," and "there is no suggestion of translating the metaphysical unity into social equality." This reluctance to cancel difference in favor of sameness is exemplified even in the case of the "renouncer" *(sannyasin)* and those "liberated while alive" *(jivanmukta)* who have transcended *samsara:*

> The freedom conceded to the "renouncer" *(sannyasin)* and even the liberated *jivanmukta* is carefully channeled. Even in negation and in renunciation, he remains bound to that same order from which he is freeing himself. For the existence and fundamental validity of this order constitutes the precondition for the possibility of liberating oneself from it. . . . The *sannyasin* continues to

draw his legitimation from that very *dharma* from which he is liberating himself.[31]

What surfaces here are philosophical problems of considerable magnitude which resist easy settlement and which certainly cannot be ad-
judicated through the facile invocation of formulas (such as Eurocentrism or anti-Eurocentrism). In Indian thought, transcendence of difference
(or equality) has itself to be justified in light of a differentiated *dharma*,
which is precisely the opposite of modern Western thought where difference or distinction is radically put on the defensive (as in need of
justification). What is called "Europeanization" or "Westernization"
of the world is to a large extent the militant extension of egalitarianism or the principle of equivalence to other parts of the globe (with
capital serving as the currency of equivalence). Liberty here is not ad-
verse to equality, because it basically means freedom of choice (where
all choices are equivalent or of equal value). Whatever their intrinsic
merits may be, the principles of equality and equal liberty are today
exported around the globe in a missionary and largely unthinking way,
without much reflection on the premises of such principles and how
they (and their consequences) might be vindicated. Non-Western societies, which are not readily swayed by these principles, are quickly
dismissed as illiberal and undemocratic. India in particular—given
the long legacy of "homo hierarchicus"—is likely to be denounced
as a major obstacle on the road to world democracy (in a not very subtle resurrection of Orientalism).

As it seems to me, exiting from Orientalism in our time requires
more than an exchange of blind charges and counter-charges; above
all, it requires a serious rethinking of such basic philosophical categories as equality (or sameness) and difference. Perhaps, in reacting
against Buddhism, traditional Indian (or rather Hindu) thought has
tended to privilege difference too much over sameness (and being over
nonbeing), forgetting the more complex legacy of the "ontology of
openness" deriving from the Vedas. But the problems are reciprocal
or cross-cultural. As Ernesto Laclau and Chantal Mouffe have persua-
sively pointed out, the two principles of equivalence and difference
presuppose each other and need to be articulated jointly, but in a way
that resists synthesis, yielding only reciprocal destabilization.[32] What
this points up is an enormous task looming ahead of us in the wake of
Orientalism: the task of genuine dialogical learning on the level of
basic frameworks, beyond the limits of assimilation and exclusion. By
being willing to shoulder this task, Wilhelm Halbfass's work makes an
important contribution to cross-cultural understanding which can serve
as a guidepost illuminating future endeavors.

WESTERN THOUGHT AND INDIAN THOUGHT

Some Comparative Steps

Rudyard Kipling's famous saying about the "twain" cultures which shall "never meet" today strikes us as quaint and old-fashioned. In an age of jet travel and rapid communication, boundaries between cultures are liable to erode and perhaps to vanish altogether. In the political and economic spheres, there is much talk about the global market and about the emerging new world order, conceptions that pay scant attention to cultural differences and none whatever to Kipling's celebrated hiatus between East and West. Yet, behind the facile rhetoric of globalism, distinct cultural accents or biases can readily be detected: in particular the bias of a Western-style universalism deriving from European Enlightenment thought (with its offshoots of free enterprise and political internationalism). Seen from this angle, globalism does not so much eradicate as intensify cultural divisions and fissures, especially the fissure between a hegemonic culture (of Western origin) and the array of not-yet-assimilated and perhaps unassimilable indigenous cultures.[1]

Thus, in its effects contemporary globalism does not by itself falsify Kipling's observation, although it does place it in a new context, thereby sharpening the issue underlying his dictum. Simply put: contemporary trends transpose Kipling's saying from the propositional into the interrogative mode. Under the relentless impact of globalism, indigenous cultures are increasingly pushed into a context of cross-cultural encounter or confrontation, an encounter that forces them to interrogate both themselves and their competitors (the chief competitor in most settings being the West). In many third world societies—bruised already by many decades of colonial domination—confrontation involves an intense questioning of self-identity, a process that often gives rise to a profound identity crisis. In large measure, the new world order can be seen as a codeword for a universalized identity crisis, whose severity, to be sure, varies from place to place. Although by no means immune from this crisis, Western culture tends to enjoy a cushion of complacency provided by its hegemonic position.

This chapter explores one facet of the ongoing cross-cultural confrontation: the relationship between India and the West, more particularly between Western and Indian "thought" (a broad spectrum of ideas ranging from philosophy to social theory and literature). No attempt is made to give a broad historical overview of the relations between India and Western culture—something which would vastly exceed the confines of a single chapter and which has also been done expertly by others.[2] Rather, this chapter seeks to sketch some general directions and configurations of thought, something one might call a metaphysical *"Gestalt"* (which is entirely different from a coherent or transparent system). Still, historical background is not irrelevant to this undertaking. In talking about a *Gestalt* of Indian thought and Western thought one clearly has to guard against oversimplification and especially against what today is called "essentialism." In exploring the correlation, the suggestion here is not that there is some eternal essence to India or the West which merely has to be uncovered behind historical contingencies (seen as the veil of *maya*). Yet, denial of essences does not entail the assumption of a *tabula rasa*. Whatever *Gestalt* may be discerned is surely the result of a protracted process of historical self-formation, a process involving imaginative discovery and invention proceeding both from intracultural and from cross-cultural contestations.

I

The lure of essentialism is not the only hazard besetting the enterprise attempted here. Even when one recognizes history's role, one still has to face up to conceptual-theoretical quandaries endemic to cross-cultural inquiry. Clearly, such inquiry requires at least two distinct terms or configurations which are not identical but which are also not so incommensurable as to preclude comparison. In the case of Indian thought and Western thought, problems quickly surface. According to some observers, the two modes of thought are separated by a radical gulf which cannot be bridged. Whatever else they may be, Vedic teachings and *darshanas* bear no resemblance to Western philosophy, which is predicated on rational argumentation. According to an opposing view, thought is bound to obey the same rules irrespective of geography or historical setting. Among others, this view has been articulated by Daya Krishna, the eminent Indian philosopher (influenced perhaps by Western analytical reasoning). What "I wish to make clear," Daya Krishna writes at one point, "is that the Indian philosophical tradition is 'philosophical' in the same sense as the Western philosophical tradition is supposed to be." What is attractive in this outlook is the effort to take Indian thought seriously and to rescue it from esoteric punditry. Unfortunately, its merits are offset by its drawbacks, especially the drawback of universalist in-difference: the tendency to equate philosophy (or "philosophy proper") with Western analytical standards.[3]

It is assumed (without elaborate demonstration) here that the two modes of thought are distinct without being incommensurable and thus permit fruitful comparison. But what is the stipulated distinctness? Can it at all be pinpointed, or is it completely submerged in a welter of multiplicity? Even without specialized study, we all realize that Western thought and Indian thought are not holistic structures readily reducible to a single denominator. A brief glance at history reveals Western thought to be an enormously complex fabric of heterogeneous strands that range from Platonism and Aristotelianism over Stoicism and Scholasticism to modern empiricism, rationalism, materialism, idealism, and pragmatism (to mention only some perspectives). The same complexity prevails on the side of Indian thought. Apart from the great religious-metaphysical divisions of Hinduism, Buddhism, and Jainism, there are the famous philosophical "schools" (Daya Krishna prefers to call them "styles of thought"[4]) whose tenets are continuously rehearsed in pertinent textbooks: there we read about the *Samkhya* school with its dualism of spirit and matter, about *Vaisesika* with its focus on empirical particularism, about *Nyaya* with its accent on logical atomism, about *Advaita Vedanta* with its celebration of metaphysical monism, about *Mimamsa* with its stress on exegesis, and about *Yoga* with its devotion to spiritual practice. Using Western-style terminology, one might say that the classical Indian schools range from idealism to empiricism, from essentialism to nominalism, from universalism to extreme particularism and even atomism, and from theism (in its varieties of mono-, poly-, and henotheism) to extreme modes of agnosticism.

As it appears from this overview, distinctness is in danger of being drowned in multiplicity and also in a kind of nondistinction that frustrates comparison. For comparative study to proceed, sameness of features has to be clearly recognized but also bracketed on some level. Thus, to take some prominent features, Western empiricism and *Vaisesika* teachings may be too closely related (perhaps even identical) to facilitate comparative assessment; the same may be true of *Nyaya* logic and Cartesian rationalism. As a result, distinctness has to be somehow distilled or crystallized out of the array of heterogeneity and nondistinction. Yet, in this process of distillation, one obviously has to proceed with extreme caution to avoid the pitfalls of caricature and cultural stereotypes. At this point, let us single out a few comparative

approaches which are dubious or unhelpful because of their stereo-
typed treatment of distinctness.

One such approach—supported by professional philosophers and
also enjoying a kind of popular vogue—is built on the premise that
Western thought is rational and scientific while Indian thought is intuitive and mystical. In my view, this approach is a bad case of "Orientalism" (in the sense articulated by Edward Said[5]). Many Western-
ers love to talk about the mysterious Orient, very often in a somewhat
condescending or paternalistic vein. Conversely, however, many Indians tend to see the West or Western thought exclusively in terms of
scientific and technological rationality. Apart from its "Orientalist" fla-
vor, the approach is unhelpful for comparative purposes because it
construes distinctness in too steep or exclusivist terms to permit cross-
cultural learning or contestation. In addition, the approach neglects
long-standing and important counter-trends on both sides of the cultural divide. Thus, prominent features of Western thought elude the
label of a scientific or instrumental rationalism: Plato's "ideas" transcend scientific formulas just as Aristotle's "entelechy" escapes technical blueprints; neither Thomas Aquinas nor Hegel were scientific ra-
tionalists in the manner of Jeremy Bentham or Karl Popper. To blur
matters further, there is the radical counter-trend of mysticism which
runs through the history of Western thought, from Teresa of Avila and
John of the Cross to Meister Eckhardt and Jakob Böhme. On the Indian side, the approach neglects the tradition of skepticism and empiricism which has strong roots in Indian philosophy (as exemplified
by the *Nyaya* and *Vaisesika* schools). In the context of Buddhist thought,
one might also mention the school of *Svatantra-Yogachara* which relied exclusively on sense perception and logical inference and treated
even consciousness as a passing, sensory phenomenon.

Another dubious approach—also considered so by Daya Krishna—
is the opposition of Western materialism and Indian (or Eastern) spiritualism. According to this widely used formula, the West is seen as
exclusively wedded to material goods and possessions while India (or
the East) has preserved the legacy of the human spirit and the higher
"spiritual" aspirations of humankind. Apart from being a staple in certain kinds of popular literature, the opposition surfaces occasionally
in the more nuanced writings of "Indian renaissance" thinkers, including Tagore and Swami Vivekananda (a fact that does not in any
way diminish their other remarkable achievements).[6] Again the approach is too stereotypical and exclusionary for comparative purposes,
and perhaps it also suffers from a reverse kind of Orientalism. Western thought, one can hardly forget, has been deeply marked by Christian spirituality, and the Protestant Reformation as well as Enlighten-

ment thought cannot be understood in abstraction from these Christ-ian-spiritual roots. One need also recall that Hegel talked of the cen-trality of spirit in history, manifest in the steadily unfolding march of the "world spirit." On the other side, one cannot ignore the nonspiri-tualist or materialist stand in Indian thought: one of the oldest schools of philosophical materialism was founded before the time of the Bud-dha by Brihaspati and his disciple Carvaka. Considering all these fac-tors, one can hardly find fault with Daya Krishna when he writes: "On-tologically, the characterization of Indian philosophy as 'spiritual' is completely erroneous."[7]

Daya Krishna also raises objections to several other characteriza-tions of Indian thought or philosophy, objections which I find in part (though not always) plausible. One of the "myths" about Indian phi-losophy, in his presentation, is the allegation that it is wedded to the "authority" of Vedic texts rather than the pursuit of truth, and thus gives priority to *auctoritas* over *veritas*. As Daya Krishna shows, this allega-tion is far from the mark. Despite a certain respect, perhaps even rev-erence, shown to classical sources, none of the mentioned schools or "styles of thought" rely in their arguments simply on past authority; in fact, he notes (perhaps overstating his case), the major writings of these schools "are not, even in form, a commentary upon Vedic texts." On the other side of the fence, one can probably not entirely brush aside certain authoritative features marking Western thought: the respectful attention commonly accorded to the texts of Plato and Aristotle (and perhaps Thomas Aquinas).

Another characterization that Daya Krishna considers mythical and that he spends considerable effort in combatting is the view that In-dian thought or philosophy is uniquely geared to liberation, release-ment, or *moksha*. In his treatment, this view is a "complete misun-derstanding" of the actual situation. *Moksha,* he notes, is neither the "exclusive" nor the "predominant concern" of Indian philosophy; ac-tually, many of the Indian schools and thinkers "are not concerned with it even marginally." On this point, I am much more hesitant to follow Daya Krishna's lead. It seems that the notion of 'moksha' touches on deep issues in philosophy as such, particularly on the theory-praxis nexus. In his dismissal of the notion, Daya Krishna may be swayed too much by his sympathy for Western "analytical" philosophy with its narrow focus on rational cognition (and its neglect of theory-praxis re-lations).[8] Curiously, I tend to embrace his objection—but for differ-ent, even opposite reasons. All genuine philosophy (and not just its Indian variant) is on some level concerned with *moksha*—a fact that renders the latter again an element not of distinctness but of nondis-tinction unhelpful to comparative inquiry.

II

The preceding discussion has pinpointed shortcomings in a number of comparative approaches, shortcomings that may end up in caricature or cultural stereotypes. The point of the criticism has not been that there are no kernels of truth in these approaches, but that these kernels have not been properly located or assessed. The main criticism of the discussed formulas, however, had to do with their suitability for comparative inquiry. As indicated before, such inquiry has to steer between the twin dangers of exclusivist distinctness and nondistinction, of radical difference and sameness. While nondistinction frustrates the possibility of contestation, exclusivism foils mutuality or reciprocal engagement. In order to make headway in this domain, we do well to heed Aristotle's reminder that comparison requires a faculty of imagination transcending factual observation. Differently phrased: comparison involves the interpretive creation of a new framework or frame of reference which transgresses the explicit self-understanding of each of the respective terms or configurations, thereby yielding insight into their (not immediately evident) correlation. In contemporary terminology one might say that comparative inquiry explores the explicit self-understanding of a given perspective in the direction of its nonthematized underpinnings or its covert "otherness" (which is not simply its negation). Comparative inquiry is most fruitful—and contestation most intimate—where the otherness of the compared perspectives is reciprocal, that is, where each perspective is seen as the "other" side of the other.[9]

For present purposes, the comparative framework I want to suggest (in a very tentative fashion) relies basically on the distinction between "text" and "context" or between rational "discourse" and "life world." As is well-known, the notion of the life world derives from Continental phenomenology where it was delineated as the backdrop to rational-intentional analysis. Building on phenomenological insights, the distinction between discourse and life world has been articulated (though with different accents) by Jürgen Habermas in several of his writings. Regarding the distinction between text and context or between "context-free" and "context-sensitive" rules I follow basically the lead of A. K. Ramanujan, the Indian poet and philosopher, who introduced this framework in his stimulating essay "Is There an Indian Way of Thinking?"[10] It must be noted, however, that the correlation of text and context or discourse and life world is not the distinction between environment and thought or between "infrastructure" and "superstructure" (to use Marxian terminology). Context and contextual life world are not seen here as underlying structures which causally determine particular modes of rational discourse or textual argumentation. Differently put: context and text stand not in the external relation of explanation and prediction, but in the relation of reciprocal otherness and mutual entwinement.

As a trained linguist, Ramanujan in his essay distinguishes between two kinds of grammatical rules, namely, rules that are context-free or universally applicable and those that are context-sensitive or contextually guided in their application. Proceeding boldly from grammar to culture, Ramanujan finds an analogous distinction on the plane of cross-cultural comparison. "I think cultures (may be said to) have overall tendencies," he writes, "tendencies to *idealize,* and think in terms of, either the context-free or the context-sensitive kind of rules. . . . In cultures like India's, the context-sensitive kind of rule is the preferred formulation." Seeking to shore up this view, the essay gives examples from Manu's legislation where rules are typically made contingent on caste and status: some rules apply only to brahmans and not to others, and even among brahmans the scope of rules depends on time and circumstance. Skipping a few centuries, the essay also refers to the great Indian epics—*Ramayana* and *Mahabharata*—where each individual story or narrative is embedded in a larger metanarrative, which contextualizes and gives meaning to each tale. Thus, the point of the Nala story in the *Mahabharata* is illuminated and made intelligible by its insertion in another tale where the hero likewise is initially humiliated and persecuted and only finds vindication after painful trials.[11]

In illustrating the meaning of context sensitivity, Ramanujan does not limit himself to India's classical period. Moving freely across disciplinary boundaries, his essay offers in fact a splendid display of (what David Tracy has called) "analogical imagination." Invoking the canons of literary theory, Ramanujan uses the vocabulary of tropes to illustrate his point: he speaks of the prevalence of metonymy (part for whole) in Indian thought and literature. For example, the term *man* does not designate there a being which stands apart from nature, but one which "stands in" for nature. Seen as "man in nature" or "man in context," he notes, the human being is "continuous with the context s/he is in." The same point can be made with the help of Peircean semiotics. In semiotic terms, Indian thought, according to the essay, accords primacy to indexical signs over symbolic devices, with indexes taken to be signs where signifiers and signified "belong in the same context," that is, where the signifier is not externally related to the signified but is itself the carrier of signification. (Thus, a figure of Shiva or Ganesh does not so much symbolize something else, but rather "indicates" its own meaning.) Turning to the fields of logic and sociology, Ramanujan explicates context sensitivity by pointing to the pervasive Hindu concern with *jati*, that is, with "the logic of classes, of genera and species, of which human *jatis* are only an instance." Each *jati* or class, he writes, "defines a context, a structure of relevance, a rule of permissible combinations, a frame of reference." More specifically, on the social or sociological level, context sensitivity also surfaces in family and interpersonal relations where Indians are said to develop a "self-we regard" (opposed to egocentrism) and a kind of "radar conscience" which "orients them to others, makes them say things that are appropriate to person and context."[12]

Ramanujan's arguments are impressive for their perceptiveness and sheer imaginative brilliance; they certainly deserve close attention among those concerned with comparative inquiry. The essay is made even more remarkable by its willingness to step into the debate over modernity and modernization (or Westernization), that is, to enter the arena of comparative development theory. In contrast to the context sensitivity of Indian culture, Ramanujan presents Western thought as oriented basically toward a "context-free" or decontextualized model. "Egalitarian democratic ideals, Protestant Christianity," the essay states somewhat pointedly,

> espouse both the universal and the unique, insist that any member is *equal* to and *like* any other in the group. Whatever, his context—birth, class, gender, age, place, rank, etc.—a man is a "man" for all that. Technology with its modules and interchangeable parts, and the post-Renaissance sciences with their quest for universal laws (and "facts") across contexts intensify the bias toward the context-free.

From this assessment of Western thought and culture, the essay derives some implications for the process of modernization and social development, implications that are captivating in their acumen and logical elegance: "One might see 'modernization' in India as a movement from the context-sensitive to the context-free in all realms: an erosion of contexts, at least in principle. Gandhi's watch (with its uniform autonomous time, governing his punctuality) replaced the almanac."[13]

III

Reflecting on his essay, I am attracted to Ramanujan's general line of argument. In large measure, the distinction between context freedom and context sensitivity can be translated into the opposition between rational discourse and life world, with the former marked by its attachment to universal validity claims (characteristic of modern Western thought) and the latter denoting the experiential underside of reason. Seen from this vantage, the process of modernization can be grasped as involving the progressive erosion of the life world in favor of rational discourses, of amorphous experience in favor of rationally transparent "systems" (of thought and action). Although I appreciate on the whole Ramanujan's perceptive insights, I cannot refrain now from voicing some reservations, thus proceeding from exposition to a more critical interpretation.

One reservation or qualm has to do with certain political or social-political accents manifest in the essay. In many of its passages (though not uniformly), the essay tends to treat the context freedom of Western thought mainly in pejorative or derogatory terms. In the process of modernization, the move toward the context free is portrayed chiefly in its negative effects, its erosive impact of traditional contexts. To the extent that this is the case, Ramanujan does not seem to appreciate fully the relation between context freedom and social-political freedom or emancipation. Sensitivity to context, in his treatment, is sometimes in danger of lapsing into a nostalgic traditionalism. "The Indian Constitution," he writes at one point, "made the contexts of birth, region, sex and creed irrelevant, overthrowing Manu." This may be seen as a prominent instance of contextual erosion or disintegration. But this fact is unlikely to be bemoaned by people who have been traditionally discriminated against on the basis of "birth, region, sex and creed"; for them, the Indian Constitution may offer a haven of freedom (perhaps also a new context of everyday life).[14]

Next to these more political qualms, there are some philosophical reservations or misgivings, which may be more weighty in the present context. As a linguist and poet, Ramanujan takes his supporting arguments chiefly from literature and semiotics, but is not always sufficiently attentive to philosophical issues (as would seem to be required in a discussion of the "Indian way of thinking"). His essay interprets some basic features of Indian thought or philosophy in a manner that seems dubious and misleading, namely, as reflecting a desire for context freedom. "In 'traditional' cultures like India," he notes, "where context-sensitivity rules and binds, the dream is to be free of context. So *rasa* in aesthetics, *moksha* in the 'aims of life,' *sannyasa* in the life-stages, . . . and *bhakti* in religion define themselves against a background of inexorable contextuality." In Ramanujan's presentation, *moksha* means a "release from all relations"; *sannyasa* (or renunciation) in his view "cremates all one's past and present relations," while *rasa* denotes a "generalized essence" and *bhakti* "denies the very need for context."[15]

Here Ramanujan's otherwise so perceptive account seems to go astray. One reason for my critical reaction derives from the structure of Ramanujan's own argument. If Western modernity is characterized by context freedom and if modernization involves an erosion of context or steady decontextualization, then traditional Indian thought cannot in the same breath or in the same sense be described as aspiring to a context-free model. If the latter description were granted, then traditional Indian thought would have to be seen as an instance of Western modernity or as an anticipation of the goals of modernization. This cannot possibly be the point of Ramanujan's essay. Apart from concerns about consistency, critical qualms also proceed from substantive considerations. As one can plausibly argue, the invoked features of Indian thought and culture are not at all geared toward context freedom, but rather toward re-contextualization, that is, toward a contextual relationship on a new and deeper level. Without pretending to a full elaboration, the following comments may for present purposes suffice.

As indicated, Ramanujan presents *moksha* as involving a "release from all relations." In my opposing interpretation, the term denotes not so much a rupturing of relationships as the discovery of a more genuine relation and attunement to the basic fabric of things (to *brahman* or the order of the universe). Seen as a move toward context freedom or decontextualization, one may ask, what exactly is it that would be freed or liberated in *moksha,* an isolated, nonrelational self or ego? But this is precisely what is left behind in *moksha.* Similar considerations apply to the other terms or features. Thus, *sannyasa* does indeed imply a loosening of the immediate bonds of family life and the household, yet not in favor of a self-contained egotism, but for the sake of gaining a deeper bond with *dharma* and the web of being. And what is *bhakti* if not the search for a complete union with the divine, involving an intense devotion and surrender to a higher power? *Rasa* in aesthetics, finally, is far removed in my view from denoting a decontextualized essence and more akin to a heightened appreciation of the beautiful and the sublime.[16]

Moving beyond the features cited in Ramanujan's essay, one might illustrate the aspect of recontextualization or deepened context-sensitivity by pointing to some other key ingredients of classical Indian philosophy like the notions of *dharma, brahman, atman,* and *sunyata.* Again, by context I do not mean here a contingent environment externally related to a given text or discourse. Instead, the term refers to the "other" side of discourse, to an implicit background of thought and action that can never be fully foregrounded or be transformed into a target of conceptual representation, but that for that reason is not simply an absence or a lack. The notion of *dharma* is a case in point. *Dharma*—one might say—is not a universal principle, a categorical imperative amenable to abstract-conceptual formulation; instead, what the term suggests is more like an elusive path or way of life (similar to the Chinese *tao)*, which distinctly structures human life but cannot definitively be charted in advance. In a similar vein, *brahman* is not simply a universal category or a foundational essence akin to Platonic ideas; instead, *brahman* remains forever a background and horizon of all determinate, discursively articulated categories and arguments. For the same reason, *brahman* cannot be reduced to a logical concept (in the sense of Descartes's "clear and distinct" ideas) nor to a unified holistic structure in which all parts would be neatly subsumed or summed up—all of which does not render the notion nugatory or a synonym for empty negativity. In turn, *atman* should not be seen as an individualized self or an ego cut loose from all relationships. If the saying *tat tvam asi* is correct, and if it is true that ultimately *atman* is *brahman*, then the boundary between self and nonself, between the individual soul and the context of being cannot be neatly or definitively drawn.[17]

Venturing into more hazardous terrain, similar claims could be made even for the Buddhist notion of *sunya* or *sunyata*. On my reading, the term should not be construed as counseling context freedom or a strategy of decontextualization. At least in the formulation of Nagarjuna and the Madhyamika school, *sunya* is basically just a manner of approaching *brahman* through *via negativa*, by saying "not this, not that" *(neti neti)*. In this sense, *sunya* is not simply nothing or an empty void, but a way of talking about ontological being or reality *(prajña-paramita)*, where being always remains behind our backs *(vis a tergo)*, a background which can never be fully conceptualized or rendered present to mind. This aspect is also reflected in the theory of the non-dual character of *sunya* and *prajña-paramita*, the notion that being cannot be split into "subject" and "object" poles. According to the Yogachara school, it is necessary to overcome the illusions of "subject" *(pudgala-nairatmya)* and of "object" *(dharma-nairatmya)*; the first illusion leads to *kleshavarana*, the second to *jñanavarana*, which are both forms of *avidya* or ignorance. One should also note the Mahayana thesis of the "dependent origination" of all things; in postulating a general relationism, this thesis clearly militates against the notion of a causal determination of some objects by others as well as of parts by whole (or of appearances by an objective-essential reality).[18]

What all the discussed elements or features illustrate is a pervasive mode of context sensitivity—the latter taken not in the sense of contextual conformism but of a liberating type of recontextualization. Seen

against this background, Western thought—here I agree with Ramanujan—can indeed be described as marked by a *tendency* toward
context freedom or *de*contextualization, that is, by an effort to render
all background into a conceptually accessible presence or foreground
(or life world into discourse). To be sure, exceptions to this tendency
and even counter-trends are not lacking in the history of Western
thought. Yet, what today is witnessed as the relentless "Westernization" of the globe would not have been possible without the strategy
of an emphatic bracketing of geographically confined cultural contexts. While the process of Westernization is today "undergone" by
most non-Western societies in painful and agonizing ways, Western
culture is not exposed to a reverse movement of similar magnitude
and vehemence.[19] For this reason—despite the presence of counter-
examples—Ramanujan's overall schema appears to be both plausible and fruitful for comparative inquiry seen as an imaginative and
heuristic enterprise.

To be sure, Western culture (like that of other societies) is not an
invariant, transtemporal essence, but the product of a protracted historical development. Ramanujan's account is somewhat brief on this
point, but could readily be fleshed out under the rubric of a history
of Western metaphysics. The movement toward context freedom was
not yet noticeable among the pre-Socratics (which may be a reason
for Heidegger's preoccupation with their thought). Decontextualization began to emerge slowly in classical Greek thought, as can be
seen in Plato's equation of being with logos and in Aristotle's formulation of a propositional logic. Incipiently or in their implications,
these initiatives heralded an epistemic turn predicated on a subject-
object bifurcation, although both Plato and Aristotle still remained
imbued with pre-Socratic leanings (hence Plato's alleged penchant
for mysticism). Subsequent developments yielded a progressive subjectivization of philosophical premises. With the Stoics the subject of
cognition was internalized; with Christianity it was spiritualized; with
Renaissance and Enlightenment thought it was radically individualized (centered in an ego) and rationalized (linked with the ability of
a calculating or instrumental rationality). German idealism—especially as formulated by Hegel—elevated spiritual subjectivity into a
universal goal or *telos* for all humankind. In his studies of the history
of philosophy and religion, Hegel rejected as underdeveloped or primitive (or "Indian") the notion of a 'preconceptual being' or a background which cannot be rendered accessible and transparent to reason or rational subjectivity.[20]

As it happens, the long trajectory of Western thought toward context freedom has been profoundly challenged (though not reversed) in

our century from *within* Western thought itself. Wittgenstein's turn to language contextualized human reason and the subject of cognition by making them a function of grammar or a prevailing "language game." With still greater force, a similar turn was performed by the strand of Continental thought known as the "phenomenological movement," a strand that reaches from Husserl over Heidegger to Merleau-Ponty and Derrida. While Husserl initially introduced the notion of the life world, Heidegger launched a basic assault on the primacy of the subject (or epistemic consciousness) by presenting human existence as a "being-in-the-world," that is, a creature inextricably and irremediably contextualized in the fabric of being and of language. Under the label of *monde vécu,* the life-world focus became a staple in French phenomenological thought, especially in the work of Merleau-Ponty who proceeded to submerge intentional subjectivity increasingly in the density (or "flesh") of contextual relationships. Derrida, finally, is well known for his "decentering" of the subject and his "deconstruction" of all univocal textual meanings in favor of a basic cross-textuality where meaning is indefinitely deferred by the multiplicity of possible interpretations and the inexhaustible otherness of language itself.[21]

To close with a personal statement: my own intellectual background is that of Continental phenomenology, and it is this background which has opened the way for me to India and cross-cultural inquiry. I believe—or perhaps it is more a fond hope—that we are approaching a propitious moment in the history of philosophy (what in German is called a *"Sternstunde")* where Western and Eastern thought for the first time can become partners in a genuine global dialogue, which often is liable to have the character of intense mutual contestation. This dialogue implies a learning process where each partner exposes itself to alienating otherness and thereby gains its own bearings, obviating the lure of an intellectual melting pot. Learning from otherness does not (and should not) entail effacement of cultural distinctness. On the side of Western thought, I do not believe that its decontextualizing thrust can simply be reversed (which would be a naive construal of the "end" of Western metaphysics). Neither the movement of Western science nor that of individual human emancipation can simply be canceled or suspended. But there may be room for a sustained reciprocal questioning of premises and objectives leading both to deepened self-understanding and to a more ready acceptance of cultural diversity. In terms suggested by Ramanujan's essay, this interchange may also involve a process of recontextualization both of Western and of non-Western cultures, namely, in the context of an emerging global democracy.

MODERNIZATION AND POSTMODERNIZATION

Whither India?

We hear much talk these days about the emergence of a new world order, an order presumably ushering in an era of global peace and prosperity, replacing the earlier arms race among superpowers and the nuclear balance of terror. Seen as an antidote to global anarchy, this vision of order surely has an appealing ring: feuds among states are to give way to a unified structure of humankind, narrow national self-interest to shared concern for our "global village."[1] Unfortunately, on closer inspection, the brightness of the vision quickly begins to dim, especially when attention is drawn to the motivating forces behind global unity. In large measure, global unification seems to be propelled by the dictates of the global market or world economy, a market that, in turn, is governed by the interests of leading industrial or postindustrial nations. On a more general (and more theoretical) plane, one may ask in which language or idiom the global vision tends to be articulated. Unsurprisingly, this language is typically of Western origin, reflecting specifically the aspirations of Western modernity with its bent toward rational universalism.[2] From its inception, modern Western thought carried a teleological imprint marked by a dialectical twist: the opposition between advancement and regression, between development and non- or underdevelopment. Confronted with the Western model, non-Western countries or cultures were expected to catch up sooner or later with the postulated *telos,* or else to suffer defeat and obsolescence.

The present chapter shall explore the issue of development and modernization in a particular context, though broader comparative conclusions can readily be drawn from the inquiry. The focus shall be on India as one of the most prominent "developing" countries today. The choice of focus is prompted by several considerations. There is, first of all, an autobiographical motive having to do with this author's repeated visits to India during the past decade. A more important impulse is the political weight of India as the most populous functioning democracy in the present world. Finally, there is a cultural consideration:

claims to superiority on the part of Western modernity appear in a particularly wistful light when viewed against the backdrop of one of the oldest living civilizations (whose culture has radiated powerfully throughout much of Asia and the Orient).

The accent in the following will not be placed on the analysis of empirical indices of development, but on the theoretical understanding of the meaning of development and modernization as such. The discussion will concentrate primarily (though not exclusively) on theoretical formulations or conceptions that have gained prominence and perhaps notoriety during the last half century. The first section of the chapter will review once again the developmental model articulated by modernization theorists during the period after World War II. As will be shown, this model gave rise to numerous challenges and rejoinders, which, however, often bypassed one of its central features: its narrowly empiricist or positivist outlook. It was chiefly this feature that became the target of a new wave of postempiricist theorizing which under the banners of phenomenology, hermeneutics, and critical theory raised the developmental debate to a quasitranscendental level. Curiously and perhaps unexpectedly, this move further fueled and intensified existing controversies by lending them philosophical depth: closely linked with a turn to language, postempiricism called into question crucial premises of Western modernity, thus triggering a confrontation between "modernity" and "postmodernity" projected onto a global scale. Throughout this chapter room is given wherever possible to arguments of Indian philosophers and social theorists, to counteract the conceit of a Western monopoly of the development debate. This attention to Indian thinkers forms the heart of the concluding section which adumbrates a loosely postmodern view of modernization (or a vantage of "postmodernization").

The Development Syndrome

In the decade after World War II, a major effort was launched by the Social Science Research Council to formulate a broadly comparative and global model of social analysis concentrated on the parameters of economic, social-political, and cultural development. In many respects, this model today is only of historical interest; yet, in the eyes of many observers, recent dramatic events in eastern Europe and the former Soviet Union seem to lend it renewed saliency. At the time of its initial formulation, the model was spawned not solely by academic concerns, although the influence of the positivist "unified science" movement can hardly be discounted. Undergirding and buttressing academic initiatives were the political constellations of the postwar period. In the words of eminent Indian philosopher Daya Krishna:

> The imperial responsibilities of the United States after the Second World War, coupled with its competitive role on a global scale against a country with a different political system, led American political scientists almost inevitably to view their field in a comparative perspective. And once things begin to be viewed in that way, specially from the vantage point of a superpower with global responsibilities for client and protégé states, the distinction between the "developed" *we* and the "underdeveloped" *they* gets built into the way issues are seen, questions are asked, and theories formulated.[3]

With greater attention to economic motives, this assessment is seconded by the Indian political theorist Thomas Pantham who notes that, during the immediate postwar era,

> it was widely recognized that the economic development of the less developed countries (LDCs) and their participation in international free trade would facilitate the rebuilding of the war-shattered economics of the industrial nations. Such economic development of the LDCs, it was further realized, depended on their social, cultural and political modernization; the LDCs, in other words, were required to follow the footsteps of the advanced industrial nations.[4]

The central features of the modernization model have frequently been recapitulated; I restrict myself here to a brief sketch. In large measure, the model was heir to theories of social evolution formulated by prominent sociological thinkers during the preceding century. Following in the footsteps of neo-Darwinian concepts of natural selection, human societies were seen as quasi-organic structures seeking to increase their survival chances through the enhancement of internal complexity and external-environmental adaptability. Taking a leaf both from Spencer and from Durkheim, modernization theorists viewed social evolution as a process of differentiation evident in the division of labor and growing "subsystem" autonomy, a differentiation requiring ever renewed efforts of system integration to insure effective environmental control. On the cultural level, Comte and strands in Marxism furnished the formula of a steady "demythologization" of world views, that is, of the progressive rationalization and secularization of society and thus of the ascendancy of science and technology over traditional beliefs.

In the years immediately following World War II, the diverse ingredients of evolutionary thought were pulled together and systematically elaborated by a leading American sociologist or social theorist:
Talcott Parsons. Blending evolutionary principles with Weberian notions of social action, Parsons presented society as a holistic though
differentiated structure whose diverse elements or "subsystems" were
designed to perform distinct functions for system maintenance, thus
securing societal survival. In the field of social evolution, his work portrayed society as moving along a trajectory of "evolutionary universals," that is, along a path leading from the ideal-typical patterns of
early or primitive society to patterns characteristic of modernity. Foremost among these typical processes were: the abandonment of social
"diffuseness" in favor of the increasing differentiation and specializa-
tion of structures and functions; the change from ascriptive assign-
ments of status to individual-personal achievement; the movement
from "affectivity" to affective neutrality (that is, from mythic-religious
engagement to secularism and science); and finally, the advancement
from particularism to universalism (or from local-parochial bonds of
kinship to general or global rule systems).[5]

Although formulated on a high level of abstraction, Parsonian systems theory exerted a profound influence on social and political scientists at the time. Most of the comparative political scientists heeding the call of the Social Science Research Council (SSRC) were in
some form adepts of "structural functionalism," although the latter was
suitably modified to meet specialized research needs. As articulated
in successive SSRC volumes, social change around the globe followed
basically the trajectory of Parsons's evolutionary universals, that is,
the path leading from primitive kinship groups to modern, Western-
style complexity. To be sure, members of the comparative research
team differed in their precise use of vocabulary. Sometimes the terms
evolution, development, and *modernization* were used interchange-
ably as designations of the Parsonian movement; sometimes the terms
were differentiated, often along the lines that 'evolution' referred to
material-biological underpinnings, 'development' to economic and
political stages of growth, and 'modernization' to changes in socio-
cultural beliefs. Typically, however, the various levels were treated as
complementary, with material and economic advances seen as the
primary requisites for political, social, and cultural innovation.

A good example of a differentiated vocabulary linked with an overarching developmental formula is Lucian Pye's *Aspects of Political
Development,* a study that in many ways summarized the outlook of
comparative research sponsored by SSRC. According to Pye, political
progress had to be viewed as "one aspect of a multi-dimensional process

of social change" and as "intimately associated with other aspects of social and economic change," all of which could be termed "development syndrome." Modernization, in this context, referred to a profound transformation of traditional ways of life, namely, to the process "in which tradition-bound villages or tribal-based societies are compelled to react to the pressures and demands of the modern, industrialized and urban-centered world." Pye added, quite candidly,

> This process might also be called Westernization, or simply advancement and progress; it might, however, be more accurately termed the diffusion of a world culture—a world culture based on advanced technology and the spirit of science, on a rational view of life, a secular approach to social relations. . . . At an ever-accelerating rate, the direction and the volume of cross-cultural influences has become nearly a uniform pattern of the Western industrial world imposing its practices, standards, techniques, and values upon the non-Western world.[6]

Regarding the historical trajectory of political development, SSRC-related studies were united in the assumption of a movement from primitive diffuseness to modern complexity. Instructive in this respect is Gabriel Almond and Bingham Powell's study *Comparative Politics: A Developmental Approach,* which encapsulated in concise fashion the basic political components of the modernization model. Adopting a streamlined version of Parsonian functionalism, the study portrayed political development as occurring along two main tracks or dimensions: a structural-systemic and a normative-cultural track. Viewed from the systemic angle, development pointed in the direction of a growing differentiation of subsystems and their concomitant re-integration for purposes of system maintenance and adaptation; however, on the normative-cultural level, social change involved progressive cultural secularization and the adoption of anonymous-universal rule systems. Properly joined together, the two perspectives supported the distinction of at least three main stages of political evolution: "primitive," "traditional," and "modern" systems, with the latter type further subdivided into liberal-democratic and authoritarian or totalitarian variants.

In the presentation of Almond and Powell, primitive systems were characterized by the submergence of politics in kinship relations or by the presence of at best "intermittent political structures" displaying a "minimum of structural differentiation" and sustained by a "diffuse, parochial culture." Structural differentiation was further advanced in traditional societies which witnessed the emergence of specialized governmental or "output" structures to which members of society were uniformly subjected (giving rise to what the authors called a "subject culture"). Modern systems finally were distinguished by the full panoply of differentiated subsystems, including both output and political "input" or "infrastructures" (comprising interest groups, parties, and communication media), a process undergirded by the flourishing of "participant" modes of political culture. Echoing themes struck both by Parsons and by Pye, the study extolled the universalizing thrust of political modernization and Westernization. "It is through the secularization of political culture," we read, "that these rigid, ascribed, and diffuse customs of social interaction [i.e., of parochial culture] come to be overridden by a set of codified, specifically political, and universalistic rules. By the same token, it is in the secularization process that bargaining and accommodative political action become a common feature of the society, and that the development of special structures such as interest groups and parties becomes meaningful."[7]

The implicit optimism permeating the early modernization model sponsored by SSRC was not borne out by real-life experiences in developing or third world countries. Barely two decades after the war, it became increasingly evident that political development around the globe did not follow the smooth path of a simple Westernization or a "diffusion" of (Western) world culture. The political regimes of developing countries were increasingly rent by turmoil and profound tensions, especially the tension between the "revolution of rising expectations" and the inability of modernizing elites to meet them. Under the impact of these experiences, the assumption of steady progress and cultural dissemination gave way to a harsher emphasis on regime stability, output capabilities, and crisis management. In the words of Thomas Pantham:

> The actual trend of socio-economic and political changes in the "new states" did not bear out the optimistic, evolutionary assumptions of diffusionist modernization. Economic development lagged behind peoples' expectations and there was no mistaking of the signs of the limits of growth. . . . [The] "dislocations" of social mobilization and the explosion of political participation were seen as dangerous "crises," the containment of which became the preoccupation of the revisionist school of political developmentalists.[8]

Among the chief spokesmen of the revisionist outlook were Samuel Huntington, Ithiel de Sola Pool, and (to some extent) David Apter. According to Huntington, the primary need in postcolonial, developing societies was "the accumulation and concentration of power, not its dispersion—and it is in Moscow and Peking, and not in Washington, that this lesson is to be learned." This view was seconded by Pool when he noted that, in developing countries, order and stability depend "on somehow compelling newly mobilized strata to return to a measure of passivity and defeatism from which they have recently been aroused by the process of modernization." Pushing this point a bit further, Apter questioned the feasibility of cultural diffusion and the application of Western standards to the non-West. Although the departure from diffusionism has sometimes been described as a radical change or "normative reversal," revisionist arguments can still be reconciled without difficulty with the prevailing functionalist or systems paradigm: without abandoning functional-empirical premises, revisionists shifted the accent from systemic processes to output performance and from feedback mechanisms to efficient policy making (where efficiency was measured by utility calculations).[9]

Given its global or universalist ambitions, the sketched modernization model—both in its diffusionist and in its revisionist variants—was also applied to the Indian subcontinent by Western social scientists, most prominently by Myron Weiner. While initially highlighting a gradual-cumulative process of "nation-building," Weiner detected in postindependence India tendencies of fragmentation which required a shift to political integration and output efficiency. There is also evidence that aspects of the model were attractive to segments of the modernizing elite in India wedded to the rapid diffusion of Western ways of life—foremost among them the first prime minister of the newly emerging country, Jawaharlal Nehru.[10] On the whole, however, the modernization model quickly encountered a barrage of criticisms articulated by intellectuals in developing countries (supported by some Western scholars). Critical attacks concentrated chiefly on two main defects of the model: first, its built-in asymmetry and political-economic inequity; and second, flaws pertaining to internal-theoretical consistency or coherence.

The first attack was at the heart of so-called *dependency* theory which charged Western modernizers with obfuscating the gulf separating development and underdevelopment, a gulf deriving from the structural dependency of "peripheral" countries on Western "center" nations in control of the world market. By restricting developing countries to the production and export of primary goods and materials, Western industrial nations slanted the world market of the rich against the poor, in favor of advanced capital-intensive economies against labor-intensive economies in the third world. As formulated chiefly by Latin American intellectuals, dependency theory carried strong Marxist-Leninist overtones, a feature which, apart from properly accentuating power differentials, also engendered intrinsic problems or drawbacks. Chief among these drawbacks was the curious "dependency" of the theory on the modernization model it opposed: together with that model, the theory often presented development as an empirical-predictable sequence of stages predicated on economic requisites (modes of production), although this sequence was now seen not as a smooth transition but as punctuated by revolution or a global class struggle.[11]

Despite its Latin American moorings, arguments akin to *dependencia* were also sometimes advanced by Indian intellectuals, though typically with some priority given to equity considerations over economic determinism. Exemplary in this category were early writings by Rajni Kothari who advocated an alternative to the "West-dominated world system" which would more equitably balance relations between center and periphery.[12] Regarding internal consistency or coherence, the modernization model was subjected to searching scrutiny by numerous critics, including Daya Krishna who launched a radical philosophical assault. Broadly sympathetic to the analytical school of thought, Daya Krishna found the propositions of the model both empirically unfounded and logically untenable. One defect of the model apparent at a first glance was its haphazard and confusing use of terminology. Terms such as *modernization* and *social development* were often used indiscriminately, although both were "neither clearly defined nor demarcated from what is usually regarded as economic or political development"; hence it was never quite clear whether the two terms carried the same meaning and how they are related to political and economic processes of change. Turning to the so-called requisites of political development sometimes stipulated by defenders of the model, Daya Krishna examined a number of such preconditions—including participation, conversion functions (that is, interest articulation, interest aggregation, and the like), and output capabilities—and judged all these criteria to be marred by logical incongruity and lack of empirical warrant. Taking up a question raised by Charles Tilly (in one of the SSRC studies) as to whether the difficulties of the model were ultimately surmountable, Daya Krishna answered (with Tilly):

> "For my part, I do not think the difficulties are surmountable." But if the difficulties are not surmountable, it can only be so because in principle it is impossible to do so. But if it is impossible in principle, then the whole enterprise is doomed to failure from the start, and it is no wonder that we have not been able to find any sure footing amongst any of the criteria that have been offered by many thinkers.[13]

In probing the concept of development itself, Daya Krishna perceived serious barriers obstructing its application to human and political life and also to the humanities and social sciences. The barriers were clearly evident in the field of art. For how could one meaningfully compare the artworks of modernity with those of Greek antiquity and (even more so) with the masterpieces of India and China? More specifically: "How shall we determine which is greater or more developed, and in terms of what?" The same barriers were noticeable in the fields of religion and philosophy; for in neither case was it possible to speak properly of "cumulative growth or development." If anywhere, the notion of cumulative growth was germane only to the natural sciences as they have developed in the modern era (and there only on the level of cognitive analysis, not the level of the examined objects). Growth patterns pertaining to the natural sciences, however, could not be transferred—even by analogy—to the field of the human sciences (the latter term comprising the spectrum from history to politics). Quoting a phrase from Robert Nisbet's reflections on history and historical knowledge, Daya Krishna noted that "there is no historical evidence that macro-changes in time are the cumulative result of small-scale, linear micro-changes." A similar absence of a linear or cumulative process characterized the arena of political life, the field specifically chosen as target by modernization theory. According to Daya Krishna, politics not only was recalcitrant to the stipulated developmental syndrome, but it also was actually governed by criteria which were foreign to mainstream modernization literature:

> The crucial question which therefore remains to be answered is whether the realm dealt with by the science of politics is of such a nature as to permit the application of the concept of "development" to itself. And our answer to this question is in the negative, for the simple reason that the only relevant distinction here is between "good government" and "bad government," and not between a "developed polity" and an "undeveloped polity," as many contemporary political scientists seem to think. . . . Perhaps the "body politic" is really like "the body" which has a thousand ways of being ill, but only one way of being healthy.[14]

Modernity and Emancipation

Although perhaps overstated, Daya Krishna's critique pointed up serious shortcomings in the dominant modernization model, especially the weakness of its philosophical premises. Empirical or positivist in orientation and inspired by evolutionary paradigms of the last century, the model was theoretically vulnerable and unable to withstand rigorous philosophical scrutiny. As it happens, at the time of the sketched debate, positivist empiricism was under siege from a number of quarters, a siege that highlighted both its internal inadequacies (illustrated by the problem of paradigm shifts) and its general inability to account for its own premises (which could not themselves be empirically derived). In the field of human and social sciences, this siege manifested itself in the ascendancy of various postempiricist or "postbehavioral" modes of theorizing, which owed their allegiance chiefly to the philosophical perspectives of phenomenology, hermeneutics, and critical theory. In critiquing positivism, these perspectives jointly (though in different ways) drew attention to the implicit underpinnings of human knowledge and action, thus shifting the level of analysis from contingent occurrences to the transcendental or quasitranscendental "conditions of possibility" (to use a Kantian phrase).

With respect to historical development, this shift dramatically raised the stakes of ongoing discussions, namely, by making modern science or knowledge itself a target of inquiry in need of philosophical grounding; while previously modernity had functioned simply as unquestioned yardstick for developing societies, this yardstick now became itself a focus of critical attention. In seeking to ground this yardstick, most spokesmen of postbehavioral perspectives were drawn to the trajectory of the Enlightenment legacy, that is, to the notion of a progressive 'awakening' of humankind from immaturity and from the constraints imposed by intellectual and political tutelage. In line with this legacy, the accent was placed not on contingent-empirical variables but on the movement of human emancipation or the growth of autonomy and self-determination, which politically translates into a process of liberalization or liberal democratization.[15]

In a trenchant manner, arguments of postbehavioral spokesmen were prefigured in a text written by the founder of contemporary phenomenology, Edmund Husserl, half a century ago. In his *Crisis of European Sciences and Transcendental Phenomenology,* Husserl attacked modern empirical science for forgetting its transcendental underpinnings in human intentionality, an intentionality that ultimately had its moorings in the experiential matrix of the life world. While critically challenging modern science, the text did not dismiss modernity itself but rather salvaged it on a deeper level, namely, as a stage in the progressive unfolding of rational reflection and moral autonomy. For Husserl, rational reflection had its beginnings in classical Greek philosophy, a moment in history when humankind first stirred from its dogmatic or mythological slumber. According to the text, Greek philosophy signaled the "breakthrough and developmental beginning of a new human epoch, seen from the standpoint of universal human-ity," namely, the epoch of a humankind that "seeks to live, and is only able to live, by freely determining its existence and its historical life on the basis of rational insight in the pursuit of infinite tasks" and by seeking a "deeper and comprehensive grasp of the world unfettered by myth and the whole tradition."

In Husserl's presentation, this breakthrough characterized Western civilization—it was the *"telos* inborn in European culture"—but ulti-mately it implied a universal calling, by revealing an "essential di-mension of humanity as such, its *entelechy."* Although an inborn *telos,* rational reflection was not an instant achievement but required a long process of historical maturation. With the advent of the Cartesian *cog-ito* and Kant's critical philosophy, classical and medieval ontology could not longer be maintained in its taken-for-granted form; likewise, with the onset of phenomenology, Enlightenment views of reason had to undergo further refinement. Geographically, rational analysis was at first the trademark of European or Western culture; but its critical momentum was bound to radiate from the center to non-Western cul-tures through a steady contagion. As Husserl noted (in a somewhat harsh passage), the rational bent of Europe or the West "is recognized in us by all other human groups too"; it is this bent that, "quite irre-spective of considerations of utility and despite their unbroken com-mitment to cultural self-preservation, becomes for them a motivation steadily to Europeanize themselves, whereas we (if we understand our-selves properly) would never Indianize ourselves, for example."[16]

Despite a deepened attention to the life world, phenomenology as a variant of later postbehavioralism never quite abandoned Husserl's transcendental élan; devoted to the analysis of "essential" meaning structures in social and political life, phenomenological social sci-ence was bound to present itself as an inquiry geared to the pursuit of "infinite tasks." To this extent, Schutzian phenomenology shared some common ground with the program of "critical theory" as ar-ticulated by the Frankfurt School (despite the latter's relative distance from Husserl's legacy). This commonality is particularly evident in the case of Jürgen Habermas whose writings pushed the critical the-ory program deliberately into both a quasi-transcendental and a his-torical-evolutionary direction. Quasi-transcendental leanings sur-faced early on in Habermas's work and became a mainstay of his conception of communicative reason. In a manner hearkening back to Husserl's *Crisis* volume, Habermas's *Knowledge and Human In-terests* chastised positivism for its neglect of cognitive underpinnings in the matrix of human intentionality, a matrix that now was rede-fined in terms of three knowledge-guiding "interests" (undergirding

respectively the endeavors of science, hermeneutics, and emancipatory critique).

Reformulated in a steadily refined and universalist idiom, the same
quasi-transcendental leanings serve as a pillar of Habermas's subsequent writings on language and communication. In the field of language theory, these writings extended Chomsky's notion of a deep-
seated 'linguistic competence' into the domain of speech performance
and communicative interaction—a move undergirding the framework
of a quasi-transcendental or "universal pragmatics." In terms of this
framework, every native speaker must be intuitively endowed with a
basic "communicative competence" (as condition of possibility of
speech), a faculty that supports not only the performance of diverse
utterances but also, in these utterances, the articulation of crucial "validity claims" universally present in speech as such: the claims to truth,
normative rightness, truthfulness, and comprehensibility. In Habermas's words: "The meaning of the validity [of utterances] consists in
their worthiness to be recognized, that is, in the guarantee that intersubjective recognition can be brought about under suitable conditions.
I have proposed the name *universal pragmatics* for the research program aimed at reconstructing the universal validity basis of speech."[17]

As in the case of Husserlian phenomenology, Habermas's reconstruction of universal requisites was not meant to support a static essentialism. Paralleling arguments in the *Crisis* volume, rational faculties for Habermas denoted both necessary preconditions *and* teleological
guideposts for the growth of human knowledge and insight. Simultaneously with the analysis of universal rule structures, Habermas embarked on studies of developmental processes both on the individual
and on the collective-social levels, studies that perceived rationality
as moving basically along the trajectory from latency to manifestness.
Given his postbehavioral yet (emphatically) social-scientific ambitions,
Habermas's approach in this domain was indebted both to evolutionary
and neo-evolutionary theories (from Spencer to Parsons) and to phenomenological and hermeneutical concepts of culture and normative
purpose. This combination emerged clearly in his *Legitimation Crisis,*
a work that—while focusing on crisis potentials in "late-capitalist" societies—offered also a theoretical scheme of social-political development as such. According to this scheme, development occurs typically along two tracks: the tracks of "system integration" and "social
integration," the former referring to advances in systemic differentiation and steering (or output) capacities, and the latter to the cultural
domain of the life world.

Regarding sequential patterns, the scheme replicates the modernization model on the systems level, while supplementing it with cul-

tural considerations. Thus, we encounter again the three stages of political development familiar from Almond and Powell: the stages of primitive, traditional, and modern systems (the latter now subdivided into early modern and late modern phases). While in primitive societies system and life world were still diffusely blended in kinship relations, traditional societies witnessed the emergence of political steering systems, coupled with a weakening of mythic beliefs; modern society, finally, heralds the differentiated autonomy of the economic market as well as the ascendancy of universalist cultural norms (with a potential clash between system and norms as manifest in late capitalism). In a theoretically refined manner, the two-track scheme was resumed in Habermas's *Theory of Communicative Action,* which depicted modernization as a tension-laden movement occurring simultaneously in the fields of instrumental-technical and communicative-cultural rationality. As in the previous study, the motor of development was located in the process of "rationalization" seen as the advancement of rational reflection or "reflective learning." Elevated to a normative principle, such reflective learning constitutes for Habermas the hallmark of "modernity," a stage of human maturation permitting the autonomous cultivation of science, ethics, and art.[18]

Although couched in a distinctly Western idiom, Habermasian critical theory has been attractive to many third world intellectuals for a number of reasons. The chief reason undoubtedly is Habermas's strong commitment to emancipation and liberating critique, an aspect that resonates with persistent struggles against colonial and postcolonial elites as well as against entrenched forms of stratification. Another motive is Habermas's (relative) attention to culture and to the legacy of human or cultural sciences, a feature that seems amenable to cross-cultural comparisons. In India, the Habermasian framework has been greeted by a number of intellectuals, including Thomas Pantham and philosopher Sundara Rajan. In "Habermas' Practical Discourse and Gandhi's *Satyagraha,*" Pantham discusses "interesting parallels" between Habermas's notion of 'communicative action' and Gandhi's engagement in *satyagraha* in the pursuit of moral-political goals. Both Habermas and Gandhi sought to recover the "public sphere" seen as an arena of practical involvement in opposition to the usurpation of politics by technocratic or managerial elites; both also aimed at a consensual resolution of conflicts that would reintegrate ethics and politics.

However, for Pantham, the chief parallel resides in their shared emancipatory élan. "The goal of Habermas' critical theory," we read, "is human emancipation from ideological deceptions or self-deceptions (i.e., from systematically distorted communication) as well as from technocratic domination and the scientization of politics." From Habermas's vantage, contemporary society fosters increasingly the conversion of "practico-political" issues into issues of "technical manipulation and control," which entails a growing divorce of politics from morality and ethics. To counteract this tendency, Habermas advocates the revitalization of cultural-normative concerns, and especially the strengthening of practical discourses through which prevailing interests can be screened, rendered transparent, and perhaps even transformed—a goal that is not too far removed from Gandhi's accent on nonviolent struggle and *satyagraha*. While acknowledging some important divergences, Pantham summarized the similarities between the two positions in these terms:

> A critical-emancipatory concern is common to both Gandhi and Habermas. They are concerned with the legitimacy crisis of the socio-political structure of exploitation and violence as well as our ideological self-deceptions and the tyranny of dogmatic beliefs. Habermas objects to the reduction of practico-political questions into the technical or technocratic model of politics, which eschews ethics and morality. Gandhi also condemns the divorce of politics and economics from ethical standards and moral principles. Both Gandhi and Habermas seek to reclaim the freedom or autonomy of the individual from the technocrats of social power.[19]

On a more abstractly theoretical level, Habermasian arguments have been adapted and further pursued by Sundara Rajan, in a string of publications starting with *Innovative Competence and Social Change*. As the author acknowledged, the notion of 'innovative competence' was indebted to the "communication-theoretical model" of Habermas and especially to the latter's concept of communicative competence. In addition to the Habermasian framework, the study also invoked Schutzian phenomenology as a cognate (postbehavioral) approach to the analysis of the cultural life world. "If this alignment between the theory of communicative competence and [Schutzian] social theory could be defended," Sundara Rajan observed, "then I suggest that we may have a possibility of carrying over a transcendental point of view into the domain of social theory."

Regarding social and political development, *Innovative Competence and Social Change* relied in part on evolutionary models from Spencer to Parsons (though stripped of their positivist determinism), and in part on the Habermasian scheme of a double or multiple trajectory of modernization. In line with Habermas's tripartition of cognitive interests (corresponding to the validity claims of empirical truth, rightness, and truthfulness), Sundara Rajan portrayed development as moving along the three axes of growing steering efficiency, cultural communication, and self-reflection or self-expression. In terms of the study, every society, no matter how simple or complex, "has to face, and in a measure successfully solve, three basic types of tasks: (1) task of survival; (2) task of maintaining the structure and normative order of the group; (3) task of making possible for individual members a tolerable degree of personal fulfillment and happiness." Accordingly, innovative competence can be differentiated into the three strands of adaptive, interactive, and expressive innovation, strands that reflect the central goals of every society, namely, efficiency, justice, and happiness. Approximation of these goals involves a process of progressive differentiation coupled with reciprocal integration and ultimately with universalization:

> If at all we can speak of the goal or ultimate objective of socio-cultural evolution, as a terminus of the process, it may be described as an optimal balance of these three [dimensions] — an order of balance which may be said to be a "cultural climax.". . . [Hence,] the omega point of cultural evolution is a single universal culture in which there would be perfect balance of efficiency, justice and happiness. It is not merely different social types but the universalization of these types in the form of a single culture that may be said to be the ultimate goal of cultural evolution.[20]

The notion of 'innovative social change' was carried forward in Sundara Rajan's subsequent book, *Towards a Critique of Cultural Reason,* a work that blended Habermasian motifs with arguments derived from Ricoeur's transcendental hermeneutics. Adopting the Habermasian distinction between life world and discourse or between ordinary interaction and communicative reason, the study postulates a differentiation between two basic levels of social practices: the levels of situation-bound context and of decontextualized or transcendental universality. Blending this distinction with vocabulary drawn from Ricoeur's hermeneutical theory, Sundara Rajan juxtaposed the two semiotic dimensions of "signification" and "symbolization," where signification means the "expression of contextualized and situation-specific meanings" and symbolization denotes the emancipatory "transcendence of such contextuality" within the communicative process itself. As he recognized, articulation of this distinction implied a departure from orthodox Marxism which tended to equate culture with ideology and, more specifically, to reduce universal symbolization to modes of distorted signification or communication (to be unmasked through a "hermeneutics of suspicion").

Countering such a reductive approach, Sundara Rajan stressed the genuine quality of symbols and their possibly liberating or transformative effects. In terms of the study, "culture" was not simply a contingent or restrictive life-form, but a synonym for essential features of social life as such; to this extent, culture could be described as "the architectonic of the symbolic," which points to "general or universal meanings." Where such meanings are evoked, the text observes, we are in the presence of

> symbols of transcendence. I am noting that from this point of view, culture is the domain of symbols of transcendence. In so far as such symbols operate in discourse, i.e. in so far as culture is active in the experience of individuals, the finite individual is able to transcend the contextuality and existential boundedness of his life. In traditional formulation, in culture life is *aufgehoben*—that is, transcended and preserved in a higher form. If this is so, it is in the domain of the symbolic that finite transcendence takes place.

As one should note, symbolization for Sundara Rajan was not only potentially liberating but also a "condition of possibility" of cultural understanding in the Kantian sense. Pursuing this line of argument (beyond the confines of Kant's own critical inquiry), the study projects the outline of a "critique of cultural reason" which alone can serve as "the foundation of historical knowledge."[21]

Elaborating on the implications of this approach, *Towards a Critique of Cultural Reason* made a distinction between two dimensions of communicative practices: semantic meanings and intentional actions. In both cases, the bifurcation of contingent context and universality was said to be operative. In the domain of semantic meanings, Sundara Rajan—following Ricoeur—differentiated between ordinary speech and written text (a variant of the Habermasian correlation of speech and discourse). While everyday speech was said to be contextual or context-bound and to reflect the semantic process of signification, written texts were seen as relatively context-free in the sense that ordinary expressions are elevated or "sublated" into universal meanings through a process of semantic transformation whereby "symbolization transcends signification." A similar movement of transcendence was detected in the field of intentional action where the process of sublation points from ordinary modes of interaction to the level of "exemplary" or "epochal acts," the latter seen as the hallmark of politics in the strong sense. Just as texts—the term taken as stand-in for a broad cultural field (from art and literature to ethics)—are able to thematize essential meanings and address universal human needs, so epochal acts are capable of disclosing universal political longings shrouded or obscured by limited historical settings. In Sundara Rajan's words, by virtue of exemplary deeds a community

> comes to self-consciousness in terms of what it aspires to be. The exemplary act reveals a vision of the good life as the community in its historical and contextualized vicissitudes, in its moments of humiliation and defeat has nevertheless obscurely felt within, as a vague and unnamed aspiration and hope. The exemplar clarifies this longing, responding to the hope in bringing to consciousness the demands that it entails; he, as it were, de-contextualizes the meanings of its historical experiences and thus anticipates the form of the world that an obscure and confused longing was intending in the depth of its misery and defeat.

The Challenge of "Postmodernity"

At the time of the publication of Sundara Rajan's study, some premises of his approach were already under close scrutiny in the West. Despite its appealing emancipatory élan, Habermasian critical theory at that juncture was under severe pressure from a number of quarters and for several reasons. One prominent reason was the partial complicity of his framework with earlier modernization theory, as manifest in his endorsement of growing system differentiation and capability and his overall teleological or stage model of social development. In the eyes of many critics, Habermas's evolutionary outlook dovetailed too neatly with the progressive ascendancy and domination of Western science and technology around the globe. This complicity was not (or not sufficiently) offset by his attention to the life world and to normative-cultural concerns. Although constituting a clear advance over the positivist focus on psychological attitudes, "culture" in Habermas's scheme was still an intentional domain attached as a supplement to empirical science (and following like the latter a teleological trajectory).

As it happens, the "transcendental turn" undergirding this scheme has been paralleled in recent decades by another trend: the so-called "linguistic turn" or turn to language, where language is assigned a more emphatic, contextualized meaning than it is accorded in rational "discourse." The resurgence of language has been accompanied by a more pronounced accent placed on "culture" seen as a reservoir of mostly latent, only partially articulate or intentional meanings—a conception which was favored and promoted for some time by cultural anthropologists. As a close corollary, this accent entailed a reassessment of the notion of 'tradition' and its status in the process of social change. In opposition to universal or transcendental formulas, both culture and tradition came to be seen as historical phenomena necessarily couched in local, vernacular idioms.[23]

Together with its universalist bent, Habermasian critical theory was also suspect for its relentless modernism. In line with his teleological schema, Habermas was led to champion with growing vigor the accomplishments of Western modernity or of the "philosophical discourse of modernity," a discourse that he perceives as marked by commitment to rational enlightenment and by the growing differentiation of cultural "value spheres" (science, ethics, and art). To this extent, his outlook seemed to downplay the intrinsic tension or "dialectic of enlightenment" characterizing the modern age, an aspect that had been powerfully propounded by some of the early spokesmen of the Frankfurt School program.[24] Building in part on such earlier initiatives, recent intellectual trends in the West have mounted a concerted assault on the modernist trajectory, assailing Western rationalism and universalism as synonyms for "logocentrism" and as smokescreens for "Eurocentric" designs of global domination. Prominent among these trends are the perspectives of poststructuralism and deconstruction, whose proponents are sometimes grouped together as "postmodernists" or advocates of an incipient "postmodernity."

In his *Postmodern Condition*, Jean-François Lyotard denounced all the trajectories of modernization—that is, the teleological accounts of modern history, including the account of human emancipation— as high-flown "metanarratives" out of touch with the basically circumscribed, historically contingent character of language. As he observed, modernity as a process (that is, modernization) invariably presents itself in terms of "some grand narrative such as the dialectics of spirit, the hermeneutics of meaning, the emancipation of the rational or working subject, or the creation of wealth." By contrast, the chief trademark of the postmodern outlook is its "incredulity" toward such accounts, its skepsis toward all continuous or progressive teleologies of history. Relinquishing universal schemes, postmodernity— in Lyotard's view—insists on the dispersed and heterogeneous character of historical episodes and cultural "language games," thus lending support not to holistic theories but only to a "pragmatics of language particles" and to political activity only "in patches—local determinism." In explicit opposition to Habermasian communication, the study privileged the role of "dissension," coupled with "sensitivity to differences" and an "ability to tolerate the incommensurable." Accordingly, the basic "principle" underlying the study was struggle or contestation: for, "to speak is to fight," and speech acts "fall within the domain of general agonistics."[25]

Theoretical accents of this kind are pervasive in contemporary literature, from Derrida's celebration of *différance* to Deleuze's stress on heterogeneity and Foucault's notion of 'micropowers.' Rejection of historical teleology was particularly pronounced in Foucault's *Archaeology of Knowledge,* which shifted the focus from historical evolution to paradigmatic ruptures, discontinuities, and epistemic breaks. As Foucault observed, the notion of discontinuity "assumes a major role" in contemporary historical inquiry; whereas previously seen as a "stigma of temporal dislocation that it was the historians' task to remove from history," discontinuity now surges forth as a central issue blocking holistic overviews. The political implications of antiholism were spelled out by Foucault in a subsequent interview which underscored the role of decentralized practices and local resistances; political analysis, he notes there, should be concerned not with total systems but with "power at its extremities," with "those points where it becomes capillary, that is, in its more regional and local forms and institutions."[26]

In the American context, antiholism surfaces frequently in the guise of a neopragmatic particularism or of a postmodern cultivation of (counter-) cultural diversity. Adopting a pragmatic stance, Richard Rorty tends to privilege local narratives over Habermasian quasi-transcendentalism; in lieu of the global trajectories of modernization, he commented at one point, it would be preferable to endorse "those untheoretical sorts of narrative discourse which make up the political speech of the Western democracies" and hence to be "frankly ethnocentric." In the cultural (or counter-cultural) domain, the characteristic preferences of postmodernity (or a prominent strand in postmodernity) have been eloquently stated by Cornel West in "The New Cultural Politics of Difference," where we read: "Distinctive features of the new cultural politics of difference are to trash the monolithic and homogeneous in the name of diversity, multiplicity and heterogeneity; to reject the abstract, general and universal in light of the concrete, specific and particular; and to historicize, contextualize and pluralize by highlighting the contingent, provisional, variable, tentative, shifting and changing."[27]

As briefly sketched here, postmodern trends carry important—and largely salutary—implications for the issue of development. In opposition to universal categories derived from Western modes of discourse, postmodern antiholism seeks to give voice to local or vernacular idioms and thus to empower the marginalized, in particular the poor masses in third world countries trying to resist Western global control. The former president of Senegal, Leopold Senghor, captured this emancipatory thrust when he said that "we Africans do not wish to be mere consumers of civilization." This saying resonates deeply with a formulation that Deleuze used to characterize Foucault's contribution to contemporary social theory: "You have taught us something absolutely fundamental: the indignity of speaking on someone else's behalf."[28] To avoid this indignity, ethnic and other (sub-)national groups in the third world must have the opportunity to articulate their hopes and grievances in their own vocabulary, which implies a valorization of indigenous cultural and linguistic traditions and ways of life.

To be sure, such valorization can also give rise to narrow self-enclosure or to ethnic parochialism; under socially and economically stressful conditions, Rorty's benign ethnocentrism can readily give way to virulent forms of chauvinism and ethnic-religious "communalism." This is the dark or perilous side of postmodernity, an aspect rendering it vulnerable to modernist attacks. To counter this danger and the lure of cultural narcissism, postmodern localism or particularism must be construed in a radically porous and open-ended manner, one that encourages multiple types of engagement and interaction, both between marginalized groups and ethnic communities and between traditional cultures and the modern West (whose presence cannot simply be exorcised). Seen from this angle, Lyotard's "agonistics" loses some of its militant and atomistic quality, making room instead for a struggle for mutual recognition or a process of "agonal dialogue"—a process that seems to concur with Seyla Benhabib's notion of 'interactive universalism' (and with Merleau-Ponty's earlier conception of a 'lateral universalism'). Under these auspices, tradition and modernity are no longer binary opposites or poles of a historical trajectory, but rather ways of life intimately entwined with each other, a correlation finding expression in diverse forms of critical traditionalism and naturalized (or traditionalized) modernism.[29] Instead of pursuing these matters on an improperly abstract level, the final part of this chapter is devoted to theoretical initiatives on the Indian subcontinent that illustrate the potential of a non-Western approach to development or to (what one may call) "postmodernization."

Postmodernization in India?

Among contemporary Indian theorists concerned with development issues, Foucauldian and postmodern influences are particularly evident in the writings of Tariq Banuri. In "Modernization and Its Discontents," Banuri has zeroed in on a crucial feature of modernization models: their glorification of "modernity" based on the assumption that modern culture is inherently superior to other life-forms or "ways of seeing the world." In Banuri's view, there is a deep-seated crisis of development or modernization theory, that derives not simply from errors in detail, but from basic inadequacies of a philosophical, epistemological, and ontological sort. Differentiating between "personal" and "impersonal" maps or world views, the essay finds modernization models attached to Western modernity which, in turn, is addicted to a hierarchical postulate: the "impersonality postulate" whereby impersonal relations are intrinsically privileged over personal relations. In this formulation, impersonality characterizes a culture in which everyone maintains anonymous relations "with other people, with the natural environment, and with knowledge," whereas concrete experiential bonds in all three dimensions are the hallmark of a "personal map," which is "context-specific" while the impersonal stance is abstract, decontextualized, or "universal."

While most actual cultures reveal a blend of the two dimensions, the distinctive trait of Western modernity is its attempt to bifurcate the two and place them in an asymmetrical hierarchy. Seen from this angle, the trajectory of modernization theory globalizes this hierarchy: "It has the confessed task of 'rationalizing' the whole world, of placing the world in a conceptual grid." Its primary objective is "not pedagogy but control; not helping to understand the world, but rather helping to maintain existing (often oppressive) structures of power." Appealing to Foucauldian vocabulary, Banuri's essay castigates the "hegemonic panopticism" inherent in "Western liberalism's method of binary opposition," that is, in its hierarchical rather than dialectical correlation of modernity and tradition, of universality and contextuality. Offering a summary diagnosis of the malaise of modernization, Banuri argues that "many of the seemingly insoluble problems of today's world stem precisely from the implicit assumption of a dichotomy and a hierarchy between the impersonal and the personal spheres of culture, and that in our search for solutions we need to replace this hierarchy with the notion of a tension or a dialectic between the two."[30]

In moving from diagnosis to prescription, Banuri does not advocate a radical, antimodern separatism, but rather something like an agonal or tensional dialogue. Such a tensional approach, in his view, is liable to show that concrete social systems always reflect "an admixture of the personal and impersonal perspectives," notwithstanding the "overemphasis of the modernization approach on the latter," and also that "a perfectly coherent and logical argument could be based on the 'personal' map just as easily as on the modernizers' exclusive reliance on impersonal arguments." The basic moral-political upshot of this approach is the correction of cultural asymmetry: the replacement of the modernizers' assumption of the superiority of the modern life style with "the earlier notion of the moral as well as socio-economic worth of different cultures and value systems." To accomplish this correction or redress, however, a basic shift of focus is necessary, namely, a shift from the universal discourse of "impersonal" (Western) experts to the indigenous or vernacular idiom of third world societies. Both theoretically and practically, such a turn is designed "to deny the validity and legitimacy of universal and objective definitions" and thus "to transfer the power of defining the problems and goals of a society from the hands of outside experts into those of the members of the society itself."

Foucault's stress on local resistance gains relevance here. In Banuri's account, the resistance of "traditional" cultures to modern values and practices can be understood as an attempt "to retain control over their own actions and their own environments"; from this angle, whatever development or social change takes place, will occur "as the result of resistance, protest, and challenges from below, rather than from an imposition from above." Banuri in this context formulates a "vision of the future in the Third World" couched in terms of a "decentralized polity, economy, and society"; decentralization here implies a strengthening of local government "whether at the level of the village, a group of villages, small towns, or possible subdivisions of large cities." Such a decentralization, in Banuri's view, is able to link up with the Gandhian legacies of self-reliance and nonviolence. In contrast to the wantonly aggressive character of instrumental modernism, "the shift in perception away from this universal and impersonal perspective towards one based on direct human connections can help create the notion of sustainable development as a fundamental human value, and therefore also the basis for popular resistance against violence."[31]

A similar outlook (though with slightly more polemical accents) has been articulated by Ashis Nandy in several of his writings. In frontal opposition to modernization seen as progressive adaptation to Western hegemonic culture, Nandy at one point defined progress or development as "expansion of the awareness of oppression in society." The concrete implications of this definition were spelled out in a manifesto or third world "credo" titled "Cultural Frames for Social Transformation." According to Nandy, emphasis on indigenous culture or cultural traditions is urgent in the face of the relentless Westernization and uniformization of the world. As in Banuri's work, resort to native culture implies for Nandy "a defiance of the modern idea of expertise," an idea that demands that even resistance be "uncontaminated by the 'inferior' cognition or 'unripe' revolutionary consciousness of the oppressed." Given the hegemonic status of Western modernity, the manifesto adds, resistance to oppression has to involve "in our part of the world, some resistance to modernity" itself; in particular, resistance must challenge the connotative meanings of concepts such as "development, growth, history, science and technology," concepts which have become in the third world "not only new 'reasons of state' but mystifications for new forms of violence and injustice."

The stance toward social transformation outlined in the manifesto is termed "critical traditionalism," a phrase evoking the liberating potential present in "living traditions" and meant as counterpoise to all forms of complicity with modernization (including a "critical modernism" loyal to Western hegemony). In Nandy's view, such a liberating potential is not a monopoly of Western modernity but can also be found in Indian culture; for many features of traditional Indian thought—including "many of its Puranic and folk elements"—can be and have been used as a "critical base." According to the essay, a chief representative of critical traditionalism was Gandhi who, in many of his writings and speeches, was "by far the most consistent and savage critic of modernity," while refusing to retreat into a nostalgic archaism. Gandhi, we are told, rejected "modern innovations such as the nation-state system, modern science and technology, urban industrialism and evolutionism," yet without abandoning traditional notions of "the state, science and technology, civic living and social transformation." The central feature in Gandhi's outlook was his opposition to oppression, in the past as well as in the present. In Nandy's words:

> Gandhi's movement against the tradition of untouchability [was] the other side of his struggle against modern imperialism. . . . Unlike Coomaraswamy, Gandhi did not want to defend traditions; he lived with them. Nor did he, like Nehru, want to mesmerize cultures within a modern frame. Gandhi's frame was traditional, but he was willing to criticize some traditions violently. He was even willing to include in his frame elements of modernity as critical vectors.[32]

With some concessions to liberal humanism, a stance congenial to Nandy's has been propounded in recent writings by Rajni Kothari (who like the former works at the Centre for the Study of Developing Societies in Delhi). Together with Nandy and Banuri, Kothari in these writings links the search for political alternatives and a properly "humane world order" with resistance to Western global hegemony; secular modernization or development, in his view, has produced a basic asymmetry both in global in and domestic society, a split that divides north against south, urban against rural populations, and Westernized elites against indigenous masses. As he wrote in *Transformation and Survival,* the contemporary crisis of development results from a steadily "sharpening dualism (a) between the imperial centers and peripheral societies and (b) between the rich and the poor of the world."

Like Nandy, Kothari locates the core of genuine development not in an expansion of technocratic or managerial controls but in liberating transformation; such transformation, he emphasizes, has to do with "the problem of freedom in human affairs and of democracy and the institutions that sustain it." To unleash this liberating potential, Kothari's prescription urges a strengthening of local self-government and an invigoration of indigenous cultures and grassroots movements, especially among marginalized groups. As his *Rethinking Development* observes, the focus on ethnicity and native cultures "is a response— including reaction—to the excesses of the modern project of shaping the whole of humanity (and its natural resource base) around three pivots of world capitalism, the state system and a 'world culture' based on modern technology, a pervasive communications and information order and a 'universalizing' educational system." While supporting ethnicity and local cultures, however, the study does not endorse any kind of ethnocentrism or self-enclosed chauvinism, an enclosure that is at the heart of contemporary "communalism" and the upsurge of intercommunal violence. Honoring liberal-humanist impulses, Kothari's work instead subscribes to open-ended engagement among cultures and to an agonal "dialogue among people" *(lokayan),* an engagement that alone can pave the way to equal respect among religious and cultural groups and to an alternative world order.[33]

As in the case of Nandy, Kothari's outlook resonates with aspects of Gandhi's legacy, especially with the themes of self-reliance and nonviolence; according to *Rethinking Development,* it was Gandhi's *Hind Swaraj* that best articulated "the moral imperative of treating people as a source in the recovery of a humane order." Gandhian affinities are pervasive among Indian writers working in this field, although there surely is not (and cannot be) anything like a Gandhian orthodoxy.[34] What is typically invoked in contemporary writings is an image of Gandhi not as a modernizing nation-builder but rather as a critical traditionalist, that is, as a figure able to combine reliance on indigenous Indian traditions with the aspiration for liberating transformation. In this respect, Gandhi is clearly an unparalleled political and intellectual figure in our century, someone who has lessons to teach not only to India, but to the world at large.

Wherever possible, Gandhi sought to articulate his views in the vernacular idiom of Indian languages and through appeal to indigenous traditions. Thus, the notion of *swaraj* (self-rule) was borrowed from the tradition of *arthashastras* but, in the context of our century, acquired the connotations of resistance to colonial hegemony and of local governance recalcitrant to centralized managerial control. Similarly, the concept of *ahimsa* (nonviolence) paid tribute to ancient Buddhist and Jain teachings (as well as to the Sermon on the Mount) but now gained strategic significance in the political process of liberative-transformative struggle. As is well known, one of Gandhi's favorite classical texts was the *Bhagavad Gita;* in line with the teachings of the text, he perceived himself as a *karmayogin,* one pursuing the path of right action. While often applauding his political struggle, Western observers are likely to be perplexed by the yardstick of this struggle, which Gandhi described in terms of *satyagraha* (practice of truth), a notion far removed from Western-style "interest-articulation" or "interest-aggregation" (to borrow terms from modernization theory). Western writers also tend to praise his commitment to interethnic and interreligious peace, but they fail to detect the source of this commitment: far from reflecting a secularist indifference or "tolerance," his search for ecumenical peace was itself part of his striving for *moksha* (liberating salvation) whose sparks he saw present in every genuine religious experience.[35]

In the modern Indian context, Gandhi was not alone in exemplifying a religiously grounded ecumenicism. In many respects, a cognate outlook was shared by leading figures of the "Indian renaissance"—including Rabindranath Tagore, Sri Aurobindo, and Vivekananda—whose life work exhibited an alluring blend of rootedness in Indian traditions and cross-cultural or global generosity.[36] By way of conclusion, I want to draw attention to still earlier sources of critical traditionalism or a nonexclusionary reading of native legacies, specifically, the liberating-transformative spirit evident in *bhakti* poetry and some of the Puranic literature.

During my last visit to India I was fortunate enough to watch an evening performance by an Odissi dance group (a performance held in celebration of the annual "Shreeya Chandaluni"). The dance drama was based on "Lakshmi Purana," an Orissa poem, written by the sixteenth-century *bhakti* poet Balaram Das. The story of the drama centered on the worship of goddess Lakshmi performed by housewives in Puri annually in November. One year, Lakshmi decided to go into the city disguised as an old woman, in order to observe the level of devotion. Going from house to house, she was increasingly discouraged and dismayed, noticing the prevailing religious superficiality and even apathy among the women. Finally, she came upon the house of an untouchable family, finding the woman prostrated on the ground praying fervently "Mahalakshmi." Overjoyed, the goddess entered the house and shared a meal with the woman. This event was reported to Lord Jagannath (another name for Vishnu or Krishna), who is the presiding deity in Puri. Denouncing her ritual impurity, Jagannath ordered the goddess out of the temple. However, Lakshmi fully rose to the occasion. With the help of divine architects, she had a new palace constructed for her near the sea. At the same time, she had the temple in Puri cleared of all contents, including every morsel of food. Faced with this desolation and deprived of sustenance, Jagannath and his brother were eventually forced to go into town begging for food. Having been ignored at every house, the nearly starved gods finally came to the palace of Lakshmi, whom they entreated to return but who proved obstinate. In the end, Lakshmi consented to come back to Puri, but only on the condition that in the temple there would be no distinction of caste and that everyone would be allowed to enter freely. Couched in a traditional idiom, this poem tells a story that concurs with the Gandhian legacy and, more important, with the ecumenical aspirations of humankind.

SUNYATA EAST AND WEST

Emptiness and Global Democracy

What if being itself happened through
self-withdrawal?
　　　　　—Heidegger, *Beiträge zur Philosophie*

It is commonplace today to speak of globalization, of the steady emergence of a worldwide community or "cosmopolis."[1] It is equally commonplace to note the directional bent of this process: its close linkage with Westernization, that is, with the progressive modernization of all societies under the aegis of Western political, economic, and scientific ideas. In recent years, the most compelling manifestation of this bent has been the dramatic upsurge of Western-style democracy in many parts of the world, from South America over eastern Europe and South Asia to Tiananman Square. What impressed Alexis de Tocqueville over a century ago as a near-providential event—the democratization of European societies—has today assumed worldwide proportions and significance. Yet, something curious happens in the midst of this global process: just when Western democracy is reaching its farthest extension, it unexpectedly encounters resources of a distinctly non-Western or Asian provenance, resources that have lain in wait there for a long time. Just at a time of triumphant affirmation and emphatic insistence, democracy discovers in its own core a kind of negativity or nonaffirmation, something that Eastern thought has traditionally described as "emptiness" or *sunyata*. Thus, upsurge and global outreach are strangely coupled in this area with a sense of recoil, absence, and (perhaps) enigma. This constellation surely deserves closer scrutiny. The following proceeds cautiously into the sketched terrain, in an effort to gain a better grasp of this puzzling kind of East-West encounter in our time.

To be sure, encounter here does not mean a smooth blending or merger of perspectives. Despite areas of overlap, the meeting of cultures is likely to be marked by contestation, struggle, and agonism that matches the tensional relation between absence and presence, emptiness and affirmation. Eastern or Asian thought is bound to be challenged by the progressive-historical thrust of democratization and by the assertion of individual human rights (as endemic to liberal democracy); conversely, Western thought is prone to be upset or thrown into disarray by the radical tenor of political nonfoundationalism (as implicit in *sunyata*). Perhaps it is in this arena that the distinct accents or contours of East and West can most poignantly be discerned, contours that otherwise are only dimly indicated by the opposition between action and nonaction, ego-self and nonself *(anatman)*, self-seeking and self-abandonment.

The approach of this chapter is dictated by the need to keep the distinctness of philosophical and cultural traditions clearly in view, while at the same time preparing the ground for a reciprocal dialogical encounter or agonal conversation. In a first step, the notion of 'emptiness' or *sunyata* is examined as it has been bequeathed to us by Eastern or Asian thought in a long succession of formulations. A second step then turns to parallel conceptions in recent Western thought, with special attention to developments in contemporary political theory. As shown here, one of the important features of the latter has been the discovery of a hollow or negativity in the heart of democracy, more particularly the articulation of popular-democratic sovereignty in terms of an "empty place." The chapter concludes with a discussion of the possible implications of Eastern and Western contributions in this area for the prospects of global democracy.

I

In a sense, emptiness as negativity exceeds geographical boundaries, and thus also the division of East and West. The view that being relates somehow to nonbeing just as life is entwined with death belongs, no doubt, to the general patrimony of humankind. Nevertheless, much depends on the construal of this correlation. In traditional Western thought, emptiness has typically been seen as a mere lack or remedial privation and hence as antechamber to the investigation of substantive reality (being as such). To this extent, Eastern thought is distinguished by its pervasive bent to elevate emptiness itself to a central concern both of theoretical reflection and of practice. As one should note, emptiness here denotes not simply a vacuum or empty space; nor does it coincide with logical negation (in both its universal and in its determinate forms). In Western-metaphysical terminology, emptiness may be said to occupy an ontological or perhaps practical-ontological status. Far from serving (as in Hegel's philosophy) as a vacuous preamble to conceptual determination, the term signals an absent-present matrix allowing conceptual distinctions to arise in the first place (while simultaneously placing them in jeopardy). In addition, the term harbors a practical-transformative quality in the sense that emptiness "empties" or liberates humans from attachment to "ontic" things and ultimately from attachment even to emptiness itself (thus sidestepping every form of nihilism). In all these respects, emptiness—no longer one category among others—ruptures the bounds of Western-style conceptual metaphysics, assuming instead the role of an emblem of liberation.

Within the ambience of Eastern thought, emptiness forms part of a diversified and widely disseminated tradition. Traces of the notion can be found in ancient Indian culture, especially in Vedic texts stressing the equivalence of being and nonbeing and the nonsubstantial character of being itself. The idea of nonattachment to things and to the fruits of action was one of the central lessons of the *Bhagavad Gita,* furnishing the backbone for the Indian legacy of *karma yoga.* The most prominent articulation of the notion, however, occurred in Buddhist thought. One of the principal teachings of the Buddha Sakyamuni—one of his four "noble truths"—was the cessation of embroilment in self-seeking desire *(nirodha)* as a stepping-stone to mature enlightenment. Together with the principle of self-abandonment or no-self *(anatman),* Sakyamuni's truth became the cornerstone of all subsequent Buddhist schools or sects through the centuries.

In philosophical terms, the most innovative and fruitful development of emptiness or *sunyata* occurred no doubt in Mahayana Buddhism, chiefly due to the influence of Nagarjuna, one of its great founding thinkers (second century). Radicalizing traditional formulas, Nagarjuna extended the notion of no-self to cover the nonessentialism or lack of self-nature *(svabhava)* of all things or beings; simultaneously, by construing emptiness as an ongoing self-emptying process affecting *sunyata* itself, Nagarjuna cleared the path for the finely calibrated "middle way," which pointed beyond the opposition of sameness and diversity, of the nondistinction of nothingness and the manifold character of distinct phenomena. By the time of this innovative renewal, Buddhism in its Mahayana version was already beginning to infiltrate China where it soon flourished in a variety of schools, all dedicated to the pursuit of the middle way. Among these schools, the most radical and innovative was the Ch'an sect which traced its lineage back to Bodhidharma (fifth century), an Indian monk who had traveled to China and who, in response to a question by Emperor Wu-ti ("What is the supreme meaning of the sacred truth?"), had answered: "Vast emptiness—nothing sacred." Under the label of *Zen,* the Ch'an approach came to Japan some six centuries later, especially due to the efforts of the great religious thinker Dogen, founder of the Soto school and author of the *Shobogenzo.*[2]

In the present context, no attempt will be made to review in detail this complex historical trajectory; instead, attention is given briefly to some climactic episodes, first to the contributions Nagarjuna and Dogen and next to the most prominent contemporary offshoot of Zen Buddhism in Japan: the so-called Kyoto School (represented by such figures as Nishida, Hisamatsu Shin'ichi, Nishitani, and Masao Abe). Nagarjuna is well known as the writer of the *Madhyamaka-Karika* and also as the reputed author of a lengthy commentary on the "Sutra of Supreme Wisdom" *(Maha-prajñaparamita-shastra).* In his writings and teachings, Nagarjuna never denied the idea of a supreme "reality" (what the earlier Upanishadic tradition had termed *"brahman");* what he did deny was that this reality could be substantialized or converted into a target of conceptual knowledge without jeopardizing its ultimacy. At the same time, he vigorously rejected the tendency, prevalent among some sects or schools, to treat partial phenomena as ultimate givens, that is, the tendency to absolutize relative elements by elevating the conditioned to the status of the unconditional.

Once the essential fixity of phenomena was put aside, all that could be maintained—according to Nagarjuna—was the intimate relationism of all relative phenomena, a relationism captured in the doctrine of the reciprocity and "dependent co-arising" of all things or beings *(pratitya-samutpada).* Moreover, it was only in and through this web of phenomenal relationships that ultimate reality showed itself—but showed itself precisely in the mode of absence, emptiness, or *sunyata.* As he pointed out in his *Karika* as well as his Sutra commentary, the point of the middle way was to liberate from false attachment or clinging both to ultimate essences and to relative things and even from clinging to emptiness itself (which required a double process of emptying or a *sunyata-sunyata).* Once false clinging was abandoned, the world was able to emerge in its "suchness" *(tathata)* or basic nirvana character *(dharmadhatu).* In the words of the *Karika* freely rendered: "Everything stands in harmony with him who is in tune with *sunyata*— which is not a rejection of reality or understanding but of the misconstrual of the sense of the real or the error of misplaced absoluteness which is at the heart of clinging and the root of conflict and suffering."[3]

While favoring the characteristic Ch'an or Zen mode of stylistic abruptness, Eihei Dogen followed Nagarjuna's middle way both in his teachings and in his monastic practices. Regarding practice, Dogen counseled a distinctly nonattached or nonclinging kind of action, that is, an activity completely unconcerned with benefits or the accomplishment of ulterior goals: the activity of "just sitting" or "nothing-but-sitting" *(shikantaza)* whereby self-seeking is set aside in a manner resembling a resolute "dropping off of body and mind." Yet, while embracing the traditional Buddhist doctrine of self-abandonment, Dogen's teachings did not simply substitute self-denial for selfhood, but instead sketched a middle path pointing beyond both ego-self and no-self *(anatman)*. As he wrote in *Shobogenzo Genjokoan:* "To study the Buddha-way means to study the self; but to study the self means to forget it. Forgetting the self implies to be enlightened by all things," which, in turn, means "to drop off body and mind, of oneself and others."

Awakening through detachment from self and no-self carried over to the attitude toward the world and worldly phenomena, that is, toward the relation of *samsara* and *nirvana*. Although the motto of non-clinging requires awareness of the emptiness or nonsubstantiality of phenomena, this awareness for Dogen could not serve as basis for a new kind of attachment; rather, by relentlessly "emptying itself," *sunyata* pointed the way toward the reemergence of phenomena, that is, toward the world in its "suchness." To this extent, Dogen endorsed the answer that an old master gave to the question "What is the nature of the great, pure and bright spirit?" when he replied: "Mountains, rivers, and the great earth; sun, moon, and the stars." The same attitude is evident in Dogen's comments on Sakyamuni's reference to the "flowers of emptiness" or the "flowers of the empty sky." As he observed in a chapter of *Shobogenzo:*

> Buddhas and ancestors alone know the blooming and falling of the flowers of emptiness and of the flowers of earth, as well as the blooming and falling of the flowers of the world; they know that the flowers of emptiness, the flowers of earth, and the flowers of the world are the real *sutras*. This is the touchstone for learning the Buddha-way. Because the vehicles of Buddha-ancestors are flowers of emptiness, the buddha worlds and buddhas' teachings are none other than the flowers of emptiness.[4]

The insights of Nagarjuna and Dogen have been preserved and further developed in our century by the so-called Kyoto School, especially by its founder and leading representative, Kitaro Nishida. What is striking and distinctive about Kyoto thinkers, including Nishida, is their determined attempt to bridge the gulf between Eastern and Western thought, that is, to articulate traditional Zen teachings in a manner cognizant of central strands in modern Western philosophy and thus accessible to Western-educated readers. This bent is particularly evident in the writings of Nishida with their repeated invocations of the teachings of Kant, Hegel, Kierkegaard, James, Bergson, and Husserl. Yet, despite this display of broad philosophical erudition, study of Western texts for Nishida was not so much a goal as an avenue or vehicle for the renewed elucidation of Eastern thought, especially of the legacy of Mahayana and Zen Buddhism.

A central ingredient of this legacy is the notion of emptiness or *sunyata*. In a string of essays and books written during the prewar period, Nishida sought to recapture this notion under the label of *absolute emptiness* or *absolute nothingness (zettei mu)*, always in close confrontation with the tradition of Western logic, epistemology, and ethics. One of his last manuscripts, completed shortly before his death in 1945, attempted to delineate the "place" *(basho)* of nothingness as the site of a religious world experience nurtured by Zen. Emerging out of a probing meta-critique of Kant's critical philosophy, this site was shown to be located beyond the dichotomies of subject and predicate and of noumenal and phenomenal realms; in traditional terminology, the "place" could only be circumscribed in paradoxical language, namely, as the contradictory unity of opposites, as the tensional entwinement of identity and nonidentity, of the one and the many, of self and no-self. Nishida in this context appealed to Nagarjuna's middle path (of affirmation through negation) and also to the passage in the *Diamond Sutra:* "Because there is no Buddha, there is Buddha;/Because there are no sentient beings, there are sentient beings." Regarding the status of selfhood, his manuscript basically endorsed the road of self-finding through radical self-negation, which is the path common to all schools of Mahayana Buddhism (including Zen and Pure Land). In Nishida's words:

> The self, we must say, possesses itself through its own self-negation. It has its existence in a bottomless self-negation that is inconceivable either in the direction of the grammatical subject or in the direction of the predicate. Its nothingness is grounded in the contradictory identity of the creative world, which is self-transforming through the dialectic of its own negation and affirmation. . . . I believe this is the meaning of the ancient Buddhist saying, "Because there is No Place in which it abides, this Mind arises."[5]

Largely under the influence of Nishida, other Kyoto thinkers continued the exploration of the significance of *sunyata,* while at the same time deepening and steadily intensifying the cross-connection between Western and Buddhist thought. In pursuing the latter connection, these

thinkers—most of them students of Nishida—shifted the attention progressively from German idealism and early phenomenology to the
works of more recent Continental philosophers, including Heidegger
and the French existentialists (as well as to aspects of Nietzsche's teachings). The foremost exponents of the Kyoto perspective after Nishida
are Hisamatsu Shin'ichi, Keiji Nishitani, Hajime Tanabe, and Masao
Abe; almost invariably the publications of these thinkers reflect the
strong concern with emptiness and its status or articulation in the context of contemporary East-West philosophical discourse.

Thus, in addition to numerous books on religion, aesthetics, and
the Japanese tea ceremony, Hisamatsu is known for a study titled *Oriental Nothingness* (1939), which clearly reflected Nishida's inspiration. Likewise, together with writings devoted to Aristotle, his teacher
Nishida, and the problem of nihilism, Nishitani has published such
works as *God and Absolute Nothingness* (1948) and *Religion and Nothingness* (1956; now available in English). Somewhat more distantly related to Nishida, Hajime Tanabe has gained broad recognition chiefly
through *Philosophy as Metanoetics* (1946; now translated into English), a study that explores the issue of self and no-self or self-seeking
through self-denial along Buddhist (here Pure Land rather than Zen)
lines. Finally, apart from translating into English works by Dogen and
Nishida and commenting on his teachers Hisamatsu and Nishitani,
Masao Abe is widely respected as the leading contemporary proponent of Western–Far Eastern and Christian-Buddhist dialogue, a reputation that is grounded, among other things, in such publications as
Zen and Western Thought (1985) and "Kenotic God and Dynamic
Sunyata," in *The Emptying God: A Buddhist-Jewish-Christian Conversation* (1990).[6]

Needless to say, the perspectives of Kyoto thinkers—especially on
the topic of *sunyata*—are far from being congruent or convergent (the
differences between Nishida and Tanabe have in fact given rise both
to theoretical and to personal conflicts). Instead of attempting to survey the entire panorama, discussion here will be limited to Masao Abe,
surely the most well-known living representative of the Kyoto School
and also the one most readily accessible to students of Western philosophy.[7] A student both of Hisamatsu and of Nishitani, Masao Abe
has taught at various places in Japan, but has spent a major portion of
his professional life in the United States; hence, his grasp of central issues in Western philosophy and of Western religious beliefs is subtle
and profound. Although addressing themselves to a variety of concerns, Abe's writings almost invariably revolve around the topic of
sunyata and about the process of self-finding through self-negation or
self-emptying.

This feature is clearly evident in the essays collected in *Zen and Western Thought*. The central essay carrying the same title elaborates the basic difference between Western and Eastern (specifically Buddhist) thought in terms of their respective focus on positivity or negativity, on being or emptiness. According to Masao Abe, classical Western thought—as represented by Plato and Aristotle—concentrated on essential ideas or substantive "being" as the ground of all things. "In the philosophy of Aristotle," he writes, "which can be called the highest peak attained by Greek thought, . . . 'Being' as such, i.e. absolute *Sein,* which is the ground of the existence of beings, is established as the fundamental principle. The history of Western metaphysics after Aristotle has been erected on the extension of this concept of 'Being.'" Aristotle's focus on substantive being involved a reformulation of Platonic essentialism—with its segregation of ideas and phenomena—by relocating the moving force (as *energeia)* in existing phenomena themselves; in this manner, he arrived at the notion of *'ousia'* as the ground that "makes the existence of beings possible." Aristotle's ontology persisted through the Middle Ages in Christian scholasticism (especially the work of Thomas Aquinas), but was radically challenged and unhinged by later Enlightenment thought, particularly by Kant's critique of traditional metaphysics. In lieu of Aristotelian being, Kant placed the philosophical loadstone in human consciousness or subjectivity, specifically in transcendental consciousness seen as emblem of noumenal freedom and as fountainhead of universal norms: "In Kant, the philosophical thought of the West reached a definite turning point. The metaphysics of substantive 'Being' became that of the subjective 'Ought.'"[8]

In Masao Abe's view, traditional Western philosophy is largely (with a few exceptions such as Meister Eckhart) impaled on the two dilemmatic horns of metaphysics: substantive-objective being or subjectively grounded will and freedom. However, a different philosophical approach has prevailed in the East, especially in Buddhist thought as initiated by Sakyamuni and later developed by Nagarjuna and Mahayana Buddhism. "Rooted in the tradition of religious self-realization going back to the time of the Buddha," Abe notes, "Nagarjuna philosophically established the standpoint of absolute 'Nothingness' which transcends both being and non-being." Together with the notions of being and subjective 'ought,' he adds, *sunyata* should be seen as one of "the three fundamental categories for human thought, and accordingly for human existence itself." In opting for emptiness, Nagarjuna took a stand both against essentialism or substantialism and against a metaphysical nihilism which clings to nonbeing as a new foundation. In Abe's words, he rejected as illusory not only "the 'eternalist' view" but also the opposite skeptical or nihilistic view which holds that "emptiness and non-being are true reality." In proceeding in this manner, Nagarjuna staked out the terrain of the "middle way" for all future Mahayana Buddhism, a path that was already adumbrated in the passage of the *Prajñaparamita-sutra,* which states: "not being, and not not being." This passage clearly pointed both to the negation of substantive being and to the movement of double negation which is the genuine abode of *sunyata* and the core of *prajña* wisdom. As Abe elaborates, emptiness for Nagarjuna was not simply a vacuum or abstract negativity. It entailed a recovery of phenomena and a sense of "wondrous being":

> Precisely because it is emptiness which "empties" even emptiness, true Emptiness (absolute Nothingness) is absolute reality which makes all phenomena, all existents, truly *be.* . . . "Nothingness" thus made absolute by Nagarjuna as the basic principle which truly discloses reality as such is here affirmed to be the *third* fundamental category, differing from both Aristotelian "Being" and the Kantian "Ought."[9]

Nagarjuna's insights, in Abe's presentation, were theoretically deepened and practically or existentially concretized in Zen Buddhism with its method of "directly pointing to the human heart." Following the middle path, Zen applied the notion of self-emptying *sunyata* even to Buddhahood and the goal of reaching *nirvana.* To the extent that Buddhahood or the Buddha mind is itself an emblem of *sunyata,* the former cannot be the target of a clinging attachment; instead, Zen involves complete deliverance, which implies getting "free even of the Buddha himself." The same view extends to *nirvana* and the interrelation of *nirvana* and *samsara* (ordinary life). According to Abe, *nirvana* cannot be objectified or conceptualized; above all, it cannot be "sought for teleologically." Rather, as the abode of self-emptying *sunyata,* it is "absolute actuality realized here and now" and as such is "beyond the duality of means and end, subject and object, being and non-being."

From the Zen perspective, Buddhahood and *nirvana* are neither substances nor ideal essences; to this extent, they involve a repudiation of "being" and also of "substantive thinking" (along the lines of traditional Western ontology). Being wedded to nonattached action or simply to nonaction *(wu-wei),* Zen also transcends the standpoint of morality or attachment to normative "ought." However, all these denials should not be taken as a simple endorsement of negativity, but rather as a gateway to the recovery of phenomena through *sunyata,* that is, to the suchness of all things in the domain of *samsara-nirvana*. The entwinement of singular and universal in Zen Buddhism, Abe observes, is expressed in the terms *thusness* or *tathata* which indicate the place where "everything is truly *as it is."* This thusness, he adds, "is nothing other but another term for *Dharmata,* that is, the universal nature of the dharmas (particular things). Further, in Buddhism, *tathata* and *Dharmata* as the universal is realized as nonsubstantial and nonrational 'emptiness.'. . . [which renders it] radically different from the universal in Western thought which is not nondual with the particular because of its transcendent and noumenal character."[10]

With a few exceptions (as indicated), emptiness was never accepted by traditional Western thinkers as a basic category of philosophical inquiry. While Plato and classical ontology rejected the notion of 'absolute negation' *(ouk on)* as unthinkable, Hegel and German idealism demoted nonbeing to the status of a vacuous preamble in the process of conceptual determination. To this extent, there looms up a profound and long-standing difference regarding the understanding of nothingness "between the West and the East, especially as exemplified in Buddhism." According to Abe, some tentative steps toward a rapprochement on the part of the West have been undertaken in recent times, particularly due to the initiatives of Nietzsche and Heidegger, both of whom (he says) have "seriously dealt with the question of 'non-being' or 'nothingness' *(Nichts)* which cannot be categorized as either 'Being' *(Sein)* or 'Ought' *(Sollen)."* In terms of the essay, the first Western thinker who "clearly realized the cul-de-sac" of traditional metaphysics was Nietzsche, with his keen insight into the progressive devaluation or self-emptying of the highest traditional values. In overturning the entire system of established values, Nietzsche was the first "to grasp 'non-being' in a positive sense," namely, in the form of an "active nihilism"; in so doing, he detached thinking both from substantive being and from ideal ought, although his own preferences led him to embrace the categories of "life" and "will to power."

This initiative was continued by Heidegger who, like Nietzsche and "indeed more radically than Nietzsche," focused on the problem of nothingness and thereby "opened up a standpoint extremely close to Zen." Moving beyond traditional ontology, Heidegger—in Abe's account—tried to probe "the meaning of 'Being' itself *(Sein selbst)* which is disclosed by passing beyond Aristotelian 'Being' to its root source through the realization of 'nothingness.'" At another point in the volume, Abe credits Heidegger with taking the issue of nothingness "not only with utmost seriousness, but perhaps with the most profundity in Western history." This seriousness is revealed in his emphasis on *Nichts* or self-emptying nothingness as the corollary or requisite for any disclosure of being as such: "In order to penetrate 'Being' itself, not just the 'Being' of beings, Heidegger insists that nothingness *(das Nichts)* be realized at the bottom of our own existence."[11]

The application of emptiness even to Buddhahood or the traditional concept of Buddha nature is elaborated in the same volume in a commentary on Dogen. In one chapter of his *Shobogenzo,* Dogen reflects on a passage from the *Nirvana Sutra* which customarily had been taken to say: "All sentient beings without exception have the Buddha-nature; *Tathagata*-Buddha is permanent with no change at all." In this rendition, Buddha nature appeared as a timeless essence or substance in which all beings partake or share in a proprietary manner. Departing radically from this view, Dogen's chapter translates the passage boldly as follows: "All are sentient beings, all beings are the Buddha-nature; *Tathagata* is permanent, non-being, being, and change." In this reading, Buddhahood is no longer a substance inhabiting or manifesting itself in beings; the latter do not *have* or display some essence, but *are* directly what the Buddha nature is, namely, a mode of emptiness or *sunyata* beyond being and nonbeing. For Dogen, Abe observes, "the Buddha-nature is *not 'something' at all,* even in the negative sense such as something unnamable, something limitless, and so forth. In other words, it is *not substantial* at all. . . . Since the Buddha-nature is not substance, 'what' is immediately the Buddha-nature and the Buddha-nature is immediately 'what.'"

This means that Buddha nature for Dogen is not akin to Spinoza's *natura naturans,* that is, to a source or ground from which all beings immanently proceed or emanate; nor is it a transcendental demiurg fabricating things in sovereign fashion. Rather, beings are themselves empty and hence empty themselves directly into Buddha nature. Thus, a pine tree, for example, is neither a divinely created product nor the manifestation of an ideal substance, but rather simply a mode of "what," a "mode without modifier." For this reason, a pine tree is able to exhibit suchness, to be "really a pine tree," neither more nor less. In the words of an older (Chinese) Zen master, "Mountains are mountains, waters are waters." Returning to the sutra passage, Abe notes that Dogen's rendition does not establish a substantive identity of beings and Buddha nature, but only a coincidence in *sunyata.* From this perspective, the notion of Buddha nature converges with "no-Buddha-nature" *(mubussho),* as Dogen himself stipulated. The same chapter of the *Shobogenzo* expresses this view explicitly, saying: "Since the Buddha-nature is empty it is called *mu* (no-thing)."[12]

The notion of a coincidence in *sunyata* is further developed by Masao Abe in a succinct essay titled "Emptiness Is Suchness." Countering the widespread portrayal of Buddhism as a form of sheer negativism or nihilism, Abe accentuates the affirmative quality of emptiness. He writes: "I think that 'everything is empty' may be more adequately rendered in this way: 'Everything is just as it is.' A pine tree is a pine tree; a bamboo is a bamboo" in the same way as "you are you; I am I." Through the quality of suchness, the singularity and unique difference of all beings is preserved, but not in the mode of a rigid separation or segregation, due to the lack of a stable core of beings. Thus, everything is indeed "different from everything else"; and yet, while everything and everyone "retain their uniqueness and particularity, they are free from conflict because they have no self-nature. This is the meaning of the saying that everything is empty." Segregation and possibly conflict arise among human beings because of their endowment with self-consciousness and hence the lure of an attachment to selfhood in the sense of ego identity. Through self-consciousness, Abe notes, humans are induced to erect a wall between self and others and between self and the world.

In Buddhism, such segregation is considered "ignorance" (avidya) since it cuts us off "from the reality of suchness" both of the world and of ourselves. Selfhood as ego consciousness is termed ignorance because it tries to make the self into an object for the self (as subject), which is an impossible and self-defeating goal. Once the latter fact is perceived, the ego looses its props and finally collapses into emptiness. At this point, the awareness of "no-self" looms up and the realization that "there is no unchanging, eternal ego-self"—a realization pointing the way toward an awakening to suchness. As Abe points out in another context, this awakening to suchness follows a kind of (non-Hegelian) dialectic moving from ego-self to no-self to double negation. Invoking again the early Chinese Zen master, Abe comments on the transformations implicit in the saying "Mountains are mountains, waters are waters." Initially, mountains and waters are objectified or reified from the vantage of a self-centered subject or "ego-self." The predicaments deriving from this subject-object split give rise to the collapse of the centrality of the ego self, which also means a denial of the object world (mountains are not mountains, waters are not waters). Awakening to the emptiness of ego self and the self-emptying of no-self finally leads to insight into the "unattainability" of the "true self" or into true selfhood as unattainable:

> To realize that the true Self is really unattainable is to realize that the true Self is empty and nonexistent. . . . The true Self is realized only through the total negation of no-self, which is in turn the total negation of the ego-self. Again, the total negation of total negation is necessary to attain the true Self as the great affirma-

tion. . . . This movement from the realization (A) that the true Self is unattainable, to the realization (B) that the unattainable itself is the true Self is a crucial turning point.[13]

II

Having delineated in brief strokes Buddhist teachings regarding *sunyata*—with a special focus on Masao Abe—discussion turns now to some parallel developments in Western thought. As indicated, Abe (together with other members of the Kyoto School) finds in recent Western philosophy promising signs of an incipient nonfoundationalism, that is, of a departure from traditional (rationalist or empiricist) metaphysics. The leading thinkers typically invoked in this context are Nietzsche and Heidegger (and subsidiarily French philosophers from existentialism to deconstruction). In Abe's writings, Nietzsche is frequently singled out as an intellectual pioneer, mainly because of his promotion of an "active nihilism" and his keen insight into the self-emptying character of dominant traditional values; yet, Nietzsche's role is critically circumscribed by his attachment to "will to power" and his (presumed) reluctance to suffuse affirmative will with radical negativity (or the "great death" of the ego). To this extent, Heidegger is said to mark a further advance over Nietzsche and in fact is credited (as mentioned) with having reached a standpoint "extremely close to Zen." Still, Abe's endorsement of Heidegger is hedged in again by numerous qualifications or critical reservations.

In the essay "Zen and Western Thought," Heidegger's thinking of being *(Denken des Seins)* is said to stop short of the emptiness of nonthinking. The commentary on Dogen lists several major divergences between Zen and Heidegger's understanding of time and temporality, especially the aspects that Heidegger's temporality is construed existentially (from the angle of *Dasein)* and that the linkage of "being and time" is not extended to the equivalence of time and being. The same text opposes Dogen's view of emptiness to Heidegger's emphasis on being *(Sein)* and "ontological difference." In contrast to Heidegger's approach, Abe notes, "Dogen does not make an ontological difference, not because he is unaware of the essential difference between Being and beings, but simply because he deliberately denies the idea of *Sein,* which is apt to be considered as something substantial, as ontologically distinguished from *Seiendes.* Hence his emphasis on the idea of 'no-Buddha-nature.'"[14]

It cannot be my task here to assess Abe's critical reservations (many of which appear dubious or problematical).[15] Instead, I want to sketch briefly some of Heidegger's main lines of argument regarding nothingness

(das Nichts), lines that place his thought indeed into the close proximity of Zen (without submerging it in the latter). The notion of 'self-
abandonment' or of the 'great death' of the ego-self was at least adumbrated in Heidegger's *Being and Time* in the discussion of "being
unto death" or "being toward death." In Heidegger's portrayal, death
or nonbeing was not merely the antithesis or external limit of *Dasein*
or human being, but rather formed its inner limning or "innermost possibility"; far from denoting a terminal endpoint, death or nonbeing was
intrinsic to *Dasein* in its suchness (so to speak). In recognizing this impending nonbeing, Heidegger observed, *"Dasein* discovers its innermost potentiality of being where the very being of *Dasein* is at stake."
Exploration of nothingness was intensified or radicalized in subsequent
writings, starting with the essay "What Is Metaphysics?" (composed
shortly after *Being and Time).*

Countering modern science's exclusive concern with "positive"
knowledge, the essay shifted attention resolutely to the domain of non-
positivity or nothingness. Non-positivity, again, was not simply a synonym for antithesis or for logical negation (deriving from the semantic "not"), but rather denoted a "metaphysical" power permeating
positivity itself. In language approximating Abe's conception of "dynamic *sunyata,"* the essay spoke of the "nihilating" quality of nothingness and of the intrinsic "suspendedness" of *Dasein* in nonbeing,
a suspension implying exposure not to an alien domain but to *Dasein's*
own suchness as present absence. In Heidegger's pointed formulation:
"Nothingness designates not merely the conceptual opposite of beings, but is an integral part of their being. It is in the being of beings
that the nihilation of nothingness *(das Nichten des Nichts)* occurs."
Similar arguments pervade his so-called *Beiträge zur Philosophie (Contributions to Philosophy),* written about a decade after *Being and Time.*
As Heidegger observed in *Beiträge,* traditional Western thought has
tended either to bypass nothingness or to treat it as equivalent to negativity, which then gave rise either to a "pessimistic nihilism" or to a
"heroic" counterposture (centered on will to power). Transgression of
this traditional outlook required a turn toward nothingness as nihilation, and thus to a self-nihilating or self-emptying kind of nihilism. In
Heidegger's words:

> Nothingness is neither negative nor is it a goal or endpoint; rather,
> it is the innermost trembling *(Erzitterung)* of being itself and thus
> more real than any (ontic) being. . . . What if being itself hap-
> pened through self-withdrawal and thus in the mode of refusal?
> Would such a refusal be simply nothing or rather the highest gift?
> And is it due to this nihilating refusal of being itself that "noth-

ingness" acquires that enabling potency on which all doing or creating depends?[16]

Concern with nihilation and transgression of the ego self is also a prominent feature of Heidegger's later writings, especially of his commentaries on the poetry of Hölderlin and Trakl with their recurrent focus on exile, estrangement, and radical transformation. His essay on Trakl, "Language in the Poem" (composed barely a decade after the war), concentrates on the distant peregrinations and profound mutations of the poetic "soul" or self—faithful to one of Trakl's lines which reads: "Strange is the soul on earth." As Heidegger points out, the term *soul* in Trakl's usage does not designate an inner substance or fixed entity; as a corollary, strangeness does not mean the self's displacement into the world from a realm of permanent essences. Rather, the soul's strangeness on earth implies the need for a distant wandering or journeying, which points not toward a safely familiar abode, but toward a painful dislodgement or nihilation in the precinct of "death." In Trakl's poetry, the strange soul is repeatedly described as "mortal" or "silent" and even as "pale" and "dead." In one of his poems, the stranger's soul is called upon by a thrush "to go under" *(in den Untergang)*, while another poem, "Seven-Song of Death," speaks starkly of "man's decomposed or rotting *(verwest)* form."

As Heidegger comments, however, going under and decomposition are part of the stranger's journey and thus not simply synonymous with negativity or a terminal limit of life. "Death," he writes, "denotes here poetically that 'going under' or undergoing into which the strange soul is called"; its death signals "not decay but instead the trespassing or leaving behind of the decomposed figure of man." In terms of the essay, this decomposed figure stands basically for traditional humankind, for what Nietzsche called the "last man," or (in Buddhist language) for the self-attached ego self. The fate (or *karma*) engendering the decomposition derives centrally from divisive segregation, from the rupture between ego and alter ego and between humans and world. In Heidegger's words:

> The curse weighing on decomposing humankind consists in the fact that the latter is struck apart by discord among sexes, tribes and races *(Zwietracht der Geschlechter)*. In this discord each party abandons itself to the unleashed fury of the disjointed and utter wildness of animality. It is not difference as such but discord which is the curse. In the turmoil of blind wildness, discord carries humankind into irreconcilable division *(Entzweiung)*, thereby exiling each party into stark isolation.

To overcome divisiveness requires a further nihilation, namely, a self-emptying of mutual negation through decentered relationship. Trakl pointedly presents the stranger's soul as "Other to the others," that is, as alternative to the decomposing humankind. The path sketched by this alternative is that of a generation "whose difference journeys ahead out of discord into the gentleness of a simply entwining (*Zwiefalt*), thus following the stranger's footsteps."[17]

Heidegger's comments on Trakl carry distinct political connotations or implications, although these implications are not fully thematized in his essay. As it happens, attention to nihilation and emptiness is not narrowly restricted to Heideggerian philosophy (and its offshoots in French "deconstruction"), but surfaces prominently also in strands of contemporary social and political theory. One domain where nihilation has strongly come to the fore is in versions of late-Marxist or post-Marxist theory, a fact that is not surprising given the indebtedness of Marxism to the Hegelian dialectic (of thesis-antithesis-synthesis or affirmation-negation-double negation). Yet, in our present postmetaphysical setting, Hegel's legacy clearly has to be radically reformulated, to prevent negation from slipping into logical denial and synthesis into an apotheosis of "spirit" (as ideal essence). A similar reformulation has to be applied to Marxist thought, given the tendency of the latter to substantialize or "essentialize" social class formations, and especially to treat the proletariat as a compact identity (or as concrete carrier of the world spirit).

The effort to deconstruct or "de-essentialize" Marxist categories has been undertaken above all by Ernesto Laclau and Chantal Mouffe in their innovative and tightly argued *Hegemony and Socialist Strategy: Towards a Radical Democratic Politics* (1985). Pointing to the untidy and "multifarious" character of contemporary social struggles and relations, Laclau and Mouffe there challenge the lingering "Jacobin imagery" operative in traditional or orthodox Marxism, a feature evident in its addiction to grand eschatological schemes and especially to the "monist aspiration" to capture "the essence or underlying meaning of History." As the authors note, this kind of essentialism or "foundationalism" has been disrupted in our time due to a series of political and economic developments as well as new theoretical initiatives. Jointly, these practical and intellectual changes have produced a "crisis" for traditional socialist dialectics: "What is now in crisis is a whole conception of socialism which rests upon the ontological centrality of the working class, upon the role of the Revolution (with a capital "r"), as the founding moment in the transition from one type of society to another and upon the illusory prospect of a perfectly unitary and homogeneous collective will that will render pointless the moment of politics."[18]

In an effort to pinpoint the transformation of traditional dialectics, *Hegemony and Socialist Strategy* offers an overview of the development of Marxist thought (after Marx), from the initial establishment of Marxist "orthodoxy" over the stages of revisionism and syndicalism to the strategic innovations of Lenin, Gramsci, and their successors. As formulated by Kautsky and others, orthodox Marxism was characterized by an essentialist view of social class struggle, and especially by its attachment to an "essentialist apriorism" on several levels—as evident in its reliance on a compact and unified social agent (the proletariat), its teleological conception of history (economic determinism), and its endorsement of a privileged policy instrument (state socialism). Revisionism modified this doctrine by allowing for a greater degree of political intervention, a modification intensified by syndicalism's acceptance of broad social 'blocs' transgressing economic class lines. The notion of social blocs was carried forward in Lenin's formula of "class alliance" (chiefly of workers and peasants), a formula, however, which by no means affected the "ontological centrality" assigned to the proletariat, manifest in the leadership role of the proletarian "vanguard" party.

In the account of Laclau and Mouffe, the first crucial break with Marxist essentialism occurred in the work of Gramsci, especially through his elaboration of the notion of 'hegemony.' Extricating himself from the legacy of fixed class identities, Gramsci focused on more ambivalent groupings termed "historical blocs" whose social role was determined not solely by economic factors but also by cultural and political capabilities; as a corollary, bipolar class struggle was replaced by a complex antagonism revolving around the attainment and contestation of social hegemony. Yet, despite these theoretical advances, the study detects a serious limitation in Gramsci's initiative, namely, a tendency to ascribe the ultimately unifying power of hegemonic structures to an "ontologically" construed class identity (a tendency manifest in his notion of 'war of position'). Overcoming this limitation requires a still more resolute effort to jettison essentialism and economic determinism, a step that brings into view a more intricate welter of antagonisms. As the authors observe, antagonism in its radical meaning does not merely refer to the confrontation of different empirical groups or structures but (more important) to the tensional correlation between presence and absence, between empirical positivity and destabilizing negativity. Equating negativity with a counterpositive "equivalence" subverting all substantive distinctions, they write: "The *ultimate* character of this unfixity [of the social], the *ultimate* precariousness of all [positive] difference, will show itself in a relation of total equivalence, where the differential positivity of all its terms is dissolved. This is precisely the formula of antagonism, which thus establishes itself as the limit of the social."[19]

Seen as the limit of social structures, antagonism testifies to the inability of hegemony to erect itself into a permanent regime or into a closed, fully integrated system; permeated by negativity, hegemony remains exposed to the polysemy of meanings and to the shifting parameters of social-political options and goals. In the view of Laclau and Mouffe, social life is precariously lodged at the crossroads of presence and absence, of positivity and negativity. Given its embroilment with negativity and antagonism, they observe, society cannot attain "the status of transparency, of full presence," which means that "the objectivity of its identities is permanently subverted"; as a result, the "impossible relation" between presence and absence must be seen as "constitutive of the social" itself. One should note, however, that thematization of absence or negativity does not involve a simple lapse into negativism or nihilism. Just as social hegemony can never be fully stabilized (or essentialized), so negativity or negative equivalence cannot be turned into a totalizing enterprise, for the simple reason that negativity is not merely logical denial but rather a nihilating force, which, in contesting positive integration, simultaneously nihilates or empties itself, thus canceling its own predominance.

What emerges into view at this point is a middle path of social life, a path steering a difficult course between nothingness and positivity or—in the authors' words—between two kinds of "social logics": the "opposed logics of equivalence and difference." Viewed from this middle path, neither of the two logics is able to hold complete sway or achieve foundational status without jeopardizing the integrity of social life; differently phrased, full positive integration as well as total rupture or dissolution only signal the extreme poles or terminal end points of a spectrum whose basic fulcrum points to the entwinement of positivity/negativity in "their reciprocal subversion." This reciprocal entwinement is particularly important in modern democracy with its simultaneous resistance both to totalitarian domination and to radical polarization (where each party operates as the negation of the other). Translating the interplay of social logics into the more traditional vocabulary of liberty and equality, Laclau and Mouffe assert the importance of their correlation in a modern democratic context: "The precariousness of every equivalence demands that it be complemented/limited by the logic of autonomy. It is for this reason that the demand for *equality* is not sufficient, but needs to be balanced by the demand for *liberty,* which leads us to speak of a radical and *plural* democracy."[20]

The role of negativity or emptiness in social-political life has also been explored, and further clarified, in the writings of Claude Lefort, particularly through his elaboration of the distinction between political framework and partisan politics or between "polity" (or "the political") and policy. In Lefort's treatment, the term *politics* in its generic sense refers to overt political activities and power strategies amenable to observation and empirical analysis, while *polity* or the *political* has to do with the constitutive, quasi-transcendental setting or matrix of political life. Whereas study of manifest political behavior and events is the province of political science and sociology, inquiry into the underlying framework or matrix has traditionally been the task of political philosophy and metaphysics.

Probing beneath the surface of contingent phenomena, Lefort comments, philosophical inquiry of this type raises the question "of the constitution of the social space, of the *form* of society, of the essence of what was once termed the 'city.'" Exploration of constitutive underpinnings in this context involves both the assignment of meaning to political events (what Lefort calls *"mise en sense")* and their staging in a public forum or a social-political space *(mise en scene).* Attention to "the political" seen as a generative setting or space-time schema derives not merely from speculative whim but from a kind of metaphysical urgency; in Lefort's view, it reflects philosophy's "oldest and most constant inspiration." Philosophers, he notes, have always refused to "localize the political *in* society," that is, to reduce it to overt empirical data while neglecting the constitutive "shaping" *(mise en forme)* of political life manifest in meaning assignment and staging in a public forum. As he adds, such a shaping of society implies not only a discrimination between true and false, just and unjust, but it extends to the distinction between the visible and the invisible, presence and absence, being and nonbeing. To this extent, inquiry into the political involves ultimately "an investigation into the world, into being as such."[21]

While paying homage to the objective of traditional political philosophy, Lefort voices strong reservations regarding past construals of the political, particularly their proclivity to substantialize or essentialize the constitutive framework of political life. As he notes, traditional political metaphysics has tended to postulate the concrete embodiment of the public space, specifically its manifest localization in such representative figures as kings, emperors, and princes. Thus, during the *ancien régime* (and in some places beyond its demise), monarchical rule functioned as the holistic instantiation or representation of the political as such, with ultimate sovereignty—seen as quasi-transcendental, constitutive power to "shape" society— being directly inscribed in the king's body or person. Against this background, postmonarchical or postrevolutionary developments signal a sharp break with traditional representational thought (and hence a move toward postmetaphysics). While not canceling the political and its philosophical articulation, modern democracy does herald the withdrawal of sovereignty from a place of manifest domination and inscription to a more subterranean or oblique mode of implication.

As Lefort observes in *Democracy and Political Theory,* modern democratic regimes testify to "a highly specific shaping *(mise en forme)* of society," such that "we would try in vain to find models for it in the past, even though it is not without its heritage." The specificity of the democratic shaping is said to reside chiefly in the relocation of sovereign power and representational inscription, namely, from a site of overt rule to an absent site or a site of absent presence—that is, to a site of emptiness (which is not synonymous with vacuity or categorical negation). "Of all the regimes we know," Lefort asserts, modern democracy is "the only one to have represented power in such a way as to show that power is an *empty place* and to have maintained a gap between the symbolic and the real." Without encouraging anarchy, emptiness of the democratic public space means "that [ultimate] power belongs to no one; that those who exercise power do not possess it; that they do not, indeed, embody it."[22]

In Lefort's portrayal, modern democracy accentuates the built-in tension between politics and "the political," not by banishing the latter altogether, but by transforming it into the latent or hidden underside of politics. Seen as an empty place, democratic sovereignty cannot be manifestly actualized by any individual or group in society. What is manifest or visible in democracy are only the partisan strategies, the mechanisms of government, and the individuals or groups wielding political authority at a given time; but the constitutive matrix or space-time schema of the polity remains hidden. In Lefort's words, democracy might even be described as the institutionalization of a "society without a body" or a society that "undermines the representation of an organic totality." This does not mean that totalizing conceptions or ambitions have completely subsided in modern, postrevolutionary times. Translated as "rule by the people," democracy is sometimes identified with a populist regime where "the people" at large directly exercise sovereign power, thus visibly embodying the public space. Closely associated with rule by the people during the last two centuries has been the investment of public power in such holistic entities as the nation or the nation-state.

As Lefort points out, the vanishing of concrete bodily representation by kings or princes leads to the emergence of new regimes in which "the people, the nation and the state take on the status of uni-

versal categories." Conceptions of this kind, he notes, are the outgrowth of a nostalgic regression, that is, of an effort to recapture and
resubstantialize a public space that, in democracy, is destined to remain empty and latent. In its more virulent form, resubstantialization
is at the root of political fundamentalism and totalitarianism in our
age. Under totalitarian auspices, the idea of popular sovereignty has
repeatedly given rise to (what Lefort calls) "the phantasy of the People-as-One," to the quest "for a substantial identity, for a body which
is welded to its head, for an embodying power, for a state free from
division." At this point, a "logic of identification" is set in motion which
hearkens back to the traditional logic of representational embodiment:
the presumed identity of the populist movement or party with "the
people" generates the image of "a homogeneous and self-transparent
society, of a People-as-One."[23]

III

At this point, I would like to return to East-West relations in our time.
The conception of democratic staging as an empty place resonates
deeply with the Buddhist notion of *sunyata* (as outlined above). As in
the case of Buddhism, democratic emptiness does not denote nihilism
or sheer negativity but rather a kind of inner lining or hidden foil allowing democratic politics to emerge in its suchness. If *sunyata* is seen
as a core ingredient of Buddhism (at least in its Mahayana version),
then contemporary politics offers the spectacle of a curious East-West
encounter: just at the time when Western-style democracy is experiencing a worldwide affirmation allowing us to speak of a process of
global democratization, democratic politics discovers in itself a non-
actuality or hidden hollow, a hollow whose understanding can be
greatly assisted by the rich Buddhist legacy of *sunyata.*

To be sure, encounter of cultural traditions is never entirely free
from complicating factors. One complication derives from misper-
ceptions on both sides. While Western democratic theory is often exclusively focused on overt electoral behavior (to the neglect of constitutive staging), Buddhist thought in turn has sometimes not been
entirely faithful to the nonsubstantiality of suchness as disclosed
through the self-emptying impact of *sunyata.* As is well known, some
Japanese Buddhists have on occasion tended to reinvest emptiness
with an array of substantive categories, especially with an essentialist conception of nationhood or nation-state. This tendency is clearly
documented in the case of branches of the Nichiren school of Buddhism; but it also surfaced in the confines of the Kyoto school both
before and during the war—a fact that still is the source of intense

controversy today. As one observer comments, with special reference to Haijme Tanabe's notion of a 'species community' comprising believers (but the reference could be broadened): "The theory of species is regarded by many as having helped develop an intellectual climate supporting the feelings of racial superiority and the conception of 'manifest destiny' borrowed from Western colonialism that prevailed in Japan during the 1930's. Whether Tanabe himself should be held partly responsible for the disastrous consequences of this conception has been a topic of debate."[24]

Without entering this debate, let us consider at least briefly the dangers and predicaments besetting any overt politicization of Buddhism, that is, any attempt to transform Buddhism from a stance of vigilant nonattachment into an instrument of manifest politics. These predicaments are clearly evident in a country such as Sri Lanka where Buddhist religion—although enjoying a majority status—has been beleaguered for some time both by Western colonizers and by opposing segments of the population. As Stanley Tambiah has shown in his instructive study *Buddhism Betrayed?* the response of Sinhalese Buddhists to real or perceived threats has moved through a number of stages, mainly from an early endeavor to "restore" the integrity of traditional beliefs to a steadily intensified politicization of group solidarity. According to Tambiah, restorative efforts during the early postcolonial period involved chiefly the strengthening of Buddhist tenets through eradication of colonial inequalities; the recognition of Sinhala as official language; the creation of Buddhist universities; and the elevation of Buddhism to "foremost" status in the country.

During more recent decades, however, nationalism and other "secular" ideas increasingly moved to the forefront of the struggle. By this time, Tambiah comments, "the primary slogans, for monks as well as laity, were the unity and sovereignty of the 'motherland,'" while their major identity derived from their status as "sons of the soil." In his account, the late eighties may be seen as marking

> the final shift of "political Buddhism" from a more localized religiosity of earlier times primarily enacted by monk-laity circles in villages and towns . . . to a vocal and sloganized "religiousmindedness," which has objectified and fetishized the religion and espoused a "Buddhist nationalism," even as regards the monks themselves, so that important tenets of their religion regarding detachment, compassion, tranquility, and non-violence and the overcoming of mental impurities are subordinated and made less relevant to Sinhala religio-nationalist and social reform goals.

Under the aegis of a "militant, populist, fetishized form" of Buddhism, traditional emptiness or *sunyata* does not so much empty itself, but rather gives way to an overt political strategy which serves as a "marker of crowd and mob identity," as a "rhetorical mobilizer of volatile masses," and as an "instigator of spurts of violence."[25]

By comparison, the main thinkers discussed in these pages have (for the most part) resisted the lure of outright politicization. Masao Abe, in particular, has carefully maintained the reticent, nonpositive quality of *sunyata*, rejecting its submergence in overt partisan platforms. In political terms, Abe—largely under the influence of his teacher Hisamatsu—has been active in various socially concerned lay organizations (especially a lay society which treats Buddhism as a vehicle of selfless "awakening" in a cosmopolitan setting).[26] Still, even such subdued forms of social engagement need occasionally to be screened against embroilment in strategic politics. Apart from his ample contributions to the philosophy of religion, Abe has also written various essays of a more political character, essays whose formulations are at least sometimes ambivalent or misleading. A case in point is "Sovereignty Rests with Mankind" (a paper included as a chapter in *Zen and Western Thought*). Despite the captivating élan of its overall message, some passages seem unduly programmatic, as evocative of a political platform. "All of mankind on this planet," the opening lines announce, "has entered into an age when it must realize that it now is based on the clear realization of itself as 'mankind,'" as "a community with a single destiny—one living self-aware entity."

The imperative style of these lines is underscored in a subsequent passage which seems to issue universal marching orders for our age: "The age of nation-states as the bearers of history must proclaim its end, and the age of mankind must begin." Equally problematic, from the vantage of contemporary democratic theory, is Abe's employment of the term *sovereignty* in application to global society or humanity at large. To be sure, his use of the term is cautious and circumspect. "What we must establish now," the essay states, "is not an international confederacy in the sense of a league of sovereign nations. Even less should it be a world empire based on one great sovereign state." Still, despite these caveats, democratic sovereignty is not clearly portrayed as empty or self-emptying; instead, the essay speaks of "a unified cooperative human community in the complete sense of the term" and of a "sovereign authority of mankind" as a substitute for national sovereignty.[27]

However, recognition of the emptiness of popular sovereignty, is only part of the problem. What remains open or at issue is the difficult and tensional relation between affirmation and denial, between presence and absence, or (in Lefort's terms) between politics and the political. In this respect, Masao Abe has provided significant guideposts, especially by pointing to certain traditional limitations of Buddhist thought (which are only the obverse of the activist limitations of Western life). By emphasizing emptiness and detachment, his *Zen and Western Thought* notes, Zen Buddhism in the past has tended to neglect or bypass other dimensions of reflective inquiry, such as epistemology and ethics, which in the West have provided the groundwork for the rise of science and the articulation of a normatively guided praxis. "Precisely because of its standpoint of Non-thinking," he writes pointedly, "Zen has in fact not fully realized the positive and creative aspects of thinking and their significance which have been especially developed in the West."

By the "positive and creative aspects of thinking" Abe means basically the domains of empirical research ("substantive thinking") and practical ethics ("subjective thinking"), domains that, under the metaphysical labels of "being" and "ought," have strongly been cultivated and "conspicuous" in the West. Due to the neglect of these domains, Buddhist "non-thinking" is often said to harbor the danger of "degenerating into mere not-thinking" and, in practical terms, of "losing its own authentic freedom" by "sinking into a mere non-ethic or antiethic." To counter this danger, Abe counsels an interpenetration of positive and negative elements through a cross-fertilization of hitherto disparate cultures. In his words:

> If Zen intends to be a formative historical force of the human world as a new "world religion" in the "One World" which is coming, Zen must take up its historical task to place substantive thinking and subjective thinking, which have been refined and firmly established in the Western world, within the world of its own Non-Thinking. . . . However, to carry out this task, just as the Western notions of "Being" and "Ought" are being forced into a basic reexamination through present dialogue between Zen and Western thought, Zen too must internally embrace the standpoints of Western "Being" and "Ought" which have been foreign to itself.[28]

To be sure, the burden of reorientation cannot entirely rest on Buddhist thought, but must fall with equal weight on Western preoccupations with science and praxis, especially in the context of an emerging global democracy. As previously indicated, exclusive concern with empirical indicators and practical programs tends to shortchange the realm of constitutive staging (which is beyond the pale of pragmatic engineering). In this respect, contemporary democratic theory can learn much from the tradition of Zen Buddhist teachings, from Nagarjuna to the present. Basically, the notion of popular sovereignty as an "empty place" is bound to remain an empty slogan unless it is nourished by the Zen legacy of self-abandonment, self-awakening, and radical transformation. In this respect, Masao Abe's comments on the future of humankind—despite certain problematic formulations—still retain their force and cogency. What is wrong with existing nation-states and established political structures, in his view, is precisely their neglect of emptiness and self-denial. "Sovereign states," he writes, "do not know self-negation"; instead, they take as their guiding principle "a position of self-affirmation and self-assertion" through which, in times of crisis, "the position of 'mankind' is overlooked and destroyed."

In arguing for a global sovereignty, Abe realizes that the meaning of the term must itself be transformed; for it can no longer be a "self-affirmative, self-assertive sovereignty," but must be "a sovereignty which always is based in self-negation," one that "takes wisdom and compassion as its principles rather than authority and justice." What renders such a transformed sovereignty possible is the transformation of the ego, in the form of a "self-awakening of the original self." This change in turn renders feasible a new moral and political "cosmology," an "ethics of mankind" in which humans are fully responsible both to each other and to the nonhuman (ecological) universe. To conclude with some lines by Masao Abe, written in the form of a poem:

> We must place mankind within a new cosmology
> Which has extricated itself from anthropocentrism.
> Is not the boundless "expanse of self-awakening,"
> Which gives life to both self and other
> As it sets up the distinction between them—
> Is not this precisely the foundation of a new human society?[29]

DEMOCRACY AND MULTICULTURALISM

In this concluding chapter I want to return to 1492. In recounting the Spanish conquest of America and the ensuing subjugation or annihilation of the native Americans, Tzvetan Todorov advances an important thesis to the effect that "there exist two major forms of communication, one between man and man, the other between man and the world." In large measure, Todorov's account of the conquest revolves around the relation or conflict between these two modes of communication, with the Indians cultivating resonances with the world and the Spaniards interhuman discourse. The "exemplary history" of the Spanish conquest, he writes, teaches us "that Western civilization has conquered, among other reasons, because of its superiority in human communication; but also that this superiority has been asserted at the cost of communication with the world." Being heir to the Spanish colonizing effort, modern Western thought tends to conceive communication as "only interhuman," a conception predicated on the notion that "world" cannot be a grammatical subject or a partner in dialogue. While granting the possibility of an evolutionary ascendancy, Todorov considers the latter conception as "perhaps a narrow view of the matter," one that unduly flatters "our feeling of superiority in this regard."

Properly construed, communication in Todorov's view should be extended to include, alongside intersubjective relations, the interaction that occurs "between the person and his/her social group, the person and the natural world, the person and the religious universe." This second type of communication played a crucial part in Aztec culture, which interpreted "the divine, the natural, and the social through indices and omens, and with the help of that professional, the prophet-priest." By privileging world communication, the Indians were unable to cope with, and ultimately fell prey to, the rationalizing, disenchanting discourse of the Spaniards; in fact, it seems as if "everything happened because the Mayas and the Aztecs lost control of communication." Summarizing his findings on this score, Todorov's study offers an assessment that is judicious as well as haunting and portentous:

> The Spaniards win the war. They are incontestably superior to the Indians in the realm of interhuman communication. But their victory is problematic, for there is not just one form of communication,

> one dimension of symbolic activity. . . . The encounter of Mon-
> tezuma with Cortés, of the Indians with the Spaniards, is first of
> all a human encounter, and we cannot be surprised that the spe-
> cialists in human communication should triumph in it. But this
> victory, from which we all derive, Europeans and Americans both,
> delivers as well a terrible blow to our capacity to feel in harmony
> with the world, to belong to a preestablished order; its effect is to
> repress man's communication with the world, to produce the il-
> lusion that all communication is interhuman communication; the
> silence of the gods weighs upon the camp of the Europeans as
> much as on that of the Indians. By winning on one side, the Eu-
> ropeans lost on the other; by imposing their superiority upon the
> entire country, they destroyed their own capacity to integrate
> themselves into the world. . . . The victory was already big with
> its defeat.[1]

Beyond their focal concern, Todorov's comments carry a broader
significance. Uncannily, the Spanish-Indian encounter appears in many
ways as a precursor of recent and contemporary developments, now
projected onto a global scale. While, as Todorov says, the Spaniards
managed to impose their superiority "upon the entire country" (meaning America), Western culture today is in the process of imprinting its
mark upon the entire world. And since this process of globalization is
primarily an interhuman encounter, we should once again not be sur-
prised that the "specialists in human communication" (now including
radar and telecommunication) should triumph. To be sure, the spirit
of Western culture today differs from that animating the conquistadors. Whereas—apart from the quest for lucre—Spanish colonizers
aimed at (or justified their conduct in terms of) religious conversion
and evangelization, modern Western culture is dedicated to the yard-
sticks of science and democracy, both secular in character. Yet, the
difference is deceptive, disguising a deeper linkage.

On this point again, Todorov provides telling clues. Devoted to the
model of world communication, he notes, Aztec culture gave a large
space to religious belief, which seems to be paralleled by Spanish missionary zeal. But here a crucial contrast surfaces, one that separates
that zeal sharply from all kinds of "pagan" religion. "What matters
here," he writes, "is that Christianity is, fundamentally, universalist
and egalitarian. 'God' is not a proper noun: this word can be translated into any language, for it designates not a god . . . but *the* god."
In seeking to be universal and egalitarian, Christian religion—like
modern science—transcends all local or regional kinds of faith and
thereby is intolerant (despite its egalitarianism). While Aztecs managed to worship many divinities and even were willing to integrate

Christ into their own pantheon, this option was not available to Christians, and in fact was harshly refused by Cortés, for a basic reason: the Christian god "is not one incarnation which can be added to the rest; it is *one* in an exclusive and intolerant fashion." This fact, Todorov notes wryly, contributed "not a little to the Spaniards' victory: intransigence has always defeated tolerance."[2]

Examined from our contemporary vantage, the story of the Spanish conquest is instructive in ways that are not fully articulated in Todorov's study. Apart from pointing to continuing dangers of imperialism (cloaked today behind "one-world" formulas), the story brings into view a tension or tensional opposition which is not merely accidental but has a basic or paradigmatic status: the opposition between the egalitarian universalism of modern Western culture and the array of particular ethnic cultures and religious traditions, that is, between a rationalized world view and indigenous life worlds. To the extent that it forms part and parcel of the Western syndrome, modern democracy—meaning here liberal-egalitarian democracy—necessarily stands opposed to alternative cultures and life-forms, both at home and abroad, notwithstanding pragmatic attempts at accommodation. Being wedded to universalist principles (of equal liberty), modern democracy cannot readily accommodate radical cultural diversity, just as little as modern science can integrate alchemy (or Christianity accept the pagan pantheon).

This chapter explores this tensional nexus of democracy and multiculturalism, paying attention both to issues in democratic theory and to some concrete political experiences in our time. Taking a leaf from Todorov, one might say that the tension involves two modes of communication: intersubjective (linking speaking subjects or agents), and "worldly" or holistic. Using slightly different terms, the first might be described as linear and horizontal, the second as circular and (in a sense) vertical. A preliminary word of caution: in taking world communication seriously, the point is not to endorse ethnocentrism or to ignore or downplay dangers of communal repression and aggression. While troubling and far from imaginary, these dangers (in fairness) must be complemented by perils lurking from the opposite side. Despite a complacent sense of moral "superiority" in the West, universalist ambitions are far from blameless, having often entailed violent or destructive consequences—a fact amply documented by the Spanish conquest.

I

In recent American discussions, the issue of multiculturalism is often styled as a debate over curricular structure and reform, with defenders

of mainstream education arrayed against advocates of postmodern pluralism or heterogeneity. Approached from this angle, the issue is largely
(or only) of academic interest; reduced to curricular wrangles, the
sharper edges of multiculturalism are likely to be dulled or ignored.[3]
In a more direct and tangible fashion, the issue penetrates into contemporary ethical-political and constitutional theory in America, but
again in a manner that rarely touches on the deeper level of cultural
paradigms and existential life-forms. In the scholarly literature in this
field, multicultural concerns surface primarily in the form of a controversy over the nature and status of the ethical bond in the public
arena, that is, over the relative weight to be assigned to formal rules
of justice vis-à-vis more substantive conceptions of the "common
good." Customarily, the controversy boils down to the opposition between two major camps labeled respectively "liberalism" (or liberal
universalism) and "communitarianism," with the first camp sponsor-
ing universal principles derived from individual or interhuman consent, and the second a more historically nurtured vision of holistic
goodness. In terms of philosophical inspiration, the first camp draws
its impulses chiefly from Kant and his neo- or post-Kantian heirs, while
the second relies on insights culled from Aristotle, Hegel, and recent
versions of cultural and linguistic contextualism. In the vocabulary of
moral theory, the first perspective may be said to subscribe to a "de-
ontological" ethics revolving around individual "rights" and freedoms,
while the second centerstages the cultivation of "virtue(s)" in the context of a moral-political community.[4]

It is beyond the scope of these pages to review in detail the liberal-
communitarian controversy, something that has been done frequently
and expertly by many others. Rather, a few salient features of this debate will be highlighted before proceeding to arguments that appear
to be more revealing with respect to multiculturalism. One feature that
can hardly be overlooked is the somewhat abstract or ahistorical character of the debate, the tendency on both sides to treat "liberalism" or
"communitarianism" as invariant essences or ideal types which can
be instantiated at any time or place. Although useful for polemical purposes, this essentializing tendency blends out significant aspects of lo-
cality and history (quite apart from downplaying multiple modes of
syncretism or overlap).[5] What is most important, theoretical essentialism sidesteps the historical situatedness of the debate, the fact that it
arose in a distinct historical setting and for distinct reasons. Without
oversimplifying unduly, one might say that the debate arose in the context of—and in response to perceived quandaries besetting—American liberal democracy, with one side seeking to shore up and vindicate the core tenets of that democracy and the other side pointing to

weaknesses with the intent of providing remedies or antidotes for such defects. Seen in this light, it is clear that the debate was carried out on the terrain and under the auspices of liberal universalism, with communitarianism playing at best a subsidiary or remedial role. Moreover, placed on this terrain, communitarians often were tempted to adopt the vocabulary of the host paradigm with its built-in polarity, which accounts for their proclivity to replace individual with communal goals or ego identity with collective identity. (In this manner, one might add as an aside, communitarians misconstrued the fabric of traditional life-forms whose porous, unsystematic character eluded the individual-collective bifurcation.)[6]

Despite such shortcomings, the sketched debate has managed to bring to the fore a number of issues that are bound to reverberate in present (and future) discussions of multiculturalism. Commonly, two main dimensions are singled out for purposes of differentiating the two camps: one is the dimension of existential-ontological premises; the other that of ethical or metaethical doctrine. In the first domain, the distinction is between the autonomous ego and the situated human being or—to use Michael Sandel's phrase—between the "unenumbered self" and a historically and culturally contextualized self. (Liberals generally do not deny psychological and sociological differences among individuals, but only their relevance under the rubric of rational-moral agency.) In the second domain, the contrast is between formal-universal rules and concrete moral relationships, or between a "procedural republic" (to borrow from Sandel again) and a republic of ethical life (or *Sittlichkeit*). The two dimensions are obviously closely linked; their combined force throws into sharp relief the contours of liberal universalism, but also its intrinsic dilemmas.

These dilemmas are epitomized in the thesis of liberal impartiality, that is, the claim that formal-procedural rules (of justice) are devoid of any intrinsic conception of goodness and hence are basically "neutral" vis-à-vis competing versions of the "good life." Although emphatically asserted, this claim is clearly misleading. In order to gain a foothold for universal rules, liberalism has to disassemble or disaggregate traditional life-forms into autonomous, decontextualized units (of individual subjects) who then serve as constitutive agents of rule formation. (Thomas Hobbes was the first master thinker along these lines.) Yet, such a disaggregated rule system cannot possibly be neutral toward a life-form untouched by disaggregation. In the language of Todorov: interhuman communication among autonomous agents cannot possibly subsume under its own rule the mode of world communication, or it cannot do so without inflecting damage or violence on the latter. Needless to say, the pretense of liberal neutrality has been challenged and debunked by numerous able critics. As Chantal Mouffe has observed: "Once it is recognized that the existence of rights and a conception of justice cannot exist previously and independently of specific forms of political association—which by definition imply a conception of the good—it becomes obvious that there can never be an absolute priority of the right over the good."[7]

This debate today is somewhat dated. In the meantime, the battle lines have shifted and new arguments have been introduced which are more directly pertinent to multicultural concerns. Instructive in this respect is the work of Iris Young, especially *Justice and the Politics of Difference.* As Young makes clear at the beginning of her study, her approach steers a course between and beyond the alternatives of atomistic individualism and collectivist communitarianism by taking more seriously the existence of ethnic and cultural groups and their diversity. While liberal universalism tends to abstract from distinct cultural traditions and beliefs (in the interest of normative neutrality), prevalent modes of communitarianism integrate such traditions into a unified or collective world view (often linked with the modern nation-state). Although appreciating the critical-reflective quality of liberal ethics, Iris Young finds incongruous a normative yardstick that "stands independent of a given social context and yet measures its justice"; without relinquishing concern with equity and the rule of law, her study advances a view of justice more sensitive to historical and social contexts, especially to the rich texture of cultural life-forms. In terms of this view, liberal universalism and egalitarianism need to be tempered and corrected through closer attention to cultural heterogeneity and the "politics of difference." She writes:

> The principle of equal treatment originally arose as a formal guarantee of fair inclusive treatment; this mechanical interpretation of fairness, however, also suppresses difference. The politics of difference sometimes implies overriding a principle of equal treatment with the principle that group differences should be acknowledged in public policy . . . in order to reduce actual or potential oppression. Using examples from contemporary legal debate, including debates about equality and difference in women's liberation, bilingual education, and American Indian rights, I argue that sometimes recognizing particular rights for groups is the only way to promote their full participation.[8]

In shifting the focus to cultural groups, Young's study departs sharply from liberal accounts of social pluralism, accounts in which groups figure merely as aggregates of individuals or as combinations for the pursuit of shared interests. Instead, Young places the accent on historically grown life-forms, with each being differentiated from other groups by virtue of "cultural forms, practices, or way of life." Under the impact of modern individualism and utilitarianism, she notes, Western social and political theory has tended to construe groups "either on the model of aggregates or on the model of associations," both of which are "methodologically individualist concepts." In this usage, the term *aggregate* refers to a classification of people according to some substantive-empirical attributes, such as skin color, gender, or age. Apart from other defects, this model neglects the deeper existential wellsprings of cultural life-forms, the fact that cultural groups are defined not by extrinsic attributes but by "a sense of identity," that is, by shared practices and historical experiences.

As distinguished from aggregates, "associations" are voluntary combinations formed for the promotion of particular interests. Although more practice related, associations share a crucial premise with aggregates: like the latter, the association model "implicitly conceives the individual as ontologically prior to the collective, as making up or constituting groups." This premise, however, has been debunked by the main strands of "poststructuralist philosophy" which have exposed as illusory the metaphysics of a "unified self-making subjectivity." Following this line of deconstructive theorizing, Young's study not surprisingly (and quite sensibly) invokes some Heideggerian insights regarding human "being-in-the-world." While membership in associations, she notes, derives from arbitrary choice, group affiliation by contrast "has the character of what Martin Heidegger calls 'thrownness': one *finds oneself* as a member of a group, which one experiences as always already having been." Yet, existential affiliation does not signify an inescapable fate, nor does it support the reification of group life. "From the thrownness of group affinity," Young adds,

> it does not follow that one cannot leave groups and enter new ones. . . . Nor does it follow from the thrownness of group affinity that one cannot define the meaning of group identity for oneself; those who identify with a group can redefine the meaning and norms of group identity. . . . The present point is only that one first finds a group identity as given, and then takes it up in a certain way. While groups may come into being, they are never founded.[9]

As presented in her study, a politics of difference involves a commitment to justice and the rule of law coupled with a firm recognition and promotion of cultural life-forms and group diversity. As Young points out, liberal Enlightenment principles—enshrined in the American Constitution—aim at equal legal treatment and at human and political emancipation construed as an exodus from parochial group loyalties. Under liberal auspices, justice means a focus on rights applicable "equally to all," while group differences are reduced to "a purely accidental and private matter." Liberalism thus construed, she concedes, has been "enormously important" in the history of modern politics by providing weapons in the "struggle against exclusion and status differentiation" and by making possible "the assertion of equal worth of all persons." Yet recent decades have brought to the fore the downside of this liberal program by showing the oppressive aspects of a homogenizing universalism. In Young's account, by construing liberation as the "transcendence" or "elimination of group difference," liberalism subscribes to a conception of justice that implicitly embraces an "ideal of assimilation," that is, a melting-pot vision of social integration. From the vantage of a politics of difference, by contrast, recognition of equal worth "sometimes requires different treatment for oppressed or disadvantaged groups."

Young's study at this juncture points to the upsurge of such a differential politics in the American context—as exemplified by the black power movement (with its celebration of African-American culture), the native-American movement (with its stress on red power), the emergence of gay cultural expression, and more radical, gynocentric strands in the feminist movement (with their opposition to a liberal-humanist feminism). What emerges from these diverse movements and initiatives is not a denial of emancipation but rather a reformulation of the sense and direction of liberation, where the latter means no longer liberation from, but rather in and through, culture and cultural diversity. As opposed to an assimilationist ideal, the politics of difference to this extent sponsors an outlook of "democratic cultural pluralism." In this vision, Young writes, the good society "does not eliminate or transcend group difference"; rather, it entails "equality among socially and culturally differentiated groups who mutually respect and affirm one another in their differences."[10]

No doubt, this linkage of equality and difference is startling and unconventional, and likely to be suspect from a liberal vantage. As indicated before, modern liberalism arose mainly as a reaction against caste and status hierarchies, against social and legal arrangements that defined rights and obligations differently for different groups. Hence, privileging equality over difference carried historically an emancipatory promise. In our time, however, this privilege has become dubious and has strongly been called into question by insurgent groups—for several reasons. In Young's account, there are three main aspects that render liberal difference blindness oppressive in its consequences. First, such blindness "disadvantages groups whose experience, culture and socialized capacities differ from those of privileged groups." Being wedded to the assimilationist goal, liberal policy aims to integrate all social groups and cultures into "mainstream" rules of conduct. In the pursuit of this policy, established or mainstream groups are able to define the rules and standards of this integrative process (and even to portray these rules as culturally neutral). Compelled to measure up to established standards, marginal or previously excluded groups inevitably are disadvantaged in the general competition (as is illustrated in the field of affirmative action).

Second, and as a corollary, difference blindness "allows groups to ignore their own group specificity" and thus promotes or perpetuates "cultural imperialism" by granting universal sway to the norms and standards of privileged or mainstream groups. Last, subordination of marginal or previously excluded groups to mainstream standards produces an internalization of cultural inferiority, that is, an "internalized devaluation by members of those groups themselves." Faced with established standards of conduct, Puerto Ricans or Asian Americans are prone to be "ashamed of their accents or their parents," just as African-American children come to despise their deprived neighborhoods and feminists "seek to root out their tendency to cry, or to feel compassion for a frustrated stranger." In light of these and related experiences, a politics of difference is liable to be liberating and empowering by reclaiming cultural identities or ways of life ostracized or marginalized by the dominant culture. To this extent, such a politics signals an advance over assimilationism, just as "radical democratic pluralism" moves beyond a pluralist liberalism which privatizes difference. In Iris Young's words:

> The vision of liberation as the transcendence of group difference seeks to abolish the public and political significance of group difference, while retaining and promoting both individual and group diversity in private, or nonpolitical, social contexts. . . . Radical democratic pluralism acknowledges and affirms the public and political significance of social group differences as a means of ensuring the participation and inclusion of everyone in social and political institutions.[11]

As one should note—and as Young repeatedly emphasizes—recognition of group differences in the public realm must not be confused with a return to social hierarchies or to invidious sorts of cultural prejudice and exclusivism. From the vantage of radical democracy, pluralist politics completely rejects the lure of "essentializing" cultural groups or of endowing them with invariant (empirical or cultural) traits. While traditional politics, in devaluing some people, assumed an "essentialist meaning of difference" and defined groups as having "different natures," Young notes, a democratic politics of difference construes difference "more fluidly and relationally as the product of social processes," that is, as the outgrowth of cultural practices in interaction with other practices. Seen in this light, democratic multiculturalism assigns to cultural difference a transitive, transformative, and emancipatory meaning rather than confining it to an "exclusionary" mode. In the latter mode, assertion of group distinctness implies the denial of other groups and thus obeys the antinomial frame of self versus other, thesis and negation.

As Young observes, the nondemocratic and "oppressive" meaning of difference signals an "absolute otherness, mutual exclusion, categorical opposition," thereby submitting difference to the "logic of identity" where the dominant group embodies the norm from which others deviate. Construed as categorical opposition, difference not only represses interactions between groups but also differences *within* groups; thus, in a curious reversal, difference as exclusion "actually denies difference." In contrast to this outcome, radical democratic pluralism adopts a flexible, open-ended stance; its understanding of group difference sees the latter as "indeed ambiguous, relational, shifting, without clear borders that keep people straight," as "entailing neither amorphous unity nor pure individuality." Most important, differential politics conceives difference neither in terms of passing individual interests nor under the rubric of timeless categories or attributes; instead, it focuses on the porous character of cultural traditions and on the "relations between groups" and between groups and public institutions. As Young comments, ably summarizing this part of her analysis:

> Difference now comes to mean not otherness, exclusive opposition, but specificity, variation, heterogeneity. Difference names relations of similarity and dissimilarity that can be reduced to neither coextensive identity nor nonoverlapping otherness. . . . Difference no longer implies that groups lie outside one another. To say that there are differences among groups does not imply that there are not overlapping experiences, or that two groups have nothing in common.[12]

II

In her study, Young discusses the implications of democratic difference chiefly with reference to salient issues in American domestic politics: specifically women's liberation, bilingual education, and native-American rights. In an epilogue, she suggests that arguments of her book might be extended to other societies and even to the international or global context, leaving the matter, however, to broad hints. As it happens, multicultural pressures are felt today in several industrial countries and—perhaps most acutely—in non-Western societies rent by the conflict between modernizing life styles and indigenous cultural traditions. Among industrial countries, a prominent example is Canada, marked by the rift between Anglophone and Francophone communities (not to mention the upsurge of native-American claims to autonomy).

Several aspects render the Canadian case noteworthy. One is the high political saliency of cultural pluralism and diversity. More than elsewhere (in the West), multiculturalism has been the topic of intense public and constitutional debates, which may have to do with the fact that Canada has never fully subscribed to the assimilationist or "melting-pot" ideal of its neighbor. In 1967, a Royal Commission on Bilingualism and Biculturalism (established a few years earlier) issued a report that focused attention both on rights of citizenship and on problems of cultural diversity. Largely in response to this report, the national government four years later announced an explicitly "multicultural" policy, which, while stressing equal rights of all Canadians, sought to protect the distinct life-forms or cultures of minorities. A similar outlook was embodied a decade later in the Canadian Charter of Rights and Freedoms which, while clearly centerstaging the liberal principle of equal individual freedom, also made reference to the "preservation and enhancement of the multicultural heritage of Canadians." Subsequent efforts to implement these provisions led to repeated clashes and attempts at compromise, so far without clear results.[13] Apart from political wrangles, another important feature of multiculturalism in Canada is the sustained attention it has received from top-rate intellectuals and social theorists, most prominently from Charles Taylor, one of Canada's leading philosophers.

Although often labeled a "communitarian" and hence accused of collectivist tendencies, Taylor's approach in *Multiculturalism: Examining the Politics of Recognition* is highly nuanced and circumspect. Like that of Iris Young, his argument completely sidesteps established school doctrines, especially the conundrums of individualism-collectivism. In his contribution to *Multiculturalism*—an essay titled "The

Politics of Recognition"—Taylor pays ample tribute to the liberal legacy of individual freedom enshrined in the idea of a general human "dignity." As he points out, the collapse of feudal regimes wedded to social hierarchy (governed by the principle of honor) gave way in modernity to the notion of 'dignity,' now used in "a universalist and egalitarian sense," where it refers to an "inherent dignity of human beings" or a "citizen dignity" uniformly shared by everyone. This notion was further deepened, but also complicated, by the postrevolutionary stress on a differentiated "identity," and particularly by the romantic idea of an inwardly constituted "authenticity" lending distinctiveness both to individuals and historically grown cultures.

As formulated by Herder and his heirs, the maxim of authentic identity centerstaged "originality" of life styles on two levels: that of the individual person among other persons, and that of a "culture-bearing people among other people." In their combination, the accents on dignity and individual authenticity were in danger of lapsing into a monological solipsism, a danger that was (or can be) averted only by the realization of the need for mutual recognition, a need deeply embedded in the experience of cultural life-forms. According to Taylor, individuals (even in modern societies) are able to become "full human agents" capable of self-understanding and of defining their identity only through dialogue or dialogical exchange, that is, through the employment of "rich human languages of expression." In earlier, more compact societies mutuality was directly built into the social fabric and hence could be taken for granted. This is no longer the case on the plane of inwardly derived, authentic life styles. In Taylor's words: "The development of an ideal of inwardly generated identity gives a new importance to recognition. . . . What has come about with the modern age is not the need for recognition but the conditions in which the attempt to be recognized can fail. That is why the need is now acknowledged for the first time."[14]

The sketched key notions of the modern era have spawned a complex and tensional legacy. In Taylor's presentation, modernity has given rise to two competing conceptions of public life: that of liberal universalism (anchored in rights) and that of cultural distinctiveness. With the move from feudal hierarchy to dignity, he writes, has come "a politics of universalism emphasizing the equal dignity of all citizens" and dedicated to the progressive "equalization of rights and entitlements." In modern (Western) democracies, the principle of "equal citizenship" and of growing equalization has become a central if not the chief governing maxim. On the other hand, the notion of 'authenticity' or 'authentic identity' has buttressed the emergence of a different conception: a "politics of difference" focused on individual and cultural distinctiveness. Thus, whereas the politics of universalism seeks to safeguard a general human sameness (termed "equal dignity"), the politics of difference insists on the need to recognize the "unique identity of this individual or group," their differentiation from everyone else.

By seeking to secure unique distinctness to everyone alike, the latter politics obviously harbors an inner paradox. Rigorously construed, Taylor notes, the politics of difference requires us to give general assent to what is not universal but particular. That is, it insists on paying homage to what is universally present—that everyone has an identity—"through recognizing what is peculiar to each." Hence, a universal demand here "powers an acknowledgment of specificity." The contrast between the two types of modern politics is obvious and quite naturally fuels tensions and mutual accusations. While the politics of dignity seeks to promote nondiscrimination among all citizens in a "difference-blind" manner, the politics of difference often redefines nondiscrimination as requiring differential treatment based on individual and cultural distinctness. The two modes of politics, Taylor states, hence

> come into conflict. For one, the principle of equal respect requires that we treat people in a difference-blind fashion. . . . For the other, we have to recognize and even foster particularity. The reproach the first makes to the second is just that it violates the principle of nondiscrimination. The reproach the second makes to the first is that it negates identity by forcing people into a homogeneous mold that is untrue to them.[15]

The reproach leveled by advocates of difference is actually not only directed at assimilation as such; its edge is sharpened by prevailing power differentials and the largely fictional character of liberal universalism. In light of existing political asymmetries, the supposed difference blindness of liberal politics appears often as a thin disguise of cultural dominance or imperialism, that is, as the motto of a "hegemonic culture" to which minority or suppressed cultures are required to adapt. Seen from this vantage, liberal universalism is liable to be charged with harboring a particularist bias, that is, with instantiating a "pragmatic contradiction: a particularism masquerading as the universal." To exemplify these problems more concretely, Taylor at this point turns to the situation in Canada, as it has emerged especially in the wake of the Canadian Charter of Rights and Freedoms and of the so-called Meech Lake accord (which aimed to recognize Quebec as a "distinct society").

As he points out, Canadian politics in our century—like Western politics in general—has been dominated by two conflicting conceptions of public life which have overshadowed the protracted constitutional debates of recent decades. In Taylor's interpretation, the Canadian charter basically centerstages individual rights and entitlements in a manner similar to the Bill of Rights of the American Constitution. To this extent, Canada like the rest of the Western world—and "perhaps the world as a whole"—is following the "American precedent" of a liberal, rights-based universalism. Relying on this aspect of the charter, opponents of the Meech Lake accord (with its promise of cultural distinctness) in essence sponsored the priority of rights over "goodness," that is, the principle that individual rights together with nondiscrimination provisions must always "take precedence over collective goals." Inspired by "profound philosophical assumptions" traceable to Kant, this conception of politics understands dignity to consist chiefly in human "autonomy," that is, in "the ability of each person to determine for himself or herself a view of the good life." Promoted "with great force and intelligence" by prominent thinkers in the United States, the postulate of self-determining individual autonomy forms the core of what Michael Sandel has called the "procedural republic" with its privileging of procedural rules (including judicial review) over substantive goals or shared forms of life.[16]

While appreciating its "profound" assumptions and also some of its concrete effects, Taylor does not ultimately subscribe to this procedural model. As he indicates, liberal universalism is not as innocently neutral or nondiscriminatory as it claims to be. In the Canadian case, application of proceduralism does not impartially enhance or cultivate a distinct Francophone culture but rather undercuts or demolishes the latter. Generally speaking, political society cannot remain "neutral" between those seeking to maintain cultural traditions and those wishing to "cut loose" to promote individual self-interest. To this extent, proceduralism can be charged with being "inhospitable to difference" (or at least reducing difference to private preference). For committed Quebeckers, what was at issue in constitutional debates was not only an individual right to bilingualism but the "survival and flourishing of French culture" seen as a shared "good" and its preservation for both present and future generations.

Pursuit of this goal, in Taylor's account, is not so much illiberal as inspired by a different conception of public life: a politics of difference. From the vantage of Quebeckers dedicated to cultural distinctness, public life can be organized "around a definition of the good life," without entailing a depreciation or disenfranchisement of dissenters or non-Francophone Canadians. What is involved or presupposed in this conception is a distinction between two levels of rights: a level of basic or "fundamental" rights construed along the lines of liberal universalism (and the Canadian charter), and a level of cultural rights or shared concerns which permit public regulation. Whereas the former requires uniform treatment and should "never be infringed," the latter allows for cultural diversity. On this view, Taylor notes, a society with shared or common goals can still be "liberal," provided it is also capable of "respecting diversity"—especially when dealing with dissenters—and of maintaining "adequate safeguards for fundamental rights." As is evident throughout, Taylor's own sympathies are with such a differential view of politics purged of regressive-collectivist traces. Properly construed, he adds, a politics of difference is

> willing to weigh the importance of certain forms of uniform treatment against the importance of cultural survival, and opt sometimes in favor of the latter. . . . Although I cannot argue it here, obviously I would endorse this kind of model. Indisputably, though, more and more societies today are turning out to be multicultural, in the sense of including more than one cultural community that wants to survive. The rigidities of procedural liberalism may rapidly become impractical in tomorrow's world.[17]

One should note that Taylor's endorsement of differential politics is qualified in several ways. Apart from insisting on basic liberal safeguards (on the level of fundamental rights), his essay also takes exception to an uncritical acceptance of all kinds of cultural diversity, something occasionally demanded by radical multiculturalists (including proponents of "subjectivist neo-Nietzschean" theories). In Taylor's view, uncritical acceptance of this sort is ultimately a form of condescension, because it does not derive from a "genuine act of respect." Moreover, not being based on concrete study and evaluation, bland acceptance does not actually challenge hegemonic beliefs or transgress familiar premises and hence turns out to be in fact ethnocentric. In his words, the peremptory demand for acceptance is "paradoxically—perhaps one should say tragically—homogenizing," for it implies that we "already have the standards" to make cross-cultural judgments. Thus, differential politics (in the sense of a laissez-faire multiculturalism) can "end up making everyone the same."

These comments are not meant to give comfort to the opposing camp bent on sanitizing Western culture against contamination with alien beliefs. Returning to the theme of mutual recognition, Taylor stresses the need for a critical dialogical interaction among cultures along Gadamerian lines. "What has to happen," he writes,

is what Gadamer has called a "fusion of horizons." We learn to
move in a broader horizon, within which what we have formerly
taken for granted as the background to valuation can be situated
as one possibility alongside the different background of the formerly unfamiliar culture. The "fusion of horizons" operates through
our developing new vocabularies of comparison, by means of
which we can articulate these contrasts.

From this perspective, the claim to attention and respect on the part
of other cultures operates in the form of a presumption—to the effect
that, having animated societies over long stretches of time, such cultures have presumably something to teach to the rest of the world. Although the presumption is not invulnerable, it cannot be dislodged
without close engagement and a serious effort at understanding. Phrased
differently, the presumption requires not a "peremptory" acceptance
of all cultural beliefs and practices but "a willingness to be open to
comparative cultural study of the kind that must displace our horizons
in the resulting fusions." Refusal of the presumption couched in these
terms can only proceed from cultural "arrogance, or some analogous
moral failing."[18]

III

The presumption stated by Taylor implies a readiness for cross-cultural engagement and certainly a rejection of any kind of Eurocentrism
or Western cultural imperialism. Seriously applied, the presumption
unhinges prevailing hegemonic relations, including the taken-for-
granted superiority of modern Western life styles. Although focused
on constitutional provisions and specific cultural demands, the debates in Canada brought to the fore some of the deeper—quasi-meta-
physical and existential—implications of contemporary multiculturalism. As it happens, Taylor was by no means the only prominent
intellectual to participate in these debates; his initiative was paralleled
by a host of other thinkers whose arguments further sharpened underlying issues.

    In comparison with Taylor's liberal-Hegelian leanings, some of these
thinkers were willing to tackle the status of Western modernity itself,
adopting for this purpose either non- or premodern or vaguely postmodern sources of inspiration. Particularly noteworthy in this regard
is philosopher George Parkin Grant, whose work for some time had
called into question the progressive sway of liberal proceduralism. As
he pointed out in *English-Speaking Justice* (1974), the liberal infatuation with rights and procedures was liable to obscure broader meta-

physical or postmetaphysical questions about the "good life," especially the questions of what rights are good for or of the "goodness" of justice itself. Such questions had been part and parcel of public ethics in classical or traditional philosophy; eclipsed in our time, they were bound to surface again in an age saturated with "English-speaking" conceptions of rights and individual self-interest. Although banished from official discourse, philosophical thinking could not avoid raising again issues such as: "What is it about human beings that makes liberty and equality their due?" and "Why is justice 'our good' even when it is not convenient?" The inability or unwillingness of proceduralism even to address these issues, in Grant's view, was part of the "terrifying darkness which has fallen upon modern justice."[19]

The implications of these issues for Canada in general and Quebec in particular were discussed by Grant in a number of writings, particularly in his somewhat melancholy *Lament for a Nation* (1965). According to Grant, the basic difference between Canada and the United States resided in the former's conservative bent, that is, in Canada's greater attachment to historical contexts and cultural traditions. What distinguished Quebec in the Canadian setting was the particular intensity of cultural loyalty, that is, the determination of Quebeckers to hold on to "the roots of their civilization through their church and city—which more than any in the West held a high vision of the eternal." As Grant was well aware, of course, this loyalty was now under siege, given the steady inroads of modern individualism and proceduralism. Although entailing (or promising) the advantages of greater personal freedom, these benefits were bought at the price of cultural defoliation—particularly the denuding of public ethical life in favor of technological progress and the instrumental pursuit of self-interest.

In light of this defoliation, the "vaunted freedom of the individual to choose" was in danger of collapsing either into the necessity of "finding one's role in the public engineering" or the compulsion of "retreating into the privacy of pleasure." Under liberal auspices, moreover, pursuit of self-interest was conceived as a universal principle which, "inhospitable to difference" (in Taylor's phrase), was bound to erode the distinction not only between Quebec and the rest of Canada but between Canada and the United States; for rules of efficient conduct "must after all be the same in Chicago, Hamilton, and Düsseldorf." Despite overtones of premodern nostalgia, what rendered Grant's argument in *Lament for a Nation* loosely postmodern (at least in a Heideggerian sense) was his association of liberal modernity with the spirit of technology construed as the underlying "metaphysic of the age." However, a still more overt postmodern edge can be found in his accent on cultural resistance to visions of cultural hegemony: under the

impact of the relentless and near-inescapable ascent of liberal universalism, the only option left for dissident or marginalized cultures
(such as Francophone Quebec) was to embark on a policy of resistance, in an effort to deflect at least the most blatant forms of assimilation and cultural uniformity.[20]

Having reviewed prominent strands in the Canadian discussions,
let me turn finally to the broader global implications of contemporary
multiculturalism, that is, to the tension between liberal-Western universalism and cultural loyalties in a worldwide setting. The tension is
clearly evident in many of the (so-called) developing societies where
"nation-building" along Western lines has led to the juxtaposition of
two highly diverse, nearly incompatible life styles and political discourses: on the one hand, secularism, legal proceduralism, and individual rights; on the other hand, the complex fabric of vernacular traditions and indigenous cultural beliefs. The abruptness of the juxtaposition
accounts in good measure for the volatile, near-explosive character of
political conditions in large parts of the Near East and Asia.

In the Near East, a central issue is the confrontation or accommodation between secular constitutionalism and Islamic notions of theo-
cratic government and divinely sanctioned law; in parts of Asia, sec-
ular-liberal politics collides with Hindu visions of *ramarajya* or else
with political demands grounded in Buddhist, Confucianist, or Shinto
beliefs. Under provocation, the unsteady mix of life-forms and discourses can readily tilt in one or the other direction, although political contexts constrain the available range of options. Given Western
global hegemony in economic, military, and scientific domains, long-
range trends augur ill for the maintenance of indigenous practices or
vernacular narratives. To grasp the effects of prolonged cultural imposition, one does not have to venture far afield. A telling case is the
fate and present condition of the "forgotten minority," that is, the native-American communities in North America, particularly in the United
States. With some adjustments, a similar story can be told about (postindependence) developments in Central and South America, where the
rhetoric of liberal proceduralism (with an accent on property rights)
has often been used to erode, disaggregate, and even destroy native
communities.[21]

The fate of native Americans provides a sobering reminder of the
downside of modern universalism, a reminder that offers no vindication for xenophobia or ethnic self-seclusion. No doubt, the hazards of
our age are immense on all sides and can only be met if responses rise
to the level of contemporary challenges. Our time is urgently in need
of political imagination and a readiness for experimentation (qualities
that often are in short supply). Clearly, to avoid the pitfalls of com-

munalism as well as universalist assimilation, new paths need to be explored on the levels both of institutional arrangements and of political reflection. With regard to public institutions, proponents of liberal individualism sometimes assert the superior and indeed incorrigible or irreplaceable character of existing Western structures and procedures, an assertion that neglects the variety among Western regimes as well as the long period of experimentation preceding prevailing arrangements. In a democratic setting hostile both to ethnocentrism and to universalist leveling, cultivation of diversity cannot rely solely on existing procedural safeguards, although the latter must not lightly be discarded.

More than ever in politics, democratic multiculturalism provides the opportunity and the need for institutional inventiveness and flexibility. Jean Cohen has correctly noted, "Different models of democracy are compatible with the principle of democratic legitimacy." Among the diverse possibilities of institutionalizing or giving public recognition to cultural diversity, attention might be given—and is sometimes in the literature—to such institutional devices as the extension of individual rights to group or collective rights (especially rights of ethnic and cultural minorities); the establishment of "ethnic federalism," that is, a regime that grants a degree of autonomy and self-government to ethnic groups within a broader constitutional framework; the promotion of "consociational" policies (in Arend Lijphart's sense) involving the consensual or agonal interaction between group leaders in multiethnic societies; and finally the diversification of parliamentary government through novel forms of bicameralism (or multicameralism) allowing representation of different constituencies. None of these devices is free of problems; hence, all need to be carefully screened and calibrated to insure the democratic character of multiculturalism.[22]

On the plane of theoretical reflection, multicultural politics forces a reconsideration of many issues that were presumed to be settled under Enlightenment or post-Enlightenment auspices. In important ways, this reconsideration inserts itself into the contemporary questioning of the status of "modernity" (which has no truck with a facile antimodernism). One way to approach these issues is by returning to Tzvetan Todorov, and especially to his differentiation between two chief modes of communication. As will be recalled, Todorov's *Conquest of America* distinguishes between human and world communication: the former intersubjective and horizontal in character and privileged by the conquistadors, the latter holistic and vertical and favored by the Aztec culture. As will also be remembered, Todorov sees a tragic trade-off at work in the European conquest, in the sense that the

victory of interhuman communication was already "big with its defeat" in terms of the atrophy of world communication or the ability to
relate to nature and the "religious universe." This trade-off in a nut-
shell captures crucial features of modern Western history.

Ever since the rise of contractarian theories in early modernity, interhuman (or subject-subject) communication has been at the heart of
Western conceptions of social and political life, while "world" has
been progressively distanced into a target of objective-scientific analysis. To be sure, the manner of conceptualization has been progressively refined during recent centuries, though without changing the
basic direction. Thus, contractarian assumptions still surface in a new
guise (prompted by the "linguistic turn") in contemporary versions of
"speech-act" theory and especially in the model of communicative rationality and "communicative action" (formulated by Habermas). In
tune with modern rationalist accents, communicative action theory
clearly privileges interhuman speech or discourse, while adopting an
"objectifying" attitude toward nature (and an aesthetic attitude toward
the self). To this extent, the theory cannot claim to be comprehensive
or to offer a universally applicable account of language and of the
range of communicative relations. As Alessandro Ferrara has noted,
the conception of communicative rationality and of a consensus among
equal partners "presupposes a *modern* frame of reference. It would
make no sense to speak of rational agreement on the soundness of a
validity claim within a tradition-oriented culture. Furthermore, the distinction of three kinds of validity claims presupposes the differentiation of objective, social, and subjective worlds—a differentiation which
takes place only with modernity."[23]

Although prominent (and valuable in many respects), the primacy
accorded to interhuman communication today is no longer unequiv-
ocal or undisputed; as it happens, several intellectual developments
are afoot aiming at a retrieval of the world dimension. Particularly
noteworthy in this respect is Husserl's turn to the "life world" and (still
more important) Heidegger's insistence on the worldliness of human
life and his portrayal of human *Dasein* as a "being-in-the-world," that
is, as a creature intimately enmeshed in a complex, multifaceted context. As one should note, the term *world* for Heidegger does not signify an external container (a *res extensa*) amenable to objectifying
analysis, but rather a constitutive feature of *Dasein* itself—the latter
no longer seen as a subjective ego but as a participant embroiled in
the ongoing happening or disclosure of "being." Without neglecting
interhuman speech or discourse (on the level of human co-being or
Mitsein), world relations in this framework extend to a nonobjectify-
ing engagement with nature as well as an attuned sensitivity to the

"call of conscience" (as *vox Dei),* that is, to a multilayered fabric of experiences (with "being" simultaneously disclosing and concealing itself in all these dimensions).

World communication in this sense was further developed and fleshed out in Heidegger's later reflections on language, where language is seen no longer as a mere means of human communication but as an inexhaustible reservoir or endowment allowing human thought and speech to proceed in the first place. As we read in Heidegger's "Language," if attention is fastened on speech acts seen as outgrowth of human intentions or designs, then language "can never appear as anything but a mode of expression or human activity"; however, speaking—including interhuman speech—is "not self-subsistent" but is embedded in, and arises out of, "the speaking of language itself." For Heidegger, this speaking of language establishes a primordial space for world communication or world experience, a space making room for the interactive entwinement of human life and nature, and of human finitude and the divine. A similar view of language is developed in the conclusion of *Truth and Method* where Gadamer comments on the "speculative" quality of language, that is, its character as an image or mirror of world relations (in a holistic sense). Language is speculative, he writes, "in that the finite possibilities of a word are linked with the intended sense in a direction toward the infinite"; for to speak means "to correlate what is said with an infinity of the unsaid in a comprehensive nexus of meaning that alone grants understanding.[24]

These considerations clearly have a bearing on multiculturalism, given that cultures are life-forms or forms of world-communion where meaning is structured along horizontal as well as vertical-holistic lines. What additionally needs to be taken into account here is the close linkage between cultures and vernacular or indigenous languages, a linkage that resists streamlining under the auspices of universalist discourses. At this point concerns are likely to be voiced again regarding communalism or ethnocentric myopia, concerns that are not spurious given the widespread upsurge of ethnic antagonisms and violence in our time. As will be remembered, liberal universalism arose precisely as a corrective to feudal parochialism and to the proliferation of status distinctions in feudal society. To this extent, liberalism heralded an emancipation from parochial bondage and from the fetters of social inequality; in Kant's celebrated phrase, Enlightenment signaled a release from external tutelage and an ascent to the level of a self-governing maturity. Yet, there are reasons to believe that our age holds out the challenge of a new and different kind of maturity, one where freedom is willing to recognize and cultivate cultural diversity (without restoring invidious hierarchies).

What has been called "lateral universalism" may precisely be a corollary of this mature stance where universal principles are no longer found beyond concrete differences but in the heart of the local or particular itself, that is, in the distinct topography of the world. This view resonates with another aspect of Heidegger's later work: his accent on the "four-fold" topology of being, that is, the capacity of every individual thing to gather in itself all the constitutive dimensions of the world. This conception, in turn, resonates with a view prominent in Asian thought, that of the "suchness" of all beings as an emblem not of self-centered seclusion but of an in-gathering hospitable to all other beings. In the context of Zen Buddhism, Keiji Nishitani elucidates suchness with the help of the (medieval) notion of "circuminsession," stating that, by virtue of this circuminsessional relation, every individual being is the ground of all others and that hence all things "are gathered together and as such render possible an order of being, a 'world.'" A similar outlook is expressed by Lao Tzu in the *Tao Te Ching,* in a passage which is sometimes (wrongly) interpreted in terms of a narrow parochialism:

> There is no need to run outside
> For better seeing,
> Nor to peer from a window. Rather abide
> At the heart of your being.[25]

NOTES

Introduction

1. Thomas Pantham, "Some Dimensions of the Universality of Philosophical Hermeneutics: A Conversation with Hans-Georg Gadamer," *Journal of Indian Council of Philosophical Research* 9 (1992): 132.

2. See Hans-Georg Gadamer, *Heideggers Wege: Studien zum Spätwerk* (Tübingen: Mohr, 1983), especially 17; also his *Das Erbe Europas* (Frankfurt-Main: Suhrkamp, 1989). Based on a personal communication, Graham Parkes reports Gadamer as saying in 1985 that "Heidegger studies would do well to pursue seriously comparisons of his work with Asian philosophies." See Parkes, ed., *Heidegger and Asian Thought* (Honolulu: University of Hawaii Press, 1987), 5.

3. See Otto Pöggeler, "West-East Dialogue: Heidegger and Lao-tzu," and Paul Shih-yi Hsiao, "Heidegger and Our Translation of the *Tao Te Ching*," in Parkes, ed., *Heidegger and Asian Thought*, 47–78, 93–103.

4. For some of the historical background, see Parkes, "Introduction," in *Heidegger and Asian Thought*, 5–7. See also Martin Heidegger, "Zur Seinsfrage," in *Wegmarken* (Frankfurt-Main: Klostermann, 1967), 217–18; trans. William Kluback and Jean T. Wilde as *The Question of Being* (New York: Twayne, 1958), 106–7. The 1969 address by Koichi Tsujimura, "Martin Heideggers Denken und die Japanische Philosophie," can be found in *Japan und Heidegger, Gedenkschrift der Stadt Messkirch zum 100. Geburtstag Martin Heideggers* (Sigmaringen: Thorbecke Verlag, 1989), 159–65.

5. Heidegger, *What Is Called Thinking?* trans. J. Glenn Gray (New York: Harper & Row, 1968), 52. The reference is to a letter fragment which Friedrich Nietzsche sent to Georg Brandes on January 4, 1889.

6. Jacques Derrida, *The Other Heading: Reflections on Today's Europe,* trans. Pascale-Anne Brault and Michael B. Naas (Bloomington: Indiana University Press, 1992), 24, 29, 38–39. Derrida's philosophical work has repeatedly served as a springboard for comparisons of Western and Eastern thought; compare, e.g., Robert Magliola, *Derrida on the Mend* (West Lafayette, Ind.: Purdue University Press, 1984); Harold Coward, *Derrida and Indian Philosophy* (Albany: State University of New York Press, 1990); Harold Coward and Toby Foshay, eds., *Derrida and Negative Theology* (Albany: State University of New York Press, 1992).

7. Edward W. Said, *Orientalism* (New York: Vintage Books, 1979), 1–3.

8. Ibid., 41, 203–4.

9. Ibid., 5, 24, 71. For references to a "real" or "true" Orient compare also 21–22, 67, 203. These references are offset, however, by this passage (322):

> It is not the thesis of this book to suggest that there is such a thing as a real or true Orient (Islam, Arab, or whatever); nor is it to make an assertion about the necessary privilege of an 'insider' perspective over an 'outsider' one. . . . On the contrary, I have been arguing that 'the Orient' is itself a constituted entity, and that the notion that there are geographical spaces with indigenous, radically 'different' inhabitants . . . is equally a highly debatable idea."

Regarding a move beyond the noted polarity, compare also this passage (326): "I would not have undertaken a book of this sort if I did not also believe that there is scholarship that is not as corrupt, or at least as blind to human reality, as the kind I have been mainly depicting. Today there are many individual scholars working in such fields as Islamic history, religion, civilization, sociology, and anthropology whose production is deeply valuable as scholarship." Said referred approvingly especially to the work of Clifford Geertz.

10. See, for example, the chapter "Knowledge and Interpretation" in Said, *Covering Islam: How the Media and the Experts Determine How We See the Rest of the World* (New York: Pantheon Books, 1981). There, Said notes (155): "We can say tentatively that knowledge of another culture is possible, if two conditions are fulfilled. . . . One, the student must feel that he or she is answerable to and in uncoercive contact with the culture and the people being studied. . . . The second condition complements and fulfills the first. Knowledge of the social world, as opposed to knowledge of nature, is at bottom what I have been calling interpretation." In this context Said refers approvingly to Gadamerian hermeneutics (157).

11. As he wrote at one point: "No facile compromise or reconciliation, miscalled 'synthesis,' but a relentless exposure to the tension between the scientific consciousness [of the West] and the legacy of the past is the way we can learn to address the right questions to our religious tradition and be rewarded by the answers truly adequate to our present situation." See J. L. Mehta, "Problems of Inter-Cultural Understanding in University Studies of Religion," in *India and the West: The Problem of Understanding* (Chico, Calif.: Scholars Press, 1985), 125.

12. See Pantham, "Some Dimensions of the Universality of Philosophical Hermeneutics," 131–33; and Mehta, "The Will to Interpret and India's Dreaming Spirit," in *India and the West*, 199–200. Speaking on behalf of the non-Western intellectual, Mehta asks in another essay:

> Can we simply turn our backs on our own past, just discard it, and appropriate the final fruits of Western self-understanding as *the* inner telos of man universally and as such, or shall we reject the spiritual-philosophical endeavor of the West altogether as of no consequence and seek to entrench ourselves into a specifically Indian philosophizing, in the language of the past and supposedly undistorted by the alien world of meanings embodied in the English language we employ for the purpose? Or shall we begin to *understand* both in their mutual otherness, to learn the language of each and so to evolve ways of thinking and talking which will be truly appropriate to our membership of both worlds? ("Understanding and Tradition," in *India and the West*, 159)

Compare also his essay "'World Civilization': The Possibility of Dialogue," in Mehta, *Philosophy and Religion: Essays in Interpretation* (New Delhi: Manoharlal Publishers, 1990), 33–48.

Chapter 1. Modes of Cross-Cultural Encounter

1. See Tzvetan Todorov, *The Conquest of America: The Question of the Other,* trans. Richard Howard (New York: Harper & Row, 1984), 133–37. As Todorov writes (133): "If the word genocide has ever been applied to a situation with some accuracy, this is here the case. It constitutes a record not only in relative terms (a destruction on the order of 90 percent or more), but also in absolute terms, since we are speaking of a population diminution estimated at 70 million human lives." Regarding Columbus's voyage and its effects, compare also Djelal Kadir, *Columbus and the Ends of the Earth: Europe's Prophetic Rhetoric as Conquering Ideology* (Berkeley: University of California Press, 1992); John Dyson, *Columbus—for Gold, God, and Glory* (New York: Simon & Schuster, 1991); Zvi Dov-Ner, *Columbus and the Age of Discovery* (New York: Morrow, 1991); and Stephen Greenblatt, *Marvelous Possessions: The Wonder of the New World* (Chicago: University of Chicago Press, 1991).

2. The standard of mutual recognition derives from Hegel, especially from his account of the "struggle for recognition" as presented in his *Phenomenology;* see G. W. F. Hegel, *Phenomenology of Mind,* trans. J. B. Ballie (New York: Harper & Row, 1967), 228–40. Regarding

"emancipatory care" and "letting be" see Martin Heidegger, *Sein und Zeit* (11th ed.; Tübingen: Niemeyer, 1967), par. 26, 121–22. Compare also Stephen K. White, *Political Theory and Postmodernism* (Cambridge: Cambridge University Press, 1991), 55–74.

3. George M. Foster, *Culture and Conquest: America's Spanish Heritage* (Chicago: Quadrangle Books, 1967), 10–14. He adds the following (15–16):

> The same type of simplification or "stripping down" of Spanish culture is apparent in political and economic planning. It was possible to draw up for Spanish America what the rulers thought to be an ideal Spanish political and economic system, one which could disregard the rights and privileges acquired over the years in Spain by individual cities or groups or social classes. New World forms could be modeled after those thought to be the best or most useful, and forms which bothered the central government could be largely ignored.

4. Todorov, *The Conquest of America,* 248. As he continues somewhat pointedly: "Egalitarianism, of which one version is characteristic of the (Western) Christian religion as well as of the ideology of modern capitalist states, also serves colonial expansion: here is another, somewhat surprising lesson of our exemplary history." On the conquest of Mexico and Peru see Eric Wolf, *Sons of the Shaking Earth* (Chicago: University of Chicago Press, 1962), and William H. Prescott, *The Conquest of Peru* (New York: Mentor Books, 1961).

5. Todorov, *The Conquest of America,* 30, 42–43.

6. Ibid., 127, 132, 145 (in the above I have corrected for gender bias). As Todorov adds, somberly reflecting on the future of European colonialism (145):

> Far from the central government, far from royal law, all inhibitions give way, the social link, already loosened, snaps, revealing not a primitive nature, the beast sleeping in each of us, but a modern being, one with a great future in fact, restrained by no morality and inflicting death because and when he pleases. The "barbarity" of the Spaniards has nothing atavistic or bestial about it; it is quite human and heralds the advent of modern times.

7. *The Conquest of America,* 175.

8. John Leddy Phelan, *The Hispanization of the Philippines: Spanish Aims and Filipino Responses, 1565–1700* (Madison: University of Wisconsin Press, 1959), 4–9, 136.

9. Todorov points to the curious historical coincidence that Columbus's voyage took place in the same year in which the Muslims (Moors)—as well as the Jews—were finally expelled from Spain. "The year 1492," he writes, "already symbolizes, in the history of Spain, this double movement: in this same year the country repudiates its interior Other by triumphing over the Moors in the final battle of Granada and by forcing the Jews to leave its territory; and it discovers the exterior Other, that whole America which will become Latin" *(The Conquest of America,* 50).

10. Compare William W. Cash, *The Expansion of Islam* (London: Edinburgh House Press, 1928); Bernard Lewis, *The Arabs in History* (4th ed.; New York: Harper & Row, 1966); Hamilton A. R. Gibb, *Studies in the Civilization of Islam* (Princeton: Princeton University Press, 1982).

11. See Bernardino de Sahagún, *Historia general de las cosas de Nueva España* (Mexico City: Porrua, 1956), vol. 3 "Prologue." The passage is cited in Todorov, *The Conquest of America,* 222. Compare also St. Augustine, *The City of God,* ed. Vernon J. Bourke (Garden City: Doubleday, 1958), books 1, 2, 6, 7, pp. 39–77, 119–43. On *chresis* or *usus justus* as practiced by the early Christian church, see Paul Hacker, "The Christian Attitude Toward Non-Christian Religions," *Zeitschrift für Missionswissenschaft und Religionswissenschaft* 55 (1971): 81–97.

12. The above citations are all taken from Todorov, *The Conquest of America,* 43. Apart from journal entries, Todorov himself quotes from *The Life of the Admiral Christopher Columbus* (New Brunswick, N.J.: Rutgers University Press, 1959), 26, 62.

13. Todorov, *The Conquest of America,* 151–53, 160, 168, 171. The passages from Sepúlveda are taken from his *Democrates secundo: De las justas causas de la guerra contra los Indios* (Madrid: Instituto F. de Vitoria, 1951), 20, 33. For the rejoinder of Las Casas, see his *In Defense of the Indians,* trans. Stafford Poole (De Kalb: Northwestern Illinois University Press, 1974), 40. Compare also Las Casas, *The Tears of the Indians,* trans. John Phillips (first published in 1656; new ed., New York: Oriole Chapbooks, 1972). The translation by John Phillips was originally dedicated to Oliver Cromwell as an inducement to military action against Spain and against Spanish supremacy in the New World. Actually, Cromwell needed little coaxing as he had already sent out an expedition two years earlier to attack the Spanish possessions in the West Indies. How far Cromwell himself was from the Spanish conquistadores can be gauged from the savagery he committed against his non-Puritan countrymen, against the Catholics in Ireland, and against the generals of the failed expedition against Spain (who, on their return, were thrown into the Tower of London).

14. Lloyd and Susanne Rudolph, *The Modernity of Tradition* (Chicago: University of Chicago Press, 1967), 119–20, 137–38. The more recent conversions in Tamil Nadu and elsewhere are discussed—usually from a narrowly Hindu point of view—in Devendra Swarup, ed., *Politics of Conversion* (Delhi: Deendayal Research Institute, 1986).

15. Crawford Young, *The Politics of Cultural Pluralism* (Madison: University of Wisconsin Press, 1976), 71. Compare Rupert Emerson, *From Empire to Nation* (Cambridge, Mass.: Harvard University Press, 1960), 95–96; Ronald Cohen and John Middleton, *From Tribe to Nation in Africa* (Scranton, Pa.: Chandler Publishing Co., 1970); and Partha Chatterjee, *Nationalist Thought and the Colonial World* (Delhi: Oxford University Press, 1987). The definition of the term *assimilation* is cited in Milton M. Gordon, *Assimilation in American Life* (New York: Oxford University Press, 1964), 62, and in Crawford Young, *The Politics of Cultural Pluralism,* 15–16. See also Edward H. Spicer, "Acculturation," *International Encyclopedia of the Social Sciences* (New York: Crowell, Collier and Macmillan, 1968), 1: 21–25.

16. See Nathan Glazer and Daniel P. Moynihan, *Beyond the Melting Pot* (Cambridge, Mass.: Harvard University Press, 1963), v; Milton M. Gordon, *Assimilation in American Life,* 159; and Michael Novak, *The Rise of the Unmeltable Ethnics* (New York: Macmillan, 1971). Regarding cultural pluralism, see M. G. Smith, "Social and Cultural Pluralism," in Vera Rubin, ed., *Social and Cultural Pluralism in the Caribbean* (Annals of the New York Academy of Sciences no. 83, January 1960), 763–77; and regarding a confederation of cultures, see Horace M. Kallen, *Culture and Democracy in the United States* (New York: Boni and Liveright, 1924). Assimilation in Israel is discussed in S. N. Eisenstadt, Rivkah Bar-Yosef, and Chaim Adler, *Integration and Development in Israel* (New York: Praeger, 1970), and Judith T. Shuval, *Immigrants on the Threshold* (New York: Macmillan, 1968). Regarding the Israeli-Palestinian conflict, compare, e.g., Deborah J. Gerner, *One Land, Two Peoples* (Boulder, Colo.: Westview Press, 1991), and Haim Gordon and Rivka Gordon, eds., *Israel/Palestine: The Quest for Dialogue* (New York: Orbis Books, 1991).

17. It is under these rubrics of "integration and cultural pluralism" that Crawford Young discusses the political and cultural history of the Philippines; see *The Politics of Cultural Pluralism,* 327–67. For his comments on postindependence Latin America, see 85, and for a discussion of the process of "mestization" 436–38, 440–42. For recent challenges to the melting-pot model in Latin America, see Rodolfo Stavenhagen, *Problemas étnicos y campesinos* (Mexico: Institute Nacional Indigenista, 1979); Guillermo Bonfil Batalla, *Mexico Profundo: Una Civilización negada* (Mexico: Grijalbo, 1989); and Denis Goulet,

Mexico: Development Strategies for the Future (Notre Dame: University of Notre Dame Press, 1983), 50–56.

18. Crawford Young, *The Politics of Cultural Pluralism,* 101–3, 107–8. See also Lloyd and Susanne Rudolph, *The Modernity of Tradition,* 36–49; M. N. Srinivas, *Caste in Modern India and Other Essays* (Bombay: Asia Publishing House, 1962); and Harold A. Gould, *Caste Adaptation in Modernizing Indian Society* (Delhi: Chanakya Publications, 1988), esp. ch. 7, 143–55 ("Sanskritization and Westernization").

19. Paul Vinogradoff, *Roman Law in Medieval Europe* (2nd ed.; Oxford: Clarendon Press, 1929), 142. Vinogradoff also points to the underlying social-economic motives of the reception (143–44):

> Coming, as it did, from an age of highly developed social intercourse, Roman law satisfied in many respects the requirements of *economic* development. . . . And when the elaboration of [traditional] common law became a social necessity, the Roman system grew to be a force not only in the schools, but also in the courts. Altogether, the history of Roman law during the Middle Ages testifies to the latent vigor and organizing power of ideas in the midst of shifting surroundings.

Regarding the origins of Greek culture, compare Martin Bernal, *Black Athena: The Afroasiatic Roots of Classical Civilization* (New Brunswick, N.J.: Rutgers University Press, 1987). Regarding the syncretism of the Hellenistic period, see William W. Tarn, *Hellenistic Civilization* (London: Arnold & Co., 1927), and Moses Hadas, *Hellenistic Culture: Fusion and Diffusion* (New York: Columbia University Press, 1959).

20. Regarding Marco Polo's journey, see, e.g., *The Travels of Marco Polo,* trans. Aldo Ricci (London: Routledge & Kegan Paul, 1950), and Henry H. Hart, *Marco Polo: Venetian Adventurer* (Norman: University of Oklahoma Press, 1967). For the cultivation of Chinese tastes in prerevolutionary France, see David Maland, *Culture and Society in Seventeenth-Century France* (New York: Scribner, 1970), and Peter France, *Politeness and Its Discontents: Problems in French Classical Culture* (Cambridge: Cambridge University Press, 1992). Cultural borrowing in the form of *chinoiserie* was rudely transformed into military conquest and colonization during the nineteenth century as a result of the industrial revolution and its insatiable demand for overseas markets. One cannot bypass here in silence the ignominious story of the forced "unequal treaties" and of the later Opium War (whereby Western colonial powers sought to foist the consumption of opium on the Chinese people).

21. Heinrich Dumoulin, *Zen Buddhism: A History,* vol. I: *India and China,* trans. James W. Heisig and Paul Kittner (New York: Macmillan, 1988), 64–65, 68. As Dumoulin adds (67–68):

> During this period of assimilation there was a steady progress in the adaptation of Buddhist doctrine to Chinese forms of thought, or in the integration of the Chinese way of thinking into the Buddhist religion. Buddhist notions like *prajña, tathata* ("thusness"), and *bodhi* ("enlightenment") were sinicized, while Mahayana took on the typically Chinese notion of *wu-wei* ("nonaction"). But the deepest roots of this remarkable inner affinity between the basic ideas of Buddhism and Taoism suggest a naturalistic view of the world and of human life that inspires the Mahayana sutras as well as Chuang-tzu, Lao-tzu and other Chinese thinkers.

Compare also Erik Zürcher, *The Buddhist Conquest of China,* 2 vols. (Leiden: Brill, 1959); Kenneth Ch'en, *Buddhism in China: A Historical Survey* (Princeton: Princeton University Press, 1964); and R. H. Robinson, *Early Madhyamika in India and China* (Madison: University of Wisconsin Press, 1967).

22. Dumoulin, *Zen Buddhism,* 64, 68–69, 86–84.

23. Edwin O. Reischauer, *Ennin's Travels in T'ang China* (New York: Ronald Press Co., 1955), vii–viii, 3–4. See also *Ennin's Diary: The Record of a Pilgrimage to China in Search of the Law,* trans. Edwin O. Reischauer (New York: Ronald Press Co., 1955). Among remarkable cross-cultural journeys one should also not forget the travels of the Muslim Ibn Battuta who between 1325 and 1349 traveled from Tangier to Mecca and through the Near East to India and China; see Ross E. Dunn, *The Adventures of Ibn Battuta: A Muslim Traveler of the 14th Century* (Berkeley: University of California Press, 1986).

24. See John Rawls, *A Theory of Justice* (Cambridge, Mass.: Harvard University Press, 1971), 60–65, 126–27; "Kantian Construction in Moral Theory," *Journal of Philosophy* 77 (1980): 536; Ronald Dworkin, *Taking Rights Seriously* (rev. ed.; Cambridge, Mass.: Harvard University Press, 1978), 272–73; "Liberalism," in Stuart Hampshire, ed., *Public and Private Morality* (Cambridge: Cambridge University Press, 1978), 127; and Bruce Ackerman, *Social Justice and the Liberal State* (New Haven: Yale University Press, 1980), 11. There are, of course, significant differences between these liberal thinkers regarding the role of neutrality and public ethics, differences which have been accentuated by Rawls's turn to "political liberalism." On these differences, compare Chantal Mouffe, *The Return of the Political* (London: Verso, 1993), 102–8. Although insisting on a more argumentative or "communica-

tive" approach, Jürgen Habermas's ethical theory shares many of the assumptions of procedural liberalism, especially the primacy of (procedural) justice or "rightness" over "goodness"; see his *Moral Consciousness and Communicative Action,* trans. Christian Lenhardt and Shierry Weber Nicholson (Cambridge, Mass.: MIT Press, 1990), esp. 98–106, and for a critique my "Kant and Critical Theory," in *Life-World, Modernity, and Critique* (Cambridge: Polity Press, 1991), 105–31.

25. See William E. Connolly, *Identity/Difference: Democratic Negotiations of Political Paradox* (Ithaca, N.Y.: Cornell University Press, 1991), 160–61; Michael J. Perry, *Morality, Politics, and Law: A Bicentennial Essay* (New York: Oxford University Press, 1988), 4, 57–73. In his conclusion (184), Perry endorses an ethical outlook inspired by what Hilary Putnam has called "Jerusalem-based religions," but whose "heart" is curiously rooted "in certain Indic spiritualities (for example, in Hindu Vedanta and in Mahayana Buddhism) as well as in the semitic religions." Compare Putnam, *The Many Faces of Realism* (LaSalle, Ill.: Open Court, 1987), 60. For a critique of Rawlsian proceduralism akin to Connolly's but more fully developed, see Iris Marion Young, *Justice and the Politics of Difference* (Princeton: Princeton University Press, 1990), 4–5, 15–38.

26. Ashis Nandy, "The Politics of Secularism and the Recovery of Religious Tolerance," *Alternatives* 13 (1988): 189. As Nandy adds (185):

> To many Indians today, secularism comes as a part of a larger package consisting of a set of standardized ideological products and social processes—development, mega-science and national security being some of the most prominent among them. This package often plays the same role vis-à-vis the people of the society—sanctioning or justifying violence against the weak and the dissenting—that the church, the *ulema,* the *sangha,* or the Brahmans played in earlier times.

Compare also A. R. Desai, *State and Society in India: Essays in Dissent* (Bombay: Popular Prakashan, 1974), and Manoranjan Mohanty, "Secularism: Hegemonic and Democratic," *Perspectives* (June 3, 1989): 1219–20.

27. Niccolo Machiavelli, "Discourses on the First Ten Books of Titus Livius," ch. 4, in *The Prince and the Discourses* (New York: Modern Library, 1950), 119. Compare also Thomas Hobbes, *Leviathan* (New York: Dutton, 1953), chs. 13, 17–18, pp. 63–66, 87–96; and John Rawls, "Kantian Constructivism in Ethical Theory," 539, 542.

28. See Machiavelli, *The Prince and the Discourses,* 119; "The Communist Manifesto" in Robert C. Tucker, ed., *The Marx-Engels Reader* (New York: Norton & Co., 1972), 336, 338–40, 344–45. In extolling industrialization, the *Manifesto* was blunt regarding the relations between advanced Western societies and third world countries (339): "The bourgeoisie has subjected the country to the rule of the towns. . . . Just as it has made the country dependent on the towns, so it has made barbarian and semi-barbarian countries dependent on the civilized ones, nations of peasants on nations of bourgeois, the East on the West."

29. See Jean-Paul Sartre, *Being and Nothingness: An Essay on Phenomenological Ontology,* trans. Hazel E. Barnes (New York: Philosophical Library, 1956), 258, 260–63, 287–89, 296–97, 364; and Jean-François Lyotard, *The Postmodern Condition: A Report on Knowledge,* trans. Geoff Bennington and Brian Massumi (Minneapolis: University of Minnesota Press, 1984), 11–13, 15–17. For a more extensive discussion of *Being and Nothingness* and *The Postmodern Condition,* see my "The Look and Interpersonal Conflict: Sartre," in *Twilight of Subjectivity* (Amherst: University of Massachusetts Press, 1981), 72–85, and "Polis and Cosmopolis," in *Margins of Political Discourse* (Albany: State University of New York Press, 1989), 10–15. (I realize that, in other contexts, Lyotard has considerably tempered the conflictual outlook.)

30. See Frantz Fanon, *The Wretched of the Earth* (New York: Grove Press, 1963), 29–30, and Cornel West, "The New Cultural Politics of Difference," in Russell Ferguson et al., eds., *Out There: Marginalization and Contemporary Cultures* (Cambridge, Mass.: MIT Press, 1991), 25.

31. Todorov, *The Conquest of America,* 250. Regarding Habermas, see especially his "Toward a Universal Pragmatics," in *Communication and the Evolution of Society,* trans. Thomas McCarthy (Boston: Beacon Press, 1979), 1–68, and *The Theory of Communicative Action,* vol. 1: *Reason and the Rationalization of Society,* trans. Thomas McCarthy (Boston: Beacon Press, 1984), 8–42. For a critical review, see my "Transcendental Hermeneutics and Universal Pragmatics," in *Language and Politics* (Notre Dame, Ind.: University of Notre Dame Press, 1984), 115–47, and "Habermas and Rationality," in *Life-World, Modernity, and Critique,* 132–59. In discussing liberal neutralism, Connolly notes that "Habermas is tempted by the wish to exclude existential issues from political theory, but, again, they seep back in. He appears to think that because an organization of public life can *resolve* or eliminate existential suffering, these issues can be excluded from public discourse." See *Identity/Difference,* 162. Regarding Gadamer, see his *Truth and Method,* trans. Joel Weinsheimer and Donald G.

Marshall (2nd rev. ed.; New York: Crossroad, 1989), and for a discussion of his later perspective chapter 2 below. Curiously, although vindicating tradition against Habermas's emancipation from tradition, MacIntyre proposes a rationalist model of cross-cultural communication akin to Habermasian discourse; see, e.g., Alasdair MacIntyre, *Three Rival Versions of Moral Enquiry: Encyclopedia, Genealogy, and Tradition* (Notre Dame: University of Notre Dame Press, 1990), 222–24.

32. Todorov, *The Conquest of America*, 247, 249–51. As he adds (251): "The anthropologist's position is fruitful; much less so is that of the tourist whose curiosity about strange ways takes him to Bali or Bahia, but who confines the experience of the heterogeneous within the space of his paid vacations." Regarding dialogue in Bakhtin's work, compare Katerina Clark and Michael Holquist, *Mikhail Bakhtin* (Cambridge, Mass.: Belknap Press, 1984), 9–12, 347–50.

33. Connolly, *Identity/Difference,* 13–14, 36–37, 166–67. Connolly in the same study (33) also uses the phrase *agonistic dialogue* to characterize his position. Compare also his *The Ethos of Pluralization* (Minneapolis: University of Minnesota Press, 1995). For a perspective which in many ways is akin to Connolly's, see Young, *Justice and the Politics of Difference,* especially 98–99 ("Postmodernist Critique of the Logic of Identity") and 163–73 ("Emancipation through the Politics of Difference" and "Reclaiming the Meaning of Difference"). In her epilogue, which briefly alludes to the global arena, Young (260) defends an "ideal of politics as deliberation in a heterogeneous public."

34. Regarding the medieval dialogue, compare, e.g., A. M. Goichon, *La philosophie d'Avicenne et son influence en Europe médiévale* (Paris: Adrien-Maisonneuve, 1951); Robert Hammond, *The Philosophy of Alfarabi and Its Influence on Medieval Thought* (New York: Hobson, 1947); and among more recent works David Burrell, *Knowing the Unknowable God: Ibn-Sina, Maimonides, Aquinas* (Notre Dame: University of Notre Dame Press, 1986).

35. Regarding the *Heptaplomeres,* see Jean Bodin, *Colloquium of the Seven about the Secrets of the Sublime,* trans. Marion L. D. Kuntz (Princeton: Princeton University Press, 1975).

36. Regarding Akbar, compare Sri Ram Sharma, *The Religious Policy of the Mughal Emperors* (London: Oxford University Press, 1940); Emmy Wellesz, *Akbar's Religious Thought* (London: Allen & Unwin, 1952); Pierre Du Jarric, *Akbar and the Jesuits* (New York: Harper & Row, 1926); Ashirbadi L. Srivastava, *Akbar the Great* (Agra: Agarwala, 1962); and S. M. Burke, *Akbar: The Greatest Mogul* (Delhi: Manoharlal, 1989). See also Wm. Theodore de Bary, *East Asian Civilization: A Dialogue in Five Stages* (Cambridge, Mass.: Harvard University Press, 1988), ix–x, 33. The citation is from Miyamoto Shoson, "The Relation

of Philosophical Theory to Practical Affairs in Japan," in Charles A. Moore, ed., *The Japanese Mind* (Honolulu: University of Hawaii Press, 1967), 7.

37. See de Bary, *East Asian Civilizations,* 123–24, 127, 138.

38. Todorov, *The Conquest of America,* 249, 254.

Chapter 2.
Gadamer, Derrida, and the Hermeneutics of Difference

1. Compare in this context, e.g., Immanuel Wallerstein, *Geopolitics and Geoculture: Essays on the Changing World-System* (Cambridge: Cambridge University Press, 1991), and Mike Featherstone, ed., *Global Culture: Nationalism, Globalization and Modernity* (Newbury Park, Calif.: Sage Publications, 1990).

2. For a perceptive discussion of Gadamer's early writings on dialogical politics, see Robert R. Sullivan, *Political Hermeneutics: The Early Thinking of Hans-Georg Gadamer* (University Park: Pennsylvania State University Press, 1989).

3. Hans-Georg Gadamer, *Wer bin Ich und Wer bist Du? Ein Kommentar zu Paul Celans Gedichtfolge "Atemkristall"* (Frankfurt-Main: Suhrkamp, 1973), 7.

4. *Wer bin Ich und Wer bist Du?* 9–12. Gadamer diminishes the starkness of the ambiguity somewhat by allowing for an occasional specificity of pronouns. Thus, he speaks (12) of the possible substitution of the "reader-ego" for the "poet's ego" and the resulting "determinacy of the meaning of thou."

5. *Wer bin Ich und Wer bist Du?* 14–18, 39.

6. Ibid. 110. These comments do not prevent Gadamer from observing at another point (113) that the multivocity or "polyvalence" of words is pinpointed or "stabilized in the course of discourse" and that hence there is "a univocity which is necessarily endemic to every type of discourse, even that of *poésie pure.*"

7. *Wer bin Ich und Wer bist Du?* 112–15. For the notion of 'phrase families' compare Jean-François Lyotard, *The Differend: Phrases in Dispute,* trans. Georges Van Den Abbeele (Minneapolis: University of Minnesota Press, 1988). Regarding "agonistic (or agonal) dialogue," see my *Margins of Political Discourse* (Albany: State University of New York Press, 1989), 16–19, 109, and also William E. Connolly, *Identity/Difference: Democratic Negotiations of Political Paradox* (Ithaca: Cornell University Press, 1991), 33.

8. Gadamer, *Wer bin Ich und Wer bist Du?* 118–21.

9. Ibid., 129–31. As Gadamer adds (133–34): "There cannot be a 'final' interpretation. Every interpretation only aims at approximation;

and its own concrete possibility would be vitiated if interpretation did
not assume its historical place and did not insert itself into the 'historical effectiveness' (Wirkungsgeschehen) of the text."

10. See Gadamer, "Letter to Dallmayr," in Diane P. Michelfelder
and Richard E. Palmer, eds., Dialogue and Deconstruction: The Gadamer-
Derrida Encounter (Albany: State University of New York Press, 1989),
96–97. The letter was a response to an essay comparing and counter-
balancing Gadamer and Derrida; see "Hermeneutics and Deconstruction: Gadamer and Derrida in Dialogue," in the same volume,
76–92.

11. Gadamer, "Hermeneutics and Logocentrism," in Michelfelder
and Palmer, Dialogue and Deconstruction, 119, 125 (in the above citations, the translation has been slightly altered for purposes of clarity). Compare also Gadamer, "Destruktion and Deconstruction," in
the same volume, 102–13.

12. Gadamer, "Die Vielfalt Europas: Erbe und Zukunft," in Das Erbe
Europas: Beiträge (Frankfurt-Main: Suhrkamp, 1989), 7, 10–11. (Author's own translation.) For an English translation under the title "The
Diversity of Europe: Inheritance and Future," see Dieter Misgeld and
Graeme Nicholson, eds., Hans-Georg Gadamer on Education, Poetry,
and History: Applied Hermeneutics, trans. Lawrence Schmidt and Mon-
ica Reuss (Albany: State University of New York Press, 1992), 221–36.

13. Gadamer, Das Erbe Europas, 13–14. Regarding Husserl, compare especially his "Vienna Lecture" (1935), in The Crisis of European
Sciences and Transcendental Phenomenology, trans. David Carr
(Evanston, Ill.: Northwestern University Press, 1970), 269–99. Compare also Martin Heidegger, Beiträge zur Philosophie (Vom Ereignis),
ed. Friedrich-Wilhelm von Herrmann (Gesamtausgabe, vol. 65; Frankfurt-Main: Klostermann, 1989).

14. Gadamer, Das Erbe Europas, 15–17, 20–24. Regarding Husserl's
notion of the life world, see The Crisis of European Sciences, 48–53.
For a discussion of successive transformations of life world and world
from Husserl and Heidegger to Derrida, see my "Life-World: Varia-
tions on a Theme," in Stephen K. White, ed., Life-World and Politics:
Between Modernity and Postmodernity, Essays in Honor of Fred Dall-
mayr (Notre Dame, Ind.: University of Notre Dame Press, 1989), 25–65.
Regarding the "underlaborer" view of philosophy, see Peter Winch,
The Idea of a Social Science and Its Relation to Philosophy (London:
Routledge & Kegan Paul, 1958), 3–7.

15. Gadamer, Das Erbe Europas, 28–30.

16. Ibid., 31–34.

17. "Die Zukunft der europäischen Geisteswissenschaften," in Das
Erbe Europas, 37–39, 42–45. For an English translation under the title

"The Future of the European Humanities," see Misgeld and Nicholson, eds., *Hans-Georg Gadamer on Education, Poetry, and History,* 193–208.

18. Gadamer, *Das Erbe Europas,* 35, 46–48.

19. Ibid., 49, 52, 57–58. Regarding Herder, compare R. T. Clark, *Herder: His Life and Thought* (Berkeley: University of California Press, 1955), and Isaiah Berlin, *Vico and Herder: Two Studies in the History of Ideas* (New York: Viking Press, 1976).

20. Gadamer, *Das Erbe Europas,* 58–62. Regarding tolerance, compare also Robert Paul Wolff, Barrington Moore, Jr., and Herbert Marcuse, *A Critique of Pure Tolerance* (Boston: Beacon Press, 1965).

21. Jacques Derrida, *The Other Heading: Reflections on Today's Europe,* trans. Pascale-Anne Brault and Michael B. Naas (Bloomington: Indiana University Press, 1992), 38–41.

22. Ibid., 14–15.

23. Ibid., 29, 76–77. Derrida offers a number of alternative formulations of the double injunction or double duty, formulations which lucidly throw into relief our postmetaphysical as well as post–Cold War situation. The *same* duty, he notes (77–79), dictates criticizing "a totalitarian dogmatism that, under the pretense of putting an end to capital, destroyed democracy and the European heritage. But it also dictates criticizing a religion of capital that institutes its dogmatism under new guises, which we must learn to identify." In a different register, the same double duty dictates "respecting differences, idioms, minorities, singularities, but also the universality of formal law, the desire for translation, agreement and univocity, the law of the majority, opposition to racism, nationalism, and xenophobia." On a more philosophical plane, the double duty dictates "cultivating the virtues of such *critique,* of the *critical idea,* the *critical tradition,* but also submitting it, beyond critique and questioning, to a deconstructive genealogy that thinks and exceeds it without yet compromising it." The latter aspect involves "tolerating and respecting all that is not placed under the authority of reason. It may have to do with faith, with different forms of faith. It may also have to do with certain thoughts, whether questioning or not, thoughts that, while attempting to think reason and the history of reason, necessarily exceed its order, without becoming, simply because of this, irrational, and much less irrationalist." Derrida's essay at another point (54–55) critiques the one-sided focus on transparent reason and "communicative rationality" associated with Habermasian critical theory.

24. *The Other Heading,* 9–10.

25. On culture theory in the social sciences, compare Fred Inglis, *Cultural Studies* (Oxford: Blackwell, 1993), and Margaret Archer, *Cul-*

ture and Agency: The Place of Culture in Social Theory (Cambridge: Cambridge University Press, 1988).

26. David Couzens Hoy, "Heidegger and the Hermeneutic Turn," in Charles B. Guignon, ed., *The Cambridge Companion to Heidegger* (Cambridge: Cambridge University Press, 1993), 188–89. In Hoy's presentation, the issue turns largely on the meaning of the "hermeneutical circle." As he writes (192):

> Deconstruction could indeed be a crucial moment in the circle of interpretation, for its techniques could be used to ensure that the alterity of the text was taken seriously enough. The circle of understanding should not be purely reconstructive, if by that is meant either that the interpreter reads only what is already familiar back into the text or that in the effort to find a unity of meaning the interpreter should overlook tensions and contradictions that are also at play. But the circle could also not be purely deconstructive, since there must first be an assumed meaning that is deconstructed, and the discovery of tension and contradiction is itself a projection of an understanding of what is really going on in the text.

27. See especially Martin Heidegger, "The End of Philosophy and the Task of Thinking," in *On Time and Being,* trans. Joan Stambaugh (New York: Harper & Row, 1972), 55–73. Regarding the issue of a Eurocentric or Graecocentric bias, see, e.g., Rainer Martin, "Heidegger and the Greeks," in Tom Rockmore and Joseph Margolis, eds., *The Heidegger Case: On Philosophy and Politics* (Philadelphia: Temple University Press, 1992), 167–87.

28. J. L. Mehta, "Heidegger and Vedanta: Reflections on a Questionable Theme," in Graham Parkes, ed., *Heidegger and Asian Thought* (Honolulu: University of Hawaii Press, 1987), 27. As he adds in a footnote (43 n. 24): "Granting the metaphysical component in Sanskrit, however, it may be instructive to investigate the correctives it has developed against this representational or objectifying element, thus exhibiting its own unique genius: a mode of utterance in which representation and the cancellation of the representative force are held in tension and balance."

29. See Raimundo Panikkar, "Eine unvollendete Symphonie," in Günther Neske, ed., *Erinnerung an Martin Heidegger* (Pfullingen: Neske, 1977), 175, and his "What Is Comparative Philosophy Comparing?" in Gerald J. Larson and Eliot Deutsch, eds., *Interpreting across Boundaries: New Essays in Comparative Philosophy* (Princeton: Princeton University Press, 1988), 130. In the latter essay, Panikkar also presents genuine comparative philosophy as an "imparative philosophy," a

term which is meant to stress (127) "an open philosophical attitude ready to learn from whatever philosophical corner of the world, but without claiming to compare philosophies from an objective, neutral, and transcendent vantage point."

30. Nirmal Verma, "India and Europe: Some Reflections on Self and Other," *Kavita Asia* (Bhopal, 1990), 121, 127, 132, 137, 144.

Chapter 3. Radhakrishnan on Being and Existence

1. Wilfred Cantwell Smith, "Comparative Religion: Whither and Why?" in Willard G. Oxtoby, ed., *Religious Diversity: Essays by Wilfred Cantwell Smith* (New York: Harper & Row, 1976), 140–41. The same essay offers a succinct synopsis of East-West contacts in these terms (142):

> The traditional form of Western scholarship in the study of other men's religion was that of an impersonal presentation of an "it." The first great innovation in recent times has been the personalization of the faiths observed, so that one finds a discussion of a "they." Presently the observer becomes personally involved, so that the situation is one of a "we" talking about a "they." The next step is dialogue, where "we" talk to "you." If there is listening and mutuality, this may become that "we" talk *with* "you." The culmination of this progress is when "we all" are talking *with* each other about "us."

2. According to Wilhelm Halbfass, Sri Aurobindo and Radhakrishnan are "the two most representative neo-Hindu thinkers of the twentieth century" who, in different ways, "exemplify the potential and the problems of neo-Hinduism"; but the "most typical" and "most successful" spokesman in his view is Radhakrishnan. See Halbfass, *India and Europe: An Essay in Understanding* (Albany: State University of New York Press, 1988), 248, 251. Compare also K. Satchidananda Murty and Ashok Vohra, *Radhakrishnan: His Life and Ideas* (Albany: State University of New York Press, 1990); Troy Wilson Organ, *Radhakrishnan and the Ways of Oneness of East and West* (Athens: Ohio University Press, 1989); and Robert N. Minor, *Radhakrishnan: A Religious Biography* (Albany: State University of New York Press, 1987).

3. See Sarvepalli Radhakrishnan, "The Religion of the Spirit and the World's Need: Fragments of a Confession," in Paul A. Schilpp, ed., *The Philosophy of Sarvepalli Radhakrishnan* (New York: Tudor Publishing Co., 1952), 3–82. Compare also his *The Hindu View of Life*

(London: George Allen & Unwin, 1927), and *An Idealist View of Life* (London: George Allen & Unwin, 1932).

4. See Radhakrishnan, "Fragments of a Confession," 4; Michel Foucault, *The History of Sexuality,* vol. 1: *Introduction* (New York: Vintage Books, 1980), 59. It is true that Radhakrishnan in 1937 had written another (but no less sketchy) autobiographical account; see "My Search for the Truth," in Vergilius Ferm, ed., *Religion in Transition* (New York: Macmillan, 1937), 11–59.

5. Radhakrishnan, "Fragments of a Confession," 6–7. He adds (7): "The prominent feature of our time is not so much the wars and the dictatorships which have disfigured it, but the impact of different cultures on one another, their interaction, and the emergence of a new civilization based on the truths of spirit and the unity of mankind."

6. "Fragments of a Confession," 8–10. Turning against traditionalists Radhakrishnan states (8): "Devotion to a master who lays down the law gives us rest, confidence and security. To minds wearied and worried by doubt, authoritarian religions give a sense of release and purpose. We cannot, however, expect rational criticism from those who have too much reverence for authority." For comments on Hindu traditionalists, including A. K. Coomaraswamy, and their critique of Radhakrishnan, see Halbfass, *India and Europe,* 254–55.

7. "Fragments of a Confession," 10. The same accent is evident in Radhakrishnan's treatment of Hinduism as anchored in "religious experience." "The Hindu philosophy of religion," he writes, "starts from and returns to an experimental basis. Only this basis is as wide as human nature itself. . . . By accepting the significance of the different intuitions of reality and the different scriptures of the peoples living in India, Hinduism has come to be a tapestry of the most variegated tissues and almost endless diversity of hues." See *The Hindu View of Life,* 16–17.

8. "Fragments of a Confession," 31–32. He adds (32): "There is an inconscient world of being from out of which different worlds form themselves under the guidance of spirit. The dualism of *purusha* and *prakriti* cannot be ultimate."

9. "Fragments of a Confession," 34–37. The citation is from Alfred North Whitehead, *Process and Reality* (New York: Macmillan, 1929), 488. Compare also Radhakrishnan's essay "Bergson and Absolute Idealism," *Mind* 28 (1919): 41–53, 275–96.

10. "Fragments of a Confession," 38–39.

11. Ibid., 39–41.

12. Ibid., 47, 49, 51, 56.

13. Ibid., 48, 50, 52, 56–57.

14. Ibid., 23–24, 26, 30, 45.

15. Regarding the oldest of these texts, see Radhakrishnan, *The Principal Upanishads* (London: Allen & Unwin, 1953). In addition to the triple canon Radhakrishnan has also written a commentary on a Buddhist classic, *The Dhammapada* (Oxford: Oxford University Press, 1950).

16. Radhakrishnan, *The Brahma Sutra: The Philosophy of Spiritual Life* (London: Allen & Unwin, 1960), 11–12. Regarding Shankara and *Advaita Vedanta* see the insightful treatment in Eliot Deutsch, *Advaita Vedanta, A Philosophical Reconstruction* (Honolulu: University of Hawaii Press, 1969). Compare also Natalia Isayeva, *Shankara and Indian Philosophy* (Albany: State University of New York Press, 1993).

17. *The Brahma Sutra,* 118–21.

18. Ibid., 122–23, 126–34.

19. Ibid., 137–38, 143, 148, 156–57.

20. Radhakrishnan, *The Bhagavad Gita* (first ed. 1948; New York: Harper Torchbooks, 1973), 12, 22–25.

21. Ibid., 26, 30–37.

22. Ibid., 38, 50–54, 58–60.

23. Ibid., 66–67, 76.

24. Ibid., 67–68, 71–73. Although Arjuna's immediate task is to engage in battle, Radhakrishnan emphasizes the long-term effect of karma yoga, namely, its inducement to nonviolence and solidarity (68–69):

> The ideal the *Gita* sets before us is *ahimsa* or non-violence and this is evident from the description of the perfect state of mind, speech and body. . . . Krishna advises Arjuna to fight without passion or ill-will, without anger or attachment, and if we develop such a frame of mind violence becomes impossible. . . . If we act in the spirit of the *Gita* with detachment and dedication, and have love even for our enemy, we will help rid the world of wars.

25. See *The Brahma Sutra,* 118–21; *The Bhagavd Gita,* 46–47.

26. "Fragments of a Confession," 38, 44, 55, 57–59, 61. Compare also the statement (57): "There is a reality which is different from existence, there is a subject which is non-object, there is a time-transcending element. Faith in such a non-object spirit means the defeat of death, and the renewal of life."

27. "Fragments of a Confession," 38–39, 57, 61. For a lengthy discussion of integral knowledge, see Robert W. Browning, "Reason and Types of Intuition in Radhakrishnan's Philosophy," in Schilpp, ed., *The Philosophy of Sarvepalli Radhakrishnan,* 173–277.

28. Regarding the erasure of being, compare especially Martin Heidegger, "Zur Seinsfrage," in *Wegmarken* (Frankfurt-Main: Klostermann,

1967), 213–53, trans. William Kluback and Jean T. Wilde as *The Question of Being* (New Haven: College and University Press, 1958). More generally on the later Heidegger, see my *The Other Heidegger* (Ithaca: Cornell University Press, 1993). Regarding deconstruction, see Jacques Derrida, *Of Grammatology,* trans. Gayatri C. Spivak (Baltimore: Johns Hopkins University Press, 1974), and *Margins of Philosophy,* trans. Alan Bass (Chicago: University of Chicago Press, 1982). Concerning the notion of *lila* and its relevance in Radhakrishnan's work, see S. J. Samartha, *Introduction to Radhakrishnan: The Man and His Thought* (New York: Association Press, 1964), 60–61. Compare also A. K. Coomaraswamy, "Lila," in Coomaraswamy, *Metaphysics,* ed. Roger Lipsey (Princeton: Princeton University Press, 1977), 148–55.

29. J. L. Mehta, "Heidegger and Vedanta: Reflections on a Questionable Theme," in Graham Parkes, ed., *Heidegger and Asian Thought* (Honolulu: University of Hawaii Press, 1987), 17. Mehta adds (28–29):

> Comparative philosophy so far has proceeded largely on the basis of an uncritical employment of these "metaphysical" concepts, assumed as obviously and eternally valid, in the understanding of "philosophies" such as those of India. But something remarkable will be seen to happen when we take seriously Heidegger's talk of "the end of philosophy" and his "overcoming of metaphysics.". . . Comparative philosophy, if we still retain the name, would then be a name for the task, infinitely open, of setting free, bringing into view and articuating in contemporary ways of speaking, in new ways of speaking, the matter of thinking which, in what has actually been realized in thought, still remains unsaid and so unthought in the traditions of the East. Otherwise, comparative philosophy will amount to no more than an unthinking attempt at perpetuating Western "philosophy" by translating Eastern thinking into the language of Western metaphysics, taken as the universally valid paradigm.

30. Halbfass, *India and Europe,* 442. He adds, drawing explicitly on Heideggerian insights (441): "Neither the language of 'science,' nor that of 'metaphysics,' nor that of 'historical understanding,' can provide the proper foundation for a dialogue in which all these ideas themselves will have to be questioned. We have to transcend 'what is European' *('das Europäische'); we have to reach 'beyond Occident and Orient.'"* Halbfass also refers to similar views advanced by J. L. Mehta in his *Martin Heidegger: The Way and the Vision* (Banares: Banares Hindu University Press, 1967).

31. Radhakrishnan, "Fragments of a Confession," 65–66. See also Radhakrishnan, ed., *Mahatma Gandhi: Essays and Reflections on*

Gandhi's Life and Work (London: Allen & Unwin, 1939). The link-age between the overcoming of metaphysics and karma yoga is not fortuitous: once metaphysics is seen to be metaphorical (and not as the cognition of essences inhabiting a transcendent world), every-thing comes to depend on proper (nonpossessive) conduct in the world.

Chapter 4. Heidegger, Bhakti, and Vedanta

1. J. N. Mohanty, "Introduction," in J. L. Mehta, *Philosophy and Religion: Essays in Interpretation* (New Delhi: Indian Council of Philosophical Research and M. Manoharlal Publishers, 1990), vi.

2. J. L. Mehta, "Life-Worlds, Sacrality and Interpretive Thinking" (1987), in Mehta, *Philosophy and Religion,* 248–49. The essay was printed earlier in T. S. Rukmini, ed., *Religious Consciousness and Life-Worlds* (New Delhi: Indian Institute of Advanced Study and Indus Publishers, 1988), 19. The essay is also contained, together with a discussion, in William J. Jackson, ed., *J. L. Mehta on Heidegger, Hermeneutics and Indian Tradition* (Leiden: Brill, 1992), 209–33. Some of the biographical background is offered by Mehta in "My Years at the Center for the Study of World Religions: Some Reflections" (1982), in Mehta, *Philosophy and Religion,* 65–82.

3. "Introduction," in Mehta, *Philosophy and Religion,* v. The Heidegger study was first written in 1962 and presented as a doctoral dissertation at Banares Hindu University. The later change of title was at least partly due to a letter that Heidegger wrote to Mehta and in which he referred to the early version as "your book on my 'philosophy.'" For this information, see Mehta's preface to *Martin Heidegger: The Way and the Vision* (Honolulu: University Press of Hawaii, 1976), xiv.

4. See "Finding Heidegger" (1977) and "A Western Kind of *Rishi*" (1977), in Mehta, *Philosophy and Religion,* 20–21, 25, 31. The two papers are joined in the volume under the heading "In Memoriam: Martin Heidegger." In view of the hostile accounts often found in the literature, it may be worthwhile to cite Mehta's portrayal of his mentor (31): "Not a pompous and clever school master bursting with 'ideas,' not an ecstatic or visionary, not an introverted *yogi* or one lost in the inner world of thoughts, not 'mad' or possessed by a demon, but down-to-earth and 'all there,' composed and collected, a craftsman and a 'maker,' alert, simple, sane and straight, aware of his limits as a thinker, kind and friendly." The essay "Finding Heidegger" is also contained in Jackson, ed., *J. L. Mehta on Heidegger, Hermeneutics and Indian Tradition,* 27–33.

5. "The Concept of the Subjective" (1966), in *India and the West: The Problem of Understanding; Selected Essays of J. L. Mehta* (Chico, Calif.: Scholars Press, 1985), 1, 16, 23.

6. "Understanding the Tradition" (1969), in *India and the West*, 138; "Heidegger and the Comparison of Indian and Western Philosophy" (1970), in Mehta, *Philosophy and Religion*, 8–10. The citations are from Heidegger, *An Introduction to Metaphysics*, trans. Ralph Manheim (Garden City, N.Y.: Anchor Books, 1961), 32, 130. Mehta offers his own translation from the German text of 1953 (a translation revised by this author at a few points in light of Manheim's version).

7. "The Will to Interpret and India's Dreaming Spirit" (1974), in *India and the West*, 186–88. See also the essay "The Concept of Progress" (1967), in *India and the West*, 69–82. There, Mehta also points to the steady debunking of the theory of progress both by theologians and by philosophers. Following Nietzsche, he writes (81): "Heidegger has traced the lineaments and genesis of this basic movement of which the outward manifestations constitute what we cheerfully call progress and which is no longer confined to the Western world. Accompanying 'progress' as its chill and deadening shadow is the spiritual night falling on mankind, 'the darkening of the world, the flight of the gods, the depradation of the earth,' as Heidegger describes it." For the Hegel citation see G. W. F. Hegel, *The Philosophy of History,* trans. J. Sibree (New York: Willie Book Co., 1944), 142–43. Compare also Hegel, *Lectures on the History of Philosophy,* trans. E. S. Haldane (New York: Humanities Press, 1955), vol. 1, 125–47, and *Lectures on the Philosophy of Religion,* ed. Peter C. Hodgson (Berkeley: University of California Press, 1987), vol. 2, 316–35.

8. Mehta, "The Will to Interpret and India's Dreaming Spirit," in *India and the West*, 194–96; "Problems of Inter-Cultural Understanding in University Studies of Religion" (1968), in *India and the West*, 118–19.

9. "Understanding and Tradition" and "The Will to Interpret and India's Dreaming Spirit," in *India and the West*, 150–51, 198. Compare also the essays "Heidegger's Debts to Dilthey's Hermeneutics and Husserl's Phenomenology" and "The Transformation of Phenomenology" (two lectures, 1987), in Jackson, ed., *J. L. Mehta on Heidegger, Hermeneutics and Indian Tradition*, 35–60, 69–88.

10. "Problems of Inter-Cultural Understanding in University Studies of Religion" and "The Will to Interpret and India's Dreaming Spirit," in *India and the West*, 130–31, 199.

11. "Problems of Inter-Cultural Understanding," "Understanding the Tradition," "The Will to Interpret," and "Beyond Believing and Knowing" (1976), in *India and the West*, 131–32, 155, 181, 213–14. Wilfred

Cantwell Smith was Mehta's colleague at the Harvard Center for the Study of World Religions and is often praised by Mehta for his innovative insights. In the field of comparative cultural and religious study, Mehta repeatedly comments critically on the work of Mircea Eliade, taking exception especially to his resort to the scientific categories of structuralist anthropology. Notwithstanding its noble aims, he observes at one point (215), when this approach "claims to arrive by the study of myth, ritual and symbols at universal, objective, synchronic knowledge about human religiousness, it seems to be pursuing a chimera."

12. "Problems of Inter–Cultural Understanding" and "Understanding and Tradition," in *India and the West,* 125, 159; "My Years at the Center for the Study of World Religions," in Mehta, *Philosophy and Religion,* 67.

13. "A Stranger from Asia" (1977) and "My Years at the Center," in Mehta, *Philosophy and Religion,* 52–53, 69. In his writings, Mehta repeatedly criticizes contemporary Indologist Paul Hacker for his addiction to scientific methodology. "For Hacker," he states at one point, "the impeccable scholar of Advaita Vedanta, Indology is a *Fach,* a field of specialized research, a *Wissenschaft* with a simple but severely austere methodology for investigating alien texts for the sake of what is objectively present in them, with all 'interpretation' ruled out of court and its place taken by theological 'utilization'" ("The Will to Interpret," *India and the West,* 183).

14. "The Hindu Tradition: The Vedic Root" (1984), in Mehta, *Philosophy and Religion,* 115–17. The essay can also be found in Jackson, *J. L. Mehta on Heidegger, Hermeneutics and Indian Tradition,* 102–19.

15. "The Hindu Tradition" and "The *Rigveda:* Text and Interpretation" (1988), in Mehta, *Philosophy and Religion,* 100–4, 109, 113–15, 275.

16. "The *Rigveda:* Text and Interpretation," in Mehta, *Philosophy and Religion,* 278, 281–82, 288–91. He writes (288):

> In a remarkable lecture, "On the Way to Language," Heidegger sought to think of language in such a way as "to bring language itself to speech as language," language as it abides in its own manner of being, as language itself speaks in the speech of man. Heidegger also often pointed out that in disclosing to us things— whatever we speak *about*—language holds back the revelation of its own manner of being, conceals it. . . . The Vedic poets knew about the play of concealment and revealment from their own experience. . . . As a Rigvedic verse says: "The poets hide the paths of truth; they keep secret their hidden names" (10.5.2).

Compare in this context Martin Heidegger, "The Age of the World Picture," in *The Question Concerning Technology and Other Essays,* trans. William Lovitt (New York: Harper & Row, 1977), 115–54, and Heidegger, *On the Way to Language,* trans. Peter D. Hertz and Joan Stambaugh (New York: Harper & Row, 1971), especially 123–25.

17. Mehta, "Heidegger and the Comparison of Indian and Western Philosophy" and "A Stranger from Asia," in Mehta, *Philosophy and Religion,* 15, 54–58. Actually, Mehta was not quite satisfied with the solution suggested above, because of a deeper discrepancy between *atman* and the "being of beings" (61–62). This is the only instance I have discovered where Mehta critically engages Heidegger's views (on the basis of a different conception of ontology). See also Martin Heidegger and Eugen Fink, *Heraklit: Seminar Wintersemester 1966/67* (Frankfurt-Main: Klostermann, 1970).

18. "Heidegger and Vedanta: Reflections on a Questionable Theme" (1978), in *India and the West,* 228, 238–39, 265 n. 24. Regarding the latter note, Wilfred Cantwell Smith in his introduction to the volume states (xvii) that in it Mehta has "propounded in passing a precious new idea potentially richly productive: a number of doctoral dissertations are suggested in this one provocative insight." For the comments on Bhattacharya see Mehta's essay "The Problem of Philosophical Reconception in the Thought of K. C. Bhattacharya," in the same volume, 160–78. The essay "Heidegger and Vedanta" is also contained in Graham Parkes, ed., *Heidegger and Asian Thought* (Honolulu: University of Hawaii Press, 1987), 15–45.

19. "Heidegger and Vedanta," in *India and the West,* 241–43.

20. Ibid., 247–50, 259–61. Mehta's main concern in the essay is to differentiate *Vedanta* from traditional metaphysics. "If," he writes (244), *"brahman* is identified with the Greek notion of being (not to speak of its scholastic variants), conceived as ground, then Heidegger's whole effort is to demolish this idea, for his entire thinking is a critique of just this single concept." Occasionally, Shankara's thought has been linked with Christian mysticism or else with Thomistic ontology. But, Mehta objects (250), insofar as the final point of reference in these comparisons is still the Greek notion of being,

> they cannot be regarded as shedding light on what *brahma-vidya* is about or what *atman-bodha* stands for. In this respect, at least, a consideration of *Advaita Vedanta* in a Heideggerian perspective perhaps offers a better chance, for the thinking of Heidegger and Shankara may be found to have a touching point somewhere in that 'region of all regions,' beyond the thought of being and non-being, in which it has its sojourn.

21. "The Hindu Tradition," in Mehta, *Philosophy and Religion,* 104–5. Compare also the comment in the same context (106) that the "inner logic" of Indian history, "this thread running unbroken from Vedic times to the present, is constituted by the single-minded, unshaken will for the preservation of the dimension of the holy in human living at all costs, leaving it to 'history' to reckon these costs at will." See also "Heidegger and Vedanta," in *India and the West,* 223. There (254), Mehta again shows his indebtedness to Heidegger, noting that "this whole process in which truth is realized in thinking experience occurs within the dimension of the holy, as Heidegger thinks it, as a sacred happening, within an experience of being 'which is still capable of a god,' which is not yet 'too late for the gods and too early for being.'" Mehta's phrasing above seems to resonate with A. L. Basham's *The Wonder That Was India* (Calcutta: Rupa & Co., 1991). Regarding Müller, see Nirad C. Chaudhuri, *Scholar Extraordinary* (New York: Oxford University Press, 1974).

22. "The Hindu Tradition" and "Life-Worlds, Sacrality and Interpretive Thinking" (1987), in Mehta, *Philosophy and Religion,* 118, 245–46, 248. See also "Beyond Believing and Knowing" (1976), in *India and the West,* 205–7.

23. "My Years at the Center for the Study of World Religions," in Mehta, *Philosophy and Religion,* 76–82.

24. "The Discourse of Violence in the *Mahabharata*" (1987), in Mehta, *Philosophy and Religion,* 255–56, 259–60, 270.

25. Ibid., 258, 263–64. Regarding the "passing while," see Heidegger, "The Anaximander Fragment," in *Early Greek Thinking,* trans. David F. Krell and Frank A. Capuzzi (New York: Harper & Row, 1984), 13–58.

26. *"Bhakti* in Philosophical Perspective" (1986), in Mehta, *Philosophy and Religion,* 206–8. Compare also "Krishna: God as Friend" (1988), in Jackson, *J. L. Mehta on Heidegger, Hermeneutics and Indian Tradition,* 121–35.

27. *"Bhakti* in Philosophical Perspective," in Mehta, *Philosophy and Religion,* 204–5, 207–9, 213–14.

28. "Problems of Inter-Cultural Understanding" and "Beyond Believing and Knowing," in *India and the West,* 129, 216. On global dialogue compare also "Postmodern Problems East/West: Reflections and Exchanges" and "World Civilization: The Possibility of Dialogue" (1978), in Jackson, ed., *J. L. Mehta on Heidegger, Hermeneutics and Indian Tradition,* 235–51, 253–66. See also *The Bhagavad Gita,* trans. Juan Mascaro (New York: Penguin Books, 1962), 62 (4.11) and 97–98 (12.18–19).

Chapter 5. Exit from Orientalism

1. Edward W. Said, *Orientalism* (New York: Vintage Books, 1979).

2. Compare Wilfred Cantwell Smith, *Islam in Modern History* (New York: New American Library, 1957), and his *On Understanding Islam* (The Hague: Mouton, 1981); J. L. Mehta, *India and the West: The Problem of Understanding* (Chico, Calif.: Scholars Press, 1985), and his *Philosophy and Religion: Essays in Interpretation* (New Delhi: Manoharlal Publishers, 1990); and Raimundo Panikkar, *Myth, Faith and Hermeneutics* (New York: Paulist Press, 1978), and his *The Intrareligious Dialogue* (New York: Paulist Press, 1978).

3. Wilhelm Halbfass, *India and Europe: An Essay in Understanding* (Albany: State University of New York Press, 1988); *Tradition and Reflection: Explorations in Indian Thought* (Albany: State University of New York Press, 1991); *On Being and What There Is: Classical Vaisesika and the History of Indian Ontology* (Albany: State University of New York Press, 1992).

4. Halbfass, *Tradition and Reflection,* 9–11. Compare Ronald Inden, *Imagining India* (Oxford: Blackwell, 1990), and his "Orientalist Constructions of India," *Modern Asian Studies* 29 (1986): 401–46.

5. Halbfass, *Tradition and Reflection,* 9–12.

6. Ibid., 14–16.

7. Ibid., 1–6. See also Louis Renou, *The Destiny of the Veda in India* (Delhi: Motilal Banarsidass, 1965). Compare in this context Guy L. Beck, *Sonic Theology: Hinduism and Sacred Sound* (Columbia: University of South Carolina Press, 1993); Som Raj Gupta, *The Word Speaks to the Faustian Man* (Delhi: Motilal Banarsidass, 1991); and Walter J. Ong, *The Presence of the Word* (New Haven, Conn.: Yale University Press, 1967).

8. Halbfass, *Tradition and Reflection,* 40–41.

9. Halbfass, *India and Europe,* 164–69.

10. Halbfass, *On Being and What There Is,* vii, 7.

11. Ibid., 7–11. See also W. V. Quine, *From a Logical Point of View* (Cambridge, Mass.: Harvard University Press, 1961), 1, and Gilbert Ryle, "Systematically Misleading Expressions," in *Proceedings of the Aristotelian Society* 32 (1931/32): 139–70.

12. Halbfass, *On Being and What There Is,* 12–14. Halbfass refers here somewhat broadly to the "work" of D. H. H. Ingalls and some of his disciples, such as B. K. Matilal. The possible reference here is to D. H. H. Ingalls, *Materials for the Study of Navya-nyaya Logic* (Cambridge, Mass.: Harvard University Press, 1951); B. K. Matilal, *Analytical Philosophy in Comparative Perspective* (Dordrecht: Reidel, 1985);

and B. K. Matilal, *Epistemology, Logic and Grammar in Indian Philosophical Analysis* (The Hague: Mouton, 1971).

13. Halbfass, *On Being and What There Is,* 13–15.

14. Ibid., vii.

15. Halbfass, *India and Europe,* 168.

16. Halbfass, *Tradition and Reflection,* 179.

17. Ibid., 146–47, 180.

18. Ibid., 162–64. Halbfass refers here to G. Cardona, "On Reasoning from *anvaya* and *vyatireka* in Early Advaita," in D. Malvania and N. J. Shah, eds., *Studies in Indian Philosophy* (Ahmedabad: Navajivan, 1981), 79–104.

19. Halbfass, *Tradition and Reflection,* 175.

20. Halbfass, *On Being and What There Is,* 15, and *Tradition and Reflection,* 36, 132, 180.

21. *On Being and What There Is,* 24–25, 19–30. Somewhat cryptically, Halbfass adds (25): "At this point, there is no need for an explicit comparison with Heideggerian ideas, in particular with his critique of the role of representational and objectifying thinking; nor do we have to discuss the applicability of his four 'limitations' (being and becoming; being and appearance; being and thinking; being and the ought). There is, however, no good reason to adopt Heidegger's own exclusion of his ideas from the interpretation of non-Western traditions." These comments need to be qualified: Heidegger did not "exclude" his ideas from non-Western traditions but simply hesitated to apply them aggressively or in an uncritical and domineering way.

22. *On Being and What There Is,* 30–33.

23. Ibid., 36, 49, 71, 143. Compare also Gustav Bergmann, *Logic and Reality* (Madison: University of Wisconsin Press, 1964), 127.

24. Halbfass, *On Being and What There Is,* 231–34. The reference here is to J. L. Mehta, "Heidegger and Vedanta: Reflections on a Questionable Theme," in Graham Parkes, ed., *Heidegger and Asian Thought* (Honolulu: University of Hawaii Press, 1987), 15–45.

25. Halbfass, *India and Europe,* 369, 375, 340–41.

26. Compare in this context Patricia Springborg, *Western Republicanism and the Oriental Prince* (Austin: University of Texas Press, 1992). The classical study in this field is Karl A. Wittfogel, *Oriental Depotism: A Comparative Study of Total Power* (New Haven: Yale University Press, 1957).

27. Halbfass, *Tradition and Reflection,* 266.

28. Ibid., 272–75.

29. After all, liberation did not signal the release of a uniform ego from contexts, but rather liberation *from* this kind of ego in the midst

of context. This point is further developed in chapter 6 of this volume ("Western Thought and Indian Thought: Some Comparative Steps").

30. *Tradition and Reflection,* 273–81.

31. Ibid., 349, 383–84. Compare also Louis Dumont, *Homo Hierarchicus: The Caste System and Its Implications* (rev. ed.; Chicago: University of Chicago Press, 1980).

32. See Ernesto Laclau and Chantal Mouffe, *Hegemony and Socialist Strategy: Towards a Radical Democratic Politics,* trans. Winston Moore and Paul Cammack (London: Verso, 1985).

Chapter 6. Western Thought and Indian Thought

1. For a more detailed discussion of the problems of globalism, see my "Polis and Cosmopolis" in *Margins of Political Discourse* (Albany: State University of New York Press, 1989), 1–21. This essay concurs broadly with the direction of successive East-West Philosophers' Conferences, if one can accept the assessment of Jeffrey R. Timm, who describes the trend as "a postmodern search for a meta-philosophical stance capable of embracing philosophical pluralism which at the same time avoids both fraudulent reductionism and debilitating relativism." See his "Report on the Sixth East-West Philosophers' Conference 'Culture and Modernity: The Authority of the Past,'" *Philosophy East and West* 41 (1991): 461.

2. For a detailed historical review of the relationship see Wilhelm Halbfass, *India and Europe: An Essay in Understanding* (Albany: State University of New York Press, 1988).

3. See Daya Krishna, *Indian Philosophy: A Counter Perspective* (Delhi: Oxford University Press, 1991), 15, n. 3. In the chapter "Three Conceptions of Indian Philosophy," Daya Krishna presents his own conception (29) as one that "thinks of Indian philosophy as philosophy proper and not as something radically different from what goes under that name in the Western tradition." The view that Eastern thought is *not* "philosophy" in the Western sense has been upheld, among others, by Edmund Husserl in his "Vienna Lecture" (1935); see his *The Crisis of European Sciences and Transcendental Phenomenology,* trans. David Carr (Evanston, Ill.: Northwestern University Press, 1970), 280.

4. *Indian Philosophy,* 13.

5. Edward W. Said, *Orientalism* (New York: Vintage Books, 1969). In Said's presentation (3), Orientalism "can be discussed and analyzed as the corporate institution for dealing with the Orient—dealing with it by making statements about it, authorizing views of it, describing it, by teaching it, settling it, ruling over it: in short, Orientalism as a

Western style of dominating, restructuring, and having authority over the Orient."

6. Regarding Vivekananda's assessment of Western, particularly American, culture, compare Tapan Raychauduri's description: "Beyond a point, he found 'this busy, meaningless, moneymaking life,' the American love of razzmatazz hollow and tiresome. They had very little concern with true spirituality." See his *Europe Reconsidered: Perceptions of the West in Nineteenth Century Bengal* (Delhi: Oxford University Press, 1988), 310.

7. *Indian Philosophy*, 6.

8. Ibid., 8, 29–30. The "analytical" (or positivist) attachment to the theory-praxis or fact-value division surfaces clearly in Daya Krishna's account when he opposes "intellectual difficulties of a purely rational and cognitive kind" to the "practical pursuit of ends which are non-cognitive, non-intellectual, and non-rational in nature" (20). The claim that "philosophy proper" can be divorced from "spiritual liberation" (32) and the implication that Western thought deals with the former and not the latter are rendered at least dubious by the examples of Socrates, Plato, Aristotle, Thomas Aquinas, Kant, and Hegel.

9. Martin Heidegger has outlined such a reciprocal otherness in his comparison of German and Greek thought; see especially his *Hölderlins Hymne "Andenken,"* ed. Curd Ochwadt *(Gesamtausgabe,* vol. 52; Frankfurt: Klostermann, 1982), 128–32. For perceptive insights on comparative philosophical inquiry, compare several of the essays in Gerald J. Larson and Eliot Deutsch, eds., *Interpreting across Boundaries: New Essays in Comparative Philosophy* (Princeton: Princeton University Press, 1988), and Richard Bernstein "Incommensurability and Otherness Revisited" in his *The New Constellation: The Ethical-Political Horizons of Modernity/Postmodernity* (Cambridge: Polity Press, 1991), 57–78. (Bernstein's paper was originally presented at the Sixth East-West Philosophers' Conference in Honolulu in July 1989.)

10. A. K. Ramanujan, "Is There an Indian Way of Thinking? An Informal Essay" in McKim Marriott, ed., *India through Hindu Categories* (Delhi: Sage Publications, 1990), 41–58. For some of his poetic works see, e.g., A. K. Ramanujan, *Selected Poems* (Delhi: Oxford University Press, 1976). Compare also Ramanujan, ed., *Folktales from India: A Selection of Oral Tales from Twenty-Two Languages* (New York: Pantheon Books, 1991).

11. *India through Hindu Categories*, 46–49.

12. Ibid., 50, 52–53. (The above has been corrected for gender-biased terminology.) On *jati*, compare the illuminating essay by Harold A. Gould on "Toward a 'Jati Model' for Indian Politics," in his *Caste*

Adaptation in Modernizing Indian Society (Delhi: Chanakya Publishers, 1988), 171–85.

13. *India through Hindu Categories,* 54–55.

14. Ibid., 55. The above does not deny the erosive effect of context freedom, but only emphasize the ambivalence or "dialectic" of enlightenment and modernization.

15. *India through Hindu Categories,* 54.

16. For a discussion of some of these terms, compare K. M. Sen, *Hinduism* (New York: Penguin, 1987), 22–26, 37–40, and Sarvepalli Radhakrishnan, *The Hindu View of Life* (London: Allen & Unwin, 1927).

17. To be sure, elusiveness of the boundary does not mean simple coincidence or identity; instead, the copula in "this is you" (thou art that) must be read in a complex, transitive sense. For the notion of a 'transitive copula' or 'transitive ontology,' compare Heidegger, *Schellings Abhandlung Über das Wesen der menschlichen Freiheit,* ed. Hildegard Feick (Tübingen: Niemeyer, 1971), 89–99. Regarding the notion of *dharma* compare also Ariel Glucklich, *The Sense of Adharma* (New York: Oxford University Press, 1994).

18. For a very thoughtful interpretation of Buddhist "liberation" not in the sense of context freedom but in that of a heightened sensitivity to the context of language, see Dale S. Wright, "Rethinking Transcendence: The Role of Language in Zen Experience," *Philosophy East and West* 42 (1992): 113–38. Regarding *sunya* and *sunyata,* compare my "Nothingness and Sunyata: A Comparison of Heidegger and Nishitani," *Philosophy East and West* 42 (1992): 37–48. For general background, see Edward Conze, *Buddhism: Its Essence and Development* (New York: Oxford University Press, 1951).

19. In Edmund Husserl's words: "There is something unique here [in Europe or the West] that is recognized in us by all other human groups, too, something that, quite apart from all considerations of utility, becomes a motive for them to Europeanize themselves even in their unbroken will to spiritual self-presentation; whereas we, if we understand ourselves properly, would never Indianize ourselves, for example" ("The Vienna Lecture" [1935] in Husserl, *The Crisis of European Sciences and Transcendental Phenomenology,* 275).

20. See G. W. F. Hegel, *Lectures on the History of Philosophy,* trans. E. S. Haldane (New York: Humanities Press, 1955), vol. 1, 125–47; *Lectures on the Philosophy of Religion,* ed. Peter C. Hodgson (Berkeley: University of California Press, 1987), vol. 2, 316–35; and the chapter on Hegel in Halbfass, *India and Europe,* 84–99. For a succinct overview of the history of Western metaphysics from the angle of subjectivization, see Heidegger, "Überwindung der Metaphysik,"

Vorträge und Aufsätze (3rd ed.; Neske: Pfullingen, 1967), pt. 1, 63–91.

21. For some of these developments, see my *Twilight of Subjectivity* (Amherst: University of Massachusetts Press, 1981) and *Margins of Political Discourse* (Albany: State University of New York Press, 1989).

Chapter 7. Modernization and Postmodernization

1. Some decades ago, philosopher Karl Jaspers foresaw the prospect of a new "axial age" in which the diversity of human cultures would merge in a comprehensive global discourse; see Jaspers, *The Origin and Goal of History*, trans. M. Bullock (New Haven: Yale University Press, 1953), and his *The Future of Mankind*, trans. E. B. Ashton (Chicago: University of Chicago Press, 1961).

2. Regarding Western universalism compare my "Polis and Cosmopolis," in *Margins of Political Discourse* (Albany: State University of New York Press, 1989), 2–8.

3. Daya Krishna, *Political Development: A Critical Perspective* (Delhi: Oxford University Press, 1979), 1.

4. Thomas Pantham, "Changing Conceptions of Development" (unpublished manuscript), 6. The political context of modernization theory was admitted even by one of its pioneers, Gabriel Almond, when he pointed to the "missionary and Peace Corps model" animating American intellectuals and social scientists during the postwar period; see his *Political Development: Essays in Heuristic Theory* (Boston: Little Brown, 1970), 21. Compare also Denis Goulet's comment:

> After World War II, with the spectacular success of the Marshall plan, development became a shibboleth for progress. It was assumed that rapid industrialization and generalized improvement in material conditions of life could be won quickly by following the formula that had worked in reconstructing war-damaged Europe, namely injecting massive foreign aid in the form of capital for investment in infrastructure in order to restore or create a modern productive economy. ("Development: Creator and Destroyer of Values," *World Development* 20 [1992]: 468)

5. See Talcott Parsons, *The Social System* (New York: Free Press, 1951), 45–67; his "Pattern Variables Revisited," *American Sociological Review* 25 (1960): 467–83; and his "Some Considerations on the Theory of Social Change," *Rural Sociology* 26 (1961): 219–39.

6. Lucian W. Pye, *Aspects of Political Development* (Boston: Little Brown, 1966), 8–9, 44–45. A few years earlier, Seymour Martin Lipset

had analyzed the "syndrome of conditions" buttressing modern or Western democratic politics, in an effort to "help men to develop it where it does not now exist"; see his *Political Man* (Garden City, N.Y.: Doubleday, 1960), 417. Roughly at the time of Pye's study, S. N. Eisenstadt defined modernization as "the process of change towards those types of social, economic, and political systems that have developed in Western Europe and North America from the seventeenth century to the nineteenth and then have spread to other European countries and in the nineteenth and twentieth centuries to the South American, Asian and African continent." See his *Modernization: Protest and Change* (Englewood Cliffs: Prentice-Hall, 1966), 1. Compare also Daniel Lerner's comment: "What America is . . . the modernizing Middle East seeks to become" *(The Passing of Traditional Society* [New York: Free Press, 1965], 79).

7. Gabriel A. Almond and G. Bingham Powell, *Comparative Politics: A Developmental Approach* (Boston: Little Brown, 1966), 60, 215–16. For more detailed treatments of cultural development, see Lucian W. Pye and Sidney Verba, eds., *Political Culture and Political Development* (Princeton: Princeton University Press, 1965), and Gabriel Almond and Sidney Verba, *The Civic Culture* (Boston: Little Brown, 1965).

8. Pantham, "Changing Conceptions of Development," 13.

9. That the shift to policy analysis did not basically disrupt the prevailing "behavioral" framework was recognized by David Easten, one of the initial proponents of systems theory; see his "The New Revolution in Political Science," *American Political Science Review* 63 (1969): 1051, 1057. Regarding the revisionist approach, see Samuel P. Huntington, *Political Order in Changing Societies* (New Haven: Yale University Press, 1968), 138; Ithiel de Sola Pool, "The Public and the Polity," in Pool, ed., *Contemporary Political Science* (New York: McGraw-Hill, 1967), 26; David Apter, *The Politics of Modernization* (Chicago: University of Chicago Press, 1965); R. A. Higgott, *Political Development Theory* (London: Croom Helm, 1983); and A. H. Somjee, *Political Capacity in Developing Societies* (London: Macmillan, 1982). Regarding crisis management, see Leonard Binder et al., *Crises and Sequences of Political Development* (Princeton: Princeton University Press, 1971); and regarding the shift to policy analysis, see Gabriel Almond and G. Bingham Powell, *Comparative Politics: System, Process and Policy* (Boston: Little Brown, 1978).

10. Compare Myron Weiner, *Party Politics in India* (Princeton: Princeton University Press, 1957); *Politics of Scarcity: Public Pressure and Political Response in India* (Chicago: University of Chicago Press, 1962); *Political Change in South Asia* (Calcutta: Makhopadhyay, 1963);

and *Modernization: The Dynamics of Growth* (2nd ed.; New York: Basic Books, 1966). Regarding Nehru, see his *The Discovery of India* (Calcutta: Signet Press, 1946), and D. E. Smith, *Nehru and Democracy: The Political Thought of an Asian Democrat* (Calcutta: Orient, Longman, 1958).

11. The nexus of dependency and modernization theory was all the greater the more closely the former adhered to orthodox or positivist versions of Marxism. Regarding leading formulations of dependency theory, compare Fernando Henrique Cardozo and Enzo Faletto, *Dependency and Development in Latin America* (Berkeley: University of California Press, 1979); André Gunder Frank, *Capitalism and Underdevelopment in Latin America* (New York: Monthly Review Press, 1967), and Immanuel Wallerstein, *The Modern World-System* (New York: Academic Press, 1974).

12. Compare Rajni Kothari, *Footsteps into the Future* (New Delhi: Orient, Longman, 1975), and his "Towards a Just World," *Alternatives* 5 (1979): 1–42. For a critique of an orthodox Marxist approach to development, see V. R. Mehta, *Beyond Marxism* (New Delhi: Manohar, 1978), and his *Ideology, Modernization and Politics in India* (New Delhi: Manohar, 1983).

13. Daya Krishna, *Political Development*, 6, 179. Compare also Charles Tilly, ed., *The Formation of National States in Western Europe* (Princeton: Princeton University Press, 1975), 619–20.

14. Daya Krishna, *Political Development*, 187, 190, 197, 201. Compare Robert Nisbet, *Social Change and History* (London: Oxford University Press, 1969), 288, and Daya Krishna, *Considerations toward a Theory of Social Change* (Bombay: Manaktalas, 1965).

15. The notion of an awakening from immaturity stems from Kant's definition of enlightenment. The absence of sufficient attention to emancipation and human freedom in the modernization model was noted by Daya Krishna when he wrote:

> Surprising as it may seem, the concept of "political liberty" plays hardly any role in discussions about political development. Lucian Pye, who has made a supposedly exhaustive survey of all the definitions offered for political development in his well-known work *Aspects of Political Development,* barely mentions it. The closest that he comes to it is perhaps in the definition of political development as the building of democracy. But that democracy in this context is hardly concerned directly with the issue of "political liberty" is revealed by the fact that neither the words "freedom" or "liberty" nor the phrases "political freedom" or "political liberty" are to be found in the index to this book. *(Political Development,* 16)

16. Edmund Husserl, *The Crisis of European Sciences and Transcendental Phenomenology,* trans. David Carr (Evanston, Ill.: Northwestern University Press, 1970), 8, 15, 274, 288 (translation slightly altered). As should be noted, historical evolution for Husserl was a transcendental trajectory and by no means reducible to biological or organicist models. Most important, the trajectory was not a predetermined or predictable process but required steadily renewed dedication. Only through such ongoing renewal, he wrote (16), can it be decided "whether European culture bears within itself an absolute idea, rather than being merely an empirical-anthropological type like 'China' or 'India'—whether the spectacle of the Europeanization of all other civilizations testifies to the unfolding of an absolute meaning, one which pertains to the sense of the world, rather than to a historical non-sense."

17. Jürgen Habermas, "What Is Universal Pragmatics?" in *Communication and the Evolution of Society,* trans. Thomas McCarthy (Boston: Beacon Press, 1979), 5. Compare also Habermas, *Knowledge and Human Interests,* trans. Jeremy J. Shapiro (Boston: Beacon Press, 1971).

18. See Habermas, *Legitimation Crisis,* trans. Thomas McCarthy (Boston: Beacon Press, 1975); *The Theory of Communicative Action,* vol. 1: *Reason and the Rationalization of Society,* trans. Thomas McCarthy (Boston: Beacon Press, 1984); and *The Philosophical Discourse of Modernity: Twelve Lectures,* trans. Frederick Lawrence (Cambridge, Mass.: MIT Press, 1987). Regarding individual development, see especially Habermas's essays on "Moral Development and Ego Identity" and "Historical Materialism and the Development of Normative Structures," in *Communication and the Evolution of Society,* 69-94, 95–129. For a more detailed discussion of Habermas's view of development, compare my *Twilight of Subjectivity* (Amherst: University of Massachusetts Press, 1981), 179–211.

19. Thomas Pantham, "Habermas' Practical Discourse and Gandhi's *Satyagraha,*" in Bhikhu Parekh and Thomas Pantham, eds., *Political Discourse: Explorations in Indian and Western Political Thought* (New Delhi: Sage Publications, 1987), 292–93, 306. Pantham stressed primarily these divergences (292):

> The main difference between Habermas and Gandhi is that while the former's practico-political discourse centers around communicative rationality and the force of better arguments, the latter's *satyagraha* is based not only on reason but also on love and self-suffering. Moreover, Habermas' practical discourse is largely a thought experiment, while Gandhi's *satyagraha* is a mode of direct action that ruptures the theory-practice dichotomy.

A more stringent critique of Habermasian critical theory, attacking the very notion of 'language' operative in its discourse model, was voiced by another Indian contributor to the same volume; see Raghuveer Singh, "Traditional Wisdom and Modern Science as Paradigms of Political Discourse," 221–37, esp. 234–36.

20. R. Sundara Rajan, *Innovative Competence and Social Change* (Ganeshkind: Poona University Press, 1986), x–xi, 87–89, 107–8. The study (103) also distinguishes between "residual" and "dormant" competences, the former correlated with reform and the second with revolution.

21. R. Sundara Rajan, *Towards a Critique of Cultural Reason* (Delhi: Oxford University Press, 1987), ix–x, 20, 22–24.

22. *Towards a Critique of Cultural Reason,* 27, 31, 33–34, 39, 43–46. For a further development of these views, see R. Sundara Rajan, *The Primacy of the Political* (Delhi: Oxford University Press, 1991).

23. The so-called "linguistic turn" has been associated chiefly with the works of Ludwig Wittgenstein, John Austin, and the later Martin Heidegger. Regarding the anthropological conception of culture, compare Alfred L. Kroeber, *Culture: A Critical Review of Concepts and Definitions* (New York: Vintage Books, 1963); Robert Redfield, *Peasant Society and Culture* (Chicago: University of Chicago Press, 1956); and Clifford Geertz, *The Interpretation of Cultures* (New York: Basic Books, 1973). Regarding the reassessment of tradition, see Edward Shils, *Tradition* (Chicago: University of Chicago Press, 1981), and Alasdair MacIntyre, *After Virtue* (2nd ed.; Notre Dame: University of Notre Dame Press, 1984).

24. See Max Horkheimer and Theodor W. Adorno, *Dialectic of Enlightenment,* trans. John Cumming (New York: Seabury, 1972).

25. Jean-François Lyotard, *The Postmodern Condition: A Report on Knowledge,* trans. Geoff Bennington and Brian Massumi (Minneapolis: University of Minnesota Press, 1984), xxiii–xxv, 4–5, 9–10. For a reformulation of some of these arguments, see Lyotard, *The Postmodern Explained,* trans. Julian LeFanis and Morgan Thomas (Minneapolis: University of Minnesota Press, 1992).

26. Michel Foucault, *The Archaeology of Knowledge,* trans. A. M. Sheridan Smith (New York: Pantheon Books, 1972), 8; *Power/Knowledge,* ed. Colin Gordon (New York: Pantheon Books, 1980), 98. Compare also Jacques Derrida, "Différance," in *Margins of Philosophy* (Chicago: University of Chicago Press, 1982), 3–27, and Gilles Deleuze, *Différence et Répétition* (Paris: Presses Universitaires de France, 1968). For a more detailed discussion of these points, see my "Democracy and Post-Modernism," *Human Studies* 10 (1986): 143–70.

27. Cornel West, "The New Cultural Politics of Difference," in Russell Ferguson et al., eds., *Out There: Marginalization and Contemporary Cultures* (Cambridge, Mass.: MIT Press, 1991), 19. However, as Cornel West adds, the new cultural politics "shuns narrow particularisms, parochialisms and separatisms, just as it rejects false universalisms and homogeneous totalisms"; thus, it simultaneously seeks to "avoid ethnic chauvinism and faceless universalism" (35, 37). Compare also Richard Rorty, "Habermas and Lyotard on Postmodernity," in Richard J. Bernstein, ed., *Habermas and Modernity* (Cambridge, Mass.: MIT Press, 1985), 165–66.

28. For Deleuze's comments, see A. Sheridan, *Michel Foucault: The Will to Truth* (London: Tavistock, 1980), 114. The statement by Leopold Senghor is cited by Denis Goulet in "Development: Creator and Destroyer of Values," *World Development* 20 (1992): 468. Goulet also refers to the Intercultural Institute of Montreal (and its journal *Interculture*) which views development mainly in critical or negative terms, namely, as "the instrument which destroys the political, juridical, economic, and symbolic meaning systems of native cultures" (469). A similar outlook is sponsored by the Cultural Survival Movement founded by David Maybury-Lewis and headquartered at Harvard University.

29. For significant early attempts to break down the opposition between tradition and modernity, compare Lloyd I. Rudolph and Susanne H. Rudolph, *The Modernity of Tradition: Political Development in India* (Chicago: University of Chicago Press, 1967), and Milton Singer, *When a Great Tradition Modernizes: An Anthropological Approach to Indian Civilization* (New York: Praeger Publishers, 1972). Apart from outright traditionalism and modernism, the options of critical traditionalism and critical modernism are discussed by Bhikhu Parekh, *Colonialism, Tradition and Reform* (New Delhi: Sage Publications, 1989), 34–70. Regarding "interactive universalism," compare Seyla Benhabib, *Situating the Self* (Cambridge: Polity Press, 1992), 3–6; and regarding "lateral universalism," see Maurice Merleau-Ponty, *Signs,* trans. Richard C. McCleary (Evanston, Ill.: Northwestern University Press, 1964), 119–20. For the notion of 'agonal dialogue,' see my "Postmodernism and Political Order," in *Margins of Political Discourse* (Albany: State University of New York Press, 1989), 95–115.

30. Tariq Banuri, "Modernization and Its Discontents: A Cultural Perspective on the Theories of Development," in Frédérique Apffel Marglin and Stephen A. Marglin, eds., *Dominating Knowledge: Development, Culture, and Resistance* (Oxford: Clarendon Press, 1990), 73–74, 78–79, 82–83, 88. Under postmodern auspices, the terms *personal* and *impersonal* are somewhat suspect (because of the possible

association of the former with modern individualism). For these and other reasons I prefer the distinction between context-specific and de-contextualized dimensions.

31. Banuri, "Modernization and Its Discontents," 76, 89, 95–99. Compare also Banuri's "Development and the Politics of Knowledge: A Critical Interpretation of the Social Role of Modernization Theories in the Development of the Third World," in the same volume, *Dominating Knowledge,* 29–72.

32. Ashis Nandy, "Cultural Frames for Social Transformation: A Credo," *Alternatives* 12 (1987): 113–17; the essay appeared also in Parekh and Pantham, eds., *Political Discourse,* 238–48. See also his "Towards a Third World Utopia," in *Traditions, Tyrannies, and Utopias: Essays in the Politics of Awareness* (New Delhi: Oxford University Press, 1987), 20–55. Compare also Nandy, ed., *Science, Hegemony and Violence* (New Delhi: Oxford University Press, 1988), Nandy, *The Intimate Enemy* (New Delhi: Oxford University Press, 1983), and his *Alternative Sciences: Creativity and Authenticity in Two Indian Scientists* (New Delhi: Allied, 1980).

33. See Rajni Kothari, *Transformation and Survival: In Search of a Humane World Order* (Delhi: Ajanta, 1988), 16–17, and his *Rethinking Development: In Search of Humane Alternatives* (Delhi: Ajanta, 1989), 185, 192. Together with some colleagues at the Centre for the Study of Developing Societies, Kothari has been instrumental in setting up and maintaining *"lokayan,"* a forum of dialogue among social activists, scholars, and policy makers. For an instructive discussion of Kothari's perspective, see Manoranjan Mohanti, "On Democratic Humanism: A Review of Rajni Kothari's Recent Works," *Contributions to Indian Sociology* (n.s.) 25 (1991): 151–60.

34. See Kothari, *Rethinking Development,* 2. Nandy refuses to label himself a Gandhian; and there are clearly also differences between Gandhi and Kothari. In the words of Mohanti: "Gandhi worked for a total replacement of the prevailing political-economic order, namely, the capitalist parliamentary system. Kothari seeks transformation by working through the existing political-economic order. . . . Thus, despite traces in Kothari of Rousseau's celebration of the civil society and M. N. Roy's new humanism and Gandhi's *Hind Swaraj* outlook, elements of liberalism permeate his thinking." See "On Democratic Humanism," 159. Closer attachment to Gandhi—and a deemphasis on Habermasian motifs—also characterizes recent publications of Thomas Pantham; see, for example, his "Beyond Liberal Democracy: Thinking with Mahatma Gandhi," in Pantham and Kenneth L. Deutsch, eds., *Political Thought in Modern India* (New Delhi: Sage Publications, 1986), 325–46.

35. For a more detailed discussion of Gandhi as a critical traditionalist, see my "Gandhi as Mediator between East and West," in *Margins of Political Discourse,* 22–38. Regarding the sources of Gandhian *ahimsa,* compare William Borman, *Gandhi and Non-violence* (Albany: State University of New York Press, 1986), and Unto Thätinen, *Ahimsa: Nonviolence in Indian Tradition* (Delhi: Navajivan Publishers, 1976). For a defense of interreligious tolerance based not on secularism but on faith itself, see Ashis Nandy, "The Politics of Secularism and the Recovery of Religious Tolerance," *Alternatives* 13 (1988): 177–94.

36. Regarding Tagore, see Krishna Kripalani, *Rabindranath Tagore: A Biography* (New York: Grove Press, 1962), and Marjorie Sykes, *Rabindranath Tagore* (Calcultta: Longmans, Green, 1943). Regarding Sri Aurobindo, see D. P. Chattopadhyaya, *History, Society and Polity: Integral Sociology of Sri Aurobindo* (New Delhi: Macmillan, 1976), and V. P. Varma, *The Political Philosophy of Sri Aurobindo* (2nd. ed.; New Delhi: Motilal Barnarsidass, 1976). Regarding Swami Vivekananda, H. Mukherjee, *Vivekananda and Indian Freedom* (Calcutta: Orient, Longman, 1986), and Tapan Raychauduri, *Europe Reconsidered* (Delhi: Oxford University Press, 1988), 219–331.

Chapter 8. *Sunyata* East and West

1. Compare Stephen Toulmin, *Cosmopolis: The Hidden Agenda of Modernity* (New York: Free Press, 1990), and Mike Featherstone, ed., *Global Culture: Nationalism, Globalization and Modernity* (London: Sage Publications, 1990).

2. Regarding Bodhidharma and general historical background, compare Heinrich Dumoulin, *Zen Buddhism: A History,* vol. 1: *India and China,* trans. James W. Heisig and Paul Knitter (New York: Macmillan Publishing Company, 1988), esp. 85–94.

3. *Karika* 24; see K. Venkata Ramanan, *Nagarjuna's Philosophy* (Delhi: Motilal Banarsidass, 1966), 40–44. Compare also David J. Katupahana, *Nagarjuna: The Philosophy of the Middle Way* (Albany: State University of New York Press, 1986), a work that dissociates Nagarjuna from the Mahayana school.

4. See *Flowers of Emptiness: Selections from Dogen's Shobogenzo,* trans. Hee-Jin Kim (Lewiston, N.Y.: Edwin Mellen Press, 1985), 52, 176, and Eihei Dogen, *Shobogenzo Zuimonki,* ed. Shohaku Okumara (Zurich: Theseus Verlag, 1992), 25, 38 n. 31.

5. Kitaro Nishida, *Last Writings: Nothingness and the Religious Worldview,* trans. David A. Dilworth (Honolulu: University of Hawaii Press, 1987), 70–71, 82. Nishida adds, in a more religious vein (93):

The human self as an individual is the self-negation of the absolute. But the more it is consciously self-forming through its own
dynamic expression—that is, volitional and personal—the more
it discovers its own absolute negation in its bottomlessly contradictory depths, and thus faces an absolute One—faces God as
God's own mirror image and opposite. At the very root of our individuality we always face the absolute face of God, and stand
in the dimension of decision between eternal life and death. It is
in that radical dimension of existential decision that the religious
question opens up.

Compare also Kitaro Nishida, *Intelligibility and the Philosophy of Nothingness: Three Philosophical Essays,* trans. Robert Schinzinger (Honolulu: East-West Center Press, 1958), and Keiji Nishitani, *Nishida Kitaro,* trans. Yamamoto Seisaku and James W. Heisig (Berkeley: University
of California Press, 1991). As Nishitani notes there (53):

Nishida's philosophy represents an attempt to construct a standpoint in response to this singular most difficult issue for contemporary thought [i.e., the relation of science and religion] by
bringing together the Eastern standpoint of nothingness and the
Western standpoint of science and philosophy (or reason and
logic). In so doing, his aim was to conceive a dialectical logic
based on the standpoint of nothingness or no-ego by delving
deeply into the spirit behind the rationalism and logic of the
West.

6. Not all the books mentioned above are available in English.
The main work in English by Hisamatsu is *Zen and the Fine Arts*
(Tokyo: Kodansha International, 1971). Regarding Nishitani, see his
Religion and Nothingness, trans. Jan Van Bragt (Berkeley: University
of California Press, 1982); regarding Tanabe, see his *Philosophy as
Metanoetics,* trans. Takeuchi Yoshinori et al. (Berkeley: University
of California Press, 1987). Compare also Nishitani, *The Self-Over-
coming of Nihilism,* trans. Graham Parkes and S. Aihara (New York:
State University of New York Press, 1990); Taitetsu Unno, ed., *The
Religious Philosophy of Nishitani Keiji: Encounter with Emptiness*
(Berkeley: Asian Humanities Press, 1990), and Taitetsu Unno and
James W. Heisig, eds., *The Religious Philosophy of Tanabe Hajime:
The Metanoetic Imperative* (Berkeley: Asian Humanities Press, 1990).
Regarding Masao Abe, see his *Zen and Western Thought,* ed. William
R. LaFleur (Honolulu: University of Hawaii Press, 1985), and John
B. Cobb, Jr., and Christopher Ives, eds., *The Emptying God: A Bud-*

dhist-Jewish-Christian Conversation (Maryknoll, N.Y.: Orbis Books, 1990).

7. On Nishitani's view of *sunyata,* see my "Nothingness and *Sunyata:* A Comparison of Heidegger and Nishitani," *Philosophy East and West* 42 (January 1992): 37–48.

8. Masao Abe, *Zen and Western Thought,* 85, 88. He adds (90): "Kant established the possibility of metaphysical knowledge not by employing theoretical reason concerned with objects in external nature, but only by appealing to reason in its practical use. Such practical use turns pure reason deeply within and roots subjective moral determination in one's will."

9. *Zen and Western Thought,* 86–87, 93–94. Even before Nagarjuna, Abe observes (101), the Buddha Sakyamuni had moved in a similar direction "by transcending both the philosophy of the *Upanishads* of the orthodox Brahmans, who considered *brahman* to be the only reality, and the standpoint of the free thinkers of that time, among whom were pluralists, skeptics, and nihilists."

10. *Zen and Western Thought,* 103, 106–7, 111–12, 116.

11. Ibid., 85, 109, 118–19, 134. The last few passages are taken from the essay "Non-Being and *Mu:* The Metaphysical Nature of Negativity in the East and the West." While acknowledging Heidegger's rapprochement, Abe adds (119): "At the same time, however, he did not depart from thinking itself, and tried to the last to stay in a kind of thinking—the *Denken des Seins* in a sense intrinsic to Heidegger. To that extent, he must be said still to differ from Zen which is grounded on Non-Thinking." This statement, however, has to be reassessed in terms of Abe's own differentiation of "non-thinking" from "not-thinking" and his claim that "non-thinking is unshackled ultimate thinking" (112).

12. "Dogen on Buddha-Nature," in *Zen and Western Thought,* 27, 38–39, 43–45. Compare also Masao Abe, *A Study of Dogen: His Philosophy and Religion,* ed. Steven Heine (Albany: State University of New York Press, 1992).

13. *Zen and Western Thought,* 4, 9–11, 223, 225–27. The last citation is taken from the opening essay of the volume, "Zen Is Not a Philosophy, but, . . ." In a later text, Abe links the awakening to suchness with the Pauline notion of the self-emptying or *kenosis* of Christ:

> We can now reformulate the notion of the new person as the true self who resurrects through the death of the old person in such a way that "self is not self" (for self as the old person must die on account of its sin); and precisely because it is not, self is truly self (for self is now alive as the new person, together with Christ). . . .

The realization of the "suchness" of everything as the basis of salvation entails the awakening of one's original nature together with the awakening of the original nature of everything else, and the emancipation from attachment to the self and others. *(The Emptying God,* 12, 30)

14. *Zen and Western Thought,* 47, 65–66, 119, 134. Regarding Nietzsche, compare also "Zen and Nietzsche," 135–51. In the later text, "Kenotic God and Dynamic Sunyata," the charge directed against Heidegger of harboring a substantive ontology (or a substantive conception of being) is qualified by this admission: "Just as the attachment to being must be overcome, the attachment to emptiness must also be surmounted. Accordingly, however important the notion of *sunyata* may be in Buddhism, following Martin Heidegger, who put a cross mark 'X' on the term *Sein,* thus rendering it as in order to show the unobjectifiability of *Sein,* we should put a cross mark 'X' on *sunyata,* and render it." (See *The Emptying God,* 27.) Compare in this context also Heidegger, *On Time and Being,* trans. Joan Stambaugh (New York: Harper & Row, 1972).

15. In my essay "Nothingness and *Sunyata"* I had tried to respond to some extent to Nishitani's criticisms of Heidegger; see *Philosophy East and West,* vol. 42 (1992), esp. 43–46.

16. See Martin Heidegger, *Being and Time,* trans. John Maquarrie and Edward Robinson (New York: Harper & Row, 1962), 307–8, 366–67; "What Is Metaphysics?" in Walter Kaufmann, ed., *Existentialism from Dostoevsky to Sartre* (New York: Meridian, 1975), 244–46, 248–51; *Beiträge zur Philosophie (Vom Ereignis),* ed. Friedrich-Wilhelm von Herrmann *(Gesamtausgabe,* vol. 65, Frankfurt-Main: Klostermann, 1989), 246–47, 266–67.

17. Heidegger, "Language in the Poem," in *On the Way to Language,* trans. Peter D. Hertz (New York: Harper & Row, 1982), 159–63, 167–68, 170–71 (translation slightly altered for the sake of clarity).

18. Ernesto Laclau and Chantal Mouffe, *Hegemony and Socialist Strategy: Towards a Radical Democratic Politics,* trans. Winston Moore and Paul Cammack (London: Verso, 1985), 1–4. For a more detailed discussion of the study, see my "Hegemony and Democracy: A Post-Hegelian Perspective," in Dallmayr, *Margins of Political Discourse* (Albany: State University of New York Press, 1989), 116–36.

19. Laclau and Mouffe, *Hegemony and Socialist Strategy,* 51–56, 61–62, 65–69, 75–77, 85–87, 115–17, 122–29, 132–33, 137.

20. Ibid., 129, 184.

21. Claude Lefort, *Democracy and Political Theory,* trans. David Macey (Minneapolis: University of Minnesota Press, 1988), 9–12,

217–19. For a fuller discussion of Lefort, see my "Post-Metaphysics and Democracy," *Political Theory* 21 (1993): 101–27; a revised version of the essay, under the title "Post-Metaphysical Politics: Heidegger and Democracy?" appears in my *The Other Heidegger* (Ithaca: Cornell University Press, 1993), 77–105.

22. Lefort, *Democracy and Political Theory,* 223–26. Together with traditional modes of embodiment, democracy also puts an end to intellectual security and to foundational warrants of beliefs and actions. "In my view," Lefort states (19), "the important point is that democracy is instituted and sustained by the *dissolution of the markers of certainty.* It inaugurates a history in which people experience a fundamental indeterminacy as to the basis of power, law, and knowledge, and as to the basis of relations between self and other, at every level of social life."

23. *Democracy and Political Theory,* 13, 18–20, 230.

24. D. S. Clarke, Jr., "Introduction," in Nishitani Keiji, *Nishida Kitaro,* trans. Yamamoto Seisaku and James W. Heisig (Berkeley: University of California Press, 1991), x. He adds: "The debate extends also to Nishida, who because of the great prestige he enjoyed could have been an effective moral critic of militaristic politics." For a detailed examination and critique of the politics of some members of the Kyoto school, see James W. Heisig and John C. Maraldo, eds., *Rude Awakenings: Zen, the Kyoto School, and the Question of Nationalism* (Honolulu: University of Hawaii Press, 1995).

25. See Stanley Jeyaraja Tambiah, *Buddhism Betrayed? Religion, Politics, and Violence in Sri Lanka* (Chicago: University of Chicago Press, 1992), 91–92. Tambiah in the following qualifies this assessment somewhat, while ascribing the above account to "some observers."

26. For some of this background, see Christopher Ives, "Introduction," in *The Emptying God: A Buddhist-Jewish-Christian Conversation,* xiv–xv, xviii. Compare also Masao Abe, "Hisamatsu's Philosophy of Awakening" and "Hisamatsu Shin'ichi, 1889–1980," *The Eastern Buddhist* (n.s.) 14 (1981): 26–42, 142–47.

27. Abe, "Sovereignty Rests with Mankind," *Zen and Western Thought,* 249–50, 253.

28. *Zen and Western Thought,* 112, 116, 119–20. A similar point is made in "Kenotic God and Dynamic Sunyata," where Abe notes that historically Buddhism has been "hasty to go beyond human reason to arrive at the non-discriminating wisdom because of the stance that human reason is merely discriminative. Thus Buddhism has not known the creative possibility of human reason developed in the modern West in terms of science." See *The Emptying God,* 35–36.

29. *Zen and Western Thought,* 250, 252–53, 256.

Chapter 9. Democracy and Multiculturalism

1. Tzvetan Todorov, *The Conquest of America: The Question of the Other,* trans. Richard Howard (New York: Harper Perennial, 1992), 61, 69, 97, 251.

2. Ibid., 105–6. He elaborates (106), "Christianity's egalitarianism is part of its universalism: since God belongs to all, all belong to God; there is not, in this regard, a difference among peoples nor among individuals." Compare also Todorov, *The Morals of History,* trans. Alyson Waters (Minneapolis: University of Minnesota Press, 1995), especially 17–33.

3. For aspects of the academic debate, compare John Arthur and Amy Shapiro, eds., *Campus Wars: Multiculturalism and the Politics of Difference* (Boulder, Colo.: Westview Press, 1995); Nancy Warehime, *To Be One of Us* (Albany: State University of New York Press, 1993); Dinesh D'Souza, *Illiberal Education: The Politics of Race and Sex on Campus* (New York: Free Press, 1991); Allan D. Bloom, *The Closing of the American Mind* (New York: Simon & Schuster, 1987); and Allan D. Bloom, *Liberal Education and Its Enemies* (Colorado Springs: Air Force Academy, 1991).

4. Compare, e.g., David Rasmussen, ed., *Universalism vs. Communitarianism: Contemporary Debates in Ethics* (Cambridge, Mass.: MIT Press, 1990); Shlomo Avineri and Avner de-Shalit, eds., *Communitarianism and Individualism* (New York: Oxford University Press, 1992); Stephen Mulhall and Adam Swift, eds., *Liberals and Communitarians* (Oxford: Blackwell, 1992); Will Kymlicka, *Liberalism, Community and Culture* (New York: Oxford University Press, 1989); and Michael Sandel, ed., *Liberalism and Its Critics* (New York: New York University Press, 1984).

5. The historical dimension has been recognized at least by some (presumed) communitarians. As Charles Taylor has noted:

> The basic error of [liberal] atomism in all its forms is that it fails to take account of the degree to which the free individual with his own goals and aspirations . . . is only possible within a certain kind of civilization; that it took a long development of certain institutions and practices, of the rule of law, of rules of equal respect, of habits of common deliberation, of common association, of cultural development, and so on, to produce the modern individual. *(Philosophy and the Human Sciences: Philosophical Papers* [Cambridge: Cambridge University Press, 1985], vol. 2, 309)

6. As Michael Sandel, a leading communitarian, candidly admitted: "Despite its philosophical failure, this liberal vision is the one by which we live. For us in late-twentieth-century America, it is our vision, the theory most thoroughly embodied in the practices and institutions most central to our public life" ("The Procedural Republic," in Avineri and de-Shalit, *Communitarianism and Individualism,* 14). That traditional life-forms are streamlined into collective identities only under the impact of modern ideologies (especially the ideology of nationalism) is widely recognized in the literature; compare, e.g., Partha Chatterjee, *Nationalist Thought and the Colonial World: A Derivative Discourse* (Minneapolis: University of Minnesota Press, 1993).

7. Chantal Mouffe, "Rawls: Political Philosophy without Politics," in Rasmussen, *Universalism vs. Communitarianism,* 222. For a still sharper attack on liberal neutrality (as defended by John Rawls, Ronald Dworkin, and Bruce Ackerman), see Michael Perry, *Morality, Politics and Law* (New York: Oxford University Press, 1988), esp. 57–73. Regarding conceptions of the self, see Michael Sandel, *Liberalism and the Limits of Justice* (Cambridge: Cambridge University Press, 1982); Charles Taylor, *Sources of the Self: The Making of the Modern Identity* (Cambridge, Mass.: Harvard University Press, 1989); Seyla Benhabib, *Situating the Self* (New York: Routledge, 1992); Daniel Shanahan, *Toward a Genealogy of Individualism* (Amherst: University of Massachusetts Press, 1992); and my *Twilight of Subjectivity* (Amherst: University of Massachusetts Press, 1981).

8. Iris Marion Young, *Justice and the Politics of Difference* (Princeton: Princeton University Press, 1990), 4, 11. Young acknowledges a number of intellectual mentors—who are appropriately diverse. Her attitude toward Habermasian critical theory (a "communicative" variant of liberalism) is instructive: while appreciating the accent on dialogue and critical reflection, she takes exception to Habermas's rationalist universalism (his concern with ideal consensus, his separation of reason and affectivity). On the other hand, she invokes selectively "postmodern" writers, including Adorno, Heidegger, Derrida, Lyotard, Foucault, Kristeva, and Irigaray (7, 106–7, 117–18).

9. Young, *Justice and the Politics of Difference,* 43–47.

10. Ibid., 156–63. Curiously, while invoking the good society and attacking liberal neutrality, Young at other points supports the liberal separation of justice from the "good life" and the primacy of rights over goodness (36, 103–4).

11. *Justice and the Politics of Difference,* 156, 164–68.

12. Ibid., 157, 169–71. In taking this approach, Young clearly rejects the notion of radical cultural 'incommensurability.' Compare in this context also Richard J. Bernstein, "Incommensurability and

Otherness Revisited," in his *The New Constellation: The Ethical-Political Horizons of Modernity/Postmodernity* (Oxford: Polity Press, 1991), 57–78.

13. On the above, see Huguette Labelle, "Multiculturalism and Government," in James S. Frideres, ed., *Multiculturalism and Intergroup Relations* (New York: Greenwood Press, 1989), 1–4.

14. Charles Taylor, "The Politics of Recognition," in Amy Gutman, ed., *Multiculturalism: Examining the Politics of Recognition* (Princeton: Princeton University Press, 1994), 25–35.

15. Ibid., 37–39, 43.

16. Ibid., 43–44, 52–58. See also Michael Sandel, "The Procedural Republic and the Unencumbered Self," *Political Theory* 12 (1984): 81–96. Among prominent American spokesmen of liberal universalism, Taylor mentions especially Rawls, Dworkin, and Ackerman.

17. Taylor, "The Politics of Recognition," 58–61. The essay gives a succinct summary of the debates surrounding the Meech Lake accord (60): "The rest of Canada saw that the distinct society clause legitimated collective goals [in violation of liberal proceduralism]. And Quebec saw that the move to give the Charter precedence imposed a form of liberal society that was alien to it, and to which Quebec could never accommodate itself without surrendering its identity."

18. "The Politics of Recognition," 66–67, 70–73. The requirements of cross-cultural understanding have been discussed by Taylor in greater detail in "Comparison, History, Truth," in Frank E. Reynolds and David Tracy, eds., *Myth and Philosophy* (Albany: State University of New York Press, 1990), 37–55, and in "Understanding and Ethnocentricity," in his *Philosophy and the Human Sciences: Philosophical Papers* (Cambridge: Cambridge University Press, 1985), vol. 2, 116–33.

19. George Grant, *English-Speaking Justice* (Notre Dame, Ind.: University of Notre Dame Press, 1985), 86–87.

20. Grant, *Lament for a Nation: The Defeat of Canadian Nationalism* (Ottowa: Carleton University Press, 1982), ix, 56–57, 75. Grant's disdain for liberal proceduralism, as well as his cultural melancholy, can also be found in the French-Canadian thinker Pierre Vadeboncoeur, known especially for his *Un génocide en douce* (Montreal: Parti pris, 1976). In Vadeboncoeur's view, modern liberal universalism inevitably dismantles traditional cultures (through a process of "gentle genocide" which cannot be reversed). In his words:

> The West continues dissolving into individuals, the hollowest [elements] of its substance, tiny, infinitesimal beings living in a state of suspension. . . . Social revolution, with a temporary success that cannot be denied, attempts a collective recovery of con-

> sciousness, but the limits of political discourse are soon clear enough—being a part, as it is, of all that can be discussed today without circumlocution, and thus subject to the deleterious effect of our reasoning. (H. D. Forbes, ed., *Canadian Political Thought* [Toronto: Oxford University Press, 1985], 418)

I am grateful to Roberta Sullivan for alerting me to these writings. For a highly nuanced (and not nostalgic) treatment of the Canadian situation, compare also Louis Sabourin, *Passion d'être, Désir d'avoir: Le dilemme Québec-Canada dans un univers en muta.ion* (Montral: Editions du Boréal, 1992).

21. On the disruption or destruction of Indian communities in Brazil and Venezuela in favor of individual or corporate property rights, see Julian Burger, *Report from the Frontier: The State of the World's Indigenous Peoples* (London: Zed, 1987); Adrian Cowell, *Decade of Destruction: The Crusade to Save the Amazon Rain Forest* (New York: Holt, 1990); Jacques Lizot, *The Yanomami in the Face of Ethnocide* (Copenhagen: International Work Group on Indigenous Affairs [Document No. 22], 1976). For similar developments in Nicaragua, see Jeffrey L. Gould, "They Don't Care about Our History: Politics and Ethnicity in Nicaragua, 1920–1980" (unpublished manuscript). Compare also Association for Endangered Peoples, "Massacre of Indians in Peru," *Cultural Survival Quarterly* 8 (1984): 8.

22. Some of the above devices, with particular reference to the former Yugoslavia, are explored by Vojislav Stanovčič in "Problems and Options in Institutionalizing Ethnic Relations," *International Political Science Review* 13 (1992): 359–79. See also Arend Lijphart, *Democracy in Plural Societies: A Comparative Exploration* (2nd ed.; New Haven: Yale University Press, 1980), and Jean Cohen, "Discourse Ethics and Civil Society," in David Rasmussen, ed., *Universalism v. Communitarianism,* 96. Regarding the issue of diverse constituencies, compare Robert C. Grady, *Restoring Real Representation* (Champaign: University of Illinois Press, 1993). See also Will Kymlicka, *Multicultural Citizenship* (Oxford and New York: Oxford University Press, 1995); Kymlicka, ed., *The Rights of Minority Cultures* (Oxford and New York: Oxford University Press, 1995); and Oliver Mendelsohn and Upendra Baxi, eds., *The Rights of Subordinated Peoples* (Oxford and New York: Oxford University Press, 1994).

23. Alessandro Ferrara, "Universalisms: Procedural, Contextualist and Prudential," in Rasmussen, ed., *Universalism v. Communitarianism,* 16. Sharpening his critique, Ferrara (17) describes Habermasian theory as a "generalization of the parochialism of modernity," adding: "The universality of the complexes of rationality brought about by

modernity is questionable, the superiority of modern rationality over that of pre-modern and primitive societies is questionable, and the factual irreversibility of modernization cannot lend normative force to the modern conception of validity."

24. Hans-Georg Gadamer, *Truth and Method,* trans. Joel Weinsheimer and Donald G. Marshall (2nd rev. ed.; New York: Crossroad, 1989), 469. See also Martin Heidegger, "Language," in *Poetry, Language, Thought,* trans. Albert Hofstadter (New York: Harper & Row, 1971), 207–8 (translation slightly altered for the sake of clarity).

25. Lao Tzu, *The Way of Life,* trans. Witter Bynner (New York: Perigee Books, 1972), 75; Keiji Nishitani, *Religion and Nothingness,* trans. Jan Van Bragt (Berkeley: University of California Press, 1982), 159; Heidegger, "The Thing," in *Poetry, Language, Thought,* 163–86. Compare Masao Abe, "Emptiness Is Suchness," in his *Zen and Western Thought,* ed., William R. LaFleur (Honolulu: University of Hawaii Press, 1985), 223–27, and my discussion of Nishitani in *The Other Heidegger* (Ithaca: Cornell University Press, 1993), 200–26. The notion of a lateral universalism was put forth by Maurice Merleau-Ponty in *Signs,* trans. Richard C. McCleary (Evanston, Ill.: Northwestern University Press, 1964), 119–20. What Sabourin calls "endogéneité" seems to point in a similar direction; see *Passion d'être, Désir d'avoir,* 112–34.

INDEX